The Musician as Athlete

The
Musician
as
Athlete

Dorothy Bishop
BA, KA (cello), MH

Kava Publications
111 - 32nd Ave. N.W.
Calgary, Alberta, Canada
T2M 2P7

Canadian Cataloguing in Publication Data

Bishop, Dorothy.
    The musician as athlete

    Includes bibliographical references and index.
    ISBN 0-9695590-0-3

    1. Musicians--Health and hygiene. 2.
Musicians--Nutrition. 3. Physical fitness.
ML 3795.B58 1991   613.7'04   C91-091752-3

Editor : Jude Carlson
Cover Design : David Ferguson

Printed in Canada

To Geof and Orin
with thanks for their patience and understanding.

Acknowledgements

This book could not have been written without the assistance of many people. Countless colleagues have offered helpful advice and assured me that this book was needed. I particularly wish to thank the following for their thoughtful comments on the manuscript: Dr. Terry Willard, Laurie Syer, and Windsor Viney. Special thanks go to Jude Carlson, friend and editor, for her boundless patience, encouragement, and skill.

Though I have depended on the efforts of many people, the faults, and opinions, in this book are my own responsibility.

I cannot give enough thanks to Geoffrey Bishop, who spent many tedious hours proofreading and many more hours looking after our son while I processed words. Finally, thanks go to Orin, for letting Mommy use his computer.

CONTENTS

LIST OF ILLUSTRATIONS

LIST OF TABLES

Introduction

"Don't worry, it's minor surgery, 99 percent effective."
Fortunately, the doctor felt that my problem was no emergency.
"Come back in six months, when it's gotten so bad that you don't
want to live with it."
I never came back. Instead I corrected my playing technique
and allowed the injury to heal. I learned how athletes warm up
and how they time their training schedules to peak for
performance. Later I learned how diet could keep me from
getting reinjured every time I ignored my limits, and how herbs
could help keep minor injuries from turning into major ones.
Meanwhile I was studying healing in general and exploring
how the mind affects the body. While my education continues,
it is time to share the results so others can get well.

This book is for three groups of people: those who have been
injured and are playing again, those whose injuries are keeping
them from playing, and those who want to keep from falling
into either of the preceding groups. The performer resembles
the athlete in motivation and impatience to get back to the job.
Worker's compensation just doesn't make up for the the joys of
performance, and your audience may forget you while you're out
sick. If you're a free-lancer, there is also a financial incentive to
stay on the job. Competitiveness tempts us all to overtrain and
to play through pain, whether we are avid amateurs,
professionals, or serious students. At the same time, we
resemble the athlete in our ambivalence toward the pressures
of work and in our temptation to deny the negative feelings
which may predispose us to injury.
On the positive side, the love of our art can speed healing.
When injured, we need to find physicians and other
practitioners who understand that a rapid return to work is
important to us. With confidence in their support of our goals,
we will be less tempted to ignore their advice in our impatience
to perform.

Music medicine is a relatively new field, and the interest which doctors are taking in musicians' problems is extremely welcome. We have much to learn from athletes, who know how to use massage, icing, psychology, and training programs to keep minor injuries from threatening careers. We also have much to learn from the less glamorous field of occupational medicine, which deals with overuse injuries resulting from endless repetition of a circumscribed motion.

Students, teachers, and performers who have suffered minor aches (we won't call them "injuries") will find that prevention and healing are based on the same principles. The body needs to be strong, flexible, and well nourished, so that the internal organs can keep the muscles and tendons healthy. Emotions and mental outlook can facilitate healing or prevent illness.

This book is divided into four sections, which present four healing modalities. Although an ideal treatment plan engages all four, some people seem to respond better to one than to another. Each section of the book stands on its own, as does each chapter, so feel free to start in the areas which seem the most interesting or urgent. By combining the strategies suggested in all four sections, it is my hope that every one of my readers can enjoy safe and fulfilling performance.

Section I deals with the functioning of a healthy body and with the sorts of problems performers might encounter in the course of their work. It outlines some of the more conventional healing options and offers exercise and training programs for recovery or the prevention of injury.

Section II addresses the contentious issues in nutrition and gives a basis for a diet which will support healthy performance. Due to the year-round nature of our work, such a diet must support good health while optimizing performance and safety.

Section III discusses herbs which have helped performers. The herbs are grouped according to the system of the body to which they are most often applied. Some herbs are considered mild enough for health maintenance, while others are appropriate only for therapy. Herbs should not be taken without advice; the technical information in this section is intended only to enable you to evaluate and question that advice.

Section IV is a brief presentation of some of the ideas which have helped me and other performers deal with emotional issues, mental blocks, and other problems which may be conducive to injury or sub-optimal performance. The topics are presented briefly, with an annotated bibliography to help the performer start exploring the many books, courses, and workshops currently available in this field.

If we are to take responsibility for our own bodies instead of giving them over to someone else's expert care, then we have to become the experts. This book can't replace medical advice. Instead, it can help the performer to become an intelligent consumer. Ideally we all should know everything in the main text, the appendices, and the books in all of the bibliographies. In practice the more we know, the healthier we can become.

Section I

Chapter 1

GEOGRAPHY AND MECHANICS
how the healthy performer is built

Fred's got bursitis. You know, an inflamed bursa. Only what in the world is a bursa? (Do I have one too?) Will Mary's shoulder exercises help him, or will they make it worse?

In order to take good care of our bodies (or repair them when necessary), we need to know how a healthy body functions. The material in this chapter will help those who are designing a fitness program or investigating a specific problem.

Physiologists divide the body into several systems, those of greatest interest to the performer being the musculoskeletal, circulatory, and nervous systems. Each is discussed briefly, with emphasis on those aspects which are relevant to performance or to performance-related injuries.

THE MUSCULOSKELETAL SYSTEM

The musculoskeletal system comprises the muscles and bones (i.e. skeleton), as well as the tendons, ligaments, and cartilage attached to them. Most of the musculoskeletal system is made of *connective tissue*, as are the walls of the blood vessels and anything else that seems to hold us together. Connective tissue is primarily *collagen*, a fiber made of long chains of proteins, with regular kinks which can straighten to allow it to stretch.

BONES
We tend to think of bones as corresponding to the joists and girders which support buildings, but a bone is a living organ rather than an inert substance. It consists of small crystals of inorganic salts separated by protein, and acts as an electrolytic reservoir to maintain physiological as well as mechanical stability. The crystals make the bone less elastic but stronger, and children's bones, with more organic material, are more flexible. A sufficiently flexible bone yields a bit when bent, to

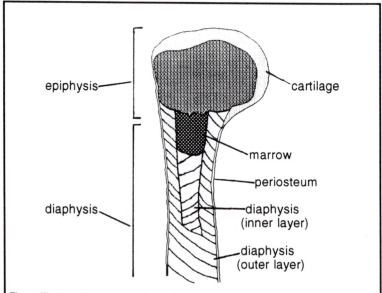

epiphysis—

cartilage

marrow

periosteum

diaphysis

diaphysis
(inner layer)

diaphysis
(outer layer)

Fig. 1: The long bones in our limbs consist of a compact, hollow, marrow-filled shaft (diaphysis) with spongy ends (epiphyses) which are covered by a thin compact layer of cartilage. The shaft consists of concentric cylinders whose fibers may lie in alternating directions for added strength. The ends distribute the force of a jarring impact. Except at the joints, bones are covered by a membrane called the periosteum.

spread stress and reduce the likelihood of cracking. Both growth and deterioration of our bones are influenced by such factors as heredity, mechanical stress, and nutrition.

All the bones in our body have names, but these are of interest, like the names of notes in music, only if we need to talk about them without pointing. Since many musicians rely heavily on the arms and hands, figure 2 shows the location of the bones of the upper limbs. The phalanges near the hand are called *proximal*, while the ones near the finger tips are called *distal*. The only skeletal connection between arm and trunk is the *sterno-clavicular articulation*, i.e. the place where the collar bone (*clavicle*) attaches to the breast bone (*sternum*). Since there is no skeletal connection between the shoulder blade (*scapula*) and the spine, we gain flexibility at the cost of stability, so it doesn't seem surprising that so many of us develop aches in the muscles between the shoulder blades.

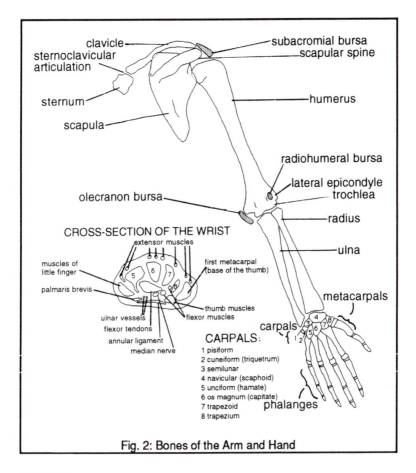

Fig. 2: Bones of the Arm and Hand

JOINTS

Joints are designed to give us flexibility, strength, and durability. Although they often are a weak point in a performer's body, they are very cleverly designed and respond well to proper care, including exercise and nutrition, with herbal support when needed.

In most moveable joints the convex end of one bone fits into the concave end of the other. Their surfaces are covered by a highly elastic tissue called *articular cartilage* (see fig. 3), which is made of connective tissue with a rather poor blood supply. Joints have a very low *coefficient of friction*, about 0.002 to 0.01. (The coefficient of friction is a measure of slipperiness, and

Table 1: Types of Joints

Classification	Example	Type of Movement Permitted*
hinge	interphalangeal (in the fingers)	rotate** in one plane
condyloid	metacarpophalangeal (base of the fingers)	rotate in two planes
saddle	base of thumb (carpometacarpal)***	rotate freely in two planes, limited rotation in third plane

Table 1. cont'd: Types of Joints

	Classification	Example	Type of Movement Permitted*
	ball-and-socket	shoulder	rotate in three planes
	gliding	intercarpal (in the wrist)	limited motion in plane of contact

*All healthy joints have some play in them, so that they can be moved passively in directions other than those listed. For example, the interphalangeal joints can be moved in the plane of the hand, a motion which can help a string player vibrate. Excessive force in any direction weakens a joint.

**The amount of rotation permitted is generally much less than 360°.

***The remaining carpometacarpal joints are severely limited in their freedom of motion.

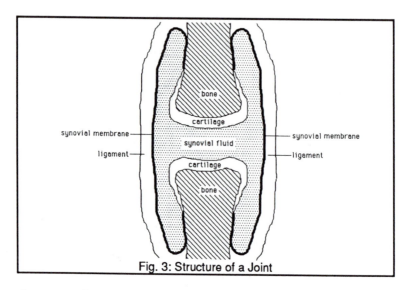

Fig. 3: Structure of a Joint

lower numbers represent slipperier surfaces. Ice on ice, one of the slipperiest combinations in the engineering world, has a coefficient of friction of 0.02 to 0.5, depending on its temperature.) They are enclosed by connective tissue (the *synovial membrane*) to keep them bathed in *synovial fluid*, which lubricates and nourishes the cartilage. This fluid is similar to plasma but contains a polysaccharide called *hyaluronic acid* and has the consistency of egg white. When a joint is bearing a load, water and salts are squeezed out through the pores in the cartilage, but protein and hyaluronic acid stay behind (*boosted lubrication*). The cartilage is somewhat elastic, making this system of lubrication even more efficient.

Cartilage feels smooth to the touch, but it is actually quite rough by engineering standards. The irregularities in the surface are in the form of dimples surrounded by bundles of collagen fibers. This shape probably traps synovial fluid (*weeping lubrication*). Cartilage gets rougher with age, though this process can be retarded by keeping the grit, e.g. calcium deposits, out of the joints. (Exercise, nutrition, and herbs can help.) Roughening can also be retarded by avoiding undue percussive force on any one joint, by not asking it to move while bearing a great weight, and by taking care of minor injuries as they occur.

What we commonly call the wrist joint is formed by the articulations of three of the carpal bones with the radius and ulna. It moves freely in two planes. The wrist has nothing to do with rotation of the forearm about itself, which is accomplished at the elbow.

The radius and ulna join the humerus to form the elbow joint. A common synovial membrane encloses all three bones. The radius rests freely in a depression of the humerus (*capitulum*, behind the trochlea in fig. 2) which lets it rotate while the ulna revolves around it. The humeroulnar joint is a hinge type joint. Friction in the elbow joint is reduced by a number of sacs (*bursae*) filled with synovial fluid.

At the shoulder joint the rounded head of the humerus fits into a depression in the scapula. The depression is deepened by a fibrocartilage rim called the *glenoid labrum*. The whole joint is enclosed in a loose articular capsule of synovial membrane and contains several bursae. Movements of the scapula and humerus are generally coordinated, with the humerus moving approximately twice as far as the scapula.

LIGAMENTS
If the bones were only flying in loose formation, perhaps held together by the skin, they wouldn't be capable of much work. Ligaments hold bones together and stabilize joints, preventing dislocations. They are a strong and flexible form of connective tissue, and contain bundles of collagenous fibers in parallel or interlaced. They sometimes form part of the container for the synovial fluid surrounding a joint. Some ligaments completely surround their joints, while others stabilize and reinforce them.

MUSCLES
Bones and skeletal muscles make up 70% of our body mass. (We are not concerned here with the smooth muscles which control the workings of our internal organs, as these muscles are normally beyond conscious control, so that the performer can't overwork them voluntarily.) Skeletal muscles enable us to move the bones at the joints. Some muscles are directly connected to the periosteum of the bone, while others are connected via tendons. Most are attached close to a joint, giving us speed at the cost of mechanical advantage. Muscles function as groups, so the muscles within each group can take turns contracting and relaxing. A muscle often pulls in a spiral

direction, so it requires assistance from other muscles either to stabilize neighboring body segments or to make the desired movement.This is called *synergistic* action.All movements are controlled by a set of opposing muscles, called *antagonists*.

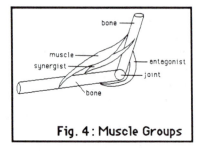

Fig. 4 : Muscle Groups

The muscles of the extremities are among our longest and have a large number of nerves running to them. The muscles get progressively finer from shoulder to fingers.

A single muscle cell may have several hundred nuclei (see fig. 5). It also has cylindrical elements called *myofibrils,* which contain the mechanical contractile mechanism. These are surrounded by *sarcoplasm,* which conducts the excitatory impulse to the center of the cell and also contains the calcium necessary for continuous effort. The source of energy is in the *mitochondria,* while oxygen is carried by a respiratory pigment called *myoglobin.*

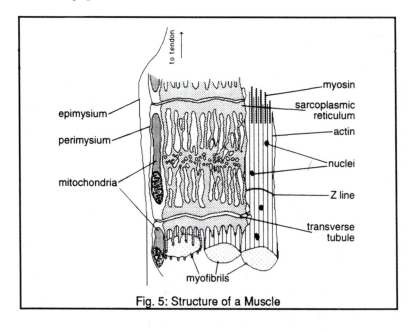

Fig. 5: Structure of a Muscle

Table 2: Types of Muscle Fibers

Slow-twitch (red)	Fast twitch (white)	FOG (fast-twitch red)
slow, sustained work, high endurance, e.g. maintaining posture	rapid contraction, low endurance	high endurance
capillaries perpendicular to fibers	capillaries parallel to fibers, in long loops	
narrow fibers, thus large surface-to-volume ratio, rich blood supply	wide fibers	rich vascularization (like slow-twitch red)
rich in sarcoplasm, myoglobin, mitochondria	rich in myofibrils	rich in myoglobin, mitochondria

Table 2. cont'd: Types of Muscle Fibers

Slow-twitch (red)	Fast twitch (white)	FOG (fast-twitch red)
innervating motor neurons have low threshold of stimulation, so red fibers are the first to contract for low-intensity work	innervating motoneurons have high threshold of stimulation, with large cell bodies, so nerve impulse is transmitted rapidly along nerve axon (faster reaction)	rapid transmission of nerve impulse, high threshold of stimulation (like fast-twitch white)
many oxidative enzymes, including citrate synthase and malate dehydrogenase, for citric acid cycle, which help avoid build-up of lactates	many active glycolytic enzymes, including phosphorylase, alpha-glycerol-phosphate, 3-phosphoglycer-aldehyde, pyruvate kinase, and lactate hydrogenase	high metabolic capacity, but rich in glycolytic enzymes
can maintain high level of activity of carnityl palmityl transferase and other enzymes which oxidize free fatty acids	high in myosin ATPase	

Sliding filament model of muscle contraction
Myofibrils (fig. 5) contain bands of overlapping thick and thin filaments that facilitate muscular contraction. The thick filaments are made of lollipop-shaped molecules called *myosin* (see fig. 6). Their tails attract each other and thus lie in the center of the filament, while the heads protrude and bind with the *actin* molecules of the thin filaments. When a muscle receives a signal to contract, the heads of the myosin molecules pull on the actin molecules, causing the filaments to slide along each other. The molecules then detach themselves from one another and reattach themselves farther along to pull again, repeating the cycle in a ratchet-like manner. Although the filaments themselves maintain a constant length, each cycle shortens the muscle by about one percent.

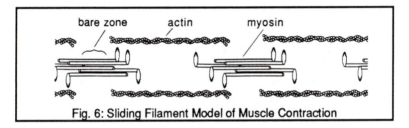
Fig. 6: Sliding Filament Model of Muscle Contraction

Factors limiting agility and strength
The detachment of the actin-myosin cross-bridges, allowing the muscle to relax, requires the presence of a chemical called adenosine triphosphate (*ATP*) which is stored in the muscles. Its complete absence produces rigor (as in *rigor mortis*). Since contraction also requires ATP, the amount available limits our agility (rapid cycles of contraction and relaxation).

If a muscle is stretched to the point where the two kinds of filaments no longer overlap, then it can't contract. On the other hand, a shortened muscle loses strength, because there is an area in the centre of the myosin molecule which has no cross-bridges (*bare zone*), and the actin filament in this area has no force applied to it. Strength is further reduced when the actin filaments overlap, since the myosin projections then pull in the wrong direction at the tips of the actin filaments. The range of length at which muscles can exert a force has a ratio of about one to three, but most motions occur in a smaller range in which the force is greatest.

As the speed of contraction increases, the power output decreases, possibly because the actin filaments slide past the myosin at such a rate that fewer cross-bridge attachments can be formed.

More muscle geography

We have about seven or eight muscles per finger and ten muscles for the thumb. The index and little fingers have straightening (*extensor*) muscles of their own, while the middle and ring fingers do not (see table 3). The ring finger is the least independent, because there are bridges between its extensor tendon and both neighbors. Although the short finger-curling muscles (*flexors*) are in the hand, the longer ones are in the forearm, and some of them even have their origin in the upper arm. The ability to move individual fingers sideways (*adduction*, spreading; *abduction*, the reverse) permits fine control, e.g. making small adjustments in intonation on a string instrument. Hand movements are made mainly by six forearm muscles whose tendons cross the wrist to insert at the base of the metacarpal bones. The wrist bones have relatively few muscle attachments, so they are freely mobile.

The *biceps brachii* normally contract about 20 to 50 microseconds before a finger movement, to act as a stabilizer. (A *biceps* muscle is any muscle that has two tendons at one end; the muscle we call the biceps is an example, and is officially called *biceps brachii* to indicate its type and location.)

Although the upper limbs together contain only about 13 percent of our body mass, moving them can generate considerable momentum, so we need muscles to stabilize the trunk while we play. The main ones are the *latissimus dorsi*, *trapezius*, and *gluteus maximus*, all in the back, and their antagonists, the *pectoralis major* and *rectus abdominis*.

TENDONS

Tendons are the fibers of connective tissue extending from the ends of skeletal muscles to attach them to bones. They form heavy collagenous bundles, held together by delicate cross-fibers. Usually the junction of tendon and muscle is an interwoven network of tendon and muscle fibers. Tendons don't contract, but they are somewhat elastic and contribute to the support of joints.

Table 3: Some of the Muscles of the Hand

Name	Location	Function
extensor carpi (3 muscles)	elbow to metacarpals	extension of fingers
extensor digitorum	elbow to phalanges	"
extensor indicis	"	extension of index finger
extensor digiti minimi	"	" little finger
extensor pollicis (2 muscles)	"	" thumb
flexor carpi (2 muscles)	elbow to metacarpals	flexion of fingers
flexor digitorum (2 muscles)	elbow to phalanges	"
flexor digiti minimi brevis	hypothenar eminence (outside of palm, below little finger)	flexion of little finger
flexor pollicis longus	thenar eminence (base of thumb)	" thumb
" brevis	"	"
opponens pollicis	"	opposition of thumb
" digiti minimi	hypothenar eminence	" little finger
palmar interossei	palm (between metacarpals)	adduction of individual fingers
adductor pollicis	betw. metacarpals of thumb and fingers	adduction of thumb
lumbricals	"	flexion, grasping
dorsal interossei	back of hand (between metacarpals)	abduction of individual fingers
abductor digiti minimi	hypothenar eminence	abduction of little finger
" pollicis longus	elbow to metacarpal	" thumb
" " brevis	thenar eminence	"

THE CIRCULATORY SYSTEM

A network of blood vessels circulates vital substances throughout the body. The *arteries* carry fresh blood from the heart, while the *veins* dispose of wastes (*metabolites*). The veins have one-way valves to keep the blood from pooling in the extremities. The arteries branch off into smaller vessels (*capillaries*) which have semipermeable walls which let food and oxygen pass out into the *interstitial fluid* bathing the cells. The capillaries return carbon dioxide and wastes to the veins.

The health of virtually every cell in the body depends on an adequate blood supply. Muscles depend on it for both efficient fuel supply and efficient waste removal. Injured tissue will heal faster when the circulation is good.

THE NERVOUS SYSTEM

Neurons are the basic units of the nervous system (see fig. 7). They contain a cell body whose membrane branches out into a large number of fine extensions (*dendrites*) which receive most of the signals from other neurons. There may also be a single long extension of the cell body called the *axon*; if the nerve is of a type which needs to communicate with distant parts of the body, the axon may be more than a meter long. It branches out at the end into *axon terminals*, which are responsible for transmitting signals.

Most nerve axons are protected by a *myelin sheath*, which acts as a kind of insulation and facilitates fast transmission of signals. It doesn't contain much *cytoplasm* (protoplasm outside a cell's nucleus). Instead, the myelin sheath is surrounded by a specialized cell (*Schwann cell*) which wraps its own cytoplasm around it. The myelin sheath is made of fatty acids and requires nutritional support for its maintenance. It is interrupted at regular intervals by *nodes of Ranvier*, which allow an exchange of sodium and potassium with the extracellular fluid so that signals can be propagated along the next segment of the axon.

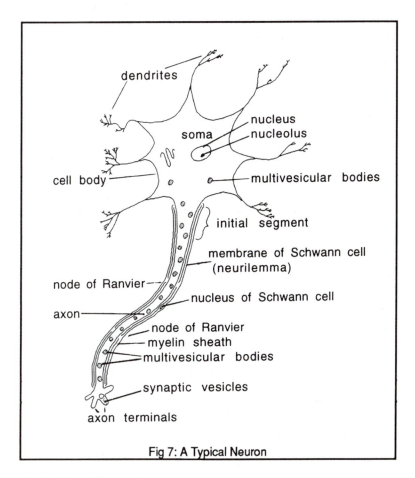

Fig 7: A Typical Neuron

labels in figure:
dendrites
nucleus
soma
nucleolus
cell body
multivesicular bodies
initial segment
membrane of Schwann cell (neurilemma)
node of Ranvier
nucleus of Schwann cell
axon
node of Ranvier
myelin sheath
multivesicular bodies
synaptic vesicles
axon terminals

Excitable cell membranes

Both nerve cells and muscle cells have excitable membranes, i.e. because the cell membrane has high electrical resistance, an electrical charge (*action potential*) can build up across it. When this charge reaches a certain level, the resistance is momentarily overcome (*depolarization*), and there is a sudden short burst of electrical current. The changes in electrical charge depend on the presence of sodium, potassium, and calcium ions in the surrounding fluid, so chemical activity outside of the cell causes action within the cell. In the gaps (*synapses*) between nerve cells, the change in one nerve cell is transmitted to the next by a process called saltatory conduction (from *saltare*, to dance). In the skeletal muscles, the impulse comes either from a nerve or from local changes in the chemistry of the muscle itself.

Some geography of the nervous system

The nervous system is conceptually divided into two parts, incoming signals (*afferent*) and outgoing signals (*efferent*). The afferent nervous system carries messages from the sense receptors in the skin about touch, temperature, and pain. It also carries messages about the degree of stretch, which are processed in other parts of the central nervous system. These messages, together with input from other sense organs (e.g. eyes and ears), and from position sensors (*proprioceptors*) in nerves and muscle spindles, form the basis for efferent signals which are transmitted along the nerves to effect a muscular contraction in response to a conscious decision to move.

The main source of nerve messages to the muscles is the *anterior horn* in the spinal cord, which is contacted directly by the brain's largest neurons, the *Betz cells* in the motor cortex. The basal ganglia of the brain, which work via the motor cortex, are responsible for coordination of different muscle groups. The cerebellum deals with feedback received during the execution of a movement.

The cerebellum may also be responsible for shifts from *current* (continuous, ongoing) control to *ballistic* control, where the details of a movement are settled at its onset so that it proceeds semi-automatically. Ballistic control gives speed to skilled movements. It may be that an inner state of relaxation facilitates this process (known as *grooving*) by letting the cerebellum inhibit muscular contraction.

The chain from finger tip to brain includes a number of nerve cells. One motor neuron branches out to innervate several muscle fibers. The *innervation ratio* (number of nerve fibers at the end of one motor neuron) is 3 to 1 in the hand, versus about 150 to 1 in the trunk. This means that we have much finer control in the hand. With biofeedback it is possible to learn selectively to control one *motor unit* (the muscle fibers innervated by one motor neuron). *Alpha* motor neurons exert coarse control, while *gamma* motor neurons exert fine control and facilitate sustained effort by letting muscles alternate.

The spinal cord contains short neurons, called *interneurons,* which either excite or inhibit other nerve cells. These modify signals from the brain to suit the specific state of the body. This helps us control both the speed and efficiency of each motion.

Stretch reflex
When a skeletal muscle is subjected to a rapid passive stretch, the stretch receptors embedded in its spindle fibers register information about the speed and magnitude of the stretch. If the stretch is dangerously rapid or large, the muscle immediately contracts to protect itself from injury. This process is called the *monosynaptic stretch reflex.* It is termed monosynaptic because only the motor neuron needs to receive the information in order to act on it. Since it thus bypasses the higher nerve centers, it is extremely quick. At the same time, the antagonist muscles are inhibited and the synergistic muscles are activated. This has the effect of reinforcing the contraction of the mucle being protected. Information is also relayed to the brain, where it is used to monitor movement. When a muscle contracts, the stretch reflex may be activated to smooth out the motion or maintain resting tension.

SKIN

A square centimeter of skin contains an average of 2 nerve endings for warmth, 13 for cold, 25 for touch, and 200 for pain. The fingertips have the greatest density of tactile corpuscles, at 100 per square millimeter. Unfortunately for the nervous performer, they also have the greatest density of sweat glands and a considerable number of oil glands.

Epithelial tissue forms the outer layer of the skin (*epidermis*), as well as the linings of all body cavities. It has no blood vessels and very little intercellular substance. Fingernails originate in the outer part of the epidermis, which also contains pigment. The next layer, the *dermis*, contains connective tissue, blood vessels, nerve endings, and glands. The *subcutaneous* layer, the deepest layer of the skin, contains fat deposits and hair follicles and connects the skin to the surface muscles. These three areas are not rigidly divided, and the components of one layer often extend into the next.

Table 4: Specialized Receptor Nerve Endings

Name	Location	Probable Function
network of Langerhans	epidermis (outer layer of skin)	
menisci of Ranvier	epidermis	
Pacinian corpuscles	dermal layer of palms (and nerves of the joints?)	sense changes in pressure, detect vibration (to 300 Hz)
arboriform terminations of Dogiel	dermal layer	
monolobar corpuscles of Meissner	papillary (outer dermal) layer of palms, some other touch-sensitive areas	sense of touch (?) (not found on all tactile surfaces)
corpuscles of Ruffini	deep in subcutaneous tissue of fingers	
articular end-bulbs of Krause	synovial membrane of finger joints	
Golgi organs	tendons	sense tension
neuromuscular spindles	most voluntary muscles	sense muscular tension; sense of touch

Chapter 2

FUEL AND RESOURCE MANAGEMENT
how the healthy performer regulates body chemistry

All of the systems of the body affect the body chemistry, which in turn affects the ability of the limbs and joints to function. Although nutrition affects body chemistry, it is mentioned in this chapter only when there are connections to a specific body part or function. Section II (Chapters 7-12) contains more information about nutrition and diet.

This chapter discusses the chemistry of several body systems and explores the importance of energy cycles to the performer.

Part I: body systems revisited

THE BONES

The chemical composition of a bone does not remain constant, even over the short term. Calcium, phosphorus, magnesium, and other minerals are continuously deposited in the bones and reabsorbed into the blood stream. During the course of the day, the body loses some of these minerals by excretion, so diet is important for maintaining strong bones. Impact exercise can reduce the loss of calcium from bones and is generally healthier than taking calcium supplements, though both may be necessary.

Bones also function as a reservoir, releasing their stored–up mineral supply to maintain the health of the vital organs. Thus, if we don't absorb enough from our food to replace losses, the bones will be among the first organs to suffer. This choice of priorities makes us live longer, but it can endanger a career.

Bone marrow is also a living tissue. Its functions include storing nutrients, and building blood cells.

THE JOINTS, LIGAMENTS AND TENDONS

The state of our body chemistry affects the health of both cartilage and synovial fluid. Though the connective tissue in cartilage has few capillaries, it requires a steady supply of all of the nutrients which strengthen collagen. As mentioned in Chapter 1, grit in the form of calcium deposits will speed up joint wear. One way to keep calcium deposits out of the joints is to regulate the intake of other minerals, as well as vitamin D. Other ways to control this process include eating slowly and chewing thoroughly.

Ligaments and tendons have a limited blood supply, so they heal more slowly than muscles and are particularly sensitive to a shortage of nutrients.

MUSCLES

Muscles need a number of nutrients in order to contract and relax. Transmission of electrical impulses across the excitable membranes of nerves and muscles depends on the presence of potassium, calcium, and sodium. The lower the external calcium concentration, the more easily the potassium and sodium ions flow across the cell membrane to produce the threshold depolarization necessary for firing. Magnesium ions compete with calcium ions, so an increased magnesium concentration can inhibit the release of acetylcholine (*ACh*), which is needed in the depolarization cycle. The metabolic pump involved in these transactions uses adenosine triphosphate (*ATP*) as an energy source, so the fuels needed in ATP energy cycles are needed here too.

Calcium is also needed for excitation coupling, the process leading to the binding of actin to myosin for muscular contraction. This calcium is returned to the muscle to be stored for the next contraction. When the muscle is at rest, the free calcium concentration is low, and the sliding of the filaments is blocked by molecules of *tropomyosin*. When the muscle is stimulated, the calcium concentration must rise, since contraction can only proceed if the calcium binds to *troponin*.

The storage and release of this intramuscular calcium again requires ATP. Calcium and magnesium inhibit the conversion of ATP by myosin which is not bound to actin. The mechanism regulating the release of intramuscular calcium is not well understood, but it is clear that blood calcium levels influence muscle tension. Blood calcium levels are tied to the levels of other minerals, so other factors in the diet will influence the calcium levels, and through them the state of the muscles.

The electrolyte balance in the blood and interstitial fluid affects muscle function in yet another way. While the red (slow twitch) muscles are believed to be supplied by capillaries which are constantly open, the white (fast twitch) muscles are nourished by capillaries whose diameter is controlled by small, smooth (involuntary) muscles called *precapillary sphincters*. The contractions of the sphincter muscles are controlled by local metabolism rather than by the nervous system. When the white fibers contract, there is a higher concentration of wastes (*metabolites*) in the surrounding blood. This makes the precapillary sphincters lose their tone, which in turn increases the blood supply to the white muscle. The resting level of contraction (*basal tone*) of the precapillary sphincters is higher for the vessels serving the skeletal muscles than for any other organ in the body. They spontaneously contract about once a minute, and the shortening of their myofilaments is relatively slow. When the body is at rest, many capillaries have no flow at all. During trills or other fast passages, the precapillary sphincters must relax to let fuel reach the muscles.

THE SKIN

The health of the skin is dependent on our nutritional state, particularly on supplies of vitamin A and zinc. Skin is an indicator of our emotional state and generally reflects the health of the body which it surrounds. It is an organ of elimination, duplicating the work of the kidneys and lungs. Keeping the skin "breathing" can reduce the strain on those organs, in turn affecting the health of every cell in the body.

THE CIRCULATORY SYSTEM

The blood has been called the fulcrum on which the see-saw of body chemistry balances. The balance is quite delicate, and if any one system deviates far from its norm then all other systems of the body will be affected by the necessary changes in the blood. Thus our muscles, for example, can be influenced by the state of our kidneys.

When the electrolyte balance is upset, some substances precipitate out into the blood and cause it to thicken, thus impeding the flow and transmission of nutrients and wastes. Some of these substances may further impede circulation by forming plaques on the walls of the blood vessels. Blood pressure is related both to the thickness of the blood and to the flexibility of the blood vessel walls, while both of these factors are influenced by nutrition. Every cell in the body is dependent on its blood supply, so anything which affects the circulatory system will affect all of our organs.

THE NERVOUS SYSTEM

Efficient nervous transmission depends on the balance of electrolytes, especially sodium, potassium, and calcium. The concentration of one electrolyte affects the concentration of the others, while all are affected by eating habits, exercise, and the efficiency of the digestive system. The myelin sheath surrounding the nerves can be robbed of its essential fatty acids and B vitamins to protect other parts of the body when supplies are low, so nervous problems may be the first signs of nutritional deficiencies.

THE ELIMINATIVE ORGANS

The accumulation of metabolites (wastes) limits our ability to do work, and their efficient removal requires good circulation. Dilation of the capillaries surrounding working muscles is increased when the metabolites themselves reduce the tone of the precapillary sphincter muscles. Thus the intensity of metabolism regulates blood flow and vice versa.

On the way to and from the capillaries, both wastes and nutrients must pass through the *interstitial fluid* which bathes every cell in the body. If the transport systems are inefficient, the interstitial fluid becomes filled with toxic sludge. In order to maintain balance, the muscles, sometimes referred to as the "toxic sponge of the body," take up some of the toxins. This process helps keep our vital organs healthier, but it doesn't do much for the efficiency of the muscles. Diet, exercise, and herbs play important roles in keeping the interstitial fluid at its optimal composition.

Ultimately wastes must leave the body via our eliminative organs, i.e. the kidneys, lungs, intestines, and skin. If even one of the eliminative organs is inefficient, the muscles will suffer.

THE ENDOCRINE SYSTEM

The endocrine system affects, and is affected by, body chemistry in many ways. The hormonal balance has a bearing on both the rate of glucose entry into the blood stream and the transformation of fat into fuel. Thyroxin increases muscle blood flow. Vasopressin helps control blood pressure, and calcium is needed for the release of this hormone from the pituitary gland. Hormones influence the kidneys, which in turn govern electrolyte balance and keep toxins out of the cells and interstitial fluid. Exercise influences both the endocrine and digestive systems, and both of these help regulate mineral levels.

Part II: ATP and the energy cycles

ATP

A compound called ATP (*adenosine triphosphate*) is the immediate source of energy for every cell in the body. It is needed for the transfer of energy from one molecule to another and is particularly important to the performer because of its role in muscular contraction. ATP is stored within each cell in small organelles called *mitochondria*.

To release energy, ATP is broken down into ADP (*adenosine diphosphate*) and free phosphate. To replenish ATP supplies, we need simply to glue the two substances back together (see fig 8). This resynthesis of ATP requires energy, which is supplied by the breakdown of fuels (proteins, fats, carbohydrates).

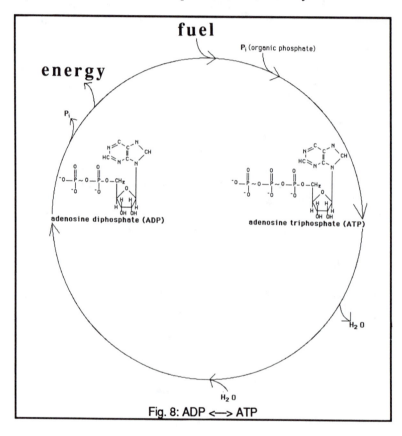

Fig. 8: ADP <—> ATP

AEROBIC CYCLE: ENDURANCE EVENTS

A muscle stores only enough ATP for a few twitches. In aerobic conditions, i.e. in the presence of oxygen, the ATP needed for further work is synthesized (from ADP and inorganic phosphate) by a process called *oxidative phosphorylation*.

The fuel for this reaction can come from carbohydrates, proteins, or lipids (fats). Muscle contains *glycogen* (derived from carbohydrates), which is a good fuel source while it lasts, but eventually the body must mobilize other fuel reserves. For high work loads the body burns mostly carbohydrates, while for long work times the body burns more fat. There is not a sudden switch from one fuel to the other.

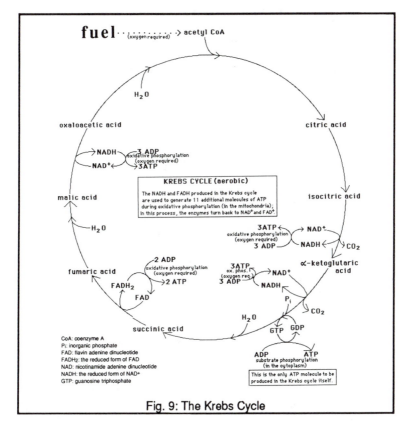

fuel $\cdots \underset{(oxygen\,required)}{\cdots\cdots\cdots} >$ acetyl CoA

H_2O

oxaloacetic acid

citric acid

$\rightarrow$ NADH
$-$ NAD$^+$ $\leftarrow$

3 ADP
oxidative phosphorylation
(oxygen required)
$\rightarrow$ 3ATP

KREBS CYCLE (aerobic)

The NADH and FADH produced in the Krebs cycle are used to generate 11 additional molecules of ATP during oxidative phosphorylation (in the mitochondria); in this process, the enzymes turn back to NAD$^+$ and FAD$^+$.

malic acid

isocitric acid

$-$ H_2O

3ATP
oxidative phosphorylation
(oxygen required)
3 ADP

$\rightarrow$ NAD$^+$
NADH $\leftarrow$ $\rightarrow$ CO_2

fumaric acid

2 ADP
oxidative phosphorylation
(oxygen required)
$\rightarrow$ 2 ATP

3ATP
ox. phos.
(oxygen req.)
3 ADP

$\rightarrow$ NAD$^+$
NADH $\leftarrow$

α-ketoglutaric acid

FADH$_2$
FAD

H_2O

P$_i$
CO_2

succinic acid

GTP GDP

CoA: coenzyme A
P$_i$: inorganic phosphate
FAD: flavin adenine dinucleotide
FADH$_2$: the reduced form of FAD
NAD: nicotinamide adenine dinucleotide
NADH: the reduced form of NAD$^+$
GTP: guanosine triphosphate

ADP ATP
substrate phosphorylation
(in the cytoplasm)

This is the only ATP molecule to be produced in the Krebs cycle itself.

Fig. 9: The Krebs Cycle

Regardless of the type of fuel available, we need oxygen to convert it to a substance called *acetyl coenzyme A* (acetyl CoA), which usually enters the *Krebs cycle* (see fig. 9) to produce ATP. (If figure 9 looks unduly complicated, bear in mind that in 1952 Hans Krebs received a Nobel Prize for describing this metabolic pathway.) The Krebs cycle generates only one molecule of ATP, but it produces a series of coenzymes (NADH and FADH) which then enter the oxidative phosphorylation pathway in the mitochondria of the cells. By utilizing further oxygen supplies, these coenzymes produce eleven additional molecules of ATP. In the process, the coenzymes are restored to a form which can be reused in the Krebs cycle.

Some oxygen is bound to myoglobin and stored in the muscles, but eventually oxygen must be supplied by the blood. There is very little waste from the Krebs cycle, since most of its byproducts are recycled continually, but there are 2 molecules of carbon dioxide which are not reused. Carbon dioxide interferes with the ability of oxygen to reach the cells, so it must be eliminated from the body. The amount of work possible in the aerobic cycle, and therefore endurance, is limited by the efficiency of both oxygen supply and carbon dioxide elimination.

ANAEROBIC CYCLE: SPRINTING

In sustained, intense exercise (e.g. sprinting), oxygen may not be supplied quickly enough to meet the energy requirements of continued muscular contraction. In these anaerobic conditions a less efficient mechanism is invoked which requires no oxygen but leaves behind messier waste products.

ATP can be synthesized without oxygen by the breakdown of PC (*phosphorylcreatine*, sometimes called *creatine phosphate*, or CP). This mechanism is quite efficient and is often used at the beginning of either aerobic or anaerobic exercise (see fig. 10). It works much like the battery in a car, getting it started until the engine can take over. Like the power from a car battery, the amount of PC available is severely limited. A muscle stores about three to five times as much PC as ATP, fast twitch fibers containing the greater amounts. Unlike the charge on a car battery, PC is replenished only when the muscle is at rest. During most of the anaerobic cycle, ATP is synthesized by *glycolysis* (the breakdown of glucose).

Muscle glycogen stores are liberated as the first source of glucose, but the supply of muscle glycogen is limited also. In the next stage, glucose is synthesized by the body, primarily from carbohydrates, and diffuses across muscle cell membranes.

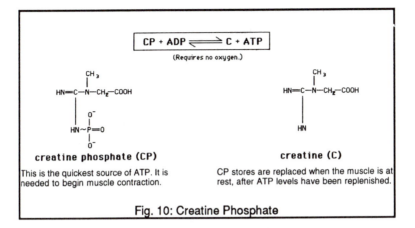

Fig. 10: Creatine Phosphate

Just as it does in the aerobic state, the glycolysis of one glucose molecule produces two molecules of ATP by a process which is called *substrate phosphorylation* because it takes place outside the nucleus (in the *cytoplasm*). In the aerobic state the end product of glycolysis is acetyl CoA, which enters the Krebs cycle to generate a further twelve molecules of ATP. In the anaerobic state, however, the glycolytic chain leads to no further ATP production, so the anaerobic cycle is much less fuel-efficient.

The second-last step in the glycolytic chain is *pyruvate*. In the aerobic state pyruvate is converted to acetyl CoA, but in the anaerobic state it is converted to *lactic acid*. This is taken to the liver to resynthesize glycogen (see fig. 11, Cori cycle), but the process is very slow. As lactic acid accumulates in the muscle, the ability to contract decreases and eventually stops. Consequently, at maximal performance we may have as little as thirty seconds of work time. We cannot sprint for as long as we can jog, for even if we ignore the pain of lactic acid buildup, the muscle will eventually cramp.

ATP levels do not fall except in cases of extreme fatigue. If the ATP concentration falls below a certain level, the muscle can go into an irreversible stretch known as *rigor*. Lactic acid production continues for a short time after quitting strenuous exercise, perhaps to repay the initial oxygen debt.

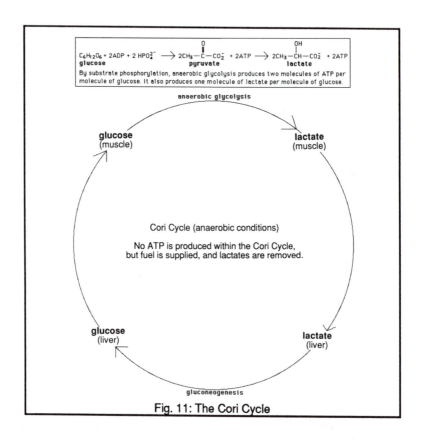

By substrate phosphorylation, anaerobic glycolysis produces two molecules of ATP per molecule of glucose. It also produces one molecule of lactate per molecule of glucose.

anaerobic glycolysis

glucose
(muscle)

lactate
(muscle)

Cori Cycle (anaerobic conditions)

No ATP is produced within the Cori Cycle,
but fuel is supplied, and lactates are removed.

glucose
(liver)

lactate
(liver)

gluconeogenesis

Fig. 11: The Cori Cycle

SPORTS AND PERFORMANCE: COMBINING THE CYCLES

To do sustained work, you must stay primarily in the aerobic cycle. There may be an initial lag in the body's response, so the muscle converts PC in the anaerobic state for a short time. Whenever a muscle's subsequent output exceeds about 50 percent of its maximum potential, some of the energy for contraction must come from anaerobic glycolysis. Between bursts of anaerobic work, you need to be able to coast and repay the oxygen debt while removing lactates. The switches between aerobic and anaerobic cycles are not immediate, but the fitter you are, the faster you can make them.

By pushing their limits, endurance athletes sometimes suffer from "bonking" (running out of muscle glycogen) or "hitting the wall" (running out of liver glycogen). The two types of anaerobic depletion sound similar but have different symptoms: in the former, the muscle becomes uncoordinated and painful, while in the latter, the whole body is affected, producing confusion, cold sweats, and shakiness along with the weak and uncoordinated movements. Eating during breaks can prevent bonking, and eating immediately will lead to quick recovery.

An endurance athlete can benefit from a program which increases oxygen uptake and utilization or establishes plentiful glycogen stores. Oxygen supplies are increased by making the heart and lungs stronger, by enlarging the arteries, by increasing the number of red blood cells, by increasing iron levels so that the blood can carry more oxygen, and by increasing the rate at which the enzymes in the muscles pick up oxygen from the blood. Endurance is limited by the stability of the blood sugar. Adequate potassium is needed also, to remove excess heat from the muscles. Diet and exercise affect all of these factors, and herbs can tone weak organs.

Are most performers endurance athletes? We do have to build enough of an aerobic base so that ordinary playing can be done in an aerobic state. On the local muscular level this means frequent repetition of the performing motions at a level which doesn't cause fatigue, e.g. slow practice, in order to increase circulation to the endurance (red) muscle fibers. Aerobic exercise (e.g. running) is also helpful, though unless you are a dancer, the level of cardiovascular exertion during performance is not likely to compare to that of a marathon runner. You could walk at a slow pace all day, if you sipped nourishing drinks, wore good shoes, etc; this does not make strolling an endurance sport. It is not usually the background playing that causes injury, though poor posture or the need to support the instrument in an awkward position for a long time may do so. These risks will be reduced by improving the aerobic base, but you will probably benefit more from a change in equipment, stretching between playing sessions, or taking Alexander lessons (see Section IV). Most injuries occur while a muscle is in the anaerobic state and unable to get rid of lactates and other metabolites efficiently enough.

Most of our playing has elements of both cycles in it. When you go back into the aerobic cycle after a "sprint," the lactic acid will convert back to carbon dioxide (via pyruvic acid) and you will get a fresh start for the next one. (This is what happens in sports like baseball which require brief bursts of speed against a background of relatively slow running.) If, on the other hand, you play trills for half an hour, the pain you feel may indeed be from "hitting the wall." With sheer will power you can keep going, though the muscle will eventually burn its own tissue for fuel. The longer you persevere in playing those trills, the longer you will need for recuperation afterwards. A trained muscle can tolerate a higher buildup of lactic acid than an untrained one, so training will heighten your anaerobic capacity. Gradually increase the strength of the muscle, the speed with which it has to move, and the time spent in this cycle.

Runners know they are in the anaerobic cycle when they are out of breath. Although that's not a useful criterion for the average musician at his instrument, we need to aim for a fitness level which allows us to stay in the aerobic cycle for all but a brief time. To prepare for a piece which feels like a marathon, train like a long-distance runner.

Chapter 3

EXERCISE
how the healthy performer gets fit

Exercise affects the whole body, so it contributes greatly to healthy performance. As a bonus, physical fitness is said to enhance creativity.

This chapter is divided into three parts. The first part shows how exercise affects each system of the body, the second part suggests some warmups, and the third part discusses a few training concepts developed by athletic coaches.

Part I: how exercise affects various body systems

Some of the effects discussed here are specific to one area of the body, while others are more general. Since each part of the body affects all other parts, the classifications below are necessarily arbitrary. Each section covers first the short term effects and then the long term ones.

BONES

short term: Exercise causes no short term structural changes in a healthy bone, unless the stress is sufficient to cause injury.

long term: Any exercise which puts a load on the bones makes them absorb calcium which might otherwise be excreted from the body. Prolonged rest leads to demineralization and weak bones.

Strengthening the muscles puts stress on the bones, which can respond by becoming stronger and larger, often rearranging their structure to form new supportive fibers called *trabeculae*. Severe repetitive strain, on the other hand, can lead to inflammation and osteoporosis.

MUSCLES

short term: During active contraction a muscle usually shortens by fifty to sixty percent of its resting length. The sheath (*fascia*) surrounding the fiber bundles becomes tense and thus promotes both stability and efficiency. Muscles generally liberate heat at a higher rate when they are shortening. The heat energy released is proportional to the work done, but the temperature is greatly dependent on the local circulation.

Adrenaline speeds up the circulation to aid delivery of fuel and elimination of waste, raises our blood sugar to provide fuel for muscles, increases cerebral metabolism to make us more alert and to improve neuromuscular response, and increases the excitability of the neurons to facilitate motor activity. Small doses of adrenaline dilate muscle capillaries, but large doses constrict them. This means that being a little nervous for a performance is a good thing, but extreme nervousness is not. Fortunately there is evidence that as little as 15 minutes' walking works better than a tranquilizer.

long term: Work requiring great effort, e.g. weight lifting, can cause measurable long-term muscular changes, including a decrease in internal fat and increases in protein and fluid. Fatty tissue reduces the efficiency of contraction by producing friction, so the loss of fat increases strength. Other forms of exercise cause changes which are too small to measure and can be inferred only by enhanced working capacity.

The capacity of the alactic (aerobic) mechanism is related to muscle mass and thus improves with strength training, while the enzymes needed to metabolize nutrient reserves and remove lactates (anaerobic state) increase in both quantity and effectiveness. Consequently, trained athletes are able to exercise at a more intense level without accumulating lactic acid, though these benefits come more slowly with age. On the average it takes about three times as long to lose muscle mass through inactivity as to build it up.

Strength training also decreases the effectiveness of the inhibitory mechanisms, because the thickening and toughening of the tissue shields the *Golgi organs* (table 4, Chapter 1) and raises the threshold at which they begin to inhibit contraction. This helps weight lifters, but it could mean loss of control or even risk of injury if the antagonists are not strong enough to balance the action of the dominant muscle. On the other hand, strength training builds up the antagonists to help control the slow lifting of heavy loads.

Endurance training increases the myoglobin content, which facilitates muscular oxygen utilisation. The mitochondria increase in both number and size, thus contributing enzymes involved in energy metabolism. Glycogen stores are not only increased, but are depleted more slowly (*glycogen sparing*). Stores of ATP and CP are increased along with the enzymes needed to utilize them.

Although the distribution of fast twitch (white) and slow twitch fibers (red) is fixed at birth (see table 2, Chapter 1), strength training increases the diameter of the muscle fibers, adds mitochondria, and causes the myofibrils to split longitudinally, so that there are more of them. These factors have the same effect as adding white fibers: we can play faster trills but could lose some endurance. The loss in endurance should be more than offset by the increased efficiency with which trained muscles extract oxygen from the blood stream. Endurance training decreases the white fibers' levels of myosin ATPase, which controls the rate of splitting of ATP, but increases the levels in red fibers, further obscuring the differences between the two types of fibers.

A certain number of our muscle fibers are dormant (latent or inactive), but with training a higher proportion of the fibers are able to contract. This phenomenon is thought to be due to the improvement in utilization of nerve pathways and transmission of impulses.

TENDONS AND LIGAMENTS

short term: Exercise produces no short term structural changes in healthy tendons or ligaments, unless the stress is sufficient to cause injury.

long term: All connective tissue, including tendons and ligaments, has some elasticity and can become more elastic with proper training. The circulation to the connective tissue may also improve. With heavy workloads over time, all connective tissue undergoes primary cellular multiplication, causing it to broaden, toughen, and gain tensile strength.

All of these changes make the tendons and ligaments stronger, more flexible, and better nourished. Wastes are removed more efficiently, and when microtraumas occur, repairs are made more quickly. Thus the tissues are less prone to injury

SKIN

Repeated trauma to the skin causes toughening of the epidermal layer, but improved peripheral circulation may help prevent calluses.

THE RESPIRATORY SYSTEM

short term: Even "non-athletic" performance has numerous short-term effects on respiration. The amount of air inhaled per minute (*pulmonary ventilation*) can increase two to five fold during sixty minutes of playing the violin. The number of breaths per minute (*respiration rate*) rises, but the amount of air inhaled in each breath (*tidal volume*) may decrease. Oxygen consumption increases two to seven fold. There is a "warm-up" factor in each case, i.e. after a while the effects become less pronounced, but mistakes cause a rise in oxygen consumption, even on repetition of the passage. There is also a correlation between the pulse rate and the melodic line. Scientists have also found increases in both pulse rate and respiratory gas exchange just before a performance.

Prolonged heavy exercise, e.g. running, can increase oxygen consumption for several hours.

long term: Regular training increases the maximal oxygen uptake and tidal volume, and decreases the respiration rate.

THE DIGESTIVE SYSTEM

short term: Hard exercise shouldn't be undertaken after a big meal, because blood needed by the muscles is preempted by the digestive organs. On the other hand, a meal with too much sugar can sometimes be worked off by exercise, which makes the body utilize the sugar as fuel and so dampens the swings in blood sugar levels.

long term: Regular aerobic exercise increases peristaltic action, thus speeding up the movement of food and wastes through the intestinal tract (i.e. reducing *bowel transit time*) and helping get rid of toxic wastes.

METABOLISM

short term: Muscular work does not increase the use of proteins, since we burn carbohydrates and fat whenever they are available. If we exercise at a steady rate, the carbohydrate contribution decreases with time, as prolonged aerobic exercise leads to mobilization of fat stores for use as an energy source.

long term: As a result of training we take in more oxygen and use it more efficiently, produce more enzymes for ATP metabolism, and burn more fat by remaining in the aerobic state longer.

Exercise may reduce tissue cholesterol levels by shifting plasma cholesterol from low density to high density lipoprotein fractions.

CELLS AND TISSUES

short term: Although there are immediate changes to the cells of the specific body parts being exercised, global cellular changes occur only in the long term.

long term: Regular endurance training causes a number of changes at the cellular level which increase oxygen uptake. There are more *oxidative enzymes* (used in the aerobic cycle to convert ADP back to ATP), proteins (especially *cytochrome C*, located in the mitochondria and used in aerobic metabolism), and *myoglobin* (used in the diffusion of oxygen from the cell membrane to the mitochondria), and there are more and bigger mitochondria (the site of the aerobic mechanism), thus increasing the surface area for oxygen utilization. The resulting gain in mechanical efficiency (more work for the same amount of oxygen consumption) means greater skill and coordination.

THE CIRCULATORY SYSTEM

short term: Although exercise increases blood flow throughout the body, the muscles receive a larger share than most organs. The ratio between working and resting muscle blood flow can be ten to one, and is even greater during maximal activity. During muscular contraction, the flow of blood to the rest of the body is decreased, and the blood pressure at the muscle rises. Rhythmic contractions increase the flow to the muscle, but sustained contraction decreases the flow by producing mechanical compression.

If the circulatory system cannot supply enough oxygen, blood lactate levels rise when the muscle is exercising at only 60 or 70 percent of its capacity. The levels should decrease within 2 to 3 minutes after resting. Gentle rhythmic contraction speeds up the removal of lactates by promoting the recirculation of venous blood.

long term: There are many capillaries which normally are closed to blood flow. Systematic training not only adds new capillaries, but permanently opens some existing ones. It also leads to structural changes in the vascular bed which improve muscle blood supply. Endurance training makes it easier to transfer oxygen from the capillaries, so we require less blood. Top athletes have an unusually high total body hemoglobin, but this may be due to increased blood volume rather than increased hemoglobin concentration. There is also an increase in the amount of another compound, 2,3-diphosphoglycerate, which is an intermediate in red blood cell metabolism and helps liberate oxygen to the tissues. This increase reflects increased fitness but is also necessary for maintenance of a given fitness level. Donating blood can lower endurance for two to three weeks.

Improved cardiovascular fitness from regular aerobic exercise benefits every part of the body. To get the full long-term benefit of aerobic exercise, it is necessary to raise the pulse rate to 60 percent of its maximum (a figure which depends on age) for 15 to 30 minutes at least 3 times a week. This may be a difficult habit to establish, but once in place, the body's homeostatic tendencies will maintain motivation. One researcher tried to find 30 exercisers willing to stop for 2 months but had to abandon his study for lack of volunteers.

THE NERVOUS SYSTEM

short term: "Paying attention" requires that the central nervous system regulate receptor sensitivity, i.e. suppress some inputs in favor of others. The sense receptors must cooperate with parts of the brain to maintain this state of attention.

long term: Repeated stimulation of the same areas in the cerebral cortex increases their dominance, so that a task becomes easier and seems more automatic. Repeating a movement induces *grooving*, i.e. the neuron fibers thicken and the dendrites enlarge, speeding conduction of impulses and reducing reaction time. Grooving may transfer some control from cortical centers to lower ones, speeding up transmission further.

General fitness affects the entire nervous system. As we become more fit we become better coordinated, enjoy improved senses of touch and hearing, have a shorter reaction time, and sleep better. We can even think more clearly, because more oxygen reaches the brain

THE ELIMINATIVE SYSTEM

short term: Sweating facilitates elimination of wastes through the skin, thus easing the load on the kidneys.

long term: Regular aerobic exercise, e.g. running, increases intestinal *motility*, i.e. wastes move more quickly through the bowels. The lungs benefit as exercise opens up more *alveoli*, the air sacs where gases are exchanged with the blood stream, thus aiding removal of carbon dioxide and increasing our working capacity. The skin "breathes" better, so it is a more efficient eliminative organ.

Part II: An exercise "routine" to help prevent some common problems

After all that theory, it's high time to get down to practical matters. If you've read straight through to here, you certainly need an exercise break!

There is no need to adhere rigidly to a daily exercise routine. Some people thrive on routine, finding that a regular exercise pattern promotes peace of mind. Others stagnate or rebel. Not only is boredom a motive for quitting, it is synonymous with reduced awareness, which means reduced benefits and increased risk of injury. It may be best to let your body tell you each day how much you need to do and which areas need the most work. But be aware that the body resists change (this is a survival mechanism called *homeostasis*), so sometimes you will have to override reluctance in favor of future benefits.

Although most of us are stiffest in the morning and might feel a need to limber up, others find that they benefit more from doing stretches at night before going to bed. It's OK to do light exercise before sleeping, and the benefits might even continue as you sleep. Have fun: it's more effective that way.

The lists of exercises below offer some ideas for varying the daily warm-up. Your body will give you others, and so will the many books on the market. Some of the books which can help are listed in the bibliography for this section. Since exercise does affect the mind, there are a few references in the following paragraphs to "bodywork" books, which are reviewed in the bibliography for Section IV (Chapter 21).

These lists contain no calisthenics, those exercises which typically require frequent repetition of fast and uncontrolled (ballistic) movements. Many athletes feel that calisthenics are more likely to injure tight muscles than to stretch them, don't add much strength, don't do anything to increase technical skill, and generally are best avoided.

You may want to include strengthening exercises, e.g. pushups or working with weights, in your routine. Even if you use mainly the smaller muscles in performance, and are concerned more with speed than with strength, you may find that strengthening the large muscles closer to the trunk allows them to take some of the load off the small muscles of the extremities. There are some suggestions in this chapter for strengthening the large muscles, but the emphasis is on warming up and stretching.

After the warm-ups and stretches, try to go out into the fresh air and get the whole body moving. A trampoline, whether used indoors or outdoors, combines aerobic benefits with toning of the lymphatic system. Swimming in warm water is soothing to painful joints. For a "bad back," avoid strokes which cause you to hold an arch in the spine, in favor of the crawl (face in water) or a gentle back stroke. Brisk walking can also limber the back, and for lower back pain, you can wear a hip belt with cushioned weights which knead the back muscles while you walk. Running is one of the best methods of building an aerobic base.

The exercises below begin with the most gentle warm-ups for each area of the body. It is not necessary to follow the given progression, though starting with the spine usually feels best.

WARM-UPS FOR THE WARM-UPS

If you're too stiff to enjoy even gentle stretching, especially in the morning, t'ai chi may allow you to limber up painlessly.

Breathing exercises can warm you up. They can also be used anytime you need to expand or integrate energy. You can make sounds to increase the effects: try saying some gentle, rapid staccato "ee" sounds when you need to wake up, or shout a loud and explosive "ha!" to get the body warm and release tensions and constricting emotions. (My editor's cats request that you check for innocent bystanders before trying this.)

THE SPINE

The spine is vital to the functioning of the limbs and trunk, and connects them to one another. It is important to stretch the spine, e.g. with gentle forward bends, before doing exercises which twist it. As with all exercises, awareness is important. Try doing the forward bend (fig. 12) entirely as a spinal stretch, rather than stretching the hamstrings and the arms. Start bending at the base of the spine and let the stretch proceed one

Fig. 12: Sitting Forward Bend

Fig. 14: Flings

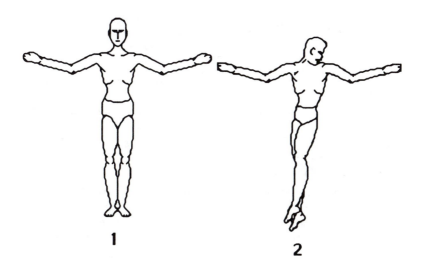

1

2

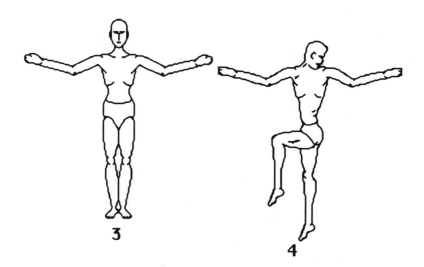

3

4

Fig. 13: The Crocodile

vertebra at a time, with the neck bending last of all. Let your shoulders stay relaxed. To return to an upright position, reverse the order, letting your spine keep lengthening all the time. Notice that we aren't calling this exercise "toe-touches;" you can touch your toes without any benefit to the spine, if your sole aim is to touch your toes. Try it and notice the difference.

Now that the spine is stretched, you may feel ready for some gentle twists. A very gentle and surprisingly effective one is called the crocodile (fig. 13). Lying on your back (*supine*) with arms outstretched, and keeping the shoulders and hips on the floor, turn the feet one way and the head the other way (repeat to the opposite side). This is followed by similar twists using other joints of the legs, e.g. crossing the ankles, or bending the knees and bringing both to one side. Move slowly, breathe, release unnecessary tensions, keep the spine stretched and the pelvis tucked, and focus on the process, not just on the goal. Other exercises which have a gentle effect on the spine include the "spine like a chain" exercise by Moshe Feldenkrais (see Chapter 21).

A more vigorous form of spinal twist (fig. 14) is done while standing up, using the momentum of swinging arms and legs (again moving them in opposite directions).

For a self-applied massage of sore back muscles, try leaning (fig. 15) against a tennis ball or an orange.

For more help with the spine, there are many alternative therapies, some of which are discussed in Section IV.

THE NECK

Thérèse Bertherat suggests an auto-massage which consists of grabbing the neck as you would grab the neck of a cat (fig. 16). If you can relax your neck while tensing your hand (of course you can, you mastered your instrument, didn't you?), this is a great way to loosen the neck muscles. Breathe deeply and enjoy.

You might begin with Moshe Feldenkrais's extremely gentle and effective version of the neck-roll, described in Chapter 21.

If you do the more conventional neck rolls (fig. 17) recommended by chiropractors, do them slowly with fewer repetitions. Keep the neck long, and imagine that your breath lubricates the spine. Begin by letting the head hang down (1,2),

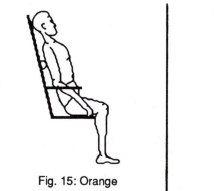

Fig. 15: Orange

Fig. 16: Cat Grip

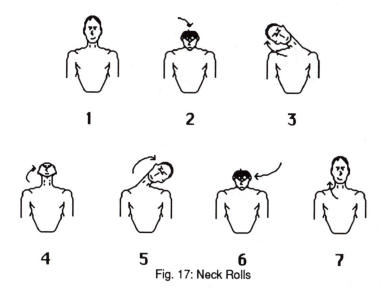

Fig. 17: Neck Rolls

then roll it until your ear rests on one shoulder (3). Continue until it hangs back (4), returning via the other shoulder (5, 6). Straighten up gradually, keeping the neck long (7). If there is pain at any stage, stop and return to the previous position. You probably need to pay more attention to keeping your neck long, but you may just need to quit for the day. If you can't do these neck rolls without pain, try the Feldenkrais ones instead.

THE EYES

Eye rolls are much like neck rolls. Rotate the eyeballs to look around in a circle (fig. 18). If you move as far as you can comfortably go in all directions, these exercises stretch the muscles of the eyeball and increase its range of motion. They should be followed by "palming" the eyes (fig 19), cupping the hands gently over the eyes to keep out light, and enjoying the warmth.

As with the neck rolls, Feldenkrais has a gentler version which seems to be at least as effective (see Chapter 21).

William Bates was the first of many authors to say that eye exercises can improve vision. His exercises include swinging the whole body back and forth (fig. 20) while letting the objects in the visual field appear to change their relative positions. Don't focus the eyes on anything, just enjoy the blur.

Bates also uses palming, suggesting that you pretend to look at a completely black field until that is what you actually do see. This relaxes your muscles so that the nerves which usually produce the "fireworks" are given a rest.

THE THROAT

The throat is associated with expression, both literally (as in singing and talking) and symbolically, so when you're nervous before a performance, your throat may tighten. Moving the trachea (wind pipe) gently back and forth with your hand (fig. 21) will reveal the tension carried in your throat and thus enable you to release it.

For an extra energy charge, move your hand a little lower and thump the sternum (breast bone) with your fist (fig. 22), like

Fig. 18: Eye Exercise

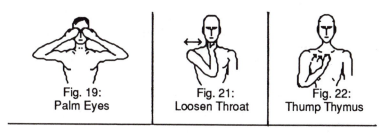

Fig. 19:
Palm Eyes

Fig. 21:
Loosen Throat

Fig. 22:
Thump Thymus

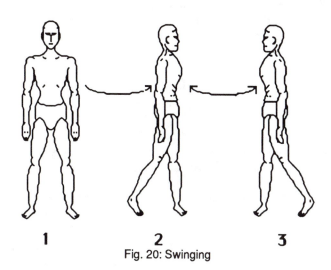

Fig. 20: Swinging

Tarzan. Some people feel that this stimulates the thymus gland.

The use of sound to expand or integrate energy is mentioned in "warm-ups for the warm-ups." You might want to experiment with sounds to help you feel the connection between the throat and the parts of the body you use in performance.

THE SHOULDERS

The shoulder joint is a complex joint, and the specific exercises needed will depend on the parts being limbered, strengthened, or healed. To release tension, try walking with light hand weights (fig. 23) and letting the hands come up over the shoulders on the forward swing (elbows bent). There are also many good exercises by Feldenkrais, Bertherat, and Anderson (see Section IV bibliography).

To stretch the shoulder blades from the back, lean on a waist-high table (fig. 24) with your hands behind your back, and then bend the knees.

Thomas Reilly suggests some unusual exercises for the shoulder: shaking hands with an imaginary person behind your back, putting the elbows above the head while the fingers crawl down the shoulder blades, kneeling and forcing the armpits toward the floor, and raising the arms from the floor at right angles to the body while lying on your stomach (*prone*).

THE ARMS

Hal Zina Bennett has developed the following warm-up for increasing awareness throughout the arm: lie on your back (*supine*), relax, raise your arms toward the ceiling, touch the fingertips of each hand, rub them together, feel the sensations in both hands, then draw the fingers of one hand down the full length of the other arm, to the sternum, caressing the arm. Repeat this three or four times per arm, then rest your arms on your chest and enjoy the feeling.

Cup one hand to hit the other arm gently, with a loose wrist, to step-up the energy after the preceeding exercise. (This is

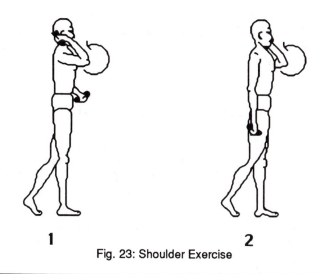

1   2

Fig. 23: Shoulder Exercise

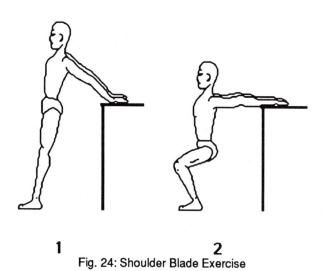

1   2

Fig. 24: Shoulder Blade Exercise

related to a massage stroke called tappotage, and also to an energizing system called Do-in.)

If you use weights to strengthen the upper arm, e.g. arm curls to strengthen the biceps, consider using the kind of weights that you can wear, so that you are not straining your hands more than you mean to.

THE FOREARMS AND WRISTS

It has been said that the keystone of hand function is the mobility of the wrist. One way to increase its flexibility is to join the palms of the hands, with the finger tips pointing up, and then maintain this orientation while gently lowering the hands (fig. 25).

To strengthen the wrist, try the "wrist twist" (fig. 26): rotate the forearm, while holding a weight of up to five pounds. Be aware that it is just this sort of thing which caused your tennis elbow. Although you probably need to do it, you surely need to stay aware of how it feels.

"Fingertip pushups" are a variation on ordinary pushups which strengthen the wrist and hand. At first these should be done against a wall rather than on the floor (fig. 27).

Put rubber bands around the curled fingers and try to open (*extend*) the hand (fig. 28). This strengthens the forearm and is important for performers who place great demands on their fingers.

The muscles for curling the fingers (*flexors*) are strengthened by squeezing a ball. Use the finger tips rather than letting the ball rest in the palm of the hand (fig. 29).

These rubber band and ball exercises add strength but not agility, although they do provide a stable platform for the safe development of agility. Doing exercises at the instrument may be far more effective in recruiting the specific muscles needed in performance.

THE HANDS

Many of the muscles used to move the fingers originate in the forearm, so some hand problems can be avoided or relieved by

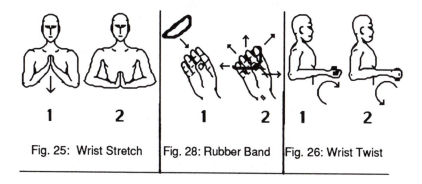

Fig. 25: Wrist Stretch | Fig. 28: Rubber Band | Fig. 26: Wrist Twist

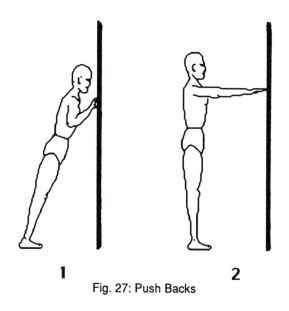

Fig. 27: Push Backs

exercises for the forearm. Or roll the rubber device illustrated in fig. 30 between the hands to increase the circulation and stimulate the acupuncture points.

Juggling the small bean bags sold to student jugglers will achieve the same thing. A lacrosse ball will provide a stronger effect if you can tolerate its weight (and if you have learned to juggle well enough to spend a minimal amount of time crawling around on the floor after the balls).

THE LITTLE GREY CELLS (THE BRAIN)

Slant board exercises (e.g. fig. 31) increase the circulation to the head and ameliorate a number of conditions ranging from a bad memory to the common cold.

Part III: some training concepts borrowed from athletes

Athletes have used the following concepts for everything from running to wrestling. They can be applied to any type of performance which makes heavy demands on all or part of the body. Take whatever seems useful, and think of the rest as a glossary to help you get through all those sports books you'll be reading late at night. There are further tips on warm-up and other aspects of training in Chapter 6.

OVERCOMPENSATION

If you consistently swing your baseball bat too low, it isn't good enough merely to swing it higher, as this will probably feel awkward and cause a hesitant and weak swing. A better strategy, called overcompensation, is to aim too high, as this gives better timing, balance, accuracy, and force. The same idea applies to just about anything, from intonation to rhythm. Its

yes   no

Fig. 29: Holding a Ball

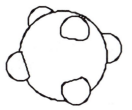

Fig. 30: Reflex Ball

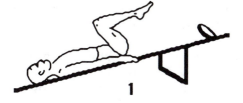

1

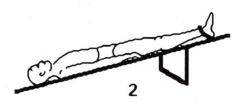

2

Fig. 31: Slant Board

immediate effect is to remove the pressure to do it right, and the longer-range effect is to allow you to find a comfortable middle where what is right also feels right.

INTERVAL TRAINING, CIRCUIT TRAINING, FARTLEK, TEMPOLAUF

It is not wise to train to exhaustion, because fatigue will affect coordination and bring bad habits, and fatigued muscles are prone to injury when they lose their ability to relax quickly. Here are some suggestions for maximizing the amount you can accomplish safely in a day.

Interval training means short bursts of exercise at high power with breaks between the bursts. When doing an exercise at maximum speed, it is best to stop before you feel the ache associated with lactic acid formation. The breaks between intervals let the muscle replenish its supplies of ATP and PC. Interval training gives you more power, a quicker recovery, and no discomfort from acidosis, so that you can do more repetitions per day.

Letting the hands hang down between bursts of activity may cause pooling of "stale" blood. Let them lie on your lap, or better yet, keep them moving gently and slowly to speed the removal of lactates.

If you take a break of more than five or ten minutes, you must warm up again. For this reason, many people prefer to use *circuit training*, i.e. rotating through a number of exercises in a single session. It also allows more efficient use of time. If each exercise stresses a different set of muscles, you can keep practising longer at a stretch. By keeping the blood circulating, athletes can use circuit training to speed the removal of lactates from the muscles they just finished exercising while they are exercising the next set. For the sedentary performer, gaining this advantage may require some thought and planning.

Instead of circuit training, you could do the same exercise continuously but vary the intensity, so that you are alternating between the aerobic and anaerobic states. This technique, called *Fartlek*, lets you use the same set of muscles all the time, since they replenish fuel stores and get rid of metabolites during the low-intensity (aerobic) phase. It also allows you to groove the skill carefully during the slow, gentle phase and to check the results during the strenuous phase.

Occasionally you do have to practise longer at performance speed, both to judge your level of preparation and to teach your muscles to work at that speed. Going through your whole program at the speed and intensity with which you intend to perform it is called *Tempolauf*. Experience will tell you how often you need to do this for best results. As in interval training, it is important to remember that resting the tired muscle completely after strenuous activity is not the best way to let it recover. Rather, cool down slowly for the safest results.

STRENGTH, ENDURANCE, SPEED, AND AGILITY

The idea of "loads and reps" comes from weight lifting, but it has been applied to many other sports. Heavier loads and fewer repetitions build strength, while more repetitions and lighter loads build endurance. To build speed, keep the load and number of reps small and maintain top speed throughout the exercise. Short bursts of speed may work better than one continuous sequence of motions.

Do endurance work in the aerobic cycle to limit the accumulation of metabolites. Trying to push on while in the anaerobic cycle will lead to fatigue, loss of skill, and possible injury. Runners find that even gentle endurance training can lead to muscle and joint injury, so they increase the length of practice sessions gradually. (Some of this may have to do with runners carrying their own weight and may not apply to all musicians.) The smaller the muscle mass involved, the more effective endurance training seems to be.

Pure aerobic training leads to a decrease in the level of glycolytic enzymes in the muscle. Since these substances are needed for anaerobic work, every practice routine should include some speed-endurance work.

Added strength does increase endurance, because subsequent exercise requires a smaller percentage of the maximum effort. Strength also gives us better control over the motions and a bigger margin of safety. On the other hand, strength without endurance is dangerous, and recovery from injury will take longer because white muscle fibers have a poorer blood supply. Doing exercise at an intensity that limits you to as few as four to six repetitions can cause muscles to hypertrophy, which is desirable only if you're into body building. If you want to increase strength without increasing muscle mass, do six to ten repetitions at a lower level of intensity.

The fast-twitch muscle fibers needed for speed and agility can be recruited only by practising fast movements with rapid changes in direction. Agility is also a function of muscular power, reaction time, coordination, and flexibility. When you want to develop a skill which requires rapid changes in direction (e.g. trills), you need to strengthen two sets of muscles. By lifting as well as lowering weights, you strengthen both the elastic and the contractile elements. Performers who need speed more than bulk should be aware that rhythmic exercises tend to build the long muscles they want to develop.

Some say the best training sequence for muscle development is strength, then endurance, and then speed. Others put strength after endurance.

STRENGTH VS. FLEXIBILITY

Performers are often concerned unnecessarily that strength and flexibility might be somehow mutually exclusive. Increased flexibility will reduce the chance of injury, by allowing the application of force over a greater range of motion. Hypermobility, where the joints to reach an unstable position, can be prevented by strengthening the surrounding muscles and developing good background tone. Strengthening muscles also increases their blood supply and thus makes it easier to develop flexibility.

Yes, there is such a thing as being "muscle-bound." A hypertrophied muscle might be less flexible, because the contractile elements (the actin and myosin described in Chapter 1) are more affected by strength training, while the elastic components (the fascia and connective tissue surrounding the fibers) are more affected by stretching exercises.

Many factors limit flexibility, including some of the body's protective mechanisms. These include the specialized nerve endings (Pacinian corpuscles) which sense pressure and pain. A highly competitive person can override such systems but does so at risk of injury.

ISOMETRICS

Isometric exercises tense the muscle without contracting it, in other words they exert force without letting the body move. They are a good tool for rehabilitation, e.g. if you have your arm in a cast, but they aren't a great tool for increasing your ability to perform safely. Isometric exercises increase isometric strength only. You need to move at the angle used in performance in order to get the most benefit from exercise. In other words, exercise by playing the instrument.

On the plus side, isometric exercises don't promote muscle growth. They might be useful for strengthening the antagonist muscles to give you more stability and control without unwanted bulk.

ESTABLISHING A TRAINING RHYTHM

Athletes recognize that the body needs cycles of exercise and rest, both in the short term and in the long term. Musicians who practise the same amount each day could benefit from this idea. It is better to alternate heavy and light practice days, varying the time spent or the intensity of the exercise. Recovery time for strained muscles improves as your fitness improves, so there is no set rule for a good training rhythm. Some athletes maintain a level of strength with just one high-intensity session every two weeks.

To prevent injury, you must be patient whenever you are increasing practice time or intensity. Make the increase gradually and be sure to include more stretching time as well. If a piece requires a new or seldom-used skill, start practising this skill gradually, even if you are already in good shape.

Muscles which are in poor condition respond more rapidly to training, so you will have to keep increasing your workload in order to continue to improve.

PEAKING

As you approach a performance date, keep increasing the load on your muscles, while always respecting your limits. In the days just before the performance, you may find it best to work harder for shorter periods of time, letting the body replenish stores and eliminate metabolites, so that your fitness is at its peak. Athletes know that they cannot maintain peak fitness all year round. Often a World Cup event as little as a week after the Olympics will produce a different set of winners, since the medalists have used this principle to best advantage and given their top performance for the main event. Musicians would find it easier to establish their optimum fitness level for critical times if they stopped thinking that they need to be at their peak every day. Mirkin and Hoffman (p. 35) suggest a maximum of six to eight weeks a year of peak performance.

Chapter 4

A LIST OF COMPLAINTS
what they call the things that go wrong

You've been doing all the exercises in Chapter 3, but something is starting to hurt. A doctor's diagnosis might give you clues about which systems to investigate, provided you know what it means. It may also give you some idea how long you can expect to take to heal, because healing time depends on the tissue involved and its blood supply (degree of vascularization). These *prognoses* are only rough estimates, and nutritional or herbal support can speed healing, as can improvements in general fitness and attitude.

Along with a diagnosis, the doctor may mention the ailment's *etiology*, i.e. an opinion on what caused the problem. This can be useful in avoiding the problem in the future, and might give you more clues about treatment. Any suggestion that you have an overuse injury, for example, should lead you to examine your technique as a performer.

Accompanying the diagnostic terms defined in this chapter are brief lists of symptoms. **These are not meant as an aid to self-diagnosis.** A brief summary of conventional treatments is included with each problem on the list. The treatments are described in greater detail in Chapter 5. Nutritional and herbal remedies generally complement the less invasive of these and may enable you to avoid such last resort treatments as surgery and drugs.

INFLAMMATION

When a tissue is injured, the body responds by activating its defense systems. The capillaries near the site dilate and become more permeable to large molecules. This helps deliver *fibroblasts* which are necessary for regeneration of tissue and *phagocytes* which digest damaged cells. The accumulation of fluid in an injured area can interfere with mobility and can produce pressure which threatens the neighboring tissue. Although inflammation is the body's repair system, it is sometimes considered desirable to diminish these side effects. When a specific part of the body is inflamed, the name given to the condition usually has the suffix, -itis. The treatments for the various kinds of -itis discussed below will thus have a certain similarity. This similarity is one reason the therapist who uses a systemic approach to inflammation probably doesn't care about the name of your complaint.

The standard treatment for inflammation is RICE (Rest, Ice, Compression, Elevation), which is described in Chapter 5. If inflammation persists, there are anti-inflammatory drugs, which are usually related to ASA (acetylsalicylic acid, e.g. Aspirin). Dosages in this context might be as high as 10 to 15 tablets per day.

MILD PAIN, STIFFNESS, SORENESS

If unaccustomed exertion leads to mild pain, use massage, heat, and relaxation to increase the circulation, and very gently stretch both the sore muscle and its antagonist.

If there is stiffness after a performance, there may be a pulled or swollen muscle. The ensuing fluid build-up can be reduced by light exercise and massage.

Soreness to the touch, lasting a few days, can mean a slight tissue rupture, which needs rest to heal. Herbal therapies can be extremely effective in containing the problem at this stage.

MUSCLE CRAMPS

When a muscle can't stop contracting, we have a muscle cramp. This can be so brief and mild that it feels like just a slight twitch, or it can be debilitating.

Etiology includes mineral (*electrolyte*) imbalance, slight injury, and obstruction of the blood supply by sustaining a contraction for too long. Rapid breathing, leading to hyperventilation, which prevents the body from using calcium, can also cause muscle cramps.

Most cramps will go away if you stretch the muscle by moving the appropriate limb segment with the other hand. Mineral supplements may prevent recurrence of cramps, but sometimes all you need to do is to drink more. Be cautious in changing your salt intake, if this is the problem, because your body will have adjusted to some extent to your present intake level and may be slow to adapt to sudden changes.

PULLED MUSCLES

A pulled muscle is one with torn muscle fibres. The pain is more localized than in ordinary sore muscles and often comes on suddenly at the time of injury.

The causes of pulled muscles include overtraining, insufficient warm-up, inattention to stretching, lack of endurance training, uncompensated force applied by an antagonist, and a poor supply of such minerals as sodium, potassium, and magnesium.

RICE is the standard treatment, followed two days later by heat to increase the blood supply and bring nutrients to the muscle. Strengthening and stretching exercises are important after the muscle is healed.

STRAIN

Muscle strain is damage to muscle tissue, somewhere between soreness and a pulled muscle.

Chronic strain comes from overuse (or frequent misuse), while an acute strain comes from a single violent force. Both can lead to fatigue and muscle spasm.

To recover from a strain, keep moving the muscle gently as soon as pain permits. Do not merely ignore the pain and keep performing, since chronic lesions often come from repeated minor injuries which the performer has decided to ignore. This can mean shortened muscles, adhesions, scarring, or fibrous growth (*fibrosis*), all of which will interfere with freedom of movement. Prevention of these problems means "listening" to the pain and doing graduated stretching and strengthening exercises.

SPRAIN

A sprain is an overstretched ligament at the extremes of its range. It can also be a torn ligament. Movement of a sprained ligament causes pain. Chronic injury of a ligament can lead to arthritis in that joint.

Treatment includes RICE, then heat, support and immobilization of the joint (splinting or a pressure bandage), and six to eight weeks rest. If the injury is not extremely severe, you can do rhythmic isometrics.

GANGLIA

A ganglion is a weak spot (*herniation*) in either the joint capsule or the synovial sheath of the tendon, forming a bulge encasing a clear, mucinous fluid. Ganglia most commonly occur in the tendon sheath on the back of the wrist, but they may appear at any tendinous part of the wrist or hand. They usually develop slowly and may bring discomfort due to pressure.

Although the etiology is not clear, performers should investigate the possibility that their technique is putting unnecessary stress on the injured point, weakening the tendon sheath.

Treatment includes applying pressure to break down the swelling, followed by a felt pressure pad to promote healing. Other methods are sucking out the fluid through a hollow needle (aspiration) followed by chemical cauterization, and surgery. None of these treatments prevents recurrence, and surgery in a joint carries the risk of scarring and loss of mobility. Spontaneous remission is fairly common, so some doctors recommend no treatment at all.

TENDINITIS

The ailment ought to be spelled "tendonitis," since it is an -itis of the tendon, but here most of the medical books just don't agree with the lay person. Tendinitis is defined as an inflammation of the tendon sheath and often also of the enclosed tendon.

Usually most of the inflammation occurs in the synovial-lined sheath (*tenosynovitis*), but sometimes, as a result of calcium deposits, the tendon is the primary site.

With tendinitis there may be inflammation or fluid accumulation, but sometimes the area remains dry and rough, causing friction which can be heard with a stethoscope. In any case, there is localized tenderness, pain on movement, and some weakness. Often the pain is worse first thing in the morning and gets better with exercise.

Tendinitis is believed to be caused by either systemic factors, such as rheumatoid arthritis, or local factors, such as trauma, strain, or strenuous unaccustomed exercise. Tendons have a smaller cross-section than the muscles to which they are attached, and this makes them more subject to injury. They also rub against bones and ligaments, and this can cause irritation. Inflammation is often caused by muscles which are chronically tight, so that they pull on the tendon even when it is not being exercised.

Conventional treatment includes one to two weeks' complete rest, and heat or cold, whichever feels better: the cold reduces inflammation, while the heat promotes flexibility. Contrast bathing (see Chapter 5) provides the best of both. When you start to exercise again, use heat before and during exercise, and cold afterwards. Ultrasound is also useful for tendon injuries, and there are drugs to treat both the pain and the inflammation. Using drugs for pain may help you relax and thus heal faster, but if you're practising, you need to know when there is pain, so you don't make things worse.

After the initial rest period, gradual stretching several times per day is recommended to keep the joint from becoming frozen. Next come strengthening exercises and more stretching. Chronic lesions can benefit from *transverse frictions*, a form of physical therapy (called "physiotherapy" in Canada). Some of the electrotherapies listed in Chapter 5 can soften scar tissue and help circulation. There is some belief that injection of corticosteroids into the tendon and sheath is helpful, though in the long run these can dry out the joint. A treatment of last resort is surgery to remove inflamed or calcific deposits, followed by physical therapy.

Tendons and ligaments take longer to heal than muscles (eight weeks or more for tendons), because they have a poorer blood supply and the needed nutrients therefore gather slowly.

BURSITIS

Bursitis is an -itis in the bursa, the lubricating sac usually found around a joint. If there is repeated stress on a joint, the bursa may produce extra fluid to protect it, sometimes causing pressure and pain. If the bursa itself is injured repeatedly, the wall may become thickened, and its lining may degenerate. Eventually there will be adhesions, calcium deposits, and muscle atrophy. The soft tissues may degenerate, limiting movement.

As in tendinitis, there is pain, localized tenderness, limitation of motion, and weakness.

Bursitis is sometimes a result of *scoliosis*, a lateral curvature of the spine, which in turn can be a result of unilateral muscular development.

Treatment includes movement to prevent formation of adhesions. Injection of hydrocortisone is sometimes recommended. As in tendinitis, heat or cold may help. (Try heat before the concert and cold afterward.) Rest, splinting, and pain-killers are not considered effective. Surgical removal of calcium deposits, followed by physical therapy, is a last resort.

TENNIS ELBOW

The fancy name for tennis elbow is *epicondylitis humerii*. The condition results from a strain or tearing of the muscles of the forearm, near the elbow. The name "tennis elbow" is sometimes applied to a stress-induced inflammation in the same area, either to the radiohumeral bursa or to the periosteum (see figures 1 and 2).

Symptoms include severe pain on the outside of the elbow, often radiating down the arm. The pain increases when gripping or actively twisting the wrist, though passive twisting seldom causes pain. There may be point tenderness at the lateral epicondyle (fig. 2), inflammaton in that region, and weakness of the wrist. The diagnosis can be confirmed by injecting an analgesic into the area and noting the disappearance of symptoms.

Tennis elbow is classified as an overuse malady with several possible causes, including rotating the forearm against resistance, as in driving screws, or violent extension of the wrist with the hand pronated, as in tennis. Treatment includes avoiding the movements which cause pain, and applying deep heat or ultrasound. Strapping the forearm can transfer the work to other muscles and allow the arm to be used sooner. A physical therapist can recommend shoulder and wrist exercises to speed elbow recovery. If the arm has been immobilized, gentle stretching should be done, when the doctor allows it. Hydrocortisone is sometimes injected, although its eficacy and safety are being questioned. Surgery is used in severe cases to release part of the muscle from the lateral epicondyle, but strengthening exercises often make surgery unnecessary.

MYALGIA, MYOSITIS, FIBROSITIS, RHEUMATISM

Myalgia is the name for muscular pain. If there is inflammation of the muscle tissues, the term myositis is used. Fibrositis refers to inflammation of the fibrous connective tissue, and can occur in muscles, tendons, ligaments, or joints. The term rheumatism is sometimes used to describe any or all of these conditions in combination.

Symptoms usually include a sudden onset of pain which is made worse by movement. Sometimes there is tenderness, especially at "trigger" points. Diagnosis is generally made by eliminating other possibilities. The symptoms may disappear spontaneously, recur, or become chronic.

Causes include *trauma* (injury), exposure to dampness and cold, and virus infection, but psychological origin is also possible, and environmental or emotional stress is considered an aggravating factor.

Treatment includes rest, heat, gentle massage, aspirin, and the injection of pain-killers or hydrocortisone into trigger points.

CARPAL TUNNEL SYNDROME

Carpal tunnel syndrome is a peripheral nerve disorder, in which the medial nerve may be under pressure by the tendons which serve the wrist and hand.

Symptoms include pain and progressive weakness of the hand. It may be aggravated by vitamin B deficiency or exposure to cold.

Possible causes include physical traumas such as direct blows or even repeated fine movements in contorted positions.

Mild cases can be relieved by rest, but recurrence is likely if the underlying problem is not solved. Surgery followed by rehabilitation can be successful in severe cases: H. G. Kollmann reported relief of symptoms in 76.2 percent of his patients.

PINCHED NERVE, HERNIATED DISC, SCIATICA, LORDOSIS

The spinal column encloses nerves which serve the extremities, so back problems can cause numb or tingling fingers. Faulty playing habits and tension can aggravate these symptoms. Sometimes it is difficult to trace the problem to the spine, and practitioners will disagree on interpretation of symptoms and tests.

A herniated disc is a rupture or bulging of the discs between the vertebrae of the spine. Since diagnosis is difficult to establish and often controversial, it is particularly important to get a second opinion before undergoing surgery.

Sciatica can be caused by any number of lower back problems which affect the sciatic nerve radiating along the leg. Those who have had sciatica are three or four times more likely to get it again. Proposed reasons for such a poor prognosis include neurophysiological memory storage, psychogenic reinforcement of pain, incomplete recovery, or a stiff spine with weak muscles. The treatment depends on the cause, which can be in the spine or in the muscles of the lower back.

Lordosis is excessive curvature of the lower spine, which can cause muscle spasms and low back pain. If there is nothing structurally wrong with the spine, exercise can often correct the posture and eliminate the problem.

Treatment for all of these back problems ranges from exercise and massage to traction and surgery. Recurrence is likely unless the underlying causes are removed. This means correcting posture and performance technique, strengthening the muscles of the abdomen, and reducing physical and emotional tension.

BLISTERS AND WARTS

A blister is defined as a fluid-filled elevated lesion on the skin. It can become infected and lead to scars or blood poisoning. Causes include persistent or repeated rubbing of an object against the skin. Treatment can include piercing with a sterile implement to draw out fluid, followed by application of disinfectant. It is usually considered best to leave blisters alone if they do not cause problems, and to allow them to heal before resuming playing. In some cases, putting plain adhesive tape tightly over the blister will allow you to resume playing immediately, though this practise has occasionally resulted in infection.

The common wart is caused by a virus. It appears in areas which are subject to trauma, such as fingers, and can spread elsewhere. It resembles a callus, but does not have the normal pattern of the fingerprints. Invasive procedures such as freezing or surgery can be painful, may cause scarring, and are not very effective, with recurrence rates as high as 35 percent. For children, the Merck Manual (a physicians' reference of diagnosis and therapy) actually recommends some "impressive manipulation" to remove the wart by suggestion. In England, doctors send patients to wart charmers. Herbalists use dandelion juice (Chapter 18).

SCARRING AND ADHESIONS

Scar tissue can form as the result of a chronic low grade inflammation, acute trauma, or surgery. It may interfere with mobility, and can be removed (by further surgery). Scar formation can often be prevented by maintaining mobility during the healing process.

Adhesions are usually post-surgical scars which bind

together two surfaces which are ordinarily separate. They often interfere with mobility, sometimes painfully so. Kneading the affected area can loosen adhesions, especially in their early stage. Ultrasound is also effective. Nutritional support is particularly helpful for this condition.

BROKEN BONES

Even if broken bones aren't an occupational hazard, they can be a major setback. A sympathetic physician can help design a cast which permits movement of uninjured parts so that the hand can be exercised, and in some cases a cast can even allow performing. The exercise can prevent atrophy and greatly shorten recovery time. In some cases, e.g. some kinds of stress fracture, a sports doctor may recommend doing without a cast.

HEARING LOSS

Hearing loss threatens people who work in a noisy environment, e.g. in front of the band's speaker. Violinists sometimes report hearing loss in the left ear. Ear plugs seem to help prevent it, but not much can be done after it occurs, and they may make it impossible to play the instrument. With advances in technology, it is increasingly likely that most performers can find a style of ear plug to meet their needs, and this practice is becoming more acceptable in the professional environment.

ET CETERA

Physicians like to diagnose, so they sometimes invent names for newly discovered conditions. Thus we have Flautist's Chin, Fiddler's Neck, Clarinettist's Cheilitis, Guitar Player's Nipple, and the controversial Cellist's Scrotum. This last condition keeps reappearing in the literature, particularly in British medical journals such as *Lancet* and the *British Medical Journal*, but most writers agree that the original diagnosis was based entirely on a hoax.

Chapter 5

CONVENTIONAL TREATMENTS
some of the options

Because musicians' needs resemble those of athletes, the injured musician who doesn't live near a performers' clinic might be well advised to visit a physician who specializes in the treatment of athletes. Today's sports physicians aim at quick recovery and avoidance of reinjury, though there is a considerable latitude in their approach. Some suggest resuming practise or performance immediately, if the pain is not too severe, because the exercise increases circulation to the injured area, heats it up, and increases flexibility. Others advise against playing through any pain at all. Most would agree, however, that if pain persists for a week, the area should rest until it heals.

It is tempting to avoid going to a doctor, lest you hear that you have to stop playing for longer than your career would seem to allow. Gabe Mirkin and Marshall Hoffman advise the athlete to seek medical treatment for traumatic injuries to a joint, severe pain, persistent pain in a joint or bone (more than two weeks), slow healing (more than three weeks), or any infection, fever, red streaks, or swollen lymph nodes. These are not meant to be minimum requirements, and any time you feel "in over your head," it is important to find help.

Most of the treatments that follow can be used in conjunction with alternative therapies, but especially if drugs are used, someone knowledgeable must co-ordinate the whole program to prevent drug-herb interactions and to monitor the effects of nutritional support on drug requirements.

Some of the treatments, e.g. icing, can be self-administered, but they should not be attempted without expert instruction.

RICE

RICE (Rest, Ice, Compression, and Elevation) is the immediate treatment for inflammation following an injury. Neither ice nor compression should be applied until any internal bleeding has ceased.

Rest is very important. Injured tissue is susceptible to reinjury and can be weakened by premature reuse. If you rest long enough, the total healing time will be shortened.

Ice stops swelling by constricting blood vessels. It should be applied for five to ten minutes, three times a day. To prevent damage to the skin, wrap the ice in a towel. A bag of frozen peas makes a good ice pack.

Compression helps contain the swelling. It should be applied for thirty minutes at a time, with fifteen minutes between applications. Take care that it doesn't cut off circulation, and remove it immediately if there is numbness, cramping, or added pain.

Elevation of the injured area drains excess fluids. Again, the treatment must be neither too extreme nor too prolonged.

CONTRAST BATHING

Contrast bathing, a variation on RICE, can be done later when inflammation is under control. Heat the area for one minute to increase the circulation, and then apply ice for two to five minutes to promote drainage. Repeat the cycle five times in a session.

MASSAGE

There are many types of massage, from Swedish massage and shiatsu to a specialty called "sports massage." Massage can increase the circulation, promote lymphatic drainage, stretch connective tissue, prevent scar formation, increase nutrition and metabolism of the musculature, facilitate removal of lactic acid and other metabolites, and stimulate cell metabolism. Kneading a muscle loosens adhesions and squeezes congestive material into the general circulation. Stroking toward the heart promotes lymphatic and venous drainage, but some styles of massage go in the other direction to release the flow of energy. Massage can be used before exercise to warm up, or afterwards to eliminate metabolites and heal micro-traumas before they become an injury.

There are some times when massage is *contraindicated* (a fancy way to say, "don't do it"). If there is an infection, massage could spread it further. If the injury is recent (within 36 hours) massaging directly over it can dislodge blood clots. There are many other contraindications, so when in doubt, consult a qualified practitioner.

PROPRIOCEPTIVE NEUROMUSCULAR FACILITATION, PASSIVE STRETCHING, ISOMETRICS

Before an injury has healed sufficiently to allow full use of that part of the body, the following techniques can stimulate nerves and muscles, and thus speed healing with little risk of further injury.

Proprioceptive neuromuscular facilitation improves the neuromuscular mechanism through stimulation of the *proprioceptors*, the afferent nerves in muscles, tendons, and joints which sense contraction, tension, and position. First the patient tries to move a joint, while the therapist offers complete or partial resistance. Next the therapist moves the joint, while the patient is passive.

Passive stretching restores mobility. Massage may precede passive stretching, to increase circulation and relax the area, thus stretching not only the muscle but all of the connective tissue.

Isometric exercise calls for tensing a muscle without moving the joint associated with it, e.g. flexing the biceps without moving the forearm. It prevents atrophy when a joint must be kept immobilized.

SUPPORTIVE STRAPPING

Strapping can allow earlier use of a limb, by transferring some of the force from an injured muscle to another area. Use a four-inch-wide elastic bandage, and take care that it dosen't cut off the circulation.

CASTING

Sometimes putting a limb or joint in a cast seems to be the only way to give it the rest necessary for healing. The drawback is that the muscles are more likely to atrophy, though isometric exercise can counter this tendency.

HOT OR COLD COMPRESSES

There is a joke about the difficulty of choosing between heat and cold in treating a chronic pain. The patient tells the doctor of following a neighbor's advice to use hot compresses, with great success. This comes as a surprise to the doctor, whose neighbor has always advocated cold compresses.

The trouble is that in spite of theoretical arguments in favor of one or the other, each seems right for some people. An understanding of the theory may, however, prevent the misuse of heat or cold where one or the other is clearly contraindicated.

Don't apply heat immediately after a traumatic injury, if there is hemorrhage, or when inflammation persists two to three days afterwards, because heat exaggerates the inflammatory response, resulting in more swelling and more pain. This is important to know, because sometimes heat feels better than cold at first, and the ill effects don't appear until a few hours later. Some people always use cold (see RICE), while others feel that ice interferes with the body's natural healing mechanism and could also kill some of the cells in the area.

After the inflammation has subsided, heat improves circulation by opening and dilating capillaries, and thus speeds healing. Manually applied heat does not usually penetrate joints and muscles, so electrotherapy may be indicated. Heat is not usually beneficial in cases of intra-articular swelling (*synovitis*), which simply need rest followed by isometrics.

ELECTROTHERAPIES

Electrotherapy can get heat into the deep tissues. It can also stimulate small muscle contractions, thus speeding healing as well as preventing atrophy. All electrotherapies should be applied by qualified personnel only.

Infrared heat can penetrate up to one inch without blistering the skin, but only a small percentage of the heat actually goes that deep. It is sometimes used for limbering up and can cause burns if misused.

Short-wave diathermy increases muscle blood flow and heats deeper tissues than infrared heat does. Although it is used to treat chronic inflammation of joints, bursae, tendon sheaths, or muscle tissue, the benefits are generally short-term.

Microwave diathermy is focused on a smaller area, penetrates deeper, and raises the temperature more than short-wave devices do.

Ultrasound produces a high frequency vibration which is converted to heat in the body. It also has the effect of a micromassage, increasing muscle blood flow and easing pain. Most of the heat is focused on the junctions between two types of tissue, e.g. tendon and bone. Ultrasound is used to treat subacute or chronic inflammation, arthritis, and nerve conditions, and is especially recommended for injuries of the tendons. Since it produces heat, some practitioners use a pulsed beam in cases of inflammation, to allow the heat to dissipate, while others use ultrasound only at the periphery of the swelling.

Galvanic muscle stimulation applies a direct current, and is used in diagnosis and muscle testing.

Sinusoidal muscle stimulation: an alternating current gently exercises or relaxes fatigued, strained, or sprained muscles.

Faradic muscle stimulation: an intermittent direct current contracts muscles. It prevents atrophy, discourages formation of adhesions, and encourages drainage of fluid.

Diapulse is a combination of short-wave and faradic stimulation, increasing blood flow as well as contracting the muscle. It has the advantage of not generating heat, so it can be used as soon as an injury occurs.

TENS (Transcutaneous Electrical Nerve Stimulation) bombards the sensory nerve endings so that a muscle can move with less pain.

DRUGS

Drugs are used to block pain, promote healing, or improve performance.

Relaxants of two types affect the skeletal muscles. Peripheral relaxants act on the junction between nerve and muscle, to block the signals which would trigger contraction. Central relaxants inhibit specific neuromuscular reflexes. Relaxing the muscle promotes healing by improving the circulation. Relieving muscle spasms also reduces pain, often allowing earlier use of the affected limb.

Beta-blockers are used to relieve performance anxiety by interfering with the transmission of certain nervous stimuli. They are generally considered neither safe nor effective in this application: performers may think they are doing better while under the influence of beta blockers, but the audio tape often says otherwise.

Enzymes sometimes are used to promote healing. Hyaluronidase may be injected into a joint to reduce the viscosity of the synovial fluid. Bromelain (ananase, which comes from pineapple) can be taken orally to reduce inflammation. Proteolytic enzymes such as trypsin or chymotrypsin are sometimes used to break down injured tissue.

Anesthetics should not be used as a shortcut to the resumption of performance, if they merely mask the damage done while performing. They do have their place in promoting healing, however, by making it easier to relax and by increasing the blood flow.

Anabolic steroids are infamous due to their abuse by athletes, but most performers are neither trying to maximize muscle mass nor working at a training level which would allow the drugs to do them any good. Anabolic steroids are occasionally used to speed the healing of muscles. These drugs are not the same as the **corticosteroids** which have been used, with limited efficacy, to heal inflamed tissue.

Chapter 6

REHABILITATION ...
... and prevention

You've injured yourself, and you've tried some of the therapies listed in Chapter 5. What else can you do to get healthy and stay healthy? An effective recovery program includes exercise, diet, herbs, and attention to the emotional factors which often aggravate performance-oriented problems.

This chapter concentrates on physical factors and exercises directly related to performance. The first part deals with ways to speed the early stages of recovery, before the injured area can be exercised. The second part discusses getting into shape again, once normal practice is resumed. The last part considers ways to stay well. The same principles apply to both prevention and rehabilitation, so this chapter is meant for the healthy as well as the recovering performer.

There is ample scientific support for prompt and careful attention to injury. Rats whose clinically-induced swelling (edema) is left untreated for two months or more develop chronic inflammation from the accumulation of excess protein. This implies that if you ignore the injury for long enough, it changes in nature and becomes harder to treat.

In designing a recovery program, it is important to balance desire with patience. Hurrying can lead to re-injury, thereby turning an acute complaint into a chronic one which takes much longer to heal. Favoring an injured area while performing can lead to injury of a neighboring area. Instead of performing prematurely, use the time-off to increase cardiovascular fitness and maintain general body strength. You will heal faster, lift depression, and decrease your chances of future injuries. Ideally, recovery should progress steadily and without major setbacks.

FIRST STAGES OF RECOVERY

Immediately after an injury, it may be inadvisable to exercise the injured area at all. If so, exercise the opposite limb and take advantage of the fact that strengthening one side of the body will also strengthen the other. Since muscular strength can deteriorate by 10 to 15 percent per week of inactivity, and flexibility is lost even faster, begin moving — very gently — as soon as swelling and pain subside.

ISOMETRICS
Some performers have found isometric exercises especially good for the first stages of rehabilitation, while others have reported that isometric exercise seemed to hinder recovery. The word isometric implies that the muscle does not change length, but in fact there is internal work done, which shortens and lengthens individual components by about three percent. The energy for tensing the muscle produces heat, which might be beneficial. Isometric exercise seems to rebuild muscle mass, so its usefulness might depend on whether you are looking for strength, or for speed and flexibility.

MENTAL PRACTICE
Mental practice means imagining that you are playing the instrument, while paying attention to (imagined) input from as many sensory channels as possible and in as much detail as possible. Mental practice can improve your coordination and timing and let you locate and eliminate bad playing habits such as poor posture or excess tension. It does engage the muscles which will be used in performance, though not enough to increase strength.

At first you will tend to make the same mistakes in mental practise that you made in performance. Break down each motion into very small components, analyze, correct, and put them back together. Eventually you will be able to complete an imaginary performance in tempo with all the details conscious and correct. When the time finally comes to return to the instrument, you may find that you've learnt a more effortless and thus safer way of playing.

RELAXATION TECHNIQUES

Take advantage of the extra time available during an extended lay-off to learn one of the many relaxation techniques. A relaxed muscle has better circulation and thus gets rid of toxins faster, and a relaxed mind is able to be more efficient and alert. The ability to relax will greatly speed progress at the instrument, once you resume playing.

The following technique has been used for recovery from sports injuries. Lie down and pay attention to all of the parts of the body in succession, starting at the soles of the feet and working upward. Relax any stiff place by imagining that it is a cube of sugar or a pat of butter, and let it melt. Then pay attention to the breath, imagining that you inhale healing energy and oxygen and exhale stale air and toxins.

Sometimes each area is first tensed and then relaxed. This is called progressive relaxation, and is a simplified version of the method used by Jacobsen (see bibliography for Section IV, Chapter 20). Some people find it annoying to be asked to tense up repeatedly while the body is becoming more and more relaxed. They might want to learn the Jacobsen method itself, a powerful tool which takes time to learn. It could be especially helpful in increasing awareness of localized tension which contributes to risk of injury in a vulnerable area.

TAPES AND BANDAGES

Tapes and bandages are sometimes used to protect the injured area from further trauma during performance. They may be of temporary benefit immediately after an injury, but in the long run they tend to weaken rather than strengthen a muscle.

GETTING BACK INTO SHAPE

Gradually resume practising once the injury has healed completely. It is tempting, especially when motivated by a need to earn a living, to begin too soon or too intensively. Will power can compensate for lack of fitness, but there will be repercussions later. A tired muscle is less elastic, i.e. it loses its ability to relax (uncontract). Stressing an out-of-shape muscle can lead to injury, which then further weakens that muscle and leads to higher risk of re-injury.

The time required for getting back into shape varies with both the performance requirements and the nature of the injury. After an extended layoff, it is best to be conservative: plan on taking at least six to eight weeks before performing again.

DEVELOPING BODY AWARENESS

Precise information about muscle tension normally goes directly to the cerebral cortex without entering conscious awareness. With increased competence in the relaxation techniques described above, it is possible to notice ever finer degrees of tension and to let go when appropriate. Kneading a tense muscle also focuses awareness on it. (This is only one of the benefits of massage; for more information read Chapter 21.) Often an injury itself can have the desirable side effect of increasing awareness. This new awareness should be nurtured, for it may improve technique and prevent re-injury.

Let awareness of the body's signals override any other principles or rules of training. In theory, a farmer could learn to lift a cow by starting with the new-born calf and lifting it every day. This notion is a variant of the "overload principle" and is similarly misapplied by musicians who move the metronome up a notch at a time to learn a fast passage. Pay attention instead, to the way the body feels, and don't go by the numbers alone. Also let the body's needs, rather than a timer, determine the length of rest periods. With a higher level of awareness, there will be less temptation to skimp on rest periods, no matter how urgent the need to get back into shape or to learn a new piece.

PAIN AS TOOL

Pain is not an enemy. It is a signal that something needs to change. Extreme pain may be telling you to put away the instrument, but even the slightest pain is an often-ignored ally. Paying more attention to a pain may make it go away, and relaxing a painful area reduces the tension which may have been the original source of the injury. On the other hand, ignoring pain can generate more tension, which in turn generates more pain. By blocking out pain, you block other useful signals as well. Openness to pain is part of a real body awareness.

WARM-UP

A proper warm-up increases the circulation and oxygen supply to the tissues and raises the muscle temperature enough to speed up chemical transmisssion of nerve impulses. This enhances flexibility and speed by allowing muscles to contract and relax faster, which in turn prevents soreness and stiffness, reducing the risk of injury.

Begin the warm-up away from the instrument with gentle aerobic exercises (no overheating) Loosen the back, neck, and shoulders, massage the arms and hands, and gently shake the wrists and fingers. Finally, play the instrument, starting slowly and easily. Feel the instrument vibrate, and notice how the movements of the limbs originate from the back. Gradually increase the intensity of playing, always staying aware of how the body feels. Let the warm-up vary from day to day in response to the body's signals.

STRETCHING

Flexibility reduces the chance of muscle injuries, joint lesions, and non-specific aches and pains. Whether a muscle is shortened from the healing process or tight from the previous day's practice, it is important to stretch it before hard use. Stretching of the hand must follow the same principles as any athletic stretch.

STRETCHING IS NOT A GOOD WARM-UP. A muscle must be warm before it can be stretched safely. Muscle is a poor conductor of heat, and a warm-up and workout must be long enough to allow the heat to penetrate the tissues. Heat is particularly important in joint injuries, and the best way to elevate joint temperature is to exercise the area. Relaxation before and during stretches is also important, because a relaxed muscle can stretch further than a tense one.

A ballistic stretch (e.g. high kicks) can elicit the stretch reflex, which in turn reduces flexibility. A ballistic stretch is also hard to control: after a sudden change of force, it takes about ten milliseconds before there is a corresponding change in the velocity of contraction. (This delay occurs as the myosin cross-bridges take time to finish the old cycle and detach themselves: see Chapter 1.) During this time-lag, you could overstretch and injure yourself.

You may apply a gentle passive stretch, using a hand or a fixed object to pull on the limb being stretched. The further you stretch, the more resistance you will meet, because the connective tissue fibers, like wool fibers, become taut when stretched.

Hard exercise shortens muscles and makes them more liable to injury, so the harder you work a muscle, the more important it is to stretch it.

BUILDING STRENGTH AND ENDURANCE

After warming up and stretching, work on rebuilding weakened muscles. To avoid re-injury, take the time to develop extra strength and endurance in the injured tissue as well as in the antagonist and synergist muscles (see figure 4, Chapter 1).

Find exercises at the instrument, designed to build up enough strength for safe performance. Regard it as a bonus if these exercises also increase the skill level, for at this point the main goals are strength and endurance. The little finger has its own muscles for independent motion, and they are often weak enough to need special attention.

If the nervous system must enlist stronger muscles to help the weak ones, then extraneous motions creep in, and these will have to be unlearned later. When working on endurance, stop at the first sign of tension or awkwardness.

WORKING ON SKILLS

It is important to regain fitness before working on skills. With complete return of both mobility and strength, you can expect to find full coordination restored. Only at that point is it possible to lay down the neuromuscular patterns for safe performance.

Some performers have found it helpful to warm up by using a slow and gentle form of the playing motion, so that kinesthetic awareness increases the skill level without strain. This strategy works only if the easier motion is also technically appropriate for faster playing.

Though this is the time for working on speed and agility, continue to start every practice session with warm-up, stretching, strength, and endurance exercises. Body awareness will tell you when you are fit enough to start the day with a fast run-through of a concerto.

STAYING WELL

All performers need to warm up, be aware, relax, stretch, and keep fit and strong. For many of us, this is enough, but there are other physical factors affecting the odds of staying healthy. Some of these factors are form, posture, breathing, working conditions, and pace of training.

FORM

Many "overuse injuries" might better be termed "misuse injuries," because they are due to poor movement patterns. Good form and a smooth technique help prevent injury, and even the best performers might benefit from an occasional review. For the injured performer, a change in technique may be more appropriate than any medical intervention. Examine your playing technique before resorting to risky or invasive procedures. The following ideas may get you started. Try them out and consult your colleagues. (Not all of them will be relevant to your particular instrument.)

Principles of movement

A good technique is consistent and simple. Inconsistent or unnecessarily complicated motion is hard to control and thus invites injury. For greatest power, let all movements originate in the large muscles, e.g. use the whole arm or even the back to make sharp, effortless strokes of the fingertips, as if you were flicking a towel. In a tight spot, you may need to gain momentum by using a backswing, that is, to start with a short motion away from the goal. This strategy also increases power, because stretching a muscle before contraction increases its maximum capability.

Circular motions are easier and more efficient than reciprocal (back and forth) ones, because stopping to change direction requires force. For stability, finish each stroke by following through. Whenever possible, swing rather than apply a constant force, so that muscles can alternate and thus do more work.

Putting force on an extended joint can cause injury, so it is better to absorb the force either by flexing the joints or by rolling. This holds both for leaping from tall buildings and for striking with the fingers.

Shoulder, arm, hand

A small adjustment in the position of the shoulder might greatly increase the freedom of the hand. The best arm position is one which generates relatively little extra tension yet makes it easy for the hand to be strong. Don't think of it as a static position, but make continuous small adjustments to allow the muscles and joints to recover, thus reducing the risk of injury to the upper arm and shoulder.

Wrist, fingers

In the wrist, *flexion* (bending toward the palm) and *extension* (the reverse) are easier than *abduction* (bending toward the little finger) and *adduction* (the reverse). For greatest finger strength, keep the wrist flat or very slightly flexed. Excessive flexion or extension limits finger motion by stretching the tendons of the long extensor and flexor muscles respectively. Abduction of the wrist also weakens the finger muscles. The wrist itself functions best when the fingers are midway between flexion and extension. Both wrist and fingers function best when the thumb is in line with the radius (fig. 2a), as in the hand's normal resting position. The fingers, especially the ring and little fingers, can press harder with less strain on the flexor digitorum muscle (elbow to phalanges) if the base of the hand is closer to the finger tips. This position makes it easy to spread fingers without flexing the metacarpo-phalangeal joint excessively. Since a small increase in angle between the metacarpals means a large separation at the finger tips, opening the hand at the metacarpals rather than the phalanges means a bigger, easier stretch.

A tendency to collapse the fingers at the distal joints (the ones near the nails) may indicate a weakness of the finger flexors of the forearm. This habit reduces speed and accuracy, weakens the joints, and increases the chance of eventual injury or arthritis. If you decide to strengthen the forearm, begin gradually, do some stretching, and include exercises for the smaller muscles of the hand.

Some surprising relationships

Looking to one side stabilizes the arm movements on that side, while creating a tendency to extend the fingers on that side and to flex the fingers on the other side. This phenomenon is called

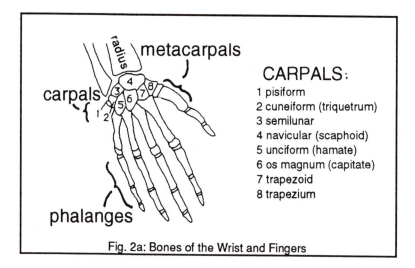

CARPALS:
1 pisiform
2 cuneiform (triquetrum)
3 semilunar
4 navicular (scaphoid)
5 unciform (hamate)
6 os magnum (capitate)
7 trapezoid
8 trapezium

Fig. 2a: Bones of the Wrist and Fingers

the "asymmetric tonic neck reflex." It implies that looking the other way increases grip strength, while looking at a hand increases its stability and makes it easier to extend the fingers. (Maybe this is why some 'cellists look at the bow during difficult passage work.)

When one hand performs an action requiring great skill or strength, the other hand "tries to help" by reinforcing the activity with its own muscular contractions. Any tension in that other hand is, of course, transferrred back to the working one, so relaxing the passive hand can facilitate the action of the active one.

Calluses

Calluses may be a sign of devotion to practise, but they can interfere with sound and lessen touch sensitivity. Skin which is tough enough not to get blisters is tough enough. Even martial arts students who learn to break bricks with the sides of their hands report that as proficiency increases and more of the force is transferred to the brick, the calluses disappear from the hands. Getting into shape gradually and playing with no more than the optimal force usually prevents calluses from becoming a problem.

Background tone and relaxation

Background tone is the tension we hold in a muscle even when we think it is relaxed. It is important for some muscles to have high background tone. The shoulder girdle, for example, forms a base for pushups, and the hand forms a base for putting weight on the fingers. Keep this in mind when getting a massage, for it can take a surprisingly long time to regain optimal background tone after a thorough hand massage has loosened all those knots.

A strong antagonist muscle helps prevent injury, but relaxing it protects it and gives you more speed and power. To learn the difference between relaxing and going limp: tense up the muscles, then let them go limp, and then bring the tension up to the optimum level for the particular job.

Whenever possible, let gravity do the work. Keep a relaxed feeling in the nape of the neck. Finally, a serene facial expression, it is said, promotes graceful movement.

POSTURE

Good posture improves performance, helps prevent injury, facilitates breathing, and increases lung capacity.

Firm but plastic postural muscles facilitate strength and freedom of movement. Let the center of gravity shift constantly, as it normally does even in sleep, but avoid violent movements.

Accuracy requires a stable base, and stability can be increased by a low center of gravity. Standing not only raises the center of gravity but may make blood pool in the legs. With less blood in circulation, the forearm muscles constrict and absorb extra-vascular fluid. To keep the blood flowing where it is needed, alternate sitting and standing during practice as your instrument permits, break frequently, and walk around during breaks.

Problems in the extremities may originate in the spine. Regain symmetry and relieve tension in the back muscles by exercising the side of the body which does less work. (Try holding your violin in the right hand for a while?)

Strengthening the muscles in the shoulder area with pushups and pullups improves posture and allows the arms to function more efficiently. The Alexander technique and other methods described in Chapter 21 also help improve posture and relieve discomfort.

BREATHING

Breathing affects performance, even in fields where the breath does not produce sound. Rapid shallow breathing increases tension, decreases awareness, and requires superfluous muscular work. On the other hand, some people find deep rhythmic breathing relaxing. Breathing with the music is said to facilitate playing. Breathe properly when practising, so that it is a habit in performance. In particular, exhale as you begin to play and at points of emphasis.

WORKING CONDITIONS

When played under cramped or unaccustomed conditions — e.g. in an orchestra pit — even well-practised pieces seem to become difficult. The phenomenon is not merely psychological. The muscle spindles adjust their response to the control signals asking for compensation, and previously grooved (ballistic) motions, which normallly occur as automatic units, may need current (ongoing) control. No amount of practice under ideal conditions will fully compensate for this loss of facility, because practising is a matter of grooving motions, and sufficiently poor conditions simply undo the grooving.

Athletes require proper equipment to prevent injury. For a musician, the equipment list may include a good chair, good lighting, reasonable sound protection, and comfortable clothes, as well as an instrument which has been kept in good condition.

Temperature affects skin sensitivity to touch, as well as the speed of propagation of the signals in a muscle. Heat prevents soreness by increasing the cellular metabolism, diminishes the risk of injury, and increases the range of motion. But too much heat, even an excessively vigorous warm-up, decreases endurance, since working muscles produce heat which must be dissipated into the surrounding air. Extreme heat reduces strength as well, because overheated muscles contract inefficiently. On the other hand, low temperatures degrade neuromuscular function, increasing the risk of accidents. To preserve internal heat and protect the vital organs, your body lets the hands cool down first. Unfortunately this survival mechanism leads to loss of both strength and dexterity in the extremities.

Fresh air helps the concentration. It also increases endurance by improving the supply of oxygen to the muscles. Fresh air during breaks has no direct effect on muscular endurance.

Negative ions in the air are said to increase strength, endurance, balance, and tranquility while decreasing reaction time. (Negative ion generators are available for the practice room.)

All body functions vary with the time of day, making practice more safe and efficient at one hour than at another. Many people have recommended specific times for efficient practising, but since these recommendations range from six AM to seven PM, it is up to each us to find our own best time slots.

Because working conditions affect performance, it is important to spend some practice time in an environment which approximates the expected performance conditions. For example, in preparation for competition in a hot place some athletes wear extra layers of clothing to let the body learn to sweat efficiently.

ESTABLISHING A TRAINING PROGRAM

Athletes have learned that they can train more efficiently by interspersing heavy days with light ones. The body needs to rest after a particularly hard workout, and the following day should either be a day off or a day of gentler training. It is simply not true that "the guy who works the hardest, wins." A good training rhythm brings greater improvement than sheer brute force and will power. Reduced practice days are ideal for mental practice.

When seeking the ideal training regime, be alert to the signs of overwork: persistent soreness, stiffness, sluggishness or other difficulties in performing, as well as a gamut of emotional symptoms ranging from nervousness and crying to depression and loss of interest in performing. Instead of feeling guilty when your body asks for a rest, let its signals guide you to the best training rhythm. Consider varying the intensity, and perhaps the length, of practice times on successive days. There is no universally accepted optimal training program: athletic coaches agree on many of the principles, but they haven't come to a consensus about the timing of rest and exercise.

Make it a rule that the harder you train, the shorter your practice time. Every time the muscles work hard, the fibers are slightly damaged (*microtrauma*) and the fuel stores are depleted. It can take a surprisingly long time for a muscle to recover completely: anywhere from 10 hours to 10 days to replenish glycogen stores, and up to 48 hours to replenish potassium stores. Tissue repair and fuel recovery do not require complete rest; in fact, they proceed faster with light exercise. This principle holds even during a practise session, so after pushing a muscle, practise the same motion gently and slowly, with the affected muscle at about the same level as the heart whenever possible.

Pacing is especially important when getting back into shape after any long break, whether due to injury or vacation. Tendinitis is more common among athletes and performers at the beginning of a season or when there is a change in the training regime. If muscles are not used to being stressed, they lose their ability to utilize oxygen efficiently. This phenomenon, called *reversibility*, takes a few weeks to manifest; it won't happen after just one day off. The grace period depends on the individual and on the sport. Endurance will deteriorate first, so a sprinter's performance in a single heat doesn't drop until his muscles have started to atrophy. Not only does performance suffer, but undertrained muscles may get sore more easily and are usually smaller, weaker, and more prone to injury.

The best way to build a skill and to protect the necessary muscles is to exercise that skill. Develop skill and strength at the instrument, by making the movements needed in performance. For many people this means practising at performing speed some of the time, though others argue that, with sufficient attention to form, the correct motions can be grooved at a slow speed. To increase agility, develop the fast-twitch muscle fibers by making fast movements. To build strength, practise against resistance, but don't neglect the agility exercises. Even weight lifters need to develop speed in order to start a lift.

A good training program can help keep injuries from recurring. And as pointed out in Chapter 3, it might also have prevented them in the first place.

Section II

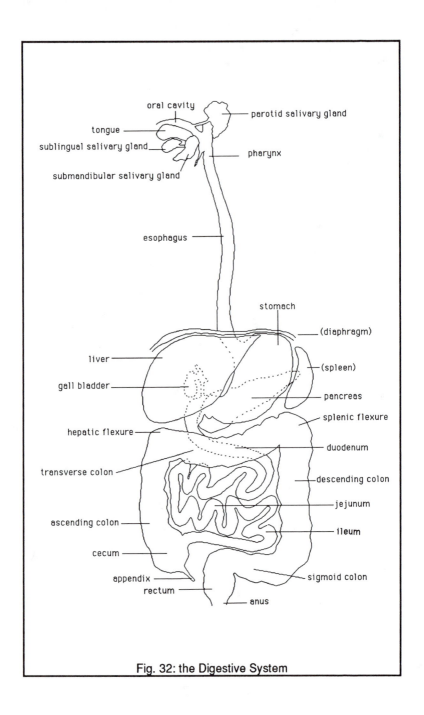

Fig. 32: the Digestive System

Chapter 7

THE DIGESTIVE SYSTEM:
what happened to that dinner?

Did mechanical trauma cause your pain, or was it an unhealthy body chemistry? The body possesses intricate and robust mechanisms for maintaining balance (*homeostasis*), so it often takes years of abuse before problems occur. Poor nutrition contributes to these problems. Good nutrition could prevent or solve them.

Before food can nourish us, it has to pass through three stages: assimilation (digestion and absorption), metabolism, and elimination. To make informed decisions about diet, we need to understand the digestive system and its role in these tasks. Chapters 7 and 8 and the appendices provide a theoretical background. For practical suggestions, see Chapters 9 through 12.

The digestive system depends on other systems, e.g. the circulatory, nervous, and endocrine systems, while these in turn depend on the digestive system and proper nutrition.

DIGESTION

Digestion transforms food into substances which the body can absorb and use. To digest food, the body secretes chemicals called *enzymes*; which break food down into molecules small enough to enter the blood stream. It is important to chew food thoroughly so the digestive enzymes can reach a large surface area.

The salivary glands in the cheeks and under the tongue secrete saliva. It is rich in enzymes, e.g. *ptyalin* (digests carbohydrates) and *mucin* (coats food with slippery mucus, speeding travel down the esophagus). Secretion of saliva also alerts the stomach to the nutritional make-up of the food, giving it time to secrete the appropriate enzymes. Ideally, all food, including liquids, should be kept in the mouth long enough for salivary secretion to take place. Although we have voluntary control over the initial stages of swallowing, the complete action is coordinated by the *medulla*, a lower area of the brain, so even at this stage digestion is dependent on the autonomic nervous system.

The muscles lining the esophagus contract in a wave-like sequence (*peristalsis*) to get the food to the stomach, and once it arrives there, the muscles of the *lower esophageal sphincter* keep the food from going back toward the mouth. The stomach secretes *pepsinogen* and *hydrochloric acid* to digest protein, and *lipase* to begin fat digestion. By adding fluids to the food, the stomach and successive parts of the digestive tract also control ion concentration. Only a few substances, e.g. alcohol, water, some vitamin C, are absorbed into the body from the stomach.

The *pyloric sphincter* is a valve which keeps the stomach contents from entering the small intestine before all particles of food are thoroughly broken up. When the food is ready, the *duodenum* (first part of the small intestine) secretes hormones to open the sphincter. The presence of food in the small intestine stimulates secretion of enzymes by the liver, the pancreas, and the intestinal wall. Again the level of enzyme secretion is regulated by hormones, so the endocrine system is crucial to this phase of digestion. Most of the pancreatic enzymes can act only in an alkaline environment, so the pancreas produces an alkaline secretion to neutralize the stomach acid. As food progresses through the small intestine, the rate of digestion decreases and the rate of absorption increases.

ABSORPTION

Up to 95 percent of all nutrient absorption takes place in the first half of the small intestine, whose walls are lined with small, hair-like *microvilli* to create a large surface area. Many nutrients can be absorbed later, but there are exceptions, e.g. iron, calcium, and other bivalent metals which must be absorbed before they combine with free fatty acids released further downstream. Some important nutrients, notably vitamin B_{12}, are absorbed only in the last part of the small intestine.

Many nutrients are absorbed by osmosis, but most are best absorbed by *active transport*, which requires energy input.

Many vitamins and most minerals require specialized absorptive systems whose specialized cells must be replaced every few days for maximum efficiency. Their replacement requires the presence of sufficient protein and folic acid. Water is absorbed in the first two thirds of the colon, and water-soluble substances, e.g. the water-soluble vitamins, can be absorbed at the same time. Bacterial action on undigested food produces toxic by-products which may also be absorbed through the colon. Some practitioners believe that most health problems are the result of the auto-intoxication which accompanies irregular bowel movements.

METABOLISM

Once absorbed, all nutrients go to the liver. Water-soluble nutrients arrive directly, but the fat-soluble ones go via the lymphatic system. The liver converts them into the substances needed by the body at a given time. Some become parts of complex molecules, such as ketones or serum proteins, while others are converted to glycogen for storage and later conversion to fuel. Many vitamins, including A and B_{12}, are stored in the liver, some to be used in enzyme systems to digest other nutrients in turn.

The body continually breaks up and re-forms its nutrient-derived substances. Many of the vitamins and minerals facilitate this process at the cellular level. For the metabolic processes to work efficiently, we need not only healthy organs, but a healthy blood stream and interstitial fluid, i.e. we need to be able to transport nutrients and wastes efficiently to and from every cell in the body. Many vitamins and minerals help regulate pH (acidity) and electrolyte levels, so they play an important role in maintaining blood and fluid composition.

ELIMINATION

The colon eliminates undigested food, parasites, bacteria, viruses, and chemical toxins which the digestive system is supposed to neutralize. The lining of the entire digestive system secretes antibodies to keep bacteria in check.

Once food enters the blood stream, metabolic proceses yield further waste products. Most of these are excreted by the kidneys, skin, and lungs, but some are returned to the colon for elimination. The bile secreted by the liver also contains substances, e.g. bilirubin and cholesterol, which may be excreted by the colon. The thyroid and spleen destroy poisons for removal. Uneliminated waste products are toxic to all the cells of the body, so a dysfunction in any of the eliminative organs may manifest itself in symptoms anywhere in the body.

OTHER BODY SYSTEMS

It is not possible to isolate the digestive tract from other body systems. Digestion starts before we even start eating: the sight and smell of food sends messages to the brain, which in turn sends messages to start the flow of digestive juices. Thus the state of the central nervous system (CNS) affects the digestive system. Our emotions affect the CNS, thereby affecting secretions and peristalsis. Ulcers in any part of the digestive system affect the associated nerve ganglia and prevent peristalsis. Hormones secreted by the stomach and small intestine affect digestion. The hormones generally have multiple functions, e.g. secretin retards stomach emptying and also stimulates secretions from the pancreas, liver, and intestines. As we progress down the digestive tract, the nervous system has progressively less influence on digestive secretions, and the hormones take over more functions. Nerves in the walls of each segment of the digestive tract control the pace of peristalsis. The sphincter muscles which control passage of food from one part of the system to the next are influenced by both hormones and nerves.

The food we eat affects virtually every system of the body. The nervous system affects the endocrine system and the digestive system. The endocrine system affects the digestive system and the nervous system. The digestive system affects every cell in the body. Some symptoms of digestive problems are fairly obvious, e.g. coated tongue, yellow skin, bloated abdomen, flatulence, constipation, chronic fatigue, and fatigue after a big meal. Others are not so easily traced to their source. Performers with any chronic problems at all would do well to look at their nutritional state.

Chapter 8

NUTRIENTS
the healthy elements in food

Is a peanut butter and jelly sandwich really healthier without the jelly? Will tofu cure my -itis? Before we can address these questions, we need to know what's inside those foods. Briefly, they contain carbohydrates, fats, proteins, vitamins, minerals, fiber, water, poisons, and some mystery factors which may or may not be nourishing. The first seven ingredients are the subject of this chapter and Appendix 1 (Vitamins and Minerals).

Nutritional information is in **bold type** when it is of specific value to the performer. This is not to imply that any single nutrient can supply all of our needs. If you want healthy hands, you need a healthy digestive system, healthy blood, healthy lungs, and a healthy liver.

CARBOHYDRATES, FATS, PROTEINS
what kind of fuel am I?

Carbohydrates, fats, and proteins are our only sources of fuel. All of the vitamins and minerals we eat merely process the fuels and facilitate the reactions which keep the body running. Most of the fuels which the body doesn't immediately need are stored as fat.

CARBOHYDRATES

The primary function of carbohydrates is to provide fuel in the form of glucose. Glucose can be converted to ATP via glycolysis, or it can be a fuel in pathways like the Krebs cycle which also produce ATP (the substance required for energy production at the cellular level; see figs. 8 - 11, Chapter 2.)

Carbohydrates are ingested as mono-, di-, or polysaccharides (from the Latin *saccharum*, sugar) of the form $C_x(H_2O)_y$. Glucose (blood sugar) is a monosaccharide (see fig. 33), and sucrose (table sugar) is a disaccharide whose complex structure

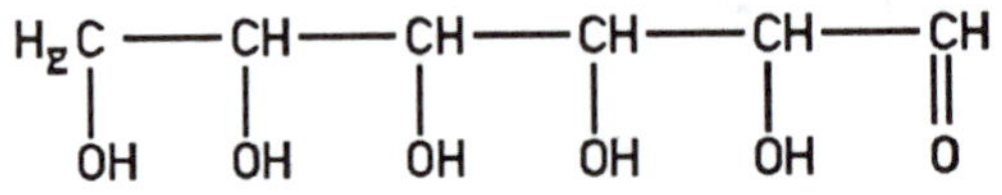

D-glucose ($C_6H_{12}O_6$)

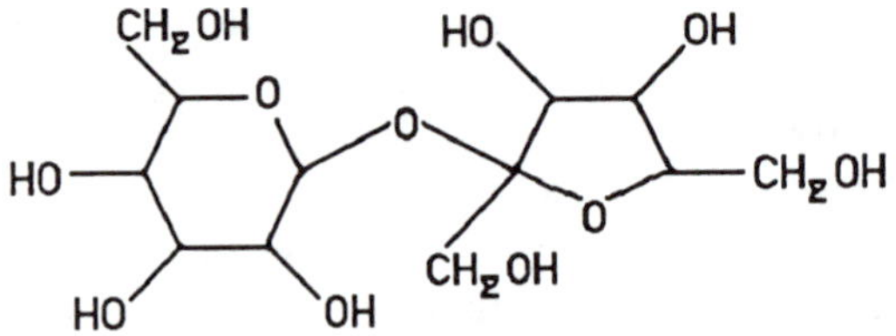

sucrose ($C_{12}H_{22}O_{11}$)

Fig. 33: Glucose, Sucrose

resembles those of starch, glycogen, and cellulose (polysaccharides). It is relatively simple to convert carbohydrates (polysaccharides) to a usable fuel (glucose, a monosaccharide). Small excess amounts of carbohydrates are stored as glycogen in the liver or muscles and converted to glucose when needed, and larger surpluses are stored as fat to meet future needs.

Carbohydrates also **lubricate joints** and form parts of DNA, connective tissues, and the glycoproteins in mucous membranes.

Complex carbohydrates are found in unprocessed grains and fresh fruits and vegetables. Although simple sugars, e.g. sucrose, are digested faster, complex carbohydrates are a superior fuel food, because their slow digestion means a steady flow of fuel. Breaking them down into simple sugars for absorption requires little energy.

North Americans typically get 45 to 50 percent of their calories from carbohydrates. Many nutritionists feel that we should reduce protein and fat intake and eat 70 to 80 percent carbohydrates, most of them natural and unrefined. A more conservative proposal is that we increase carbohydrate intake to 55 to 60 percent of caloric intake. Many people are allergic to certain grains, flours, or sugars, but most people can thrive on the gluten-free whole grains, e.g. millet and corn.

FATS

Fat is an essential part of the body structure. It is part of the cell membranes, the myelin sheath surrounding the nerves, and the white matter of the central nervous system. There must be dietary fat in the intestines, if the fat-soluble vitamins (A, D, E, and K) are to be absorbed.

Fats can be stored in the body as a source of fuel. They have the same kinds of atoms as carbohydrates, i.e. carbon, hydrogen, and oxygen, but their basic building blocks are *fatty acids* and *glycerol* (see fig. 34). Body fat is made of *triglycerides*, which contain both fatty acids and glycerol. Triglycerides can be built up from either digested fats or digested carbohydrates; the end result is the same. Fats contain more calories per gram than carbohydrates do. Although this would seem to make fats a good source of fuel, they are harder to digest than carbohydrates and require bile from the liver to separate the fatty acids from the glycerol.

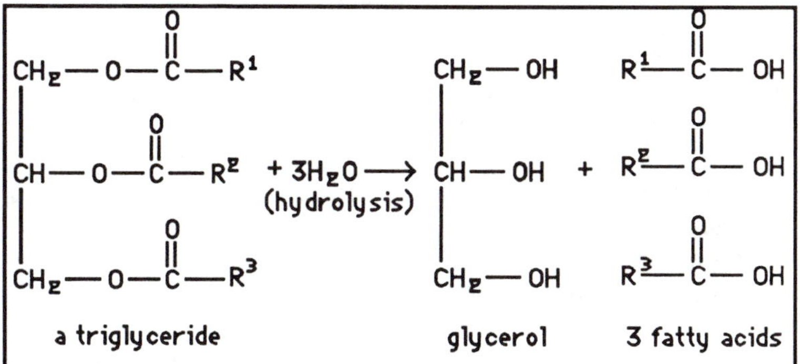

Fig. 34: Composition of Fat

There are two *essential fatty acids* (EFAs), which must be taken into the body in food form because they cannot be synthesized from other fatty acids (see fig. 35). They are called *linoleic acid* (LA), and *linolenic acid* (LNA). EFAs are found in seeds (LA, some LNA), in fish body oil (LNA), and in small quantities in dark green vegetables. Linseed oil (from flax seeds) is a particularly good source, hence the names of the acids.

The EFAs are needed for cell reproduction and repair, production of hemoglobin, and the formation of *prostaglandins*, which regulate many body processes. The EFAs help **remove**

lactic acid buildup from muscles. They even promote loss of excess weight by increasing the metabolic rate. Symptoms of LA deficiency include skin problems, water loss, poor wound healing, susceptibility to infection, hair loss, and kidney problems. Symptoms of LNA deficiency include **weakness** and **incoordination,** poor **vision,** learning problems, and changes in behavior.

Saturated fats (see fig. 36) are fats with all the hydrogen atoms they can hold (for the chemist this means the molecule contains no double bonds). Saturated fats, e.g. those in red meat and coconut oil, are recognizable by their solidity at room temperature.

Unsaturated fats must be included in the diet, because they alone contain the essential fatty acids. However, overconsumption of polyunsaturated fats (those with two or more double bonds, see fig. 35) may increase the risk of *free radical* damage (See fig. 37). Free radicals are molecular fragments with an electric charge, which combine easily with other chemicals in the body. Though they partake in many vital operations at the cellular level, free radicals can cause chain reactions which have been blamed for everything from atherosclerosis to cancer. Heat and light break down fat molecules to produce free radicals, whose presence is sometimes signalled by a rancid smell. Unfortunately, digestion also contributes to their number. Some nutritionists recommend eating only oils which have not been exposed to heat and light, and supplementing the diet with *antioxidants,* e.g. vitamins C and E.

Most North Americans eat more fat than they need. It is generally recommended that fat intake be 30 to 40 percent of caloric intake, and that the saturated fat component be no more than 10 percent of caloric intake. On the other hand, some claim that those on high fat diets (the "Stone Age Diet") have lower cholesterol levels and less arthritis than the general population.

Cholesterol (fig. 38) is widely distributed in animal tissue, so a diet which is high in saturated fats is usually also high in cholesterol. The body needs cholesterol, which forms a part of every cell membrane and plays an important role in the production of steroid hormones. Although cholesterol has become a dirty word in the popular vocabulary, there is little agreement about the effects of dietary fat intake on blood

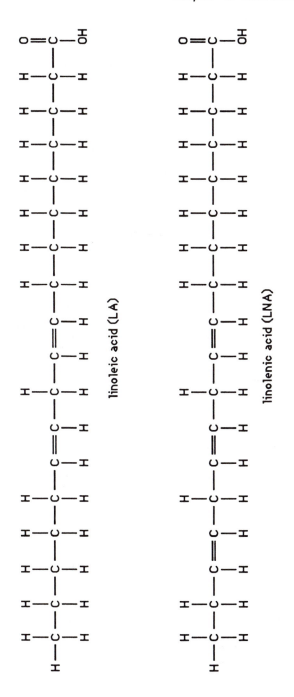

Fig. 35: The Essential Fatty Acids

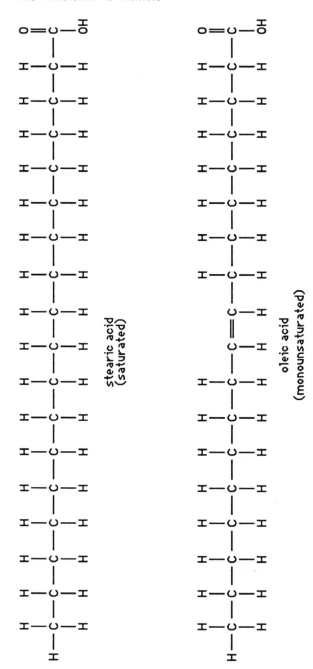

Fig. 36: Saturated and Unsaturated Fats

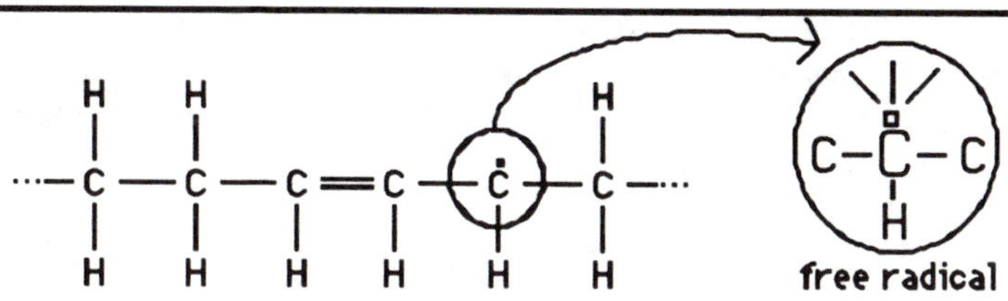

Fig. 37: Free Radical

cholesterol levels, or about those levels and the chances of heart disease. There is some agreement that the polyunsaturated fatty acids found in grains, seeds, and nuts tend to decrease blood cholesterol levels, while saturated fats may have the opposite effect. One current recommendation is that cholesterol intake be reduced to about 300 mg per day. That translates to 1 lb of ground beef, or about 10 oz of cheese, or 1/2 cup of butter, or 2/3 lb of crab, or 1/3 lb of lobster. One medium-to-large egg contains the entire daily ration, but it also contains enough of the B vitamin, choline, to keep the cholesterol emulsified, so some people consider eggs exempt from the restriction. Obviously your dietary choices will depend greatly on where you stand on this issue.

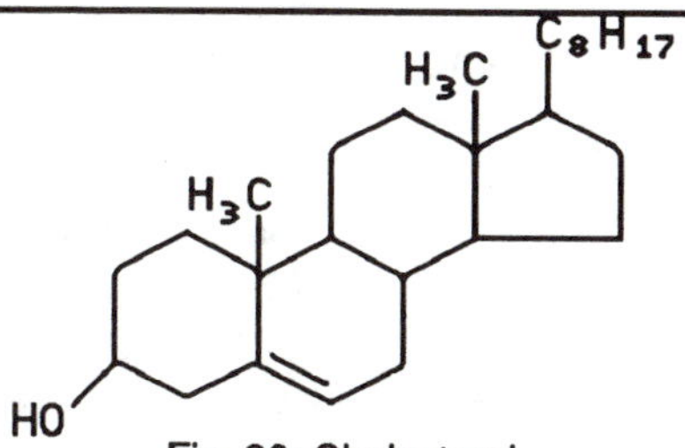

Fig. 38: Cholesterol

Cholesterol and triglycerides are *lipoproteins*, i.e. they are composed of both protein and lipid (fat) parts. Low-density lipoproteins (LDLs) carry cholesterol from the liver to the cells, while high-density lipoproteins (HDLs) take the cholesterol back to the liver, which can change excess cholesterol to bile acids and secrete it into the intestine for excretion. The HDLs are the desirable ones, and have been associated with lower risk of coronary heart disease. Though the HDL:LDL ratio is often measured, it is not clear how to change it directly by nutritional means. Some nutritionists would say that both lipoproteins and cholesterol will come into balance when the body in general is brought into balance through "proper" diet.

Regardless of the outcome of the cholesterol controversy, there are reasons to control fat intake. Excess fat in the blood stream seems to make red blood cells clump together, resulting in reduced oxygen-carrying capacity and subsequent tissue suffocation throughout the body. The clumps of red blood cells also obstruct capillaries. Overconsumption of fat means fewer calories from vitamin- and mineral-rich foods and increases the need for vitamin B_6. Excess fat intake may impede carbohydrate metabolism, raise uric acid levels, and increase the risk of heart disease, cancer, diabetes, high blood pressure, gallbladder and liver problems, obesity, and atherosclerosis.

PROTEINS

The average mass of a (dehydrated) human cell is from 65 to 80 percent protein. Enzymes, hormones, antibodies, hemoglobin, and nucleoproteins are proteins. Proteins regulate the fluid balance between blood and interstitial fluid, and dampen blood pH swings (to stabilize the acidity at a slightly alkaline level).

Like carbohydrates and fats, protein molecules contain carbon, hydrogen, and oxygen, but all protein molecules also contain nitrogen, many contain sulfur, and some contain small amounts of phosphorus, iron, zinc, or copper. The building blocks of protein molecules are amino acids, 22 of which are important in human nutrition. The body can convert some amino acids into others, but just as there are essential fatty acids, there are essential amino acids, which the body cannot build. Most animal proteins contain all the essential amino acids, whereas most vegetable proteins do not. Exceptions are millet, almonds, Brazil nuts, pumpkin seeds, and potatoes. Leafy green vegetables contain small quantities also.

In the constant process of renewal, the body breaks down an estimated 14 ounces of its own protein every day. Although much of this protein can be recycled, some of it is eliminated. To estimate your daily dietary protein need (in ounces), divide your ideal body weight (in pounds) by 100. You will have to eat approximately 4 times as many ounces of protein-rich food daily to meet this need. Thus a 100 pound person needs four ounces of protein food per day (roughly four ounces of lean meat, cheese, or nuts).

Most North Americans eat far more protein than they need. Even infants, who require protein to sustain rapid growth, can thrive on human milk, containing only three to six percent protein.

Excess protein is broken down in the liver, where the amino group (NH_2) is converted to *ammonia* (NH_3) and thence to *urea* ($CO(NH_2)_2$) which must be excreted in the urine. Sulfur from protein breakdown is also excreted in the urine, in the form of sulphate ions. Thus excess protein intake puts a burden on the eliminative organs. The loss of nitrogen and sulfur means that the protein can't be reconstructed, so you will have to meet future requirements from dietary sources. Carbon, oxygen, and hydrogen from excess protein are metabolized in the same way as those from carbohydrates or fats, though less efficiently, and amounts beyond immediate energy needs are converted to fat.

Ammonia is highly toxic, especially to the nervous system. Eating too much protein increases the risk of ammonia intoxication, whose symptoms include changes in consciousness and a flapping **tremor**. Too much protein in the diet can also cause *acidosis* (too many hydrogen ions in the blood and interstitial fluid), whose symptoms may include a vague lassitude and nausea. When the body is in acidosis the kidneys form ammonia, which combines with the excess hydrogen ions to form *ammonium* ions (NH_4^+). These are excreted in the urine, so the body does have another regulating mechanism, but overuse of this mechanism puts further stress on the kidneys.

Uric acid ($C_5H_4O_3N_4$) is a component of urine, normally excreted by an adult male at a rate of about 0.7 grams per day. It is an end product of the metabolism of *purine* (an amino acid), and its excretion rate increases with protein intake. **Uric acid crystals can be deposited in the joints**, as well as in the kidneys.

Excess protein also tends to accumulate on the capillary walls, preventing nutrients from crossing into the interstitial fluid to reach the cells.

Overconsumption of protein leads to dietary deficiencies. The ratio of calcium to phosphorus in meat (1:20) is much lower than the ratio the body needs (2:1), so diets high in meat tend to be deficient in calcium. Meat is high in calories, compared to fruits, vegetables, and grains, so the diet may be low in important vitamins, minerals, and fiber. Overconsumption of proteins, especially *tryptophan*, also increases the need for vitamin B6. These problems are aggravated by the fact that animal proteins are often associated with large amounts of fat. Symptoms of overconsumption of protein could include chronic fatigue, **arthritis**, insomnia, low blood sugar, premature baldness, depression, reduced **endurance**, arteriosclerosis, heart disease, kidney damage, and constipation.

Is it best to eliminate meat from the diet? There are many healthy vegans, who don't eat any animal products at all. Some studies indicate that vegetarians have more stamina, though it has been suggested that this finding is biased by their greater discipline, manifested in maintaining a vegetarian regimen in the first place. Vegetarian runners may have lower cholesterol and triglyceride levels than their meat-eating colleagues. Many nutritionists, even among those who espouse vegetarianism, do feel that some people may need meat, especially those people with blond hair and fair complexions. Since conversion to vegetarianism requires some knowledge of nutrition, no one should simply quit eating meat without further investigation. Those who wish to be vegetarians, or to eat very few animal proteins, need to learn about the composition of protein foods, so that their diets contain all the essential amino acids. Some vitamins, notably B12, are most abundantly found in animal proteins, so vegetarians must take extra care to obtain these.

VITAMINS AND MINERALS

Vitamins act as catalysts in fuel-burning cycles, facilitate digestion and absorption of food, and serve as chemical regulators. Vitamins must be present in the diet. Some of them can be manufactured internally, but in amounts too small to meet the body's needs. Unlike the fuel foods, the structures of different vitamins are quite varied (see Appendix 1).

The minerals are chemical elements, though most animals (including humans) cannot use them in elemental form. Plants take minerals from the soil to form the organic compounds which we can assimilate. Minerals can be grouped into three categories: the *bone minerals* (calcium, phosphorus, and magnesium), the *blood minerals* (sodium, chlorine, and potassium), and the *trace minerals* (found in the body in smaller amounts, but still vital to our health). Minerals form part of the body structure (e.g. calcium in bones), act as chemical regulators, are constituents of enzymes or catalysts for enzyme function, facilitate neuromuscular transmission, catalyze blood clotting, and help control body pH and fluid balance.

Each vitamin and mineral plays an important role in performance, from maintaining healthy nerves to strengthening muscles. Detailed information on individual vitamins and minerals is given in Appendix 1. Each nutrient affects the need for other nutrients, so it is not easy to establish a corrective nutritional program. Some approaches are outlined in Chapter 9, but it is important to consult a professional before making major changes in diet.

Is it possible to establish and maintain *optimal* health without vitamin or mineral supplements? Some nutritionists would answer yes, but others feel that most people could benefit from the right kind and amount of supplements. Nutrients are lost in transit from farm to table, and even the farm-fresh produce may have been grown in soils depleted of nutrients by modern farming methods. (Some nutrients which are necessary for human health are not needed by plants, so it is perfectly possible to grow a healthy crop which will not meet human nutritional needs.) People with a sedentary lifestyle require less food than did their forebears, so their diet may not supply enough of all the nutrients needed for optimum performance.

It is tempting to think that you can achieve optimal health by supplementing an inadequate diet with pills. Most people don't really hold this view out loud, i.e. if asked, they will admit that it might make sense to maintain good eating habits, whatever those might be. But sometimes we live as though vitamin pills were some sort of talisman protecting us against misfortune. If the subconscious is a working partner in health and in performance, then combining vitamins with what you believe to be junk food gives the unconscious a double message about your wish to be healthy. It is better to have a varied and "healthy" diet, since science surely hasn't discovered all of the nourishing factors in food. Supplements are made by isolating the active, presumably health-giving principles from food. If we knew what all of these principles were, we could theoretically stop eating food and live on pills. Many people believe that we will never achieve the necessary technology.

Therapeutic megadoses of vitamins or minerals are also controversial. I once saw the following quote, attributed to a pioneer in megavitamin therapy: "Even one medical cure shows the efficacy of a novel therapy. One should not have to prove its effectiveness over and over again to gain acceptance." Proponents of megavitamin therapies point out that the effectiveness of some mainstream medical tools is accepted on no stronger evidence. They recommend supplements because they have seen them work. Though there have been experiments designed to prove or disprove their effectiveness, it is difficult to get agreement on what the experiments show. (See the Coda for further discussion of this problem.)

When your career is threatened by some condition which others seem to have overcome with vitamin therapy, it might pay to investigate the therapy. It is often argued that people waste too much time and money chasing miracle cures. This kind of name-calling only muddies the waters. The answers to the nutritional questions are simply not yet in, and you have to take responsibility for regaining your health.

FIBER

Fiber is the indigestible skeleton which gives whole foods their shape. Though indigestible and therefore not a nutrient, fiber is needed in the diet to keep the bowels moving. It also seems to be good for the heart. Too much fiber can be irritating and may decrease absorption of some nutrients by rushing the food through the bowels (decreasing *intestinal transit time*). Fiber is found in whole grains, fruits, and vegetables.

WATER

Water is not considered a nutrient, but without it we would die in short order. How much water we need depends on exercise and diet. Some nutritionists recommend a set minimum, occasionally as high as two quarts a day, while others point out that drinking too much water upsets the electrolyte balance, washes out water-soluble vitamins, and overworks the kidneys. (Not everyone agrees that it would harm a healthy kidney.) Some athletes say that by the time they actually feel thirsty they are already excessively dehydrated and will suffer from decreased **endurance** and motor **coordination**. Dehydration inhibits the building of tissue and efficient use of energy at the cellular level, increases the concentrations of toxins (including **lactic acid**) in the blood stream, and decreases the total blood volume and thus the amount of oxygen and nutrients available. Dehydration may affect **local musculature** in **short-term anaerobic performance**, e.g. bursts of trill passages. On the other side, I've heard both mountain guides and concert artists say that too much water will weaken the limbs. I've seen nothing written to confirm this, but it's an indication that extremes of any kind are not likely to bring the body into balance.

Most nutritionists do not advocate drinking during meals. Liquid dilutes the digestive juices, slowing down digestion and leaving time for the food to ferment or putrefy. This leads to toxic wastes and gas in the digestive system. Thirst during or right after meals could be a response to too much salt or to some toxin which needs to be diluted. Since cold drinks can slow and sometimes even stop the action of pepsin in the stomach, hot tea (without tannin) might be better. Drinking water in large quantities between meals, can induce *hyponatremia* (not enough sodium), also known as water intoxication, if the electrolyte balancing mechanisms fail to keep pace with the input. Symptoms include lethargy, dizziness, and abdominal cramps. Many nutritionists recommend herbal teas or juices, since their higher electrolyte concentration matches the osmolarity of the body fluids more closely than water does. For a list of nutrient-rich herbal teas see Chapter 13. Fruit juice should be diluted by half, as it is a very concentrated source of both electrolytes and sugars. In the long term, undiluted fruit juice can aggravate blood sugar problems. Dietary sources of water also include fresh fruits and vegetables.

What is the healthiest source of water? Distilled water has its advocates, who say that the minerals in water are not digestible until processed by growing plants. They say that inorganic minerals (the ones in water) are deposited in the joints, heart, kidneys, etc, in the form of crystals which have to be flushed out by drinking distilled water. Other nutritionists say that distilled water is harmful because it washes minerals out of the body. They also point out that it is not "natural," i.e., you don't find it in rivers and wells. Instead of distilled water they advocate spring water, if it doesn't have too high a sodium content. The quality of tap water varies from place to place. It may contain chlorine (to kill germs), and maybe some germs too, as well as copper from old pipes or cadmium from many of the new ones. Since hot water may leach toxic minerals from water pipes, some people suggest drinking only from the cold water tap, and letting the tap run first if it has been shut off for several hours.

Chapter 9

WHAT THE HEALTHY PERFORMER EATS
a brief survey of nutritional theories
... and the author's biases regarding them

Now what? A diet to prevent tendinitis? How about tortellini and tomatoes, they both start with T. Bagels and bananas for bursitis? Hey, this could be all right!

Before designing the performer's diet we need a foundation — a basic healthy diet — to build on. I'm not sure there's a difference between a diet for optimum health and a diet for optimum performance, or between such a diet and one for optimally safe performance. Sometimes even a preventive diet and a curative diet are virtually identical. Chapter 11 discusses diets for some problems which increase the likelihood of injury, and Chapter 12 outlines training diets. Both chapters simply modify the framework built in this chapter.

In trying to balance some fairly extreme and contradictory views, I am constrained by my own biases. Though virtually everyone agrees, for example, that starvation or deficiency diseases would affect our work, not all physicians agree that an apparently healthy person can benefit from judicious dietary fine-tuning. Let's look at some of the positions which are actually held, as I understand them, and my reactions to them. That way you'll know where your biases fit with respect to mine.

THE BASIC FOUR

Many people believe that optimal nutrition simply requires eating daily portions of the basic four food groups (protein, grains, fruits and vegetables, and dairy products). I disagree with them on a number of counts.

First, the inclusion of dairy products as a basic food group has sparked the rumor that the whole list was first promulgated by the dairy industry. I have absolutely no evidence of this, but I do not believe daily, or even occasional, ingestion of dairy products is necessary for health, nor am I sure that it is always beneficial. For an extreme view, read *Don't Drink Your Milk* (see bibliography).

Second, the Basic Four statement doesn't say enough about food quality, e.g. how refined and processed the food is, or about the relative proportions of food from each group. I think there's a big difference, for example, between even the best whole grain bread and a bowl of cooked millet or brown rice.

Third, there is not enough said about proportions of the four groups in the diet. Some healers (e.g. Jensen, below) claim impressive results using large quantities of fresh vegetables, along with relatively small amounts of fruits, whole grains and some other protein foods.

Fourth, as discussed in Chapter 8, even the best-balanced diet may be deficient in some vitamins and minerals, so even if the basic four are accepted as a guideline, supplements might be necessary.

DON'T EXCLUDE ANY FOODS FROM YOUR DIET

Many people hold the view that no food should be excluded from the diet. This is primarily a reaction to the problems encountered with restrictive weight-reduction diets, vegetarianism, macrobiotics, cleanses, and other regimens which require an educated approach.

Since we don't know enough about nutrition to plan an optimal diet based on only a few kinds of foods, variety is good insurance. On the other hand, some foods don't agree with some people. (Usually their favorite foods, say some nutritionists.)

There are many healthy vegetarians, and vegetarianism has been practised for centuries in some cultures. However, it may not be the best diet for everyone, and those who want to switch must make the transition with knowledge, rather than merely cut out meat.

The "inclusionist" viewpoint also begs the question of what constitutes a food. Some substances which might be included under this regimen, e.g. refined sugar or coffee, might better be classified as harmful drugs than as foods (see Chapter 10). Yes, sugar cane and coffee beans are natural substances. So are poisonous mushrooms.

WONDERFOODS

Though proponents of certain "wonderfoods" seem to promise glowing health regardless of other aspects of diet or lifestyle, a diet must be considered as a whole. Using any food as a miracle drug will merely create an imbalance. If there is already an imbalance, some of these foods could nudge the body back toward the middle, provided that they form part of an otherwise sensible program. Some of the proposed wonderfoods tend to be expensive, so charges of quackery are not surprising. Furthermore, if these foods are as powerful as their proponents claim, then excessive quantities may be harmful. Exercise caution, and consult a qualified practitioner before consuming large quantities of anything.

HONEY
Many people have called honey a wonderfood. It is said to regulate the digestive system, combat **arthritis**, provide minerals, increase **endurance**, and provide quick energy.

Honey contains small amounts of phosphorus, potassium, calcium, sodium, sulphur, iron, magnesium, manganese, protein, vitamin A, some Bs, and enzymes. According to its critics, however, honey has a limited mineral content and can generate blood sugar swings (see Chapter 10). Studies supporting honey's usefulness are inconclusive. Some of the leading studies appeared only in the *American Bee Journal*, hardly an unbiased forum.

BEE POLLEN
Bee pollen may reduce **recovery time from exercise** and improve both **aerobic and anaerobic performance**. It is said to heal the digestive system and raise morale while **calming** a person without side effects. It has been recommended for **memory** loss, weight control (up or down), anemia, high blood pressure, and accumulation of toxins in the capillaries. It may also lower blood cholesterol and raise hemoglobin levels. It is a complete protein, containing all of the essential amino acids, and also

supplies most of the vitamins, possibly including B12, and large numbers of mineral salts, steroid hormones, and enzymes. Some believe that all of these elements together — plus a host of unknown factors — have a synergistic effect.

Its opponents dispute the performance claims, and point out that some people are allergic to bee pollen, though proponents say that taking small amounts will actually alleviate airborne pollen allergies.

The adventurous might wish to try bee pollen on cereal. The fermented form (fermented in the hive by the bees) is easier to digest than the pollen from the hive entrance, which has an indigestible shell.

ROYAL JELLY
Food for the queen bee, royal jelly is said to boost energy. It contains pantothenic acid (vitamin B5) and is widely used in both England and China.

GELATIN
Gelatin is derived from collagen and is almost pure protein. (It lacks tryptophan, so it is not a complete protein.) It is high in the amino acid, glycine, needed to form phosphocreatine (PC, which releases energy quickly to let a **muscle** begin work). Experiments from the 1930s and early 1940s suggested that glycine reduces fatigue in healthy people, and increase **endurance** and **grip strength**, but later research has tended not to confirm them.

BREWER'S YEAST
Brewer's yeast contains concentrated amounts of complete protein, B vitamins, chromium, selenium, nucleic acids, and enzymes. It also has RNA, which gives quick energy and facilitates cellular renewal. Brewer's yeast, if grown in the right medium, is one of the few sources of vitamin B12 acceptable to vegetarians.

Some nutritionists say that the many people with potential yeast sensitivity are better off getting their B vitamins from rice polish.

WHEAT GERM

Wheat germ is the nutrient-rich inner part of the wheat grain. It is high in vitamin E, the B complex, and protein. It may increase **stamina** by raising muscle oxygen levels, and it may support the nervous system (see Appendix 1).

Both wheat germ and wheat germ oil turn rancid, releasing dangerous free radicals (see Chapter 8), so it is important to eat these foods fresh. The germ is richer in B vitamins and protein than the oil.

KELP

Kelp is a form of seaweed which is high in minerals, including many trace minerals. It is also rich in vitamins A, B complex, C, D, E, and K, and contains many enzymes and amino acids. It has been used to cleanse the arteries, soothe the heart, and build the blood.

GREEN-LIPPED MUSSEL

The green-lipped mussel, a New Zealand shellfish, contains manganese, iodine, chromium, and smaller amounts of most minerals including all the macro-minerals. It also contains most amino acids, except taurine, and vitamins A, E, B_2, B_3, B_6, and B_{12}, and is a source of the antioxidant, SOD (superoxide dismutase). Most importantly, it contains mucopolysaccharides, a class of carbohydrates found in the human body but not often found in food. They relieve many types of **arthritis, bursitis,** and **joint problems**, generally reducing inflammation and establishing new capillaries.

SPROUTS

Virtually all seeds produce edible sprouts. Sprouting destroys enzyme inhibitors, including phytic acid. The leaves often contain amino acids which are not found in the unsprouted seed, and about 150 times more protein, up to 15 times more vitamins, and about 5 to 6 times more enzymes. Most sprouts contain vitamin C, whereas the seeds do not. The saponins in sprouts may fight Candida and **arthritis** (see Chapters 11 and 15).

BARLEY GREEN, WHEAT GRASS JUICE

Barley green is made by extracting the juice from young barley plants. It is rich in chlorophyl, beta carotene (provitamin A), and other vitamins and minerals, and some people find that it gives them more energy. Wheat grass juice is made from the first green growth of the wheat seed. It has similar properties, cleansing and strengthening the body.

CHLORELLA
Chlorella is a one-celled green alga which has enjoyed great popularity in Japan. In addition to chlorophyl, amino acids, beta carotene, and other vitamins and minerals, chlorella contains nucleic acids. It is said to speed healing from infection, strengthen the immune system, and remove toxic metals.

SHIITAKE MUSHROOM
Long eaten in China and Japan, the shiitake mushroom is becoming popular in the West, as it contains proteins, fats, carbohydrates, minerals, and vitamins (including B_{12} and D_2), as well as enzymes which lower blood cholesterol. Even the Merck Index (see bibliography for Section III) says that it is anticholesteremic. It alleviates many conditions, including **arthritis**, and is said to combat fatigue and increase the general state of health.

REISHI MUSHROOM
Another mushroom from the East, Reishi is high in germanium, an antioxidant which supports the immune system. It is used for rheumatism, ulcers, and high blood pressure.

LIVER
Liver is rich in nutrients, especially the B vitamins and iron, though it may also be rich in toxins if the animal grazed along a highway, consuming a lot of lead. Because Argentine liver has less lead than North American liver, Argentine supplements, e.g. dessicated liver pills, powder, capsules, are preferable. Liver is said to increase **endurance**, especially for anemics.

COMMON VEGETABLES AS HEALERS
According to William Borrmann and other nutritionists, the juices of many vegetables and fruits have therapeutic properties. These common foods could easily be included in a diet, but any concentrated use, e.g. juice fasting, requires

supervision. Various practitioners have made the following claims:

Potatoes heal **muscles** and **nerves** and are especially good for sciatica, in combination with such synergists as celery, carrot, parsley and cucumber.

Turnip leaves are bone builders because of their calcium content. They also benefit the **nervous system.**

Parsnips, the domestic kind, decrease **nervousness** and brain fatigue.

Endive improves **eye** conditions, including cataracts.

Lettuce combats **nervousness** and hair loss.

Grapefruit removes inorganic calcium deposits from **joints** and cartilage. Arthritics might find that citrus fruits increase pain, and people with gouty arthritis are advised to eat cherries instead.

Strawberries contain organic salicylates, so they act as pain killers.

BIOCHEMICAL INDIVIDUALITY

In 1943, the Food and Nutrition Board of the United States established the first RDAs (recommended daily amounts) of various nutrients. The RDAs were later adopted by the FDA (Food and Drug Administration), and have been periodically revised downward to reflect the eating habits of the public. The RDAs are generally sufficient to ward off the major deficiency diseases, but many nutritionists feel that the recommended levels are inadequate (see Appendix 1). There are also some nutrients which may be needed but which lack RDAs.

The term "biochemical individuality" was coined by Roger Williams to indicate that nutritional requirements vary widely from person to person. He and his colleagues argue that for this reason it is not possible to establish RDAs which will leave all or even most of us in optimum health.

Deciding what to eat is more complicated than just adding up the nutrients in various foods and looking at a chart to see whether the diet meets the RDAs. This would be true even if the charts reflected the variations (as great as 200 percent) which have been found in the composition of single food samples.

Tests to determine various nutrient levels in the body include hair mineral analysis as well as blood and urine tests, but their validity is disputed. Some people monitor symptoms of low-level deficiency (see Appendix 1), but this approach requires the aid of a competent practitioner. Richard Passwater and Michael Colgan have each written books for developing an individualized supplementation program.

MICHAEL COLGAN

Colgan's *Your Personal Vitamin Profile* suggests a basic level of supplementation, which is adjusted to meet individual needs as indicated by answers to a questionnaire. He points out that such factors as body weight, environmental pollution, eating habits, skin and hair conditions, allergies, mood, digestion, frequency of colds, joint pains, drugs, and exercise habits affect your need for nutrients. The avoidance of all salt, for example, requires an increase in iodine, while excessive salt consumption requires increases in zinc and potassium, and regular heavy exercise for long periods of time requires increases in various B vitamins, C, E, calcium, magnesium, potassium, and iron.

RICHARD PASSWATER

Passwater's *Total Protection Plan* includes exercise, proper diet, and stress reduction, as well as vitamin supplements. He starts with a basic list of supplements, a set of questions about various self-observable symptoms (from circles under the eyes to bowel regularity), and lab tests to check on blood chemistry. The questionnaire yields a total score which determines the need to increase or decrease the dosages across the board. The questions are to be answered every two weeks until a personal maximum score is reached.

COLGAN VS. PASSWATER

Colgan increases (or decreases) dosages on the basis of answers to each of his questions, while Passwater compiles a total score, based on all the answers, and increases the values of supplements across the board. The answers to Colgan's questions need to be revised periodically to adjust for the changes in skin, hair condition, lifestyle, and eating habits which often accompany improved health, while Passwater has this periodic review built into his system (initially). Passwater's formula doesn't take into account unusual individual needs for a specific vitamin, but he does suggest a look at blood chemistry, which might be a good idea. It would also be wise to find someone to help design a more personalized program than either of these.

GOING BY THE NUMBERS

Even if nutritional requirements do vary form person to person, the RDAs can indicate areas where a diet is severely deficient. The figures given in Chapter 8 suggest what proportions of a diet should be carbohydrate (say at least 70 percent), fats (say 10 percent unsaturated, 5 percent saturated), and protein (say 15 percent or at least one hundredth of our ideal body weight). With the RDAs for vitamins and minerals (see Appendix 1), we have a basis for planning an adequate diet. Rather than start from scratch, it might be a good idea to keep track of what you eat for a week or so to get some idea how close your present diet comes to these numbers.

This process is time-consuming, but there are many services that do this sort of analysis. The conclusions they come to are based on their estimates of portion size, so be sure to get a copy of the raw data after it's been tabulated. The analysis could be done by a nutritionist, nutrition-oriented doctor, or one of the following agencies. (I don't have any personal experience with these companies, so this is not an endorsement, just a way to get started.)

Advanced Medical Nutrition, Inc; 2247 National Avenue; P.O. Box 5012; Hayward, CA 94540; (800) 437-8888

Doctors Data Newsletter; Box 111; W Chicago, IL 60185

Medical Computers International; 13400 Northrup Way; Bellevue, WA 98005; (206) 644-2702

Pronovich; Box 1263; Bancroft, Ontario K0L 1C0

BERNARD JENSEN'S BASIC EATING PLAN

The controversial iridologist, Dr. Bernard Jensen (see Chapter 21), recommends the following basic nutrition program for both therapy and health maintenance: every day eat two different fruits, at least four to six vegetables (including at least two green leafy ones), one protein, and one starch, with vegetable or fruit broths and juices between meals. (Note that at least half of the daily food intake consists of vegetables.) For protein Jensen permits lean meat three times a week, eggs once a week, fish once a week, and cottage cheese once a week, with alternative suggestions for vegetarians. Starches mean whole grain cereal, baked potato, banana, or winter squash, or whole grain breads. For supplements he prefers foods, e.g. rice polish, wheat germ, and dulse. It should be possible to adopt Jensen's regimen gradually, perhaps increasing the vegetables and decreasing the protein over time, though any radical change requires supervision.

Jensen avoids pre-processed convenience foods and recommends raw foods (50 to 60 percent of the diet), the separation of starch and protein meals, fruit before breakfast, exercise, skin brushing, and a good mental attitude. He advocates periodic cleanses as therapeutic and preventive measures. Although this regimen is found in a number of his books, Dr. Jensen recommends his *Vital Foods for Total Health*, available from the author (Route 1, Box 52, Escondido, CA 92025).

MACROBIOTICS

Macrobiotics is a way of eating based on the Oriental ideas of yin and yang. The most extreme followers of this school seem to subsist on brown rice and bits of seaweed, though others enjoy a somewhat greater variety of foods. There are many books on the subject, including accounts of miraculous cancer cures. There are also tales of fanatics starving themselves by neglecting to balance their proteins. This is not an approach I'd suggest fooling around with: find someone competent or read a lot more about it than I have.

JOHN GARVY

John Garvy's booklet, *The Five Phases of Food*, applies the Chinese five-element theory to nutrition, associating every food with an element (wood, fire, earth, metal, or water). He pairs each group with an organ or system and shows the groups in a cyclical relationship, with each group strengthening the neighbor on one side and weakening the one on the other. The idea is to get into balance by favoring one group and its strengthening neighbor, and to maintain balance by eating from all five groups equally. A chart shows levels of healthfulness, from over-stimulating to strengthening, for the foods in each group. To overcome cravings for a toxic food, substitute progressively healthier foods from the same group. For sugar, which is associated with the stomach, spleen, and pancreas, the sequence might be honey, almonds, banana, apple, corn on the cob, chard, millet. For oily foods, associated with the liver and gallbladder, the sequence might be olives, chicken, trout, plum, carrot, rye. Garvy also suggests alternatives to tobacco and alcohol, meat, and excessive quantities of liquids. Each list is long enough to accommodate individual tastes. If this system represents a radical change in diet, consult someone competent in Chinese medicine or nutritional counselling.

FOOD COMBINING

Proteins, fats, and carbohydrates are digested in different places in the digestive system and require different chemical environments. Starches are digested in the mouth and small intestine, but not in the stomach, unless they remain in a slightly alkaline environment. Protein is digested in the stomach, in an acid environment. If both of these are eaten at the same meal, the body has to give priority to one, generally responding by secreting HCl when the protein enters the stomach, and letting the starch wait. Meanwhile the starch ferments. It also coats the protein, thus slowing protein digestion, which gives the undigested protein time to putrefy. The fermentation and putrefaction result in gas. Putrefactive bacteria break amino acids down into toxic substances, e.g. indol, skatol, phenol, and some of these (indoxyl, skatoxyl, phenolsulphonic acid) are subsequently found in the urine, suggesting that the toxins are absorbed from the intestines. Meanwhile, the stomach must secrete more HCl to try to keep the process going, and the body may have to draw on its sodium reserves to protect the stomach lining, a process which can result in electrolyte imbalance and ultimately affect the heart, kidneys, and joints (see Chapter 11, arthritis).

Herbert Shelton recommends "food combining" (see table 5) to avoid the problems outlined above. Many nutritionists disagree with him, pointing out that whole foods are often combinations themselves, e.g. whole grains contain both starch and protein. Shelton maintains that the enzymes in whole foods orchestrate digestive secretions for a single food in a way that the body can't manage for a mixture, so that when a whole grain is eaten, the initial secretions of the stomach contain very little HCl, but once the starch is digested, more HCl is secreted to digest the protein.

Food combining does permit a balanced diet over the course of the day. Anyone who suffers from some form of indigestion, cramping, bloating, or even tiredness after some meals might try eating this way for a while to see whether it makes a difference. Those who have adopted food combining find that in time the occasional indulgence no longer creates problems.

These rules encourage the consumption of vegetables and tend to reduce protein and starch consumption, as Jensen also recommends. Ironically, he downplays the importance of most food combinations, saying that the resultant fear of breaking the rules is bad for digestion.

THREE SQUARES VS. GRAZING

Grazing has become somewhat of a buzzword lately. The term refers to the practice of eating small amounts of food

Table 5: Rules for food combining

Rule	Comments
Non-starchy vegetables go well with proteins.	The vegetables counter fat's inhibiting effects on stomach secretions. Raw cabbage particularly aids digestion of cheese or nuts.
Eat a large raw vegetable salad with starchy foods.	No acid in the dressing, as this would slow down starch digestion.
Acids and acid fruits go with cheese, nuts, avocados.	All of these foods inhibit stomach secretion for about the same time.
Eat starches and proteins at separate meals.	Keep bread, grains, potatoes separate from meat, eggs, cheese, nuts. (see discussion for reasons).
Eat only one kind of protein at a time.*	Gastric secretions have unique timings, e.g. meat needs the strongest secretions in the first hour, milk in the last hour.
Eat fruits 15 minutes before starch meals.	Acid from apples, berries, oranges, tomatoes can be sour enough to stop starch digestion.

*This rule conflicts with the idea of combining protein foods to get all the essential amino acids at one meal, but the latest evidence doesn't support the need for that type of food combining.

Table 5, cont'd: Rules for food combining

Rule	Comments
Don't eat acid fruits with protein (exceptions: nuts and cheese).	Acid fruits inhibit stomach secretion, so acidity is right, but enzymes are missing. (No vinegar salad dressing with protein meal.) Nuts and cheese putrefy slower. (Their fat inhibits gastric secretion anyway.)
Don't eat proteins with fats.	Fat can reduce gastric tone and pepsin and HCl secretion for two hours or more. Fat-containing proteins digest slower than lean ones, but not as slowly as protein/fat combination in different foods.
Don't eat sweets with other foods.**	Sweets and sugar inhibit stomach secretions. Sugars are digested in the intestine, not mouth or stomach, so they'll ferment if held up.
Eat melons by themselves.	Like sugar, they go quickly to intestine. (Some eat them with other fresh fruits.)
Drink milk separately.	Milk coagulates in stomach, and curds coat other foods to slow their digestion. (Acid fruits may be safe, but not sweet fruits.)

**That cookie just before dinner may indeed spoil your appetite.

throughout the day rather than eating two or three large meals and fasting in between. There is evidence that food is digested more efficiently in small amounts and that grazing increases life expectancy, lowers blood cholesterol levels, and improves **athletic performance.** Small frequent meals also make food combining easier.

The most serious argument against grazing is that it may be important to rest the digestive system during the day. Other drawbacks include inconvenience and the danger that snacks will mean junk food.

HINTS FOR THE BUSY PERFORMER

You're on the run all day, from rehearsal to meeting to student to gig. Barely time to stop for a hamburger and french fries. How are you supposed to change to a healthy grazing style? It's simple, really — since you're eating only a couple of bites at a time, you need only a short break to do it.

Carry around a stash of healthy snacks. Foods for the day might include raw vegetables (easier and healthier than salads, since vitamins leak out of the cut parts of the veg — i.e. the less preparation, the more nutrition), lots of nuts (a day's supply ony — keep the rest in the refrigerator), hard-boiled eggs, fruit, rice cakes, and a thermos of something. I freeze dinners and heat them to put in the thermos. A reheated dinner which has been carried around for that long contains few vitamins and many germs, but it sure tastes good after all that raw food. It takes about two minutes to pack the day's snacks, less time than it takes to pull in and wait for a hamburger.

MAKING CHANGES SAFELY

Change eating habits gradually. A radical change in diet can put stress on the body, e.g. by releasing toxins or changing electrolyte levels. In any case, radical changes in diet are too much like New Year's resolutions — they tend to get abandoned, and repeated attempts to gain health by force merely invite ill-health.

Be cautious with vitamin and mineral supplements. All substances have toxic levels, which vary among individuals. Large doses of a single nutrient can change the need for virtually all of the other nutrients through a chain reaction (see the synergist and antagonist sections in Appendix 1.) Problems in metabolizing supplementary nutrients strain the eliminative organs, and even when metabolized successfully, megadoses of supplements ask the body to do extra work. Do not take therapeutic doses of supplements without professional advice.

Many people seeking improved health have very little trust in their bodies. I believe that our natural state is one of harmony between what we want and what we need, but that by the time many of us start on a conscious quest for optimal health, our bodies are too polluted to know what they need, and many of us have developed addictive food sensitivities. Until we have regained that natural state, we may need guidance. If it seems extremely difficult to move toward balance, there may be aggravating conditions like food allergies or low blood sugar (see Chapter 11). Garvy (above) lists substitutes for problem foods.

Any major dietary change should be made with the aid of an expert (not a book) who recognizes the pitfalls and knows how to regulate the speed of change to get maximum well-being with a minimum of trauma. Yet the eventual goal is to become independent, to reach the state of harmony between needs and wants. If your body isn't enjoying the new regimen, ask why. Is the unpleasantness a healthy sign, or a call for a change of regimen or perhaps experts? Trust an expert long enough to give the program a chance. It is never a good idea to consult several experts at once, unless they are working together.

Even for a healthy person, there are pitfalls in trusting the body. Some cleansing diets, for example, may be so bracing that it is tempting to follow them for longer than recommended. This sort of thing usually backfires a year or two down the road with some problem induced by mineral depletion. While making major changes, the body really isn't likely to be your best guide. Eventually, however, it can be just that.

Chapter 10

FOODS TO AVOID:
why the sensitive performer got sick

So what's wrong with coffee and donuts, French fries and pop? If you've been injured, or if these foods are staples in your diet, read on.

Most of the foods discussed in this chapter have little or no nutritional value, apart from calories. Some nutritionists would go so far as to call them drugs or poisons. Unfortunately they're also addictive, and eliminating them from the diet will produce unpleasant side effects and cravings. It might be best to get help kicking the habit, especially if this represents a major change in diet. Once the habit is truly broken, the cravings will abate, along with the side effects.

SUGAR

Nearly everybody eats sugar. It is a reward, our just "dessert," a consolation, a celebration, a form of companionship, and a way to make other things more palatable. A sweet dessert is our right, our social obligation, a great way to end a good meal, and a way to be generous to ourselves and to others.

Sugar is hard to avoid, since many processed foods contain it in some form, e.g. fructose, sorbitol, mannitol, dextrose. Often, adding up all the amounts hidden under these names reveals that sugar is the main ingredient in the product. Sugar addiction can start with sweetened baby foods or possibly even excessive fruit consumption and undiluted fruit juices.

What's wrong with sugar? It takes about 16 feet of sugar cane of one-inch diameter to produce one teaspoon of sugar. Sugar has virtually none of the vitamins, minerals, or fiber, enzymes, fatty acids, or proteins contained in the original cane or beet. In order to digest it, the body must dip into its own supply of enzymes, vitamins, and minerals. Thus sugar robs us of nutrients including vitamin B_6, the rest of the B complex, calcium, zinc, and chromium. The sugar in one candy bar lowers the body's calcium level for 72 hours. Sugar may accelerate the development of osteoporosis and raise blood cholesterol and triglyceride levels. Like all sweeteners, it reduces the number of T-lymphocytes in the blood, thus reducing immunity for hours after ingestion. It has been linked to cancer, atherosclerosis, heart disease (particularly coronary occlusion), and high blood pressure, as well as to delinquency and criminal behavior. Since sugar is digested very quickly, it puts stress on the pancreas. It can have a rebound effect on blood sugar levels, so sugar abuse often leads to hypoglycemia or diabetes. Finally, it hinders our ability to deal with **stress**, interferes with cell respiration, and draws water into the gastro-intestinal tract, away from the **muscles**.

Sugar withdrawal symptoms include headaches, **muscle tension, blurred vision**, rapid heartbeat, **anxiety**, delirium, depression, dizziness, hyperactivity, **inability to concentrate**, irritability, rage reaction, **tremors**, and **weakness**.

Are other sweeteners, e.g. honey, molasses, or diet aids, healthier than sugar? Although they each have their advocates, the consensus seems to be that we are better off without them: for one thing, all sweeteners depress the immune system. Aside from the unknown risks represented by artificial sweeteners which have not been on the market long enough to reveal their dangers, many side effects have been clearly established, e.g. sorbitol may alter absorption of medications, saccharin may harm the nervous system, and fructose raises blood lactate levels and may raise triglyceride levels. To prevent problems with blood-sugar regulation, limit even dried fruits and full-strength fruit juices.

SALT

Salt is found in most processed foods, especially canned foods, so many people eat far more salt than they need. A high-salt diet can lead to **muscle damage**, high blood pressure, increased sweating, chronic fatigue, blood clotting, and eventual fluid loss. Salt tablets, sometimes used by athletes to make up for perspiration losses, bypass the feedback mechanism of the taste buds, so it is easy to take an overdose. Salting food to taste is far safer.

Salt restriction could increase the chance of injury. The body will adjust eventually by retaining more salt, but a sudden decrease in salt intake can cause **cramps**. The best time to begin to cut back on salt is in the winter. Some problems, e.g. underactive adrenals, may actually indicate a need for more salt.

FRIED FOODS

Heating oil to a frying temperature makes it go rancid, releasing free radicals which are implicated in tissue damage and a host of other problems (see Chapter 8). Fried foods also raise the resting pulse rate and blood pressure.

REFINED FLOUR

The body digests refined starches, e.g. white flour and white (polished) rice very much like sugar. They have almost as few nutrients, even when labelled enriched. White flour is made whiter by bleaching it, adding one more toxic element which may attack teeth even faster than sugar does. Flour combines with water in the digestive system to make a paste that often leads to severe constipation and other bowel problems. It has also been linked with lung congestion in sensitive people.

FOOD ADDITIVES

Food additives are not food. At best they will do us no good, while at worst they may do severe harm. Though some people do advocate eating antioxidant preservatives like BHT to prevent cancer, most nutritionists would prefer the food-based antioxidants, e.g. vitamins C and E and selenium. Preservatives may indeed keep food fresher, but they might also kill the digestive bacteria in the colon.

Colorings are periodically taken off the market to be replaced with new ones, often coal tar products which subsequently turn out to be carcinogenic. (Why wait to find out? Eat by candlelight, and you won't care what color your food is.) Colorings and other food additives have been implicated in hyperactivity, various learning disabilities, and criminal behavior. Parents and prison wardens often confirm these connections, though most scientists consider them inadequately established.

Since processed foods are generally poorer in nutrients than their distant fresh cousins, eating fresh foods is the most sensible way to avoid most food additives. Frozen food is generally better than canned, and fresh food is better than frozen, both in nutritional value and in levels and numbers of additives. Any packaged food is suspect, since the preservatives in the packaging itself do not have to be listed as ingredients, even though they preserve the food inside the package.

Unfortunately even fresh foods can contain harmful chemicals. Many people know that hot dogs contain nitrates, which the stomach turns into carcinogenic nitrosamines. It is less well-known that celery and lettuce pick up nitrates from chemical fertilizers, with the same effect on the body. Organic farmers believe that if the plant is healthy enough, the pests and fungi will not harm it. (Is this why their food tastes better than produce from unhealthy plants sprayed with pesticides and herbicides?) Organic farming is hard to define, e.g. irrigation water may contain high levels of pesticides, but it is a step toward producing healthier food.

CAFFEINE

Most heavy coffee drinkers know that they are addicted to a substance which produces **anxiety**, sleeplessness, irritability, headaches, **shakiness**, tremulous feelings, lightheadedness, **nervousness**, depression, and ulcers. Coffee is diuretic but raises blood pressure. It stimulates the heart muscle and has been linked with ventricular tachycardia and fibrillation in people with a tendency to heart problems. It can raise blood levels of free fatty acids, which can lead to atherosclerosis. It can also

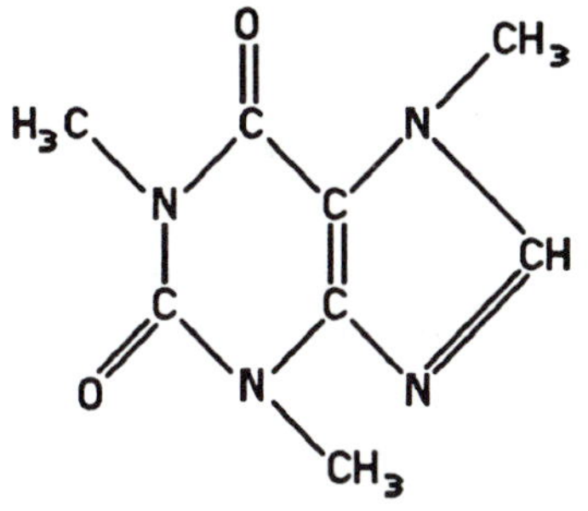

Fig. 39: Caffeine

raise blood glucose levels in diabetics but lower them in hypoglycemics, thus showing the same effects as sugar, but by stimulating the adrenals instead of the pancreas. Finally, it may promote alcoholism, produce **muscle contractions**, distort **muscular coordination**, hamper **timing**, cause growth disorders (and possibly birth defects) in children, and produce benign breast lumps in women.

There are dissenting voices of sorts, but none of them really advocate drinking coffee. Studies have shown that typists could type faster and with fewer mistakes after drinking two cups of coffee. It does relax the smooth muscles in the **lungs** and may stretch glycogen stores in **endurance** sports. Caffeine increases **alertness** and **attention**, stimulates the flow of **adrenaline**, increases the basal metabolic rate, and **relaxes some of the smooth muscles, especially in the blood vessels,** so it could be considered an ergogenic aid (a substance which increases the ability to do work). On the other hand its diuretic effect could **decrease aerobic performance.** Coffee seems to **improve visual reaction time but slow complex reaction time,** and it may improve **strength** and **local muscular endurance,** though these findings are still controversial. For the 1984 Olympics coffee in excess of the equivalent of five or six cups in a one to two hour period was considered an illegal doping agent. Reactions depend on everyday caffeine intake, so the effects of drinking coffee prior to performance vary among individuals.

Caffeine is found in coffee, black tea, chocolate, cola drinks, and many pain relievers. Withdrawal symptoms include headaches, irritability, **nervousness**, restlessness, and lethargy. Much decaffeinated coffee contains traces of the carcinogen methylene chloride.

NICOTINE

Most of us don't eat cigarettes, but nicotine is one of the most highly toxic substances in our environment. The nicotine from five cigarettes can kill a rabbit.

Smoking lowers hormone levels in both men and women. It may lead to **osteoporosis** in women, by reducing estrogen levels. It has been implicated in heart and **lung** diseases, since it increases platelet adhesion, **constricts the arteries**, increases arterial wall thickness, reduces arterial elasticity, causes arterial plaque deposits, leads to calcification of the aorta, and destroys or congests the lung's air sacs, reducing the capacity for **oxygen intake**. It disturbs the digestive system, depletes vitamin C in the blood (in neutralizing toxins from smoking), reduces the **visual field**, hampers **mental functioning**, encourages hypoglycemia (via adrenal stimulation), and increases the desire for caffeine, sugar, and alcohol.

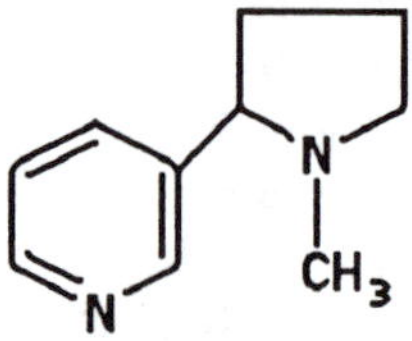

Fig. 40: Nicotine

Smoking ties up oxygen carriers in the blood with carbon monoxide, slowing down **muscle action**. It speeds up the **pulse rate** and increases blood pressure, while constricting the blood vessels, especially in the **extremities**, thus **cooling the hands** by up to 10°F.

Cadmium, a toxic metal in tobacco, raises blood pressure and lowers IQ. (see below, toxic metals).

Secondary smoke from someone else's cigarette is now known to be dangerous. It raises blood pressure, increases the heart rate, and increases blood carbon monoxide levels. Significant amounts of cadmium are inhaled along with the nicotine.

Smokers and their companions may be able to decrease the risk of problems by taking extra amounts of vitamins C, E, A, B$_3$, B$_{15}$, and lecithin, the minerals selenium, zinc, and manganese, as well as pectin, alginate, and the sulfur-containing amino acids such as cysteine (single amino acid supplementation is considered dangerous).

ALCOHOL

How unhealthy is alcohol? Moderate alcohol consumption may increase life span, reduce stress, and increase blood levels of high density lipoproteins. A small amount of alcohol may increase **self-confidence** and reduce inhibitions, feelings of insecurity, and tension, but it impairs judgement and motor performance, especially in tasks requiring **fine motor skills.** Larger amounts of alcohol reduce **gross motor skills.** A single beer decreases **heat tolerance** for up to three days and impairs **vision.** The rest of this section deals with the dangers of excess alcohol consumption, generally begging the question of how much is too much.

Alcoholism has led to pancreatitis, renal failure, cirrhosis, and gallstones. By damaging the liver, it contributes to certain types of cancer. It increases the risk of heart attack and stroke, reduces the contractile strength of the heart, raises blood triglycerides, increases platelet adhesion, and sludges red blood cells, reducing their oxygen-carrying capacity and aggravating the symptoms of **arthritis.** It is a central nervous system depressant implicated in **memory loss** and impairment of other brain functions, chronic fatigue, and toxic effects on the **muscles** and nervous system. It increases the risk of osteoporosis, bone fractures and **tooth loss.** It dilates the capillaries of the skin, at the expense of the rest of the body. It decreases peripheral vision and has led to nystagmus, an uncontrolled rapid movement of the **eye.** Alcohol increases the release of insulin from refined carbohydrates, so it contributes to hypoglycemia. This condition in turn increases the craving for alcohol, caffeine, nicotine, or sugar. Alcohol has been linked to esophageal cancer, gastritis, and ulcers. It is a diuretic, reducing **muscular efficiency** and flushing out B vitamins, calcium, magnesium, potassium, and often zinc.

Alcohol also changes the structure of the lining of the small intestine, along with its enzymes, and impedes nutrient absorption, especially of folate, B_1, B_{12}, and fat. Impairment of liver function reduces its storage capacity for vitamins A, D, and K, manganese, and copper. It may induce iron loss, through bleeding ulcers, though it is more likely to promote excess iron absorption. Alcohol may depress lactase, leading to lactose (milk) intolerance. Malnourishment in turn increases the blood levels of alcohol for a given intake.

Rats can be made to crave alcohol by feeding them too many refined carbohydrates and not enough vitamins, minerals, and proteins — sugar is one of the worst culprits. The effect is reversed by putting them back on a healthy diet: well nourished rats prefer plain water to alcohol. The same principles apply to humans, and some nutritionists claim that no one who is well-nourished can become an alcoholic. Vitamin therapy, including B_3, B_6, folic acid, C, and E, as well as herbal therapies, have helped some people withdraw from alcohol.

DRUGS

Most drugs, including the beta blockers discussed in Chapter 5, jeopardize performance quality.

Amphetamines tend to induce **shakiness** and mask pain, thus increasing the risk of injury while giving the illusion of better performance and increased energy. They also **increase recovery time for aching muscles.**

Drugs can often be replaced by herbs or changes in life-style, e.g. a fifteen minute walk may be more effective than a tranquilizer.

TOXIC METALS

Virtually everybody in the industrialized world eats, drinks, or inhales toxic metals in some quantities. Lead, cadmium, aluminum, and mercury are among the most common. Apple pectin, sodium alginate, and vitamins A, C, and E rid the body of most toxic metals.

LEAD
Lead exists throughout our environment. It is found in car exhausts (even with unleaded gas), cigarette smoke, old paint, pottery glazes, some cosmetics, shellfish from contaminated waters, and some pesticides. Even small amounts of lead in the body, at levels considered safe by many experts, can cause loss of appetite, **muscle twitches**, anemia, hyperirritability, loss of **muscle control**, mental retardation, **brittle bones, clumsiness,** behavioral disorders, decreased immunity to infection, and damage to the kidneys, **brain, and spinal cord.**

Reduce lead consumption by avoiding berries which grow near the roadside, by washing produce, and by eating country-grown organic fruits and vegetables. A high-calcium diet will decrease lead absorption, and vitamin A activates enzymes in the liver which detoxify lead. Avoid putting acid food in pottery which may contain lead-based glazes.

Replace lead-based paints, but wear a face mask and filter while scraping and cleaning the paint away. Precipitate lead out of the air with an air ionizer. And you could, of course, quit smoking.

CADMIUM
Cadmium is toxic, because it is able to displace zinc in the body. The cadmium found in foods is not generally a problem, because it exists in combination with sufficient zinc to maintain balance, though animal kidneys may contain excessive amounts. Zinc-depleted soils, food refining, and phosphate fertilizers disrupt the balance in foods. Coffee and black tea contain unhealthy cadmium-to-zinc ratios, as do alcoholic beverages. Cadmium is often found in the water supply, especially in soft water, which leaches it out of the pipes. Some paints, e.g. cadmium yellow, contain cadmium. And finally, cigarette smoke contains cadmium.

Symptoms of cadmium toxicity are subtle at first. They may include lower IQ, high blood pressure, enlarged heart, atherosclerosis, and changes in the blood vessels of the kidneys, as well as symptoms of zinc deficiency (see Appendix 1).

Zinc displaces cadmium, but excessive amounts of zinc create problems in turn, e.g. symptoms of copper deficiency (see Appendix 1) stemming from high zinc-to-copper ratios.

MERCURY

Mercury in our environment comes chiefly from pesticides, fungicides, chemical processing, and silver amalgam dental fillings. High concentrations of mercury are found in fish taken from polluted areas, especially fish that are caught when older, e.g. tuna or swordfish. Game birds may become contaminated by eating mercury-treated seed grain.

Organic mercury accumulates mostly in the fat and nervous tissues, while some inorganic mercury is stored in the kidney. Mercury displaces calcium in the nerve cells and interferes with the function of the mitochondria. The first effects of mercury toxicity are subtle changes in the mind and nervous system. Symptoms of chronic mercury poisoning include loss of fine muscle control, tremors, loss of balance, irritability, moodiness, anger, hearing and vision difficulties, depression, memory loss, and diminished intelligence.

A high calcium diet reduces mercury absorption. Vitamin C helps eliminate mercury, and seems to block the conversion of metallic mercury to the more harmful organic (methyl) form.

ALUMINUM

Aluminum is found in everyone's body, and not all people consider it harmful. It is often found in the city water supply, processed foods, and baking powder. Food prepared in aluminum cookware is another source, so this cookware is banned in some European countries.

Symptoms of aluminum poisoning may include constipation and intestinal gas, loss of appetite, nausea, skin ailments, energy loss, twitching of the leg muscles, areas of numbness, and excessive perspiration (don't remedy this with an aluminum-based antiperspirant.) Aluminum accumulates in the arteries, and some people believe that it contributes to aging, hardening of the aorta, and fatty buildup in the liver and kidneys. It has been linked with Alzheimer's disease, though no relationship has been established between dietary intake and the increased concentrations of aluminum found in the brains of Alzheimer's sufferers.

Don't use aluminum cookware, especially with acidic foods. Switch deodorants, and stop using alum baking powders. The body will gradually eliminate toxic quantities of aluminum when intake is reduced.

Chapter 11

HEALTH PROBLEMS AFFECTING PERFORMANCE
and how to deal with them

You started out with a pain in your arm, and now you've got Candida / low blood sugar syndrome (LBS) / hypertension /weight problems / premenstrual syndrome (PMS) / allergies /arthritis on top of it? Fear not. All of these conditions respond to changes in diet and lifestyle. They also affect performance, so don't try to fix your arm without correcting them.

Some practitioners consider these problems quite common, especially the undetected food allergies. This chapter discusses each one, its effect on performance, possible causes, and ways to correct imbalances and give the body a chance to repair itself.

Many of these problems can go undetected for a long time, as their sufferers think that it is normal to feel the way they do. Anyone who wants to improve performance should read the sections on Candida, LBS, allergies, and any others that seem at all likely to be relevant.

GENERAL TOXICITY

Some nutritionists say that virtually all of our health problems come from toxins in the colon or in the interstitial fluid surrounding the cells. The cells can't function efficiently when the fluid that bathes them and supplies nutrients is full of toxic wastes. They suffocate and struggle to do their jobs. Many people go on periodic fasts to allow the body to clean and rebuild itself. Fasting and cleansing diets require supervision, as they often result in a "healing crisis" which feels an awful lot like an illness. Some practitioners seem to think that you won't get well without periodic crises (sound like no pain, no gain?). Others say that you can alternate cleansing diets with programs to build up your strength, and that it is possible to avoid feeling sick during this process.

Why fast? When you fast, the body eats its own tissue. First it breaks down the injured and diseased parts, throws away the poisons, and reuses the protein molecules. In order to save the vital organs and brain for emegency rations it eats the muscles next, an expedient that unfortunately won't help your performance any. If you do stop before you lose healthy tissue, fasting might theoretically be part of a successful rejuvenation program.

What is a cleansing diet? If you're a meat-and-potatoes person, the basic diet in Chapter 9 would represent a cleansing diet. The alkaline diet described under arthritis (below) is slightly more cleansing. It is not great for those with low blood sugar or Candida. A fruit-only diet is much more cleansing, should be undertaken for no more than ten days at a time, and will probably produce headaches and other symptoms in most people unless their present diet is already quite cleansing.

There are a number of herbal cleansing programs on the market. The best ones include herbs to cleanse both the blood (Chapter 17) and the lower bowel (Chapter 14). Most include instructions for an alkaline diet to be followed during the herbal program. Reactions to these programs range from mild to violent, so don't just buy one from your local store.

CANDIDA

The yeast, Candida albicans, is found in virtually everyone's intestines, where it does not create problems as long as it is balanced by other organisms. When the Candida population grows too large, produces too many toxins, or migrates to other parts of the body, it produces a wide range of symptoms. Many factors, including stress and excess starch consumption, can make the Candida population grow. Symptoms of Candida overgrowth depend on its location and thus on the body system affected. They include fatigue, **poor memory, muscle aches, painful joints, anxiety attacks, cold hands, incoordination, inability to concentrate, cold sores, deafness,** abdominal bloating, food cravings, and fungal infections, e.g. athlete's foot.

Ever since Dr. C. Orian Truss began investigating Candida's connection with these problems, there has been an increasingly copious flow of books on the subject. Because Candida is present in healthy bodies, testing for Candida overgrowth is problematic. Many practitioners prefer to base their findings on a client's symptoms and history, e.g. past use of antibiotics or birth control pills. Many people who feel healthy, if perhaps a bit run down, and who have been taking fairly good care of themselves, actually present classic pictures of Candida overgrowth. Control of the yeast leaves them much more energetic and well than they thought possible.

There are many programs, most of them experimental, for controlling Candida. These include prescription drugs (which sometimes lead to liver damage) and over-the-counter remedies like homeopathic Candida or cows' colostrum (if it gives cows immunity, it might do the same for humans). This is a new field, some would say a new fad, so we can expect to keep seeing new remedies. Consult a qualified practitioner, since rapid killing of the yeast can release toxins which produce unpleasant and confusing symptoms of their own, and antifungal preparations which kill intestinal Candida may make the yeast migrate to other parts of the body and produce a whole new set of problems.

Diet seems to play an important role in yeast control. Some people advocate a high protein, low starch diet, while others allow whole grains but no flour. Some people forbid foods which tend to carry large amounts of Candida, including grapes and peanuts, while others question the necessity for this restriction. The choice of foods also seems to vary among individuals, e.g. some are particularly sensitive to vinegar, cheese or sugar. After the yeast is under control, the individual can determine which foods to avoid. (Unfortunately these are often favorite foods.) Food cravings will fade as the yeast subsides, and in fact, these cravings are considered a symptom of Candida overgrowth.

Candida is thought to underlie allergies, PMS, and low blood sugar syndrome. Bringing the yeast population under control often alleviates these problems.

LOW BLOOD SUGAR SYNDROME

A syndrome is a set if symptoms, and low blood sugar syndrome is the set of symptoms associated with low blood sugar (*hypoglycemia*). Since the presence of symptoms does not prove the existence of a disease, a doctor might suggest a glucose tolerance test for confirmation. The test can be quite uncomfortable for severe hypoglycemics, and there is no universal agreement on the values at which normal becomes pathological. For most hypoglycemics the consumption of sugar, especially in the form of glucose, makes the body overreact, producing too much insulin, so blood sugar levels fall sharply after an initial rise.

While many practitioners find low blood sugar syndrome quite common, most doctors are much more conservative in their estimates. As noted in the Candida section, the blood sugar problems can stem from yeast overgrowth. For this reason LBS seems like a passing fad, now being replaced by Candida. Since a typical LBS diet is quite healthy, it is probably worth finding out whether it alleviates symptoms, regardless of the label for the condition.

The symptoms of LBS include impatience, headaches, a pressing need for prompt meals, short attention span, **poor memory, shakiness,** cravings for salt or sugar, emotional swings, **tension** in the shoulders (trapezius) and calf muscles, low blood pressure, blackouts, and tiredness, especially first thing in the morning, mid- afternoon, or after a meal. Some or all of these symptoms may come and go, depending on diet, exercise, and coffee consumption. Coffee, salt, and sugar are among the substances which aggravate LBS problems and increase stress, which in turn increases the craving for these substances.

LBS can result from a congenital weakness in the pancreas, liver, or adrenals. More often it comes from eating coffee and donuts for breakfast, Danish pastry at mid-morning, and a burger, fries, and shake for lunch. Doing this every day for long enough will eventually strain those three organs, and unless they are constitutionaly very strong, the strain leads to LBS.

In the early stages, a change in diet may be enough to bring about a return to health. The diet can be supplemented with herbs to strengthen and heal the weakened organs (see Chapter 17). There are two major schools of thought on dietary

Table 6: what to avoid in LBS	
substance	comments
excess fruit	dilute any fruit juice with water
potatoes	tend to destabilize blood sugar
excess fat	digested slowly, but can destabilize blood sugar
excess protein	stresses liver, adrenals, pancreas
salt	lowers blood sugar by lowering potassium levels
alcohol	stresses the adrenals and liver
caffeine	stresses the adrenals
nicotine	"
stimulants	"
preservatives	stress the liver
sweets	sweeteners (honey, molasses) may be as destabilizing as sugar

management of LBS. The earlier approach, by Dr. Seale Harris, was a high protein diet, which evened out the blood sugar levels but placed a strain on the liver, pancreas, and adrenals, the very organs already implicated in LBS. In the long run, this diet often led to diabetes. The high complex-carbohydrate approach (see tables 6 and 7) avoids this result. The key to this approach, especially for breakfast, is eating entire high-protein grains like millet, buckwheat, or brown rice cooked only until tender. Whole grains are digested gradually, providing a continuous source of glucose rather than a massive charge which could make the body overreact and produce large blood sugar swings.

Some diabetics have found that they no longer need insulin after switching to diets of 90 to 100 percent raw foods, so this is another avenue to explore. Raw food diets have their advocates, and have been recommended for many conditions. They are not without potential problems, including reduced absorption of nutrients due in part to decreased bowel transit time. They also are likely to be very cleansing, releasing toxins into the blood stream. In short, switching to a raw food diet requires the supervision of an experienced practitioner.

Table 7: what can relieve LBS	
suggestion	comments
rest and sleep	relieve stress
aerobic ex⌁cise	increases glucose tolerance
complex carbohydrates	slow digestion stabilizes blood sugar
raw foods	"
avocadoes	mannoheptulose supresses insulin production
lemons and beets	strengthen the liver
yoghurt	better than milk, because the sugar, lactose, has been converted to lactic acid
string beans	contain levulin, which converts to levulose, a relatively well-tolerated form of sugar
garlic and onions	regulate blood sugar
brewer's yeast	rich in chromium, a part of "glucose tolerance factor" (not advised in cases of Candida or yeast intolerance)
vitamin B complex	normalizes blood sugar levels and strengthens the liver
vitamin C	increases the body's tolerance to sugars
vitamin E	supports the adrenals (Large doses only under supervision.)
nucleic acids	for severe problems (only under supervision)
calcium, magnesium, zinc	regulate stress

HYPERTENSION

Hypertension means abnormally high blood pressure. The official normal figures are around 120 over 80, increasing with age. (Many practitioners feel that this increase can and should be avoided.) High blood pressure can cause headaches, tiredness, dizziness, and **shortness of breath**. The condition is often aggravated by the stress of performance.

Anyone can learn to measure blood pressure. It may be better to do so at home than in the doctor's office, since the tension of undergoing a physical exam can temporarily raise blood pressure, causing unnecessary alarm.

A number of factors can raise blood pressure: (1) high blood volume (maybe from diluting toxins, e.g. excess salt or the by-products of allergenic foods); (2) high blood viscosity (not enough liquid for the amount of sludge, see the section on arthritis for an example of how eating too fast could be to blame); (3) constricted blood vessels (maybe cholesterol plaques, see Chapter 8); (4) reduced mileage of blood vessels, e.g. closed-off capillary beds (stress, or not enough exercise, or electrolyte imbalance causing tightening of the precapillary sphincter muscles); (5) loss of flexibility of blood vessel walls; and (6) heart pumping with greater force.

Treatment of high blood pressure should depend on the cause.

(1) If the blood volume is high, gradual moderation of salt consumption might be in order. If the increased blood volume is due to food sensitivities, e.g. if certain foods trigger a temporary weight gain (due to fluid retention) and a corresponding rise in blood pressure, these foods should be avoided. Avoid eating toxins, e.g. food additives, which the body will dilute by retaining fluids. If high blood volume is due to excess body weight, see the section on weight loss, below.

(2) If blood viscosity is high, eat slowly, drink more, take the minerals needed to rebalance the electrolytes (possibly in the form of tissue salts, see Chapter 19), eat garlic, fruits, and vegetables, and cut down on meat and refined grains. Consider going on a cleanse (under supervision, of course).

(3) If cholesterol deposits are obstructing the blood vessels, ask your doctor about chelation therapy (preferably dietary), and consider eating garlic, parsley, lecithin, selenium, and vitamin E (under supervision: large doses of vitamin E can temporarily raise blood pressure).

(4) If the blood vessels are constricted by tension, learn about stress reduction, take enough B complex vitamins, check on dietary calcium and magnesium ratios, gradually get more aerobic exercise, and get enough rest and sleep. Try biofeedback, or take cayenne, which regulates blood vessel constriction (see Chapter 17).

(5) If the blood vessel walls are inflexible, make sure the intake of bioflavonoids (a form of vitamin C) is adequate.

(6) If the heart seems to be working too hard, cut down on coffee, alcohol, and tobacco. Again, learn to cope with stress.

High blood pressure is rarely due to just one factor. Since most of the measures suggested here are healthy in moderation, it may not be necessary to establish the origin of the problem before doing something about it.

WEIGHT PROBLEMS

Body weight is such an issue today that a surprising number of people are worried about their weight even though they can't decide whether it needs to be raised or lowered. A stable weight, at any level, might be healthier than one which keeps changing. A more important measure than body weight is percentage of body fat.

Eating according to the guidelines in Chapter 9 should gradually normalize body weight, especially if combined with the appropriate type of exercise.

OVERWEIGHT
Why worry about excess fat? Overweight people are more likely to get **tennis elbow**, and too much fat between brain and finger tips slows down neuromuscular transmission: excess fat acts as a "friction brake" to inhibit the **amount and speed of muscle contraction**. Excess weight may increase blood pressure (see above) and hurt the self image (it's hard enough to get up on stage). It may reflect eating habits which are contributing to Candida, low blood sugar, or arthritis (so the programs for these conditions will tend to normalize body weight). And finally, fat is a form of energy storage — releasing that energy could lead to great performance!

Permanent weight loss requires a change in "set point," the weight toward which the body settles (determined by metabolic rate). Aerobic exercise lowers the set point, but fasting raises it. A high protein diet may lower it but carries the risk of toxin accumulation (*ketosis*). Dr. Elliot Abravanel suggests that glandular balance, as seen by the proportions of the parts of the body, determines the best diet for an individual. Constant hunger could also be a sign of specific nutrient deficiencies, and might require supplementation of these nutrients and their synergists (see Appendix 1), or herbs to improve absorption (seep Chapter 14).

Rapid weight loss has occasionally led to **bursitis,** and fat lost at any speed releases stored toxins, e.g. PCBs. Toxicity can be reduced by getting regular aerobic exercise, eating vegetable oils and vitamins C and E, and taking proper care of the eliminative organs, e.g. taking in enough fluid and fiber.

UNDERWEIGHT

Underweight people, on the other hand, may have reduced **muscle mass,** and the lack of specific nutrients could further affect performance. Fat is needed to line the nerve cells and cushion the **joints.**

Weight lifting is more effective than aerobics for gaining weight. High protein diets are just as dangerous for underweight as for overweight people. Eat complex carbohydrates for extra calories. Ask a qualified practitioner to monitor nutrient deficiencies. Food allergies (see below) could also cause weight loss.

PMS

Premenstrual syndrome (PMS) is a set of symptoms which may occur shortly before the beginning of each menstrual cycle. Symptoms vary from bloating to **shakiness** and mood swings and can be extremely debilitating. They may be due to Candida or food allergies.

The best therapy for PMS depends on its cause. You may need vitamin B₆, kelp, calcium, or hormone-balancing herbs, such as dong quai (sometimes written "tang kwei") and licorice. A very thick flow accompanied by cramps might indicate too many mucus-forming foods (usually animal proteins or refined grains) in the diet.

ALLERGIES

For a food sensitivity to be truly an allergy, the food must make the body form antibodies, but many nutritionists apply the term allergy to any adverse food reaction. Whatever the term, it is not always clear whether the culprit is the food itself, a faulty digestive system, or a combination of foods that is hard to digest (see Chapter 9, food combining.)

Reactions can be so mild that they go undetected, often manifesting themselves as addictions. Many people have experienced a tremendous increase in health by eliminating their four favorite foods for one week to two months. Don't try this experiment without supervision, especially if you have severe symptoms. Their intensity will increase about two days into the elimination program, as the toxins are flushed out of the tissues and into the blood stream. Improvements later in the week might include increased energy, better **memory**, **concentration**, sleep, mood, **strength**, digestion, **flexibility**, decreased anxiety, less hunger, greater **breathing capacity**, and loss of ear wax or circles under the eyes. Food allergies can also contribute to **bursitis, tendinitis**, or **swelling, stiffness, or redness in the joints**. After about half a year or more, most people find that they regain some tolerance to their problem foods, though they usually find it necessary to exercise moderation and to continue to monitor their symptoms.

There are many other ways to determine food allergies. Each method has its advocates and its disadvantages.

(1) Dr. Marshall Mandell suggests a five-day distilled water fast followed by a regimen of single-food meals. Mandell cautions that his method could dangerously exaggerate symptoms. Critics also point out that some foods take hours to elicit a reaction, so that it is not always clear which food was the culprit.

(2) A series of scratch tests is sometimes done, although they are not considered very accurate for food allergies.

(3) With sublingual testing (putting substances under the tongue), food enters the blood stream quickly and directly, bypassing the digestive system. This method will not identify the food sensitivities caused by poor digestion.

(4) Keep a journal, correlating food intake with symptoms. It is difficult to identify the problem food among those eaten at one meal.

(5) Dr. Arthur Coca's pulse test requires checking the pulse before and after eating. As with Mandell's plan, there may be a delayed reaction.

(6) Cytotoxic tests are done by mixing white blood cells with concentrated food samples on a slide and looking for changes in

the blood cells. Not everyone agrees that the changes correlate well with food sensitivities.

ARTHRITIS AND OTHER INFLAMMATORY CONDITIONS

Arthritis is the name of a disease, so the therapist may avoid that word, which is is just as well, since in many places it is illegal to claim to offer an arthritis cure. On the other hand, arthritis is a convenient label for a number of conditions which have often responded well to nutritional and herbal therapies, e.g. aching joints, limbs, or back. The symptoms are usually accompanied by signs of excess acidity in the body fluids. Although none of the suggestions in this section will cure arthritis, many people have found relief of symptoms following a combination of nutritional and herbal support, massage, and exercise. Like any systemic disease, arthritis is likely to attack a weak spot. Proper playing technique will make the arms and hands less vulnerable.

Some theories about alleviating arthritis are based on what arthritis sufferers have in common, e.g. excess body acidity. Two of the simpler ways to reduce acidity are eating more slowly and eating more alkaline-forming food. The first method is surely one of the safest, and eating slowly facilitates both digestion and weight control. Chew starches especially thoroughly, because saliva helps digest them. Don't gulp liquids. Sip them instead, and keep them in the mouth long enough to mix with saliva. Chew protein thoroughly, not only to break up the chunks, but also to give the stomach a chance to adjust its secretions, as one of the functions of salivary secretion is to alert the stomach to the type of food being eaten.

DOES EATING TOO FAST CAUSE ARTHRITIS?

The argument goes something like this. Large (insufficiently chewed) particles of food enter the stomach, which lacks the teeth to break them up easily. All the stomach can do is to produce more HCl to attack the food gradually. In order to protect the mucous membrane of its lining from the extra HCl, the stomach now needs more sodium, which is initially drawn from its stored reserves. Habitually eating too fast depletes the stomach reserves of sodium, which must then be drawn from the blood supply. This problem is compounded as the mucosa of the stomach thickens to protect itself, requiring still more sodium.

Once the blood sodium falls too low, sodium is taken from the interstitial fluid. This loss disturbs the balance of potassium and sodium across the membrane of each cell in the body, and some potassium leaves the cells to correct the balance. The potassium enters the blood (and lymph in smaller amounts), and there it combines with other elements, causing the blood (and lymph) to thicken. (This doesn't cause arthritis, just high blood pressure.) The loss of blood sodium also means that the relative level of calcium is too high, but instead of combining with other elements, the calcium precipitates out of solution, and becomes deposited in **joints, muscles,** and **connective tissue,** especially at the site of **previous injuries.**

With the loss of sodium, calcium, and free potassium, the body fluids become more acidic. The body attempts to correct the pH level, which is vital to a number of functions, including the ability to maintain cellular oxygen supply. The first corrective measure is removing as much excess acid as possible via the kidneys, and when the levels become too high for this mechanism alone, uric acid crystals are deposited in **joints, muscles** and **connective tissue.** The presence of crystals in these areas represents the first stage of arthritis.

Eventually the stomach becomes overworked and produces insufficient HCl, so that the chunks of food are even harder to digest. This means that any nutrients which could alleviate the arthritis are not efficiently digested. It also means that the overall pH balance is further upset, and the muscles become more acidic to compensate for the reduced stomach acidity. This change in pH affects the **flexibility** of the muscles.

Eating slowly will stop the process of acidifying, though it won't reverse it. Reversal generally requires enzymes and herbal support (see Chapter 14).

ALKALINE DIET

What is excess body acidity? Some people measure the pH of the urine to determine body acidity, but others point out that when the body's pH is becoming more alkaline, the urine may reflect this change by becoming more acidic. Benjamin Colimore lists a number symptoms to monitor, including **stiff muscles.**

A change in diet can correct the body pH. Many nutritionists recommend that acid-forming foods make up no more than 20 percent of a healthy diet for anyone, arthritic or not. Note that it is not the acidic foods which are acid-forming: on the contrary, when these are digested the end-product is generally alkaline (see tables 8 through 11).

A daily diet of four parts vegetables, two parts fruit, one part grain, and one part protein as suggested in Chapter 9 can easily stay within the 20 percent limit on acid-forming foods. The diet will be more alkaline-forming if most of the vegetables are green, if most of the fruits are juicy and sour, if most of the grains are either millet, buckwheat, or brown rice, and if some of the protein comes from almonds and pumpkin seeds. A breakfast of fruit is recommended for arthritics with stable blood sugar and no Candida overgrowth.

FOODS TO AVOID
Some acid-forming foods are best avoided altogether, e.g. red meats. (Substitute fish and some poultry. I've seen ads by the pork industry calling pork a white meat. It may look white when properly cooked, but for nutritional purposes, it is generally considered red meat, and is especially bad for arthritics.) For arthritis of the gouty type it is best to avoid the purine in organ meats, legumes, and caviar.

Like everyone else, the arthritic should avoid flour (especially white flour), sugar (especially white sugar), coffee, and processed foods.

Some people avoid hard water, since it is rich in inorganic calcium which may precipitate out into the joints. Some even recommend using distilled water to flush out mineral deposits, though it might be safest to replace these with organic minerals, perhaps in the form of herbal teas (see Chapter 13 for suggestions.)

Some people suffer arthritic symptoms when they eat members of the nightshade family, e.g. tomatoes, peppers, potatoes, and eggplant. The easiest way to test for nightshade sensitivity is to eliminate them for a week and monitor the body's reactions. It may be difficult to avoid tomatoes, as they are often found in processed foods. A very small amount can trigger a reaction, and the reaction often is delayed, so it is very important to be consistent and conscientious throughout the trial period. If you obtain great relief by the end of the week,

Table 8: alkaline-forming foods (most helpful)

food	comments
sour fruits	very alkaline-forming
umeboshi plums	quick-acting, alkaline-forming
pineapples	normalize pH
beans (properly cooked)	soak, throw out water, rinse, boil, skim off foam, simmer till soft
millet, buckwheat	
almonds	
sunflower seeds	
pumpkin seeds	

Table 9: acid-forming foods (eat small amounts only)

food	comments
meat, eggs, cheese	
most grains	except millet, buckwheat, brown rice
beans	if cooked wrong (see table 8) or poorly digested

Table 10: neutral foods (can be eaten freely)

food	comments
green vegetables	
most other vegetables	carrots may be acid forming
brown rice	

Table 11: controversial classifications

food	comments
peanuts	alkaline or acid-forming
sweet fruits	"
milk, yoghurt	"
potatoes, pasta	"
carrots	neutral or acid-forming

be very careful about trying these foods again, as the reaction may be much more severe than it was before the trial period.

Excess weight puts a strain on load-bearing joints and can aggravate arthritis in the lower extremities.

FOODS TO EAT

It is often helpful to increase the proportion of raw foods in the diet, and some people go so far as to suggest eating only raw foods. This would mean sprouting all grains, a procedure which would also produce beneficial saponins (see Chapter 15). Do not switch to a 100 percent raw food diet without supervision.

Many people recommend a concoction called "honeygar," consisting of about two teaspoons of apple cider vinegar (not wine vinegar) and two teaspoons of unpasteurized honey, diluted according to taste with a little water. This drink, taken before meals, promotes digestion of protein and calcium, stimulates flow of digestive juices (HCl, secretin, pancreatic juices, and bile), replaces sodium reserves in the stomach, and helps move the bowels. It is said to thin, yet build, the blood, recalcify the bones, and **relax the muscles** and other soft tissues while **reducing pain.**

Some forms of arthritis have been relieved by blackstrap molasses or bee pollen. Grapefruit juice may dissolve calcium deposits, and carrot and celery juices may rebuild cartilage and joints. Kelp, which can be substituted for salt, has an absorbable form of organic calcium. Irish moss has also been recommended, along with aloe vera gel and other herbs (see Chapter 15.)

SUPPLEMENTS

Fish liver oils greatly benefit the arthritic. They contain vitamin D, which increases calcium utilization and thus keeps it from falling out of solution into the joints. They also contain vitamin A, which lubricates the joints, especially if taken on an empty stomach. The best fish liver oil is Norwegian cod liver oil. For best results take it in a small amount of orange juice or milk at least an hour before breakfast. (Do not take capsules for this purpose, as the protein in the capsule is not easily dissolved in an empty stomach.)

The antioxidants, vitamins A, C, E, and selenium, as well as SOD (superoxide dismutase, the controversial enzyme), have been recommended for arthritics. These substances may decrease the number of free radicals, thus relieving pain and swelling by reducing the release of prostaglandins (see Chapter 8).

In the 1940s when cortisone drugs were first tested on arthritis, there was also very promising research into the effects of niacin (vitamin B3). Some critics go so far as to say that cortisone gained prominence only because it could be profitably sold as a prescription drug. Most studies of niacin today are concerned with its effects on schizophrenia, which can be an extreme form of the niacin deficiency disease, pellagra, but almost as a footnote the researchers note that subjects who happened to have arthritis also found relief from those symptoms. Taking enough niacin to produce a slight flush may open capillaries around sore joints. (To increase the intensity of the flush, take the niacin before meals, balancing it with the rest of the B complex during the meal.)

Researchers have found that arthritics have relatively low levels of silicon in the tissues, so some people recommend silicon supplements. Other nutrients which have been recommended include vitamins B2, B6, pantothenic acid, and folic acid, and the minerals magnesium, calcium, and phosphorus. Lecithin may dissolve the cholesterol deposits often found in arthritic nodes.

CONCLUSION

There are many types of arthritis, and each responds better to one regimen than to another, so ask a qualified practitioner to help you determine the best course of action. There is no cure for arthritis, but there are many things which give relief from symptoms. If applied under supervision, the suggestions given in this chapter will also improve general health.

Chapter 12

TRAINING DIETS FOR THE PERFORMER
preparing for a major performance

"The practices that best prepare the body for fitness and competition
are the same ones that lead to health, happiness, and longevity."
-Gabe Mirkin in *The Sportsmedicine Book*

Mirkin's point is important for anyone making extraordinary
demands on the body in the pursuit of superior performance: the
diet which furthers optimum performance is also the one which
is the healthiest in the long run. It is not a question of making a
choice between general health and high burn-out training
regimes.

The first part of this chapter builds on Chapter 9 to formulate
a daily diet and supplement plan. The next part examines
carbohydrate loading, which is used by some athletes before
major events but doesn't seem to have much to offer most
performers. The last part of the chapter will cover some tips for
the day of a performance.

YEAR-ROUND TRAINING

A BASIC DIET
One basic daily diet outlined in Chapter 9 consists of four parts
vegetables, two parts fruit, and one part each protein and
carbohydrate. The protein consists of beans, seeds, nuts, fish,
and small amounts of meat, usually poultry. The carbohydrate
is a whole grain. This diet is low in fat and high in complex
carbohydrates and fiber, a good combination for the musician/
athlete, because the energy produced per liter of oxygen is 4.92
for high-carbohydrate diets, 4.86 for mixed diets, and 4.8 for
high-fat diets. The daily diet contains primarily unprocessed
food, a fairly high percentage of raw foods, and a high
percentage of alkaline-forming foods (see Chapter 11,
arthritis). Meals are prepared with easily digestible

combinations in mind, eaten slowly, and chewed thoroughly. Water, diluted juices, and herbal teas are taken between meals. Of course you neither smoke nor drink coffee or alcohol, and you have forgotten what sugar tastes like. Some people suggest a monthly binge day. This might work, or you might need a couple of weeks to sleep it off. Even the most healthy people deviate from the ideal diet. Find a diet and lifestyle which are a joy to maintain.

THE HAAS DIET

The Haas diet, which is meant for high performance athletes, has become a popular training diet. It is a high carbohydrate diet, but Haas equates pasta with whole grains. Since white flour is digested much like sugar, pasta is not a good food for hypoglycemics, arthritics, or Candida sufferers. Whole grains have nutrients and fiber which are missing in pasta. Haas doesn't stress vegetables or any raw foods, so his is a weaker version of the "basic diet" (Chapter 9).

SUPPLEMENTS

Even an ideal diet probably won't provide all nutrients necessary for optimal performance (see Chapter 7). A good basic multivitamin-mineral tablet once or twice a day might be advisable, even if you are already healthy. Such a supplement might provide the recommended daily allowance (RDA) of each vitamin and mineral (see Appendix 1). Unless the diet includes both fish and nuts virtually every day, taking a teaspoon of cold pressed flax seed oil is the best way to get enough EFAs (essential fatty acids, see Chapter 7). If these levels of supplementation sound high, it is because many people consider the RDAs far too low for optimal nutrition and because much of our food arrives at the table virtually devoid of nutrients. As the toxicity levels in Appendix 1 show, some nutrients are toxic at quite low levels, while others have higher safety margins. Most people who have been living an unhealthy lifestyle will need more supplements at first. The exact levels are different for each individual (see Chapter 9, biochemical individuality) and are not always easy to determine. The deficiency symptoms are a start, but so many of them are so similar that they are confusing. Blood, urine, and hair analyses may be more reliable indicators but must be done by a qualified practitioner.

Smokers can increase the vitamins A, C, E, B complex, and the minerals selenium, zinc, and manganese. The supplement amounts depend on how much they smoke, but they could start with an extra 500 mg of C, 100 IU of E, 10,000 IU of beta carotene, 50 mg of a good B complex (ideally containing all of the Bs in amounts proportionate to their RDAs), 20 mg of zinc, 5 mg of manganese, and 50 mcg of selenium. Of these, the only one with a low therapeutic-to-toxic ratio is selenium, so keep this in mind when adding up the amounts needed in subsequent paragraphs. (Selenium is being used here as an antioxidant, and you could, for example, take more vitamin C instead.) Supplements that neutralize toxins make the body work harder than it would have to if it weren't being poisoned in the first place, so think of these supplements as temporary measures to be taken while kicking the habit.

Coffee drinkers can increase their iron, B complex, and chromium, perhaps starting with 5 mg of iron (in the form of 50 mg of ferrous gluconate), 25 mg of a good B complex (see smokers' paragraph), and 0.05 mg chromium (another mineral which has a narrow range of effectiveness). Brewer's yeast, if tolerated, furnishes both B vitamins and chromium.

Anyone who is **drinking** more than one glass of wine or beer a day should look at the amount of sugar in the diet. While cutting down on alcohol and sugar, increase vitamins C, E, and B complex as well as magnesium. A starting level might be 50 mg of a good B complex (see smoking paragraph), 500 mg of C, 100 IU of E, and 100 mg of magnesium (or switch to beer for more magnesium.)

Anyone who is taking **antibiotics** should take extra vitamin C, at least 500 mg a day, and acidophilus before breakfast. (Antibiotics, especially if broad-spectrum, kill all bacteria, including the ones needed in the colon. Acidophilus, the bacterium used to make yoghurt, re-establishes friendly intestinal flora.)

Insomniacs could try mild exercise and a handful of almonds before bedtime, along with a relaxation technique and a review of their emotional needs. The insomnia might be an indication of low level deficiencies. Supplements which might be needed include 50 mg of a good B complex (see smoking paragraph) and a calcium supplement containing 200 mg calcium, 100 mg magnesium, and 50 IU of vitamin D. Reishi mushrooms promote sleep without making you feel mugged upon waking.

If more than one factor is contributing to a particular deficiency, then each of these factors must be compensated for by adding the recommended doses (but don't exceed toxic levels). For example, if your drinking necessitates a supplement of 50 mg of B complex, and your smoking a further 50 mg, then you should take 100 mg of B complex.

Some non-debilitating **symptoms** also give us additional clues to deficiencies, but if you are already taking a particular supplement for a deficiency caused by life-style factors, do not raise the dosage to treat these symptoms. (You are already treating the underlying deficiency.) White spots on the finger nails might call for zinc supplements. Use one of the zinc-test solutions which let the taste buds determine your need, or take 10 mg of zinc daily until the spots disappear. Longitudinal ridges in the finger nails, ridges on the sides of the tongue, cracks in the corners of the mouth, or bumps on the backs of the arms might disappear with 25 mg of a good B complex daily (see smoker's section). And 100 IU of vitamin E daily might relieve sore spots on the tongue.

Many practitioners consider these amounts minimal for therapeutic purposes, but anyone considering taking more should do so under supervision.

PEAKING FOR PERFORMANCE

Prior to major events, an athlete might follow a training diet. Carbohydrate loading is one popular and controversial technique for increasing endurance. Some studies seem to demonstrate the effectiveness of carbohydrate loading, while others indicate that it has little effect on endurance and might be dangerous. The training level seems to affect results.

CARBOHYDRATE LOADING
The principle behind carbohydrate loading is that increasing the stores of muscle glycogen increases endurance (see Chapter 2). Exercising a muscle to exhaustion (thus depleting its glycogen) and then following a high carbohydrate diet greatly increases the glycogen stores of that muscle. Frequent glycogen depletion followed by carbohydrate loading may also teach the muscles to conserve glycogen by burning more fat. To deplete

muscle glycogen, you work the muscle till it starts to ache and gives coordination problems, and then keep working for a few minutes more.

Athletes on a carbohydrate-loading program do the glycogen depletion exercise about six days before a competition. They spend the next three days on a high protein and fat diet (low carbohydrate), to further deplete muscle glycogen. The final three days, they eat frequent small high-carbohydrate meals, forcing the muscles to load up just before competition. Some people have reported a 100 to 300 percent increase in working capacity, using this method.

Though mild exercise won't impair the effectiveness of the program, hard training depletes muscle glycogen stores, so it is best to coast during the high-carbohydrate phase. As discussed in Chapter 3, coasting also allows muscles to recover their flexibility. Anyone planning to work hard right up to the last minute should skip the high-protein/fat phase, since the muscles need carbohydrates to keep going.

Opponents of this technique caution that the muscle may not recover on time. Glycogen depletion of large muscles, may cause nausea, tiredness, headache, and irritability, as well as muscle weakness. Yet, without strict depletion, the high carbohydrate diet does not yield a significant increase in muscle glycogen stores.

Not everybody uses the high protein/fat stage of the diet, and some nutritionists consider this stage terribly unhealthy. Many people, even those in good health, find it stressful and tiring, and may suffer from low blood sugar, weakness, lethargy, and depression for several days. In extreme cases *ketosis* (accumulation of toxins brought on by severe restriction of carbohydrates) has stressed the liver and kidneys sufficiently to prove fatal. The consensus seems to be that without the high protein/fat stage, the diet is less effective but still helpful.

The high-carbohydrate phase has its dangers too. People with weak hearts may develop chest pains and an abnormal EKG (electrocardiogram). Some doctors blame this phenomenon on excessive amounts of glycogen deposited in the heart muscle, while others place the blame on loss of glycogen in the heart, as it gets diverted to skeletal muscles. Some people develop problems in the prostate, and those at risk must maintain a high fluid intake. Too much glycogen may destroy muscle fibres causing the muscle cells to break down and release myoglobin into the blood stream, which in turn can damage the kidneys. In any case, increased glycogen draws water into the muscles, and this may make them feel heavy or stiff. Fruits should be a major carbohydrate source, because they are generally high in potassium, which the muscles need in order to cope with the increase in glycogen.

Given all the side effects of all phases of carbohydrate loading, many athletes recommend that it be done no more than two or three times a year. In any case too frequent repetition lowers its effectiveness. The people who benefit most from carbohydrate loading are engaged in endurance sports, e.g. long distance running and cycling. Even tennis players find it brings little improvement, because their bursts of maximal effort are relatively short. They prefer to go on a high carbohydrate diet just one day before a major game. Prolonged work at only 60 to 70 percent of maximal oxygen uptake is also unaffected by low stores of muscle glycogen, as long as free fatty acids are released from adipose tissue.

Most of us need to command only short bursts of intense effort, so it is not clear that carbohydrate loading is appropriate. Anyone preparing a program which feels especially like a marathon might try this technique, though on the whole carbohydrate loading sounds like a bad idea. Instead, take extra care to follow the year-round diet, and leave the bingeing for the congratulatory bash.

PERFORMANCE DAY

Anyone with a favorite pre-performance meal should probably stick with it, since this is an area of such conflict and superstition. Nonetheless, your nutritional state does make a difference. For one thing, it affects the speed of lactate removal, which limits the anaerobic capacity of the muscles.

It is best not to eat a big pre-performance meal. Distension of the urinary bladder affects venous tone. Glucose in the small intestine (particularly the jejunum) affects pressure in the skeletal muscle veins. Furthermore, the higher demand for blood by the digestive system reduces the flow through skeletal muscles. With superb cardiovascular fitness, you may be able to supply both the muscles and the stomach with enough blood to do their work, but most people need to wait the two to four hours it takes to digest a meal, before performing. Since nervousness slows digestion, a warm liquid meal (perhaps prepared in a blender) might be best, sipped slowly to mix with the digestive juices in the mouth.

Most nutritionists recommend a meal high in complex carbohydrates and low in sugar, protein, and fat, though at least one study has found that a high carbohydrate meal gave no advantage. Complex carbohydrates, which are easily and gradually digested, provide the steady supply of carbohydrates needed by the central nervous system. Although some marathon runners fast before an event, low blood sugar may limit muscular endurance.

Steak is not a quick energy source, Muhammad Ali notwithstanding, and it takes long to digest. Not only does the digestive process interfere with muscular work, the breakdown products from strenuous exercise compete for the same elimination channels as the protein metabolites, though if you don't strain major muscle groups, this won't be much of a factor.

Do you need extra fluids before a performance? Anyone who perspires a lot, or maybe even breathes hard, could be handicapped by fluid loss. On the other hand, excess fluid intake can only weaken the limbs. Liquid lost in perspiration is more likely to cause potassium depletion than sodium depletion. Drink diluted fruit juice to compensate.

CODA

FADDISM, FANATICISM, EMPIRICISM
and some guidelines for evaluating nutrition experiments

Nutrition: why is this subject so controversial? Most people would agree that food affects health to some extent, but beyond that we share little common ground. Some people would have even the healthiest of us eating a pound of supplements a day, or shunning all but a minute number of foods. Others maintain that in the absence of obvious and severe symptoms of nutritional deficiency we don't need to worry about supplements. Unfortunately we can't simply ignore the arguments. While we're waiting for the experts to agree, we must continue to eat.

Why is it so difficult for the experts to agree? The possible answers to this question range from accusations of special interest (heard on both sides of most questions) to legitimate criticism of research findings. Following a look at some sorely abused labels is a discussion of some of the more thoughtful criticisms of nutritional research.

FADDISM
The Oxford English Dictionary defines fad as, "a crotchety rule of action; a peculiar notion as to the right way of doing something; a pet project ... to which exaggerated importance is attributed." Faddism is, of course, "a dispositon to pursue fads." No one has ever claimed to be *for* faddism, but most nutritionists seem to find it necessary to rail against it. Since the OED can't make it clear who is to rule on the crotchetiness of your rules, the railing continues. We all eat, so the subject of nutritional fads is an issue on which we all, implicitly or explicitly, take sides.

It is worthwhile comparing two examples of writing about faddism, one from Goodhart and Shils' imposing volume (*Modern Nutrition in Health and Disease*), and one from the controversial iridologist and healer, Bernard Jensen (*Food Healing for Man*). The first work is a cornerstone of mainstream nutrition, containing documented scientific studies on most aspects of the subject. It is revised frequently, and even the editors change from time to time. The second book is based on one man's clinical experiences. Neither Jensen nor Goodhart and Shils would advocate the "Standard American Diet" (SAD) of of coffee, donuts, steak, and potatoes, but Jensen leans further away from it than most of us do. Nothing in Goodhart and Shils seems to indicate that Jensen's diet would be unhealthy. Both parties rail against faddism, and I suspect that they'd happily apply the term to one another.

Goodhart and Shils' book has separate authors for each chapter. In Chapter 11, "Food Fads and Faddism," they are Philip White and Therese Mondeika, heads of the American Medical Association's Department of Food and Nutrition. The authors begin by identifying food faddism with mysticism. Unusual dietary patterns are, they say, doubtless adopted for "creating a spiritual awakening or rebirth," or to " provide satisfying emotional experiences for their followers," or as an "expression of disaffection, alienation perhaps, or disappointment with an environment that is becoming increasingly man made and yet increasingly foreign..." In other words, people who eat differently from the norm aren't really doing so just to be healthy. The authors' claim is unsupported, except by ambiguous pejorative phrases, like "real or imagined apprehension," and by the plea that "a line must be drawn between healthy skepticism and paranoia," because "quackery can exist within a mask of culture or religion." They dismiss such arguments as Jensen's ones against additives as "personal philosophy" rather than "debatable issues that have a basis in science," though they don't explain how to distinguish the two. "Today," they say, "experts are asked to provide evidence of absolute safety rather than evidence of hazard, an unrealistic and unattainable goal." Furthermore, they charge, "Frequently a lucrative business develops from fads and cults, as with the present-day health food enterprise." (The proponents of unprocessed food make the same charge about the convenience food industry.) The authors segue into their section on weight-reduction diets with hardly a pause for breath, thus implying that a coffee-and-grapefruit diet is equivalent to one designed to avoid food additives. From here it is but a short step to their plea against the blind acceptance of cancer cures which have been disproven by the "experts." The tone of this chapter is quite different from that of the rest of the book. Rather than presenting "just the facts," with a calm attempt at well-reasoned conclusions, this chapter is lyrical and quite entertaining. What Jensen, on the other hand, sees as a dangerous fad is the defence of food additives. In his Chapter 23, "The answer to food faddism," he says that, compared to the diet of our great-grandparents, the typical American diet is "far-out." He wonders whether food additives labeled safe can possibly have been tested for their cumulative effect over enough years, and points out that the effect of a group of additives from different foods might be greater than that of each one taken by itself, just as many vitamins are synergistic. Even in small amounts, additives could have great effect, as do some of the trace minerals. The justifications for using food additives, according to Jensen, simply don't compensate for the possibility of adding a further unnecessary burden of toxicity to our already hazardous modern environment. Rather than ask for absolute proof of safety, he suggests that we might do better to leave the additives out of our diets while the scientists are arguing. He points out that simple nutritious meals are just as convenient as additive-laden convenience foods, and usually much less expensive. He explicitly doesn't want to promote fear, but instead counsels common sense. His final word: "We don't advocate extremes, but rather the middle path to accommodate the average person living in society."

FANATICISM

The Oxford English Dictionary defines fanaticism as, "the tendency to indulge in wild and extravagant notions, *esp.* in religious matters; excessive enthusiasm." Establishment writers may be threatened by some of the alternative therapists and their supporting nutritionists, but they rarely sound like fanatics in their advice-giving state. Not so the natural healers. I think it is the frustration which comes from a lifetime of helping people and still having the validity of their work denied, which makes these people sound so like cranks. The tone of some of their books can be so proselytising and argumentative that it is tempting to throw away the content with the language. It may be that what passes as proof with these people is "strictly anecdotal" (if many decades of successful practice can really be dismissed in such a manner), but some doctors argue that much of what is practised by their colleagues is accepted on much flimsier gounds.

EMPIRICISM

The OED defines empiricism as, "Medical practice founded upon experiment and observation; ignorant and unscientific practice; quackery." I don't think these three notions are actually intended to be equivalent: they reflect three separate definitions of the word empiric.

In Goodhart and Shils, empiricism means making health decisions on the basis of the belief that "anything is worth a try," instead of "informed, systematic thinking about health."

Empiricism, as practised by Jensen and his colleagues, means basing their work on observation, experience, and tradition, as opposed to purely theoretical assumptions.

Both sides, then, agree who deserves the label. They just disagree on its value.

EVALUATING SCIENTIFIC NUTRITION EXPERIMENTS

This century has brought us volumes of research into the effects of nutrition on both general health and athletic performance. Yet every study, it seems, spawns an article or another study disproving the original findings. After reading some of the scholarly criticism, I began to list criteria by which scientists were evaluating each other's work. Some of the criteria conflict, e.g. some people insist that only single-nutrient studies are valid, while others insist that since nutrients tend to be synergistic, it is necessary to consider them in groups. From this it appears that no one study is likely to satisfy everybody.

Human beings are harder to study than rats. They tend to have longer life spans. They also travel, change jobs, break up with their mates, and generally refuse to keep all extraneous variables constant. They rebel against prolonged control over their diet, and unlike lab rats, they cheat. A stringently controlled nutrition study would have to take place in a setting where other life-style factors could be equally controlled, e.g. a prison. And even prisoners may get to leave eventually, perhaps before the effects of their diet on their children's children is at all well understood.

I made the following list for my own amusement. Anyone planning to do research among the nutrition journals may want to keep these criteria for evaluating nutrition studies in mind. Even if you stick to light reading or listening to rumors, knowing that a list like this exists could put all that conflicting advice into perspective. The items on this list came from actual published criticisms of actual published experiments. They are not just amusing quibbles; instead they reflect the struggles of scientists searching for truth.

1) Was the amount of the nutrient administered large enough to produce the desired effect? Often an investigator will claim that very large doses of some nutrient will cure or prevent some condition. A second investigator may design an experiment to test this claim, administer far smaller doses, and conclude that the claim has no validity.

This has happened, for example, in numerous experiments with vitamin C and the common cold, where investigators seem reluctant to administer the doses for which claims were originally made. If Pauling suggests several grams routinely, and more in times of stress, it isn't surprising that 100 mg administered after the onset of cold symptoms doesn't have much effect. Let's understand clearly that this doesn't prove anything. The experiment with its negative results doesn't prove him wrong, since it doesn't duplicate his conditions. On the other hand, the discrepancy in dosage doesn't prove him right. It just leaves the effect of large doses unconfirmed.

2) Was the experiment long enough to produce the desired effect? Did the nutrient have time to enter the blood stream? To build up in the tissue? A nutrient can take hours to enter the blood stream. If a meal was large or high in protein, or if the subject took a long time to digest it, then it is perfectly possible to draw false conclusions by making premature tests. Often the controversy ranges around a longer time-frame, as proponents of a nutrient claim that it isn't enough for it to be present in the blood subsequent to ingestion, but that a proper experiment would have to be carried on for months so that the nutrient builds up in the tissues of the body.

Arguments about the effects of prolonged low-level deficiencies also hinge on the time-factor: it might take years for a person to manifest clinical symptoms while depleting the stores of a nutrient. (Are certain symptoms in an older person signs of long term deficiencies, or are they the result of the natural aging process?)

3) What was the nutritional state of the subjects prior to the experiment? In particular, were their levels of the nutrient theoretically at a deficiency level? Is there general agreement on what such a level would be? Did the experimenter mean to begin the test at normal levels? Again, what would such a level be? A nutrient might increase health or performance levels until it is present at an optimum level, and then its effects would level off until it eventually becomes harmful. So the effect of the nutrient might form a curve something like this:

Of course this may be just what the experiment was meant to determine in the first place. The problem is that giving 100 people 100 mg of substance X doesn't deal with the question of where on the curve they were to begin with. And this location could be different for each person, depending on dietary history, life style, hereditary factors, etc, etc, etc.

4) What was the nutritional state of the subjects at the conclusion of the experiment? Is the scientist testing the effects of deficiency, or looking at the effects of the nutrient at levels which exceed some theoretical minimum requirement? This is the companion question to the previous one. If the subject started near the optimal level and took too much of the nutrient, for example, it might appear that this was a harmful substance. For some nutrients, the difference between too little and too much is very small.

5) How were nutritional states evaluated? Did the experimenter set some theoretical requirement and question people about their previous intakes? Or were tests done to find out how much of the nutrient was in the body? How invasive must these tests be? Are the results of hair analysis or blood tests sufficiently accurate, or are other procedures (e.g. muscle or liver biopsies) required for a clear picture? The presence of a nutrient in the urine, for example, doesn't necessarily indicate a surplus in the body. It merely means that the body is excreting a certain amount. This could indicate that more was administered than could be absorbed at once, or that some factor such as disease or improper balance of other substances is keeping the body from utilizing it properly.

6) Were there control groups of subjects? A control group is a group of people who were officially part of the study but who didn't receive any supplements. This is different from the placebo group (question 7). In theory all other factors are kept constant between the three groups, but this is difficult to achieve in human nutrition experiments. When testing a new life-saving drug there are obvious humanitarian reasons for doing without this bit of experimental protocol. But even in nutrition experiments on subjects of normal health, it is surprisingly common to leave out this group.

7) Were there subjects who received placebos? Is it clear that the placebos didn't contain other nutrients which might influence the outcome of the tests? A placebo is an inert substance which may have a therapeutic effect if the subject thinks it is supposed to. Double-blind administration of a placebo can rule out the possibility that the test substance is itself only a placebo. Both substances must be identical in taste, smell, texture, bulk, and appearance. Unfortunately, although a rat won't know what the test substance is supposed to taste like, a human just might. Though food chemists are capable of miracles of taste, texture, and appearance, we may not want to know what the fake food is doing to us. In the case of nutritional experiments, this question is important. If the placebo turns out to be beneficial, either because it puts some nutrient into the blood stream, or because it helps the body clean itself out, then it is no longer truly a placebo. Ascertaining whether this is the case requires yet another experiment. (Perhaps with the first substance as the placebo?)

8) Were there enough subjects to give the results statistical significance? Given three volunteers, two of whom dropped out before the experiment ended, we have an anecdote, not an experiment. What is the minimum number of subjects required to make a nutrition experiment valid? In human nutrition studies, the critic's answer to that question is often greater than the experimenter's answer.

9) In what form was the nutrient administered? Was it administered in the same form as in the last experiment or theoretical discussion? Were synthetic forms substituted for naturally occurring ones? Can the nutrient be digested and assimilated in the given form? Does it have reasonable absorption and excretion rates in that form? Some people argue that synthetic and naturally occurring nutrients are equivalent, while others disagree. In either case, a pill made with fillers and binders can render the contained nutrient virtually inaccessible to the body.

10) Did the experiment include a single nutrient or a number of them? Is it valid to test a single nutrient without considering its synergists or antagonists? If the experiment included a number of nutrients, were provisions made to evaluate the effects of changes in the relative amounts of the individual nutrients? Since nature has never provided food in the form of single nutrients, many people believe that single-nutrient studies can't duplicate the effects of a nutrient in the context of the food containing it. Increasing the amount of a nutrient in the absence of the substance needed for its absorption, for example, would be considered invalid by this line of reasoning. Other people insist, however, that the only way to construct a valid experiment is to test just one variable at a time.

11) Did all the subjects have identical diets, except for the nutrient(s) being tested? If not, did other dietary factors affect the results? Of course the stipulation that the whole diet be controlled should extend to other life-style factors, thus precluding long range experiments with most civilian populations. Even if all diet and life-style factors were controlled, did the chosen control levels reflect those of the population in general? Of course they already differ in one respect: they are being tightly controlled by external factors. This could either increase or decrease stress, and would affect nutrient requirements accordingly. The experiment might even be testing the effects of that diet more than the effects of the nutrient, if for example the basic diet is deficient in the nutrient or if it contains some toxic substance (e.g. mercury in tuna fish) which can be eliminated from the body with the aid of the nutrient being tested.

12) Was the subject population randomly chosen? How much is known about the subjects' previous exercise patterns, percentage of body fat, health history, mental and emotional profiles, financial and educational status, race, religion, and general upbringing? Do these and other factors affect the ability to utilize certain nutrients, or the need for them? A study done on college athletes, for example is likely to be restricted to subjects of the same age and conditioning. Even a population of soldiers or prisoners will have had similar nutritional and exercise patterns in the recent past. While these similarities limit the number of variables in the experiment, they may also limit the applicability of its findings to the population at large.

13) Are there any theoretical differences in motivation, discipline, or other factors which might differentiate the control group from the subjects? This question arises from studies comparing vegetarians to meat-eaters. In response to one study showing greater endurance among the former group, the critics pointed out that it takes a certain discipline to maintain a vegetarian regime, and that this discipline might result in better performance on endurance tests. Of course such an experiment could be conducted by selecting people to put on a vegetarian diet, but then there would be problems with compliance.

14) Does the experiment test the parameters which ought theoretically to be influenced by the nutrient? Scientific experiments aren't set up randomly to see how tweaking one variable affects a system. Rather they arise from theoretical considerations. If the body uses a nutrient in a certain way, then supplementation might produce certain effects. The experiment is designed to test this hypothesis. What specific results does the hypothesis predict? Should the nutrient increase grip strength, endurance at maximal (or submaximal) effort, recovery time, reflex time, speed, effects on mental state (subjective or testable), or resistance to disease, injury, colds, or fatigue? This point has particular relevance for the musician/athlete: if for example we never apply maximal muscular effort, then a nutrient which increases performance at this level only, perhaps even at the expense of something else like reflex time, won't do us much good, though it might do wonders for a weight lifter.

15) Are the tests designed to elicit the information they are meant to evaluate? This question is related to the previous one. If an experiment is intended to determine a nutrient's effects on a specific parameter, critics may claim that the evaluation methods don't actually test that parameter. An experimenter may intend to test the preventive powers of a nutrient, yet wait until the problem has occurred before administering it. Although the nutrient may be capable of both preventing and curing a condition, the experimenter must be consistent in specifying which property is being tested.

16) Were the testing conditions kept constant? Even after choosing appropriate subjects, diet, and tests, the experimenter may be at the mercy of nature and outside circumstances. Weather can affect an endurance run, and impending academic exams can affect stress-related parameters. Were these factors taken into account? Have they affected all groups equally?

17) Is the statistical analysis of the data valid? This is related to question 8, on the number of subjects. In an experiment with three subjects, it doesn't make sense to express the fraction 1/3 as 0.3333: the second number implies closer to 10,000 subjects. Other pitfalls include wishfully drawing a curve to fit an insufficient number of data points, or accepting results as significant even though they had a high probability of occurring at random. It is all too easy to "lie with statistics." Given the difficulty of doing rigorously controlled nutrition experiments on human subjects, and the great economic and emotional stake which people on both sides of a question may have in its outcome, it isn't surprising that statistical arguments are often used to invalidate someone else's results.

With all these conflicting criteria, do nutrition studies have any value? It can be argued that they do give us new clues about optimal diet. But whose conclusions are we to believe? Unfortunately we can't just ignore the controversies, since what we eat may affect performance. We need to locate competent guides among the many self-styled Nutrition Experts (or listen to our own bodies). Your choice of Expert will depend on your bias and desired outcome. (If there are two marriage counsellors in town, and one of them has a reputation for achieving high rates of reconciliation while another specializes in amicable divorces, then the choice of counsellors clearly reflects the desired outcome. With nutritional advisers, the situation is the same.) If an Expert tells you that your vitamin supplements are dangerous, and you disagree, you have only three options: follow the Expert's advice, don't follow the Expert's advice but continue as a client/patient (not a good idea), or find another Expert. Good luck, and *bon appétit!*

Section III

GLOSSARY of herbal terms used in section III

analgesic - pain relieving agent

antibacterial - destroying bacteria, or stopping their growth

anti-inflammatory - reducing inflammation

antimitotic - growth retardant (interfering with cell division by mitosis)

antipyretic - reducing fever

antiseptic - inhibiting or preventing the growth of harmful microorganisms

antispasmodic - relieving or preventing muscle spasm and nervous irritability

astringent - constricting agent, used to strengthen weak tissues

carminative - preventing or relieving intestinal gas

cathartic - (from Greek, *catharticos*, purification) causing the bowels to empty

demulcent - soothing or softening agent

diaphoretic - causing perspiration

diuretic - increasing amount of urine produced and excreted

expectorant - causing coughing

laxative - (from Latin *laxare*, to loosen) promoting bowel action

nervine - relieving nervous excitement by acting directly on the nervous system

purgative - strong cathartic, may cause watery bowel movements

relaxant - reducing tension

sedative - soothing, calming agent

spasmolytic - arresting spasms; see antispasmodic

stomachic - stimulating digestive action of the stomach, strengthening the stomach

tonic - strengthening or restoring tension in weak tissues, invigorating agent

vermifuge - expelling intestinal worms

Chapter 13

HERBS FOR THE PERFORMER
an alternative to drugs?

Herbs have been used since ancient times to calm nerves, relax muscles, improve memory, reduce inflammation, and tone the organs of the digestive system. Many of our modern drugs were originally extracted from herbs. Since whole herbs cannot be patented, research of their properties is not as plentiful as drug research, and most of the research on herbs is directed at isolating their active principles in order to manufacture new drugs. Nevertheless, in recent decades scientists have been studying the biochemistry of various herbs and folkloric claims for their effectiveness.

The purpose of this section is to introduce some herbal therapies, not to replace professional advice. When compensating for years of neglect and misuse, you may need to take substantial doses of herbs, especially if you continue to perform intensively during the recuperative period. Like all powerful tools, herbs need to be handled with knowledge and awareness. Licensing schemes for herbalists are less standardised than those for doctors and pharmacists, but there are self-governing bodies of herbal practitioners, and schools which are recognized by these bodies. Of course, memberships and diplomas do not guarantee quality in either a doctor or a herbalist.

Herbs are no substitute for changes in diet, lifestyle, and playing habits, but together they can make the difference between optimal performance and a sagging career.

The remaining chapters in Section III discuss applications, constituents, and toxicity of medicinal herbs. The *technical* terms for therapeutic effects are defined in the glossary. Information about constituents is given primarily for reference purposes, so if you are not a chemist, feel free to skip those paragraphs.

HERBS VS. DRUGS

Mentioning herbs and drugs in the same sentence always brings out one common reason for avoiding herbal remedies: fear of toxicity. The question is, why not take the drugs which are thoroughly researched and systematically quality-controlled? If herbs are potent enough to cure, we expect them also to have dangerous side effects. Are herbs just a separate class of over-the-counter remedies with which we can carelessly overdose ourselves? If vitamin supplements should be avoided as potentially toxic overconcentrated foods, then shouldn't herbs be avoided for the same reason? Even when the whole plant is used, therapeutic doses are often greater than the amounts found in normal cuisine. Granted, drugs are even more concentrated parts of herbs, but drugs are only taken as a last resort anyway. Why, then, use therapeutic herbs?

One answer may come from the few people who are prescribing both herbs and drugs. These practitioners include Western doctors (MDs) who have made a study of herbs and Oriental doctors (OMDs) who have studied Western medicine. The consensus among these practitioners seems to be that in acute cases drugs and surgery are the best tools, while for chronic complaints herbs build up strength and remove toxins more effectively, while putting less stress on the whole body. This distinction is approximate, since some herbs work well in emergencies, but in general it holds quite well. The injured performer might do well to investigate herbs which balance and tone the body and correct chronic conditions, before resorting to harsher drugs or surgery.

Since herbs are primarily applied to chronic ailments, it is difficult to evaluate their effectiveness. While the right remedy gives quick relief from an acute condition, chronic conditions generally improve only gradually. Not only is slow improvement more difficult to see, but there are more likely to be other contributing lifestyle factors. As health improves, the renewed energy often affects nutrition and exercise habits, so that it is no longer clear whether it was the herb or the other factors which were responsible for the return to health.

BALANCE

Just as foods can contain a number of elements which balance each other, so do many herbs. Herbalists like to take advantage of this fact, believing that the body will choose what it needs to attain a state of balance. Some herb-based drugs, on the other hand, incorporate the active substance but not the modifying one. Herbalists feel that this is a mistake, especially in treating chronic conditions, where the drug could push the body from one imbalance to its opposite. Instead, for example, licorice balances the immune system, and kelp regulates the thyroid, stimulating an underactive gland and restraining an overactive one.

Some herbs seem to have an ability to seek out the system in need of balance and to provide the proper action at the proper site. Cayenne, for example, regulates blood pressure. Not only does it raise it when needed and lower it when needed, but it also regulates it locally, stopping bleeding (lowering local blood pressure) or warming cold hands (raising local blood pressure). Lobelia, too, is so variable in its effect that herbalists have dubbed it "the thinking herb."

TOXICITY

Just as with vitamins, everything is toxic if taken in sufficient quantity: the safety of any therapeutic substance is measured by comparing its effective dose with its toxic dose. LD_{50}, one measure of toxicity, is the dose at which half of a group of experimental animals died. At other times the information on toxicity is purely anecdotal: so-and-so had a patient who took five gallons of this substance for six years, and who came in with a set of symptoms which disappeared when use of the substance was discontinued. Sometimes there is no reported toxicity. This doesn't mean that the herb is guaranteed safe: it may just mean that it hasn't been thoroughly studied. The discussions of individual herbs include the available information on toxic dosages and the bases of claims for both toxicity and effectiveness.

Herbalists disagree over the toxicity of certain herbs. Some, for example, avoid comfrey on the suspicion that it causes cancer and liver damage. Yet it was argued in the *British*

Medical Journal (3 March, 1979, p. 598) that those who have taken comfrey in the past have no cause for alarm. The authors pointed out that the liver cancer generated in experimental animals after long periods of high doses was always preceeded by liver intoxication. Since people generally take much lower dosages, and there have been no reports of liver intoxication in human comfrey users, they suggest that those dosages are probably not high enough to cause cancer. While studies of comfrey continue, some popular products containing this herb are still on the market.

Gosselin's *Clinical Toxicology of Commercial Products* gives information on some of the constituents of herbs which have been extracted to make drugs. The toxicity ratings are for the purified substance, not for that substance as modified by the rest of the herb: in some cases, the whole herb is a good deal safer, while in other cases it is not. The information is based on a number of sources, which are listed after each substance, and the results are standardized by estimating an average lethal dose for an average 150 pound man. Much of the toxicity information given under each herb in the following chapters is of this nature.

Sometimes the cleansing or detoxifying effect of a herb produces unpleasant or even dangerous symptoms. Some practitioners encourage this so-called "healing crisis," believing that it is a good sign and a necessary part of the healing process. Others try to avoid it, perhaps by adjusting the dosage or time of day for taking the herb, or by strengthening the body before further cleansing. Ask a practitioner to evaluate any symptoms which do arise, as it is not easy for the inexperienced to differentiate between a disease crisis and a healing crisis.

A 1986 study critical of the safety of herbal remedies (Consumers' Association, *drug and therapeutics bulletin* vol 24, no 25) cites numerous instances of adulteration, mislabeling, inaccurate measurement of doses, and unwanted side effects, including interactions with prescription drugs. In contrast, *Planta Medica* studied impurities in both drugs and herbal perparations ("Residues and Impurities in Medicinal Plants and Drug Preparations," *Planta Medica*, 1982, vol 44, pp 65 - 77). The herbal preparations tested generally contained lower levels of impurities than the crude drugs, and contamination of herbs was no worse than the levels found in foods which met government inspection standards.

Anyone using therapeutic herbs should seek the guidance of an experienced practitioner who would know which brands are to be trusted, which herbs are prone to adulteration, what the side-effects might be, and what quantities and combinations are considered safe. **A number of herbs are not recommended for pregnant women,** or for other conditions of which an experienced practitioner should be aware. Anyone taking drugs at the same time needs expert advice on possible herb/drug interactions. Herbal preparations are not always strictly controlled, and they do not need to carry warning labels, but in one regard, herbs are safer than over-the-counter drugs: most of them have not been government-certified, so their labels are not allowed to carry claims of therapeutic effects, thus encouraging the consumer to seek advice before buying them.

HERBAL COMBINATIONS

A good herbal combination focuses on a specific task, rather than including something for every system of the body. It might contain several herbs which work together on the primary goal, as well as herbs to eliminate toxins produced in the healing process, aid the nerve and blood supply, and soothe, nourish, and strengthen the intended site. Certain combinations of herbs have been used for many years, perhaps because they are synergistic or balance each other.

Some herbs, e.g. cayenne pepper and lobelia, are especially valuable in some of the subsidiary roles and appear in many different combinations. Cayenne opens up capillaries where needed, and carries the main herbs to the desired site, thus speeding healing. Lobelia regulates the endocrine and autonomic nervous systems, concentrating its effects on the area targeted by the other herbs in the formula.

NUTRITIONAL HERBAL TEAS

Some of the herbs sold in tea bags are quite potent. Just because they look innocent in their packaging does not mean that they can be taken indiscriminately. Some herbal teas, on the other hand, supply easily digested vitamins and minerals while meeting our fluid requirements. Though some of these herbs are available in tea bags, they are usually less expensive if bought in bulk, or better yet, cultivated in the garden.

The usual dosage is one teaspoon of dried herbs for one cup of water. Put leafy herbs in a stainless steel tea egg or unbleached cloth tea bag and cover with boiling water. (Woody stems and roots will have to be boiled.) Ten minutes is enough to maximize flavor and effectiveness, and some herbalists advise removing the herbs much sooner. Since many herbs have aromatic constituents which will be lost if they evaporate, it is best to keep tea covered until it is ready to drink.

The following teas have a mild and pleasant taste and are generally considered safe and healthy. No matter how safe a herb is, it is best to rotate a number of herbs rather than to drink the same one daily for a long time.

Peppermint tea is soothing to the stomach and can cure a mild headache (chewing fresh peppermint leaves is even more effective). For the digestion, it is often combined with **papaya.** Peppermint and **alfalfa** make a mineral-rich tea.

Rose hips are mild and **hibiscus** is tart. A blend of the two is a flavorful source of vitamin C.

Lemon grass and **oat straw** tea is rich in calcium and silicon (which may increase calcium absorption). Lemon grass has a slightly bitter, lemony flavor, and oat straw's mellow flavor smooths out the taste.

Spearmint is soothing to the stomach. It is sometimes combined with **marshmallow,** a mild, slightly sweet herb which is soothing to the mucous membranes of the digestive tract.

Echinacea and **licorice** strengthen the immune system. They have a very rich flavor and a slightly laxative effect, and they may ward off an impending cold.

Parsley and **raspberry leaves** cleanse excess mucus from the body. They are mildly stimulating to the kidneys but are considered much safer than strong diuretic herbs.

Fennel tea is soothing to the intestines and may get rid of flatulence (gas). It has a full-bodied flavor which is sometimes combined with **chickweed,** a nourishing and mild-tasting herb.

SOURCES FOR SECTION III

Since the subject of herbs is likely to be unfamiliar, the sources for some statements in this section are given in parentheses. Other statements are accepted by a large number of herbalists and are not referenced here. Some of the sources are primarily folkloric, some are anecdotal works written by healers with large practices, and some are more "scientific," but these distinctions begin to blur as practitioners see a need to understand the scientific basis of their work. Though the herbal tradition has a long empirical history, some scientific texts attempt to start over from a theoretical framework based on the ingredients of herbs. Primary sources illustrate research on the effects of herbs, much of it concerned with isolating the components and testing them on animals.

Many of the same problems encountered in evaluating nutrition research hold in the case of herbs. Human studies are rare, and well controlled ones are even rarer. Scientists don't always agree on the synergy of two components of the same herb, let alone two different herbs, a herb and a vitamin, or a herb and an exercise program.

Though herbs are gaining some credibility among North American doctors and scientists, they have much opposition. Many countries have pharmacopoeias, listing those herbs with official healing properties, and some herbs are no longer in the major pharmacopoeias. Thus physicians no longer use them, though herbalists might continue to do so. Usually the herbs have been replaced by more powerful drugs, perhaps with active ingredients originally extracted from the herbs.

Chapter 14

HERBS FOR THE DIGESTIVE SYSTEM

Digestive problems are far more common than most people suspect. Too many of us have just learned to live with fatigue after meals, gas, or bowel irregularity, to say nothing of morning breath and coated tongues. Any of these may mean digestive problems. Until they are corrected, chances are you won't be digesting the other herbs in this book any better than you're digesting your food.

Fortunately, there is help, in the form of herbs to tone the stomach, intestines, kidneys, liver, and pancreas, while subduing unhealthy cravings. Though they are discussed singly in this chapter, they are usually combined in formulas which strengthen the whole system while relieving the immediate problem.

HERBS FOR THE STOMACH

Meadow Sweet (Spirea ulmara) regulates the secretion of HCl. Many people secrete too little HCl as they get older, though this problem may be the result of years of oversecretion (see Chapter 11). Spirea has worked in either case and in many disorders of the stomach, including gastric ulcers.

CHEMISTRY: Spirea is the herb from which aspirin was originally made; it contains a large percentage of salicylic aldehyde. It also contains tannins, making it a good astringent for diarrhea, and it has antibacterial action.

TOXICITY: Though some people have theorized toxicity from the presence of salicylate and tannins, there seems to be no evidence that anyone has suffered side effects from taking this herb.

Calamus, or sweet flag (Acorus calamus) regulates the secretion of HCl, stimulates the appetite, and alleviates grain allergies, dyspepsia, or stomach ache. One constituent, alpha-asarone, has shown anti-ulcer activity. It has a bitter taste. (Many stomach tonics are called "bitters.")

CHEMISTRY: Calamus contains the volatile oils, asarone (related to myristicin from nutmeg) and beta-asarone, as well as eugenol, pinene, camphene, and caryophyllene.

TOXICITY: According to Spoerke, calamus is not considered toxic in therapeutic amounts, though larger amounts may cause drowsiness. The FDA has recommended that calamus be used only externally, though Lad and Frawley point out that the herb has been ingested in India for thousands of years.

Goldenseal (Hydrastis canadensis) is found in many formulas, where it heals the mucous membranes. It is a *tonic* for the entire digestive system, including the stomach, and is used for chronic gastritis and enteritis. Like many stomach tonics, it has a very bitter taste.

CHEMISTRY: Golden seal contains the isoquinoline alkaloids hydrastine and canadine, which give the herb its name, as well as the alkaloid berberine, which is found in a number of the herbs used as liver tonics. (Spoerke says, however, that here it is practically inert.) These alkaloids are astringents and weak antibiotics.

TOXICITY: Golden seal is toxic in large quantities. Mild symptoms include irritation of the mouth and throat. Spoerke warns of depression of the nervous system, leading to paralysis in severe cases. Even at lower dosages, golden seal robs the body of B vitamins, which must be replaced in the diet. Others warn those with high blood pressure against using it.

Roman chamomile (Anthemis flores) and **German chamomile (Matricaria chamomilla)** have similar constituents and applications. Chamomile is a soothing herb for all kinds of stomach problems, including dyspepsia and gastritis. It is both antiseptic and anti-inflammatory to the mucous membranes.

CHEMISTRY: Chamomile contains tiglic acid esters which, though mildly irritating to the mucous membranes, seem to give the herb its *tonic, carminative,* and *relaxant* properties. It also contains small amounts of apigenin, a *spasmolytic* agent, and chamazulene, which is both spasmolytic, antibacterial, and anti-inflammatory. Its alpha-bisabolol has *antipeptic* action, and inhibits stress-induced ulcers.

TOXICITY: Chamomile is not considered very toxic, though large amounts may cause vomiting. It has, however, triggered allergic reactions in people with allergies to ragweed or any member of the Compositae family of plants. Anaphylaxis (severe allergic reaction) is rare, but it can occur and is sometimes falsely attributed to aspirin.

Fennel (Foeniculum vulgare) cleanses the digestive tract of excess mucus, reduces intestinal griping and gas, and intoxicates intestinal worms, making it easier for the *vermifuge* herbs to eliminate them.

CHEMISTRY: Fennel contains volatile oils, including the phenolic ether, anethole, and the ketone, fenchone, which stimulate the digestive membranes.

TOXICITY: Fennel is not considered toxic, though the oil extracted from it may be.

Fenugreek (Trigonella foenum-graecum) is a *tonic* which eliminates excess mucus, kills intestinal worms, soothes inflamed stomachs, alleviates hypoglycemia and relieves indigestion. (It was the main active ingredient in Lydia Pinkham's remedy.) In rats, it promotes bile formation and flow, when ingested with ginger.

CHEMISTRY: Fenugreek has a high mucilage content, making it a good bulk laxative. Like cod liver oil, it is rich in protein, phosphates, lecithin, organic iron, and trimethyl-amine.

TOXICITY: Fenugreek has no known toxicity.

Calumba (Jateorhiza palmata) increases the appetite, stimulates the gastric nerve, and relieves dyspepsia and gas.

CHEMISTRY: Calumba contains the isoquinoline alkaloids, palmatine, jatrorrhizine, and columbamine. The non-alkaloidal bitter principles which may be responsible for its tonic effects include calumbin, chasmanthin, and palmarin.

TOXICITY: There is no known toxicity.

Peppermint (Mentha piperita) is a *stomachic*. Like chamomile, it contains mucous membrane irritants, which apparently relieve dyspepsia and colic. It has some *astringent* action, as it contains tannins.

CHEMISTRY: Peppermint contains volatile oils, mainly menthol, though the proportions of its constituents vary with climate and genetic factors. (The higher quality peppermint oils come from older plants.) It has tannins, which give it its astringent properties, and some nutrients, including flavonoids, tocopherols, choline, and carotenoids.

TOXICITY: The herb seems to be quite nontoxic, though the oil can be an irritant. Most herbalists do not restrict intake, though some do caution that prolonged use could harm the heart.

Papaya leaves (Carica papaya) contain papayin, a digestive enzyme which resembles pepsin, though it doesn't need an acid environment in order to become active. Papayin acts on milk protein in a manner similar to rennin, digests other proteins as well, and tends to digest dead rather than live tissue.

TOXICITY: Papaya may trigger allergic reactions, often after continued use. It may eat through the esophageal wall if taken in large amounts. It has been known to cause abortion of healthy fetuses.

HERBS FOR THE INTESTINES

Though many herbs for the stomach do heal the digestive tract as a whole, the following herbs are more specific to the intestinal tract.

Ginger (Zingiber officinale) is very effective in transporting other herbs to the abdominal area, so it is often combined with cathartic herbs. It ameliorates the griping action of strong cathartics, and it relieves flatulence, as do many of the aromatic herbs. It has been used for motion sickness and dyspepsia.

CHEMISTRY: Ginger's volatile oil, containing zingiberine, is a slight irritant. This property is probably responsible for ginger's antiflatulent action.

TOXICITY: Ginger is not known to produce toxic effects in the amounts normally taken (or tolerated), though Spoerke advises people with bowel disorders to take it with caution.

Catnip (Nepeta cataria) is a soothing herb that relieves flatulence and colic.

CHEMISTRY: Catnip's volatile oils may be responsible for its effectiveness. The herb is no longer listed in the US National Formulary, but it remains popular.

TOXICITY: Catnip has no known toxicity.

Cascara sagrada (Rhamnus purshiana) is one of the most popular *cathartic* herbs. It is relatively mild and is taken regularly over a period of time to treat chronic constipation. Although it may seem to promote dependency at first, cascara tones the intestines while stimulating peristalsis, so that eventually it will not be needed at all. It also activates the gall bladder and pancreas and is often used in diabetes.

CHEMISTRY: Cascara sagrada contains emodin, formed from anthraquinone glycosides.

TOXICITY: Large doses can be irritating, and long-term use can result in chronic diarrhea. The older the bark, the milder it is, so cascara sagrada less than a year old should be avoided. Gosselin considers it moderately toxic, since large doses can cause enteritis.

Buckthorn (Rhamnus cathartica) is another member of the same genus as cascara sagrada. It has similar applications, though it is not considered as effective.

CHEMISTRY: It also contains anthraquinone glycosides, but since it contains more emodin and is less sure in its action, it is not as popular as cascara, though the two are sometimes combined.

TOXICITY: Children who eat the berries sometimes become intoxicated and nauseous, and in severe cases may suffer kidney damage.

Turkey Rhubarb (Rheum palmatum) resembles garden rhubarb and has a similar cathartic action.

CHEMISTRY: Rhubarb contains anthracene glycosides.

TOXICITY: It is quite safe and is not habit-forming. In small doses it increases the flow of digestive juices and improves appetite.

Alfalfa (Medicago sativa) supplies extra fibre for sluggish bowels.

CHEMISTRY: It contains vitamins A, C, D, E, K and many of the B vitamins. It stimulates the appetite and is high in saponins, anti-inflammatory agents which may reduce cholesterol.

Flax seed (Linum usitatissimum) is a *demulcent* and bulk forming agent, because it contains 28 percent mucilage.

TOXICITY: Flax oxidizes relatively easily, so it may become rancid. Spoerke warns of toxicity from nitrates and linamarin, a cyanogenic glycoside, especially in immature seeds grown in warm climates.

Senna (Cassia senna, Cassia angustifolia) is a very strong cathartic which can cause severe griping or dehydration from diarrhea. It can also become habit forming. For these reasons, many herbalists do not recommend this herb, though it is found in a number of over-the-counter remedies. Unlike cascara sagrada and turkey rhubarb, it doesn't work on the nerves activating the colon, but is a local irritant.

CHEMISTRY: Senna contains anthracene glycosides, primarily sennosides, chrysophanol, and aloe-emodin.

HERBS FOR THE OTHER DIGESTIVE ORGANS

LIVER

The liver is an important organ with many functions. Although it is generally strong enough to handle the many herbs which affect it, liver cleanses often release toxins which must then be handled by the other organs, among them the much more delicate kidneys. Strong herbs for the liver are best left to an expert.

One of the milder liver tonics, **Barberry (Berberis vulgaris)**, is also a general digestive tonic. It reverses malnutriton, regulates the digestive system, and removes obstructions in the digestive tract.

CHEMISTRY: Barberry contains the alkaloid berberine, which normalizes the secretions of the liver. Berberine (also found in goldenseal) is a mild local anesthetic to the mucous membranes.

TOXICITY: Although the berries are considered harmless, the roots are stronger and may irritate the mucous membranes. In large amounts the roots can cause dangerously low blood pressure as well as heart problems. Gosselin says the toxicity of berberine is in dispute and has been rated anywhere from slightly to extremely toxic. Toxic doses depress heart action, relax blood vessels, and depress respiration rate, while stimulating the smooth muscles of the intestines and the bronchi.

KIDNEYS

Strong *diuretics* can harm a weak kidney. A gentle herbal combination is **Parsley (Petroselinum sativum)** and **Red Raspberry leaves (Rubus idaeus)**. Parsley is a mild diuretic which strengthens and detoxifies the kidneys and is mildly laxative and antimicrobial. Raspberry leaves cleanse the body of mucus. They tone as well as relax the internal organs, including the uterus and the bowels.

CHEMISTRY: Parsley contains apiol, which gives it its diuretic properties. It also contains many nutrients, including vitamins A and C and iron. Raspberry leaves contain fragerine and tannins. They are rich in nutritents, particularly ferric citrate (iron).

TOXICITY: Large amounts of parsley may be dangerous, particularly in people who are allergic to the carrot family, and should be avoided in pregnancy. (The small amounts used in cooking are not likely to be a problem.) Parsley root is more toxic than the leaves.

Raspberry leaves have no known toxicity, though excessive consumption of tannins does impede iron absorption.

DIGESTION IN GENERAL

In moderate doses, **Peruvian bark (Cinchona spp.)** augments peristalsis and the flow of digestive juices while lowering uric acid levels. It is a bitter tonic and an astringent. For digestive purposes small quantities are combined with **Virginia Snake Root**, which prevents nausea, a possible side effect.

CHEMISTRY: Peruvian bark contains about 35 alkaloids whose concentrations vary with the source of the bark. Other constituents include cinchotannic, quinic, and quinovic acids, cinchona red, and volatile oils.

TOXICITY: Because of its quinloine alkaloids, Peruvian bark is best known as a source of quinine, the anti-malarial drug. Unlike quinine, which can cause permanent deafness, Peruvian bark has produced only temporary hearing loss preceded by ringing in the ears. It may also impair sight.

Chapter 15

HERBS FOR YOUR -ITIS:
inflammatory conditions as systemic problems

To a herbalist, diagnosis of a condition is not only unimportant, but is liable to be illegal. This is fortunate when it comes to inflammatory conditions, since all too many performers have heard the experts disagree on just what it is that is inflamed, let alone whether there are sinister arthritic overtones. As in Section II, the term arthritis includes other inflammatory conditions, e.g. tendinitis, bursitis, etc.

The folk remedies for arthritis are as numerous as the disease is crippling. Though some herbal remedies have been extensively investigated, many have a long clinical history with little research support. Unfortunately, the traditional combinations, which seem to work better than individual herbs, have virtually no scientific research behind them.

The reasons for inflammation range from physical trauma to chemical imbalance. Thus swellings and painful joints might respond to anti-inflammatory herbs, blood cleansers, or relaxants of the muscles and central nervous system. Some herbs fall into more than one category, and often a herb which is used primarily for something else turns out to have anti-arthritic properties. Like a good training diet, a well-designed arthritis program will build health while improving performance.

BLOOD CLEANSERS (*ALTERATIVE* HERBS)

Blood cleansing herbs eliminate toxins and mucus from the body. They are usually combined with an alkaline diet (Chapter 11) and herbs for the eliminative organs (Chapter 14). Just as a cleansing diet can precipitate a healing crisis, so can alterative herbs.

Chaparral or **creosote (Larrea tridentata)** is a local *analgesic* which alleviates rheumatic pain, arthritis, and chronic backache. It is not considered a laxative, but increases bowel elimination. It also cleanses the lymphatic system.

CHEMISTRY: Creosote contains nordihydroquaiaretic acid, small amounts of sterols, but no alkaloids. Tyler says that none of the known constituents of chaparral have been shown to be "safe and effective" in the treatment of inflammatory conditions, but that its nordihydroguaiaretic acid, makes it an effective antioxidant. (If free radical formation plays a role in the arthritic condition, this could be important.)

TOXICITY: There have been reports of skin irritation from chaparral compresses.

Sassafras (Sassafrass albidum) relieves rheumatism, sciatica and arthritis.

CHEMISTRY: Sassafras yields a volatile oil (at least 4 ml of oil per 100 gm of crude herb) which is about 80 percent safrole (cf. Gosselin; Spoerke says 50 percent).

TOXICITY: Gosselin gives safrole a toxicity rating of 3 (the same as aspirin). It can produce vomiting, shock, cyanosis, delirium, and probably convulsions. Long term ingestion can produce changes in the liver. Though it is carcinogenic in rats and mice, the metabolism in humans seems to be different, and in any case the amounts usually ingested do not accumulate, a second criterion for carcinogenicity (Gosselin, pII-258). The oil in sassafras will induce miscarriage in the early stages of pregnancy. The safrole concentration in sassafras is low enough that ingestion of toxic levels is unlikely. Spoerke says that 5 ml of safrole is a toxic dose for adults, concluding that the maximum safe dose of the herb is 100 gm. Among the symptoms from overdose of the oil he lists nausea, vomiting, dilated pupils, cardiovascular collapse and CNS depression, while the safrol itself causes respiratory paralysis, and fatty degeneration of heart, liver, and kidneys. The herb is in trouble for another reason: it is such a potent blood cleanser that in extremely large doses it will thin the blood, so the FDA has restricted its use. Proponents of sassafras counter that, in similar doses, some of the popular soft drinks are far more toxic.

Burdock (Arctium lappa) may relieve gouty disorders, rheumatism, and sciatica. It has a long history as a blood cleanser, neutralizer of poisons, and cleanser of the lymphatic system. It is also *diaphoretic* and *diuretic* and soothes the kidneys. It appears today in the French and Spanish pharmacopeias.

CHEMISTRY: Burdock contains a bitter glycoside, arctiin, which may be responsible for its actions, though little research has been done to confirm this possibility. It also contains inulin, tannin, and a volatile oil.

Red clover blossom (Trifolium pratense) plays a dual role as a blood cleanser and salicylate-based anti-inflammatory herb. It is *antispasmodic* and a *nervine*, and removes uric acid from the body.

CHEMISTRY: Red clover blossoms contain trifolianol and trifoliin.

TOXICITY: There are no reports of toxicity, except for speculation that improper drying and storage could make the plant's coumaric acid turn into dicoumarin (an anticoagulant). In areas with high levels of molybdenum in the soil, the accumulation in the plant might reach toxic levels.

Garlic (Allium sativum) is such a valuable food that it has been recommended by healers for years as a potent blood cleanser and antibacterial agent. It limits acute platelet aggregation and formation of blood clots, may prevent coronary occlusion and atherosclerosis, reduces serum triglycerides and certain lipoproteins, stabilizes blood sugar, and normalizes blood pressure.

CHEMISTRY: Ajoene seems to be the constituent responsible for the inhibition of blood clot formation. Garlic also contains alliin and allicin (diallyldisulfide-S-oxide) which is a bactericidal principle. (Martindale lists the constituents as allyl propyl disulfide and diallyl disulphide.) It may also contain prostaglandins.

TOXICITY: Martindale cautions against giving garlic preparations to children, saying they can be fatal. Manufacturers of certain odorless garlic preparations claim to have removed the toxic constituents without reducing health-giving properties. This herb has been very extensively studied (e.g. see journals).

ELIMINATIVE ANTI-INFLAMMATORY HERBS

Eliminative herbs with anti-inflammatory properties include the diuretics **parsley, buchu, juniper,** and **couchgrass,** which work on the kidneys, as well as **balsam poplar,** a mild aid for the intestines, and **mandrake,** a strong cathartic. Some of these herbs have powerful action on their respective eliminative systems and should not be taken without qualified advice.

Parsley (Petroselinum sativum) is a mild *diuretic* (see Chapter 14). Since it purifies the blood and breaks down uric acid, it may relieve arthritis.

Buchu (Barosma betulina) dissolves kidney stones, allowing the harmful deposits to be released from the body.
CHEMISTRY: The constituents of buchu include diosmin (a benzo-pyrone) and a volatile oil which contains the phenolic ketone diosphenol (barosma camphor), which has both antiseptic and diuretic properties. Other constituents include l-menthone and hesperidin. Diosmin, which acts like the bioflavonoids in reducing capillary fragility, has been tested on rats and found effective in reducing inflammation and tissue disorganization from direct trauma or burns. Casley-Smith found a higher dosage more effective than a lower dosage in the former case, while in the latter case, only the lower dosage worked at all. He speculates that diosmin will act like other benzo-pyrones and be effective in inflammations from other causes and in other species.
TOXICITY: Buchu is a strong diuretic and should not be taken when the kidneys are weak. There are no further indications of toxicity.

Juniper (Juniperus communis) is a *diuretic* and urinary *antiseptic,* and a *carminative* and gastrointestinal antiseptic. It remedies retention of urine and assists in the production of stomach acid.
CHEMISTRY: Juniper appears in many European pharmacopeias. Its constituents include juniperin, and formic, acetic, and malic acids.

TOXICITY: Juniper is a strong diuretic which should not be used when the kidneys are weak. It should not be taken during pregnancy.

Couchgrass or **quackgrass (Agropyron repens)** is neither a common *diuretic*, nor a common anti-inflammatory, but it has been assigned both properties by a number of herbalists.

CHEMISTRY: Couchgrass contains triticin (a carbohydrate resembling inulin), mannite, and inosite, and is listed in the Polish and Swiss pharmacopeias as a mild diuretic.

Balsam poplar (Populus balsamifera) is also known as **Balm of Gilead.** Some herbalists recommend it for dryness of the intestines, as it is peristaltic, lubricating to the mucous membranes, and healing. It is also considered good for the gall bladder, since it dissolves cholesterol and then removes it by its diuretic action. It is laxative, nourishing, and cleansing.

CHEMISTRY: Balsam poplar contains salicin, as do most of the poplar species. This accounts for its anti-inflammatory properties (see salicylate-containing herbs).

Mandrake or **mayapple (Podophyllum peltatum)** may reduce inflammation which cannot be controlled with non-steroidal anti-inflammatory drugs. It has *antimitotic* properties and has been applied to warts. Mandrake has been investigated as a possible cancer drug because of its antimitotic properties, yet it relieves autoimmune diseases like arthritis.

CHEMISTRY: The podophyllum resin (podophyllin) contains the lignans podophyllotoxin and alpha- and beta-peltatins. Podophyllotoxin may be responsible for arresting the proliferation of lymphoid cells found in the synovial membrane in rheumatoid arthritis.

TOXICITY: Mandrake is a strong *purgative* and *cathartic* which can cause severe cramping and dehydration of the digestive tract. Podophyllum resin is considered extremely toxic, but the fruit of the mayapple is considered quite safe, aside from its cathartic effect.

SAPONIN-CONTAINING HERBS

Devil's claw and yucca are among the most popular and controversial anti-inflammatory herbs. They contain chemicals called steroidal saponins, which have been extensively researched because of their relationship to corticosteroid drugs (see box).

Devil's Claw (Harpagophytum procumbens), a native of South Africa, is an old remedy for arthritis and rheumatism. In African folk medicine, it is also used for diabetes, arteriosclerosis, and problems with the liver, kidneys, bladder, stomach, and intestines. It may alleviate pain in pregnant women, especially those anticipating a difficult delivery. In Indian tradition, devil's claw is thought to cleanse the lymphatic system. Most of the claims about its anti-inflammatory and analgesic effects come from the European studies discussed below. The studies also showed that it reduces elevated cholesterol and uric acid levels, but U.S. studies have failed to verify these claims. The many testimonials to this herb (anecdotal evidence) include reports from musicians who regained their ability to perform; unfortunately most of these testimonials are connected with an advertisement for a commercial preparation of the herb.

CHEMISTRY: The secondary storage roots of devil's claw contain three iridiod glycosides: harpagoside, harpagide, and procumbide.

The following are summaries of four studies using devil's claw to reduce the swelling induced in rats' paws (see journals, bibliography):

(1) Zorn studied its effects on formaldehyde-induced arthritis in albino rats. He administered fresh devil's claw tea either orally or by injection into the inflamed paw. The injections were very effective after even one administration, with no observed side effects from 1 cc given once a day for ten days. However, at 2 cc most of the rats died after three to six daily doses. The oral administration, via stomach tube, was yet more lethal even at 1 cc, so administration was stopped after six days. Nevertheless, the anti-inflammatory effect continued for up to five weeks, at which time the controls still had swollen, arthritic joints and little movement. With both

types of administration of devil's claw, joint mobility was restored. The author considered the herb as effective as the best drugs available at the time (1957). He admits that formaldehyde-induced arthritis is not considered a good model for rheumatoid arthritis, but states that all drugs which work for one work for the other, and vice versa. He planned further research to find safe effective dosages and to isolate the active principles.

(2) Eichler and Koch followed up Zorn's experiments and the subsequent isolation of harpagoside by other researchers, by investigating the anti-inflammatory properties of the glycoside itself. Their results were not as conclusive as Zorn's, but they felt that harpagoside was indeed the substance responsible and dismissed the need to search any further for explanations for the effectiveness of the herb. Their methods for producing swelling included albumin-induced edema, granuloma pouch induced by injecting Mazola oil into an air pocket, and formaldehyde-induced arthritis. Swelling induced by the second method was the only type for which harpagoside alone produced any significant results. They found little residual effect and no prophylactic effect. They also tested for analgesic and spasmolytic properties, but found none.

(3) In East Germany, Seeger continued these experiments until the customs regulations changed and he was no longer allowed to import the herb. He cites a number of experiments which indicate that devil's claw is effective in treating rheumatic diseases, arthritis, arthroses, and liver, gall bladder, kidney, and gastrointestinal tract problems.

(4) Investigating its anti-inflammatory properties, McLeod and colleagues found that devil's claw failed to reduce carrageenin-induced swelling in the rat's paw, a standard test for anti-inflammatory agents. In adjuvant arthritis introduced in rats by injecting turberculosis bacteria, the devil's claw actually seemed to potentiate the reaction.

This last account does point out one difficulty in evaluating an anti-inflammatory agent: its success varies with the methods of inducing the inflammation. McLeod maintains that his is the only acceptable way. Given the many causes for inflammation (and arthritis), it may be reasonable to suppose that the herb could work in some cases and not in others.

Yucca (Yucca glauca) goes by a number of local names, including amole, Spanish bayonet, Joshua tree, datil, Spanish dagger, Adam's needle, Spanish bayonet, and soap weed. It is found in warm, dry areas throughout Central America and the western United States, and is an old home remedy for arthritic pain. The bark is used for soap.

Moore recommends using only the dried roots, peeled, split lengthwise, and dried. Harris recommends both leaves and root, as he considers the leaf powder a good source of sarsapogenin, a potential cortisone precursor.

CHEMISTRY: As the plant matures it contains more sarsapogenin, whose molecules have fewer hydroxyl groups. It may have small quantities of other sapogenins, including markogenin, tigogenin, neo-tigogenin, neo-gitogenin, hecogenin, gloriogenin, and diosgenin in the seeds, as well as smilagenin, tigogenin, hecogenin, gitogenin, and neo-gitogenin in the leaves and roots. Harris says that yucca's saponin component doesn't have the acrid taste of other saponins, nor does it trigger sneezing.

Moore reports that "recent clinical studies have shown it to be of some use in the treatment of joint inflammations but the function is not understood. ... **Arthritis being such an idiosyncratic disorder, no single treatment will help more than a percentage of people** [emphasis mine], but if Yucca tea is effective, it can relieve pain for several days afterwards." He recommends using 1/4 ounce of the inner root boiled in a pint of water for 15 minutes and drunk in three or four doses during the day. In the absence of side effects, the dosage can be increased to 1/2 ounce per day. Potential side effects include diarrhea, accompanied by intestinal cramping: if this occurs, he suggests a lower dose the next time.

It has been hypothesized that the saponins in yucca ought to have beneficial effects on the intestinal flora, which might in turn relieve the intestinal toxicity which often accompanies arthritis. Follow up studies at the National Arthritis Medical Clinic reportedly confirmed this hypothesis. Some of the arthritic patients in the experiment gained relief of pain, stiffness, and swelling. It seemed that yucca also reduced blood cholesterol levels. No adverse side effects were reported.

Ali and colleagues report that the fresh flowers of Yucca glauca contain relatively non-toxic polysaccharides with antitumor activity. They found no such effects in the seeds, leaves, fruits, or roots.

Agave (Agave sisalana) is related to yucca as a member of the order Agavaceae.

CHEMISTRY: It contains the steroidal sapogenins hecogenin, manogenin, and tigogenin, which have been investigated as immunosuppressives. Arthritis being an autoimmune disease would thus be one of the potential applications. Other steroidal saponins isolated from agave include neo-tigogenin, sisalagenin, gloriogenin, gentrogenin, diosgenin, and yamogenin. As with yucca, the steroidal sapogenins increase with maturity of the plant and contain fewer hydroxyl groups. Hecogenin is a waste product of hemp production and is used to manufacture cortisone.

Alfalfa (Medicago sativa) contains vitamins A, D, K, C, members of the B complex, a number of trace minerals, and protein. It may reduce body cholesterol, phospholipid, and triglyceride levels (including those in the liver) while raising the levels of the (desirable) high-density lipids.

CHEMISTRY: Alfalfa contains 2 to 3 percent saponins, as well as triacontanol (a plant growth regulator), flavones, isoflavones, alkaloid trigonelline, stachydrine, and homostachydrine.

TOXICITY: Alfalfa may actually induce lupus, which like arthritis, is an autoimmune disease. Though Spoerke reports no toxicity, he says that "there is no available evidence to support its use as an antiarthritis agent."

Ginseng (Panax quinquefolium, Panax ginseng) has so many applications that its inclusion in this section gives only a small part of the picture (e.g. see Chapter 16, herbs to strengthen muscles). The Merck Index lists it as a tonic. This is an extremely well-researched herb, and the bibliography contains only a small number of the many studies which have been done on ginseng.

CHEMISTRY: The saponins in ginseng, which seem to be a mixture of steroidal and pentacyclic triterpenoids, are called ginsenosides by the Japanese researchers and panaxosides by their Russian colleagues, though these two components are apparently not completely identical. The Merck Index lists them as the biologically active constituents.

Yam (Dioscorea sylvatica, D. spp.) is spasmolytic, anti-inflammatory, and antirheumatic, so it relieves muscular rheumatism and cramps. It is especially effective with cramp bark and black cohosh in the acute phase of rheumatoid arthritis.

CHEMISTRY: Not to be confused with the sweet potato, Ipomoea batatas, yams contain diosgenin, which has been isolated by the pharmaceutical industry for partial synthesis of oral contraceptives, sex hormones, and corticosteroids. Diosgenin has been successfully tested in controlled experiments as an anti-inflammatory agent in rats, and according to the National Academy of Sciences, "is also an active anti-inflammatory agent in man." The plants contain a number of other saponins, including the closely related yamogenin, and botogenin. The steroidal sapogenins in yams have been studied since the 1940s, as some of them are closely related to cortisone. Yang and Chen have isolated as many as ten different steroidal compounds from D. collettii.

TOXICITY: Yams contain an alkaloid, generally dioscorine or a related compound. Dioscorine, related to picrotoxin, is a strong poison, causing general paralysis of the central nervous system and sometimes death. Most species of yam are toxic until the offending alkaloid is removed by soaking in water, though after this they are safe to eat. Symptoms of toxicity from untreated yams include burning pain in the mouth, throat, and abdomen, vomiting and diarrhea, and delirium, vertigo, bulging eyes, and deafness.

Ruscus aculeatus roots have anti-inflammatory activity. They also reduce capillary permeability and constrict peripheral blood vessels.

CHEMISTRY: Ruscus contains ruscogenin, related to the saponins in yams.

Birthroot or **Bethroot (trillium spp.)** is an anti-arthritic herb which also stops hemorrhages and decreases heart palpitations.

CHEMISTRY: Birthroot contains trillarin, a diglycoside of diosgenin. It also contains a glycoside resembling convalamarin, which may be the component responsible for decreasing heart palpitations.

Chinese cardamom (Costus speciosus) has been used in the commercial production of sterols. Despite its name, the plant is more popular in India than in China, and in some parts of the Far East it appears to have magical properties attributed to it. CHEMISTRY: Chinese cardamom contains diosgenin and sapogenins.

Fenugreek (Trigonella foenum-graecum) (see Chapter 14) relieves arthritis as well as indigestion. CHEMISTRY: It contains diosgenin, a steroidal sapogenin. It also contains a fixed oil, mucilage, and protein.

Sarsaparilla (Smilax spp.) is an old rheumatism remedy. It is also known as a tonic and blood cleanser. CHEMISTRY: Much of the research on this herb has been done without identifying the particular species being investigated, and some herbalists even use the name "sarsaparilla" for the wild ginseng, Aralia nudicaulis. This has led to confusion, since different species of Smilax contain different steroidal saponins. Among them are sarsaponin, smilasaponin, sarsaparilloside, and sitosterol. Other steroids, include sarsapogenin, smilagenin, sitosterol, stigmasterol, and pollinastaanol. TOXICITY: Sarsaparilla may facilitate absorption of drugs or other herbs, necessitating lower dosages. The berries of this plant are edible, and its toxicity is very low.

Stropanthus spp. contain sarmentogenin, a steroid once used in cortisone production. The use was discontinued, because the plants are scarce and difficult to grow. Plants from different geographical locations contain variants, such as sarverogenin and sarmutogenin. The species also contain cardiac glycosides and were once listed in the British Pharmacopeia as heart remedies.

Other saponin-containing herbs which may alleviate arthritis include **Hechtia texensis** (contains hecogenin), **Kallstroemia pubescens** (contains diosgenin), and **Furcraea species** (contain steroidal saponins).

SAPONINS AND CORTICOSTEROID DRUGS

A saponin is a glycoside, i.e. it consists of a sugar and another part, called an aglycone ("without sugar"). The aglycone in the case of saponins, often called a sapogenin ("producer of saponins"), is made of benzene rings (see fig. 41). Saponins (from the Latin *sapo*, meaning soap) have detergent properties, i.e. they form a colloidal solution in water, which foams when it is agitated.

When injected into the blood stream, saponins are strongly hemolytic (destroy blood cells), but when ingested orally they are relatively harmless, perhaps because digestion breaks them into sugar and sapogenin, which are not considered hemolytic.

Another reason saponin-containing herbs don't destroy blood cells may be that many of them contain both saponins and tannins. One of the tests for saponins is based on their hemolytic properties, and researchers in the late 1960s were finding that the tannins toughened the membranes of the red blood cells so that the saponins couldn't get at them, thus giving a false negative on this test.

Two classes of saponins occur in plants: the steroid derivatives (usually tetracyclic triterpenoids) and the pentacyclic triterpenoids. Though many herbs contain saponins, the steroidal saponins are relatively rare. Most of the plants containing them have been candidates for arthritis remedies. Steroidal saponins, particularly diosgenin, were used to produce steroid drugs before complete synthesis was practical.

corticosteroid drugs

Anti-inflammatory steroid drugs date back to the end of the 1940s. They are not the same as the anabolic steroids taken by weight lifters, or the steroids of the reproductive tract; steroids are widely distributed in nature and have many functions. In technical terms, a steroid is any compound which contains a perhydrocyclopentanophenanthrene nucleus. Corticosteroids, the same substances as are manufactured in the adrenal cortex, are anti-inflammatory agents. The corticosteroids are either mineralocorticoids (including aldosterone and desoxy-corticosterone), which affect fluid and electrolyte balance, or

(SAPONINS AND CORTICOSTEROID DRUGS)

the glucocorticoids (including cortisone and hydrocortisone), which affect intermediary metabolism. The difference in structure between the two affect their affinity to different receptor sites. Aldosterone, the primary regulator of sodium and potassium balance, is not available for therapeutic applications. Many of the glucocorticoids do turn out to have mineralocorticoid properties as well, and it is these which are used in the treatment of arthritic conditions, because of their anti-inflammatory activity. Cortisone, in the form of cortisone acetate, is used for rheumatoid arthritis and other collagen diseases, as well as for certain allergies. Hydrocortisone (cortisol) is used for the same purposes, as well as being injected into joints in the form of its acetate ester. It may be somewhat more effective than cortisone.

toxicity of corticosteroid drugs

Anti-inflammatory steroids can affect carbohydrate metabolism. By increasing production of glucose by the liver (*gluconeogenesis*), steroids may create a need for more insulin, thus aggravating a diabetic state. Hydrocortisone may ameliorate hypoglycemic symptoms without actually changing blood sugar levels.

Some users suffer vascular lesions and ulcers, though the ulcers may be due to the arthritis rather than to the steroids.

It is generally agreed that steroids suppress the symptoms rather than cure the disease. This means that patients must continue using them indefinitely, or as long as they tolerate them. Often the effectiveness decreases over time. If steroid treatment is to be stopped, it must be tapered off. Long-term use of corticosteroid drugs can cause irreversible atrophy of the adrenal cortex, since their presence at high levels in the body suppresses the body's own mechanism for their production. Because the adrenals stop producing their own hormones, the patient may need a temporary increase in dosage when under extra stress. Changes in sexual characteristics are also possible, even though these are usually regulated by the gonadal hormones and not the adrenal cortex.

Steroids can affect the electrolyte balance, e.g. both cortisone and hydrocortisone can cause edema through sodium retention.

(SAPONINS AND CORTICOSTEROID DRUGS)

Since it is the mineralocorticoid activity of the steroids which produces the undesired effect, there have been efforts to modify them accordingly. Betamethasone, dexamethasone, fluprednisolone, methylprednisolone, paramethasone, meprednisone, and triamcinolone have each achieved partial success in this respect.

Sometimes steroids aggravate coexisting pathological states. Some doctors recommend a complete program, consisting of regulation of diet, rest, exercise, and stress, along with physical therapy and possible splinting of the affected joint. They prescribe steroids only when other measures, including salicylates and possibly even gold treatments, have failed, and the pain and crippling are severe.

Barbiturate drugs increase the required dosage of steroid drugs.

toxicity of saponins

Saponins have an acrid taste, irritate the mucous membranes, and make people sneeze. They may impede intestinal absorption of fat-soluble vitamins (A, D, E, and K), so intake of these vitamins may have to be increased, especially A and D, as they are important to healthy joints.

Saponins interfere with vitamin E utilization, but they decrease cholesterol levels. Spoerke says "the actions of saponins are seldom specific, but in general, they are irritant substances that produce cellular damage, tissue permeability changes, and erythrocyte hemolysis [destruction of red blood cells]. Saponins may be gastric irritants and visceral vasodilators as well." Yet most authorities agree that oral ingestion of saponins results in hydrolysis to sapogenins, which don't have these properties.

Do saponins produce the same side-effects as steroids? I haven't seen any reports that they do, but neither have I seen studies to show that they don't. The main argument for using the saponin-containing herbs instead of steroid drugs seems to be the same type of argument which is advanced elsewhere: the saponin-containing herbs have balancing constituents, perhaps including the tannins, as well as a variety of saponins with slightly differing functions. It is possible that the plant

> (SAPONINS AND CORTICOSTEROID DRUGS)
> balances the ingredients better than the pharmacist does.
> Because the herb is in an organic, digestible, assimilable form,
> it may be easier on the body than any drug made from its
> constituents. Aside from such general arguments, I have no
> reason to suggest that someone who wouldn't take steroid drugs
> should substitute the herbs.

SALICYLATE-CONTAINING HERBS

Salicylates are found in members of the **willow (Salix)** and **poplar (Populus)** genera (order Salicaceae), **spirea** (order Rosaceae) from which comes the name Aspirin™, **Black Haw (Viburnum prunifolium),** and **Wintergreen.** The herbs contain salicin, a glycoside that is hydrolyzed by emulsin to D-glucose and saligenin (salycil alcohol), which is then thought to be oxidized to salicylic acid in the digestive tract. Salicylates are considered anti-inflammatory, antipyretic, and analgesic.

Balm of Gilead or **balsam poplar (Populus balsamifera)** bark is an anti-inflammatory, *antipyretic*, or *analgesic* agent. It is also applied externally as a counter-irritant in cases of **muscle strain.** The name Balm of Gilead sometimes refers to other poplar species, including **cottonwood (Populus deltoides** or **Populus candicans),** which relieves rheumatic pain.

CHEMISTRY: Balm of Gilead contains salicin and populin (benzoyl-salicin) and the volatile compounds pinene, nor-pinene, and beta-phellandrene.

TOXICITY: The concentration of salicin is considered too low to cause salicylate poisoning.

Black willow or **pussy willow (Salix nigra, S. discolor)** is a home remedy for inflamed joints and rheumatism.

CHEMISTRY: It contains tannin and salinigrin (a compound related to salicin) giving it *astringent* and *sedative* properties.

White poplar or **quaking aspen (Populus tremuloides)** is a general *tonic* and is especially good for the urinary system. It can relieve headaches caused by a sluggish liver or stomach. It may relieve rheumatism, arthritis, and swelling of joints.

Wintergreen (Gaultheria procumbens) relieves pain in lumbago, sciatica, and rheumatic conditions.
CHEMISTRY: Wintergreen contains oil of wintergreen, which can also be obtained from another genus, **Betula lenta.** Wintergreen contains a glycoside, gaultherin, which releases methyl salicylate when hydrolyzed by an enzyme, gaultherase, found in the plant. The odor of wintergreen (as distinct from that of aspirin) comes from a different constituent, an ester of enanthic alcohol. Gaultheria oil, containing large quantities of methyl salicylate, is often obtained from the related species, **Gaultheria fragrantissima.**
TOXICITY: Martindale's says the toxicity of wintergreen is about the same as ASA's, though this may apply to the oil rather than the herb. Large doses of the oil are very toxic, and can induce nausea, vomiting, pulmonary edema, convulsions, and death. Gosselin gives wintergreen oil (methyl salicylate) the same toxicity rating as ASA, i.e. very toxic.

SALICYLATE HERBS AND ASA-RELATED DRUGS

Some of the cautions associated with ASA apply to the salicylate-containing herbs as well, e.g. interference with anticoagulant drugs. The British Pharmaceutical Codex of 1934 said that salicin, found in the herbs, has virtually the same action as salicylic acid but is less irritating to the mucous membranes. It is a specific remedy for **rheumatism,** as it is longer lasting but less depressing than salicylic acid.

The mechanisms by which ASA and salicylates reduce inflammation are not completely understood. One possibility is inhibition of prostaglandin and thromboxane synthesis. It has been hypothesized that ASA reduces the heightened capillary permeability characteristic of a number of inflammatory conditions. It doesn't prevent inflammation induced by histamines or bradykinins, but it does suppress a number of antibody reactions, apparently by more than a single mechanism. It influences the metabolism of **connective tissue,** thereby reducing **joint and other tissue damage** from

(SALICYLATE HERBS AND ASA-RELATED DRUGS)
inflammation. ASA also has *antipyretic* properties, lowering the temperature only when it is too high.

ASA may suppress the inflammation from rheumatic fever, but it fails to prevent the heart damage often associated with this disease. Their analgesic and anti-inflammatory properties make ASA-related drugs effective in the treatment of **rheumatoid arthritis**. The analgesic action makes it easier to do **therapeutic exercises**. Doses are high, often 5 to 6 g daily, held just below the level which produces ringing in the ears.

Salicylate herbs are of similar therapeutic value, tend to be less irritating, and have long been used for inflammatory conditions. Recent research, however, has lead some herbalists to prefer **feverfew** (see other anti-inflammatory herbs, below).

toxicity
Pure salicylic acid is considered too irritating to take internally, so a number of derivatives have been synthesized. ASA, acetylsalicylic acid, or Aspirin™, is a member of a group of anti-inflammatory drugs whose action is similar to that of the salicylate-containing herbs. ASA and other salicylate derivatives account for more drug consumption than any other group of drugs. About 10 grams of ASA are enough to produce toxic effects, though less than 1 gram has been lethal, and people have survived as much as 130 grams. Children are disproportionately sensitive.

Salicylate poisoning from acidosis (excess acidity of body fluids) can be aggravated by the effects of ASA on respiration: it increases oxygen consumption and carbon dioxide production in the skeletal muscle by uncoupling of oxidative phosphorylation, and this in turn accelerates respiration. In itself this does not change the plasma carbon dioxide concentration, but if the rapid breathing is countered with barbiturates or morphine, then the concentration can increase (respiratory acidosis), producing weakness, fainting, and accelerated pulse.

The salts of salicylic acid, such as ASA are often irritating to the gastric mucosa, even though they were originally derived from a herb (spirea) which regulates gastric secretions (Chapter 14). Side-effects include nausea and vomiting,

> (SALICYLATE HERBS AND ASA-RELATED DRUGS)
> ulceration, and often painless hemorrhage, sometimes resulting
> in iron-deficiency anemia.
>   Methyl salicylate is absorbed through the skin, and severe
> poisoning has resulted from its external applicaton as a
> counterirritant. This is also true of herbal applications, e.g. oil
> of **wintergreen.**

OTHER ANTI-INFLAMMATORY HERBS

Feverfew (Tanacetum parthenium) has been an arthritis
remedy since ancient times. In cases of rheumatoid arthritis,
Heptinstall found feverfew superior to non-steroidal anti-
inflammatory agents like ASA for inhibiting the abnormal
secretion of substances found in the synovial fluid. Feverfew is
effective for arthritis caused by the activation of protein
kinase C rather than by calcium imbalance.
   Feverfew can also prevent migraines.
   TOXICITY: Allergic reactions to feverfew include sore mouth
and skin rash. A freeze-dried preparation may avoid these
problems.

Chamomile (Matricaria chamomilla, Anthemis nobilis) (see
Chapter 14) has a long folk history as an *antispasmodic* and
anti-inflammatory herb. Since the anti-inflammatory agents
are found in a volatile oil, much of which is lost in brewing, a
whole plant extract may be preferable to tea. Nevertheless,
drinking the tea over a long time is said to be very beneficial.
   CHEMISTRY: The anti-inflammatory effects of chamomile
come from chamazulene and alpha-bisabolol, while the antispasmodic effects come from the flavonoids and coumarin
derivatives. Jakovlev studied the anti-inflammatory effects of
matricine, chamazulene, and guajazulene, finding that the first
constituent had a greater effect, and that the second had a
longer-lasting effect than the third. He concludes that these
substances can't replace each other in chamomile preparations.
Della-Loggia reports that the bioflavonoids also contribute to
its anti-inflammatory effect. Wagner found that the
polysaccharide stimulates the immune system, but this may be

an advantage when seeking to bring the body to a state of balance.

TOXICITY: See Chapter 14 for toxicity information.

Gotu kola (Centella asiatica) is a blood purifier, body strengthener, revitalizer, and sedative. It is popular in Europe for stimulating the circulation. Other applications include slow-healing wounds and periodontal disease.

CHEMISTRY: Asiaticoside (in the form of the drug Madecassol which is extracted from gotu kola) stimulates collagen synthesis in wound healing. The sedative effect is probably due to two saponins, brahmoside and brahminoside. Madecassoside is an anti-inflammatory, and asiaticoside is a wound-healing agent that was thought to be a glycoside but is now considered an ester.

TOXICITY: Gotu kola has been injected into the muscles without side effects. I have found no studies of the tea's toxicity.

Myrrh (Commiphora molmol) is perhaps a surprising candidate for anti-inflammatory action, as it increases the body's white blood cell count. It fights infection, particularly in the gums, where its astringent action also firms up the tissue. It was an astringent and disinfectant in Egyptian embalming fluid. In Saudi Arabian folk medicine the oleo-gum resin is used to treat inflammations and rheumatic condtions. Modern research confirms its anti-inflammatory and *antipyretic* effects.

CHEMISTRY: A related plant, C. mukul, also has anti-arthritic properties, which are attributed to a steroidal compound, though Tariq speculates that the anti-inflammatory effect of C. molmol may also be due in part to a "highly significant antihistaminic effect."

Bittersweet or **nightshade (Solanum dulcamara, Solanum spp.)** relieves chronic rheumatism. The juice from S. dulcamara was used since the time of the second century physician, Galen, to heal various growths.

CHEMISTRY: The members of the nightshade family contain various steroidal glycoalkaloids which have been extracted in commercial production, e.g. solanine, demissine, diosgenin, solasodine, and solanidine. The highest concentration is in the unripe fruit. The plants also contain saponins, such as dulcamarinic and dulcamarstinic acid in S. dulcamara. (Or alternatively solaniceine, dulcamarin, and dulcamaric and dulcamaretic acids.)

TOXICITY: The members of the Solanum species include the potato (S. tuberosum), tomato, eggplant, and green pepper. Since some arthritics benefit from avoiding these foods, they probably should avoid the herbs as well. Tyler says that the steroidal glycoalkaloids are toxic, and that the free alkamines produced by hydrolysis before absorption into the body produce such symptoms as "dulling of the senses and stupefaction." Martindale warns that solanine is poisonous, although it has been used to flavor food. Spoerke says that bittersweet has no effect on rheumatism, and that just two or three unripe berries can produce burning in the throat, vomiting, decreased pulse, muscle paralysis, headache, coma and death.

Comfrey (Symphytum oficinale) is an extremely valuable herb which has become suspect. Though its rosmarinic acid may be an anti-inflammatory agent, comfrey also contains allantoin, a cell-proliferant which promotes healing but may be a carcinogen. Since some of the plants contain pyrrolizidine alkaloids, which are toxic to the liver, many practitioners have agreed not to recommend comfrey until more information is available. One alkaloid, lasiocarpine, has produced liver cancer in rats, and comfrey leaves have produced cancers of the liver and bladder (also in rats). The herb is considered safe for external abrasions and other wounds, but it speeds healing to such an extent that it must be combined with antibacterial agents to avoid infection in a deep wound.

Mulberry (Morus indica) root is anti-inflammatory, *analgesic*, and a central nervous system depressant. Chatterjee and colleagues confirmed its anti-inflammatory effect in several types and phases of inflammation, including chronic experimentally-induced arthritis.

Papaya (Carica papaya) (see Chapter 14) has anti-inflammatory properties which are probably due to its antihistamines.

Bupleurum falcatum is a Chinese remedy for gout, rheumatism, and other inflammatory conditions. Experiments have comfirmed its effectiveness.

CHEMISTRY: B. falcatum contains saikosaponins, which are pentacyclic triterpenoid saponins rather than the steroidal saponins more commonly found in anti-inflammatory herbs.

Benoit and colleagues tested 177 plants for their ability to reduce carrageenin-induced pedal edema (swollen feet) in rats. (This is one of the standard tests for proposed anti-inflammatory agents.) Three which seemed to merit further investigation (66% to 75% reduction) were **Eupatorium hyssopifolium**, **Boehmeria cylindrica**, and **Solidago flexicaulis**. E. hyssopifolium is an antidote for poisonous bites of all sorts. The Solidago genus has about 100 members, most some type of goldenrod. In spite of the suggestiveness of the name, S. flexicaulis, I have found no reports of folk remedies for arthritis, but rather references to acyclic diterpenes and to polysaccharides with anti-tumor activity.

Plagiorhegma dubium is one of the many herbs native to China which are being investigated by Western scientists. It is an antipyretic and bitter stomachic.

CHEMISTRY: P. dubium has three compounds with anti-inflammatory activity: the protoberberine alkaloid, jatrorrhizine, and the lignaneglucosides dehydrodiconiferyl-alcohol-4-beta-D-glucoside, and its isomer, dehydrodiconi-feryl-alcohol-gamma-beta-D-glucoside.

Fagara (Fagara zanthoxyloides or **Zanthoxylum zanthoxyloides)** is a West African tree which yields many alkaloids, flavonoids, terpenoids, and related phenolic substances. These include zanthoxylol, which may exert its anti-inflammatory effect by inhibiton of prostaglandin synthesis. (It also inhibits the development of sickle-cell anemia.) Another constituent, fragaramide, also reduces inflammation, perhaps in part by inhibiting prostaglandin synthesis.

Calophyllum inophyllum is an Indian plant with anti-inflammatory properties. It contains a coumarin, calophyllolide, which seems to act by reducing capillary permeability in histamine or bradykinin reactions.

OTHER HERBS FOR YOUR -ITIS

Guaiac (Guajacum officinale) reduces the symptoms of rheumatism. It is an antioxidant in food. If it has the same effect in the body, it might relieve arthritis which was caused or aggravated by the presence of free radicals.

CHEMISTRY: Guaiac contains guaiacin, or guaiac-saponin, a pentacyclic triterpenoid saponin rather than a steroidal saponin. Other constituents include alpha- and beta-guiaconic acids, guaiacic acid, and guaiaretic acid.

TOXICITY: The toxicity of guaiac is very low, though Spoerke calls it a gastrointestinal irritant.

Licorice (Glycyrrhiza glabra) "has mild anti-inflammatory and mineralocorticoid properties associated with the presence of glycyrrhizin and has occasionally been used in place of the corticosteroids" (Martindale). Unlike cortisone, it is soothing to the stomach. The Chinese herbalists say it balances the immune system.

CHEMISTRY: Licorice has another pentacyclic triterpenoid saponin, glycyrrhizin, which may stimulate interferon production.

TOXICITY: There is a big range in the rate at which people metabolise the various constituents of licorice, and retention of glycyrrhetic acid has been associated with pseudoaldosteronism (spasms and weakness, with circulatory and bladder problems; see Chapter 17, blood sugar, for a more thorough discussion).

Poke root or scoke (Phytolacca decandra, P. vulga americana) has a long folk history as an antirheumatic and is recommended for rheumatism, arthritis, anxiety, and many other ailments. The Merck Index calls it antirheumatic, and Martindale calls it mildly narcotic.

CHEMISTRY: Poke root contains triterpene saponins, tannin, phytolaccine, phytolaccic acid, and asparagine.

TOXICITY: Much has been written about the toxicity of pokeweed (poke root), though early settlers in North America often ate the leaves as a vegetable and the Indians used the roots as a blood cleanser. Spoerke says it causes a delayed reaction of nausea, vomiting, and diarrhea, and that the roots are the most toxic, then the stems, followed by the leaves, and lastly the berries. Tyler cites several deaths in children and hospitalization in adults. Studies on changes in peripheral blood cells were initiated in 1966. In May, 1979, the Herb Trade Association recommended that poke root not be sold as a tea or as a food, and that herbal preparations containing this herb carry a toxicity warning. This action was triggered by a single case of acute poisoning from a cup of tea obtained in a health food store in Wisconsin, which also resulted in a state-wide embargo.

Celery (Apium graveolens) is used in China for arthritic conditions.

CHEMISTRY: Celery is rich in organic sodium, which is thought to be utilized better than table salt, so that it tends to balance the electrolytes.

Cowberry leaf (Vaccinium vitis-idaeae) relieves rheumatic conditions and is listed in several European pharmacopeias.

Evening primrose oil contains the essential fatty acid, GLA. One theory is that GLA acts by raising prostaglandin E1 levels to a point where they can control the auto-immune activity producing rheumatoid arthritis.

Black currant seeds and **borage** are less expensive sources of GLA.

Basil (Ocinum spp.) is one of the sacred herbs of India. Although it is used both there and in North America primarily for sore throats, Lad and Frawley recognize it as a remedy for arthritis and rheumatism.

Other Western herbs they suggest for these ailments include **ginger (Zingiber officinale)**, **prickly ash (Xanthoxylum spp.)**, **alfalfa (Medicago sativa)**, **celery seeds (Apium graveolens)**, **fenugreek (Trigonella foenumgraeceum)**, **frankincense (Boswellia carterii)**, **juniper berries (Juniperus spp.)**, **mugwort**

(Artemesia vulgaris), skullcap (Scutellaria spp.), and turmeric (Curcuma longa).

Maria Treben suggests **horsetail (Equisetum arvense)** or **stinging nettle (Urtica dioica)** tea for "inflamed and deformed joints and wear and tear symptoms". For rheumatism she recommends teas of **agrimony (Agrimonia eupatoria)** leaves, **club moss (Lycopodium clavatum), corn silk (Zea mais), Wild garlic (ramsons, Allium ursinum)**, or the fresh stems of **Dandelion (Taraxcum officinale)**, or a tincture of **Speedwell (Veronica officinalis)**.

The following additional herbs are sometimes recommended for arthritis.

Beech (Fagus silvatica) has triterpene sapogenins and is listed in a number of European pharmacopeias and dispensatories but only for skin disorders.

English ivy (Hedera helix) also has triterpene sapogenins, including helixin.

Blue flag (Iris versicolor) contains the fatty acids myristic acid and oleic acid, as well as irone, and methyl myristate, and other esters.

Chickweed (Stellaria media), especially the tea, may retard chronic degenerative arthritis, though it is more effective for prolonged use if mixed with other healing plants.

Corn silk (Zea mais) is a traditional North American Indian remedy for arthritis and removes excess uric acid from the system. It contains maizenic acid.

Dandelion is valued by many herbalists for its beneficial effects on the liver. It gets rid of excess uric acid and purifies the blood, which relieves arthritis symptoms. It contains taraxerol and is found in several European pharmacopeias.

The **garden carrot** is a tonic and blood cleanser, good for all types of arthritis.

Goldenseal (see Chapter 14) is recommended for rheumatic pain.

Although **hops (Humulus lupulus)** is primarily a *nervine* (see Chapter 16, sleep), it is also used for rheumatism and inflammations.

Ginger (see Chapter 14) is a circulatory stimulant. Ginger tea may relieve rheumatism, because ginger is warming in winter and cooling in summer.

Lobelia (Lobelia inflata) (see Chapter 16, muscle relaxants) is an *antispasmodic* and blood cleanser which is good for rheumatism and arthritis.

Mullein (Verbascum thapsus) (see Chapter 17, respiration) can remove internal scar tissue, particularly in sciatica and inflamed rheumatism and arthritis.

Oregon grape (Berberis aquifolium) is related to barberry (see Chapter 14, liver). It relieves rheumatism, arthritis, and internal infections.

Peruvian bark (Cinchona spp.) (see Chapters 14 and 16) is an analgesic, nervine, and circulatory stimulant which relieves acute rheumatism.

FORMULAS

One commercially available formula combines **devil's claw, yucca, chaparral, red clover blossoms,** and **valerian root.**

Swedish Bitters is a formula which Maria Treben attributes to an "old manuscript" (quotation marks are hers), written by a Swede, Dr. Samst. Treben endorses the manuscript's claim that the formula cures a wide variety of extremely serious conditions. The Small Swedish Bitters contain **aloe** (or **gentian** or **wormwood), myrrh, saffron, senna,** natural **camphor, rhubarb** roots, **zedovary** roots, **manna, theriac venezian, carline thistle** roots and **angelica** roots, and can be bought under the name Swedish Bitters (see Treben's book for the formula). As internal medication or in compresses, it heals crippling arthritic joint deformation, swellings from bruising, hearing loss, eye strain, and many other conditions. If a compress is applied, the skin should first be rubbed with **calendula** ointment and powdered afterwards, to prevent itching. According to the manuscript, Swedish bitters also strengthens the brain and memory, gets rid of spots in front of the eyes or buzzing in the ears, improves digestion, heals warts and chapped hands, and sobers up drunks. (Two tablespoonfuls will do it "on the spot.")

The following are among the many formulas for specific types of arthritis.

(1) **dandelion root, ginger, chaparral, licorice,** and **ginseng** (for chronic and degenerative arthritis)

(2) **lobelia, ginger, yarrow, goldenseal, dandelion,** and **licorice** (for most arthritic problems, including acute, chronic, or rheumatoid arthritis, gout, lumbago, sciatica, and muscular rheumatism)

(3) **parsley, juniper, celery seed,** and **ginseng** (for chronic or rheumatoid arthritis)

(4) **Peruvian bark, ginger, echinacea,** and **licorice** (for acute and inflamed rheumatism)

(5) **white pond lily, parsley,** and **burdock** (a cleansing tea for rheumatism)

(6) **chaparral, elder flowers,** and **peppermint** (for arthritis or chronic backache — the other herbs also make the chaparral more palatable).

The following nutritious formulas may relieve arthritis during a cleansing program.

(1) **corn silk, shiitake mushrooms, green onions,** and **soya sauce**

(2) **parsley, lettuce, garlic,** and **carrot** juices (for gout and chronic and rheumatoid arthritis)

(3) **red clover blossoms, lettuce, mint** and **lemon** juice (for the same conditions)

ANTI-INFLAMMATORY HERBS AND PERFORMANCE

Inflammation is the body's healing mechanism (see Chapter 4). It causes pain, which may discourage performance (and further injury). If the pain indicates damage to the neighboring tissue, however, the inflammation should be reduced.

Ice reduces inflammation, but heat during performance makes movement safer (see Chapter 5). An anti-inflammatory herb could mimic the effect of ice, reducing the circulation and thus the swelling (see Ruscus aculeatus, for example). If this herb is in your system during performance, provide extra warmth in some other way (warm-ups, heating pad, circulatory stimulant herbs).

Chapter 16

HERBS FOR THE NEUROMUSCULAR SYSTEM
relaxing and strengthening muscles and nerves

Tense muscles degrade performance and invite injury, no matter whether the tension is due to bad practice habits, worry, or overuse trauma. Herbs and drugs are no substitute for elimination of these contributing factors, but the right herbs decrease the risk of injury or speed recovery.

Herbs can break the cycle between anxiety and tense muscles. Many antispasmodics have a nervine effect, i.e. the same herbs which relax the muscles may also calm the mind or relieve insomnia. Other herbs promote safety by strengthening the muscles so that they can work at a smaller percentage of their capacity. Since the categories overlap, the herbs are classified according to their primary application.

Since the sedative effect of the muscle relaxants varies among individuals, it would be wise to test them during heavy practice sessions rather than during performance. The herbs for the nerves are generally considered safer than tranquilizers, but it might be a good idea to make a recording while under the influence of the herbs and review the tape when their effects wear off.

DRUGS TO RELAX THE MUSCLES

Most muscle relaxants act through the central nervous system. Intravenous administration reduces muscle spasms from physical trauma or inflammation, but it can produce flaccidity. Taking the drugs orally seems to be safer, but much larger doses are required. All muscle relaxants have some sedative action even at ordinary doses. Sedation can be useful if the muscle tension is anxiety-induced, but the performer may prefer a clear mind.

HERBS TO RELAX THE MUSCLES

Kava (Piper methysticum) relaxes the skeletal muscles, gently tones the digestive system, and alleviates rheumatism. I haven't seen studies on the prolonged use of kava by performers/athletes, but the stories from both users and practitioners are extremely encouraging. To illustrate the problems of evaluating a herb with both a long folkloric history and a fair amount of research behind it, there is a more extensive study of kava in appendix 2.

CHEMISTRY: The active constituents are a group of pyrones called methysticin, dihydromethysticin kawain, dihydro-kawain, yangonin, and desmethoxyyangonin. These work better as a group than singly, and other constituents present in smaller quantities may increase their effectiveness.

TOXICITY: Kava was originally the basis for an intoxicating beverage. Scientists disagree about the effect of the brew on mental capacities but report no adverse mental effects (or any noticeable mental effects) when the herb is taken in therapeutic quantities to relax the muscles. It may, however, produce local anesthesia and inhibit the tonic stretch reflex.

Achyrocline satureioides is mentioned here only because it has a kava-pyrone in the leaves.

CHEMISTRY: The pyrone is called 6-(4'-Hydroxy-trans-styryl)-4-methoxy-2-Pyrone.

Cramp bark (Viburnum opulus) is an antispasmodic which relieves many conditions, from intestinal cramps to asthma. The Merck Index lists it as a uterine antispasmodic.

CHEMISTRY: Cramp bark contains valerianic acid, aucubin glycosides, saponins, coumarins, and cyanogenetic glycosides.

TOXICITY: Coumarin was a flavoring agent until banned by the FDA for its unfavorable reactions with a number of drugs.

Black cohosh or snake root (Cimicifuga racemosa) relieves chronic rheumatism but is primarily taken for menstrual cramps, since some of its constituents seem to exhibit endocrine activity. It appears today in the Japanese pharmacopeia.

CHEMISTRY: Cimifugin is considered the active principle of black cohosh. The herb also contains racemosin, tannin, isoferulic acid, triterpine glycosides including saponins, and a volatile oil.

TOXICITY: Black cohosh is not considered highly toxic. Spoerke reports mild nausea and vomiting, though the herb can relieve indigestion. Other possible side effects include vertigo and tremors.

Lady's slipper or **American valerian (Cypripedium bulbosum, C. pubescens)** is an antispasmodic, as well as a remedy for "excitability." The Merck Index lists it as a sedative.

CHEMISTRY: Lady's slipper contains a volatile oil and a volatile acid, as well as a bitter glycosidal principle.

TOXICITY: Those who are harvesting their own herbs should note that lady's slipper can cause a poison ivy-like rash.

Skullcap (Scutellaria lateriflora) alleviates hiccoughs, insomnia, and general nervous disorders.

CHEMISTRY: The effects of skullcap may be due to scutellarin.

TOXICITY: Although skullcap is considered a relaxant, Spoerke reports that large doses produce central nervous system stimulation, irregular pulse, hyperreflexia, confusion and giddiness.

Grindelia or **Gumweed** or **California gum plant (Grindelia spp.)** acts on both nerves and muscles, so it relieves asthma and bronchitis and is also a mild sedative. It is listed in the Belgian and French pharmacopeias. According to Martindale's, it "has been stated to exert a spasmolytic effect."

CHEMISTRY: The active components of grindelia may be in the unsaturated cyclic acids of its amorphous balsamic resins, though there are also grindelol, tannins, robustic acid, and possibly alkaloids and saponins.

TOXICITY: The resins are excreted in the urine, so human toxicity is rare. In animals, large doses produce drowsiness, high blood pressure, and decreased heart rate. The plant can accumulate toxic amounts of selenium.

Henbane (Hyoscyamus niger) can be taken in small doses for asthma, whooping cough, control of urinary and intestinal spasms, pain control, and insomnia. The Merck Index lists it as a smooth-muscle relaxant and sedative. It is found in about 15 pharmacopeias throughout the world.

CHEMISTRY: Henbane contains the two alkaloids hyoscyamine and scopolamine. In the mature plant the ratio of these is 3:1, while in younger plants it is smaller. (Trease lists the principal alkaloids as hyoscyamine and hyoscine.)

TOXICITY: Henbane acts similarly to belladonna, though it is somewhat weaker, and the higher amounts of hyoscine make it less likely to produce cerebral excitement. Gosselin considers hyoscyamine extremely toxic, as toxic to the central nervous system as atropine, the toxic agent in belladonna. Henbane is very toxic in doses as small as 20 grams of the raw plant. Symptoms include dilated pupils, increased heart rate, dryness of the mouth, urinary retention, and delirium. In Turkey, children eat henbane as part of a game. Sometimes the resultant intoxication is fatal.

Jersey tea or **red root (Ceanothus americanus)** is an antispasmodic which has also been recommended for "despondency and melancholy." It may decrease blood pressure.

CHEMISTRY: Jersey tea contains ceanothic, succinic, oxalic, malonic, orthophosphoric, and pyrophosphoric acids, and three alkaloids.

TOXICITY: Jersey tea is the main ingredient in a drug which increases blood coagulability.

Rue (Ruta graveolens) is a smooth muscle relaxant which can relieve "hysteria." It is said to remove deposits from the tendons and joints, particularly the joints of the wrists, and to have anti-inflammatory and antihistaminic properties.

CHEMISTRY: Rue contains a number of alkaloids and is the plant in which the bioflavonoid, rutin, was first discovered. (The family rutaceae also includes the citrus fruits.) Its anti-inflammatory and antihistaminic properties may be due to the presence of arborinine and furanocoumarins.

TOXICITY: Rue has caused miscarriage, and external application (as a wasp repellent) has resulted in redness, itching, and edema.

Sage (Salvia officinalis) is an antispasmodic which relieves muscle cramps and decreases salivation.

CHEMISTRY: The antispasmodic effects of sage are probably due to the constituents of its oil. It also contains the antioxidants, labiatic and carnosic acid.

TOXICITY: In large doses, sage can dry out the mouth, but otherwise it seems to have no side effects.

Virginia snake root (Aristolochia serpentaria) or Texas snake root (A. reticulata) increases circulation and soothes upset stomach. It is a nerve stimulant which relieves depression and exhaustion. A related species, **A. mollissima** may have anti-inflammatory properties.

CHEMISTRY: Virginia snake root contains the bitter principle serpentaria and a volatile oil with esters of borneol and terpene.

TOXICITY: Large doses can produce nausea. The aristolochic acid is thought to be carcinogenic.

Lobelia or Indian tobacco (Lobelia inflata) is found in about 10 pharmacopeias throughout the world. It appears in many herbal formulas in small quantities, to assist the other ingredients. It stimulates the autonomic ganglia and then depresses them, acting similarly to nicotine, and is an ingredient in lozenges for those who are trying to quit smoking, though Martindale questions its effectiveness in this application.

CHEMISTRY: Lobelia's action is primarily due to a piperidine alkaloid named lobeline, as well as to about 14 less active minor alkaloids, including lobelidine, lobelanine, and lobelanidine.

TOXICITY: Lobelia is one of today's most controversial herbs. Many herbalists consider it a great regulator of the autonomic nervous system, calling it "the thinking herb" for its apparent ability to know where it is needed. Others warn that it is highly poisonous, though there seem to be no problems with toxicity in the quantities found in commercially available combinations. The lobelia controversy reveals much about how accepted practice evolves.

LOBELIA: a controversial herb

Samuel Thompson lived in the beginning of the nineteenth century, a time of struggle between the doctors whose methods foreshadowed today's medical techniques, and other healers who preferred natural botanicals and more traditional methods. Thompson belonged to the latter group, and one of his favorite herbs was lobelia, a herb with a long and venerable history. When taken by itself in sufficient quantities, this herb induces vomiting (its popular name was pukeweed). Thompson considered this purging a healthy way to get toxins out of the body. He said that after throwing up, his patients felt that the herb had done them a great deal of good. Thompson was accused of killing one of his patients with this cure. According to Kloss, "the Judge was favorably disposed to the prosecution," but there was no evidence of any deaths, so Thompson was acquitted. His supporters claimed that neighboring doctors were jealous of his successes or believed that only a poison could heal so effectively.

Some modern herbalists believe that lobelia is safe in any amount, and that its purgative effect always leads to improved health. One herbalist went so far as to challenge a doctor to match him dose for dose in strychnine — perhaps it is fortunate that the challenge was declined. Today many herbalists consider the Thompsonian use of lobelia to be abuse. While most of them don't claim any first-hand knowledge of ill effects, Moore cites the case of one "genial addlepate" who showed up at the hospital with respiratory failure after taking massive amounts. He says, "The presumption that the patient should puke his or her brains out and then take even more Lobelia is past my understanding." Even Kloss says of the emetic treatment, "There are many conditions under which this treatment ought not to be administered ... none but an experienced Botanic Practitioner ... should undertake the use of the treatment."

At even larger doses, lobelia has extremely serious effects: at some point, if the user can manage to keep taking it, it depresses spinal cord function. Hutchens refers to the state of complete muscular paralysis as the "alarm," and says that it is not dangerous, except that any poisons administered at this time

---

(LOBELIA: a controversial herb)

are quickly absorbed. Others say that it causes fatal medullary and respiratory depression and convulsions. Grieve says that excessive doses have the effects of a "powerful acro-narcotic poison, producing great depression, cold sweats, and possibly death." Mrs. C.F. Leyel, her editor, interrupts at this point to say that herbalists "deny that it has poisonous properties and that it has ever caused death."

No problems have been observed with the small amounts of lobelia commonly found in herbal formulas. Due to the dangers of very large doses, lobelia has been listed as a poison in the United States Pharmacopea and the American Dispensatory. Many herbalists call it dangerous without specifying quantities and combinations. Lust says it is toxic. Hutchens says it is not a poison, but says it gives only temporary relief and must be used carefully, lest it do "as much harm as good." Meyers says it "is too dangerous for internal use by the unskilled," and should be administered only by those "who are best acquainted with its properties." Grieve warns that even external application is dangerous, as absorption through the skin may be sufficient to produce toxicity. Whether any of these claims are from first-hand experience is not clear. Even Moore gives only a single example without elaborating on the circumstances surrounding it. On the other side are practitioners like Christopher, who considered lobelia a staple in his work.

Is lobelia toxic? In large enough doses, of course it is, like any substance. Is it safe in the small quantities found in most herbal combinations? It certainly seems that way. Lobelia in these combinations is probably as safe as any herb in the hands of an experienced practitioner.

Licorice (Glycyrrhiza glabra) (see Chapter 11, blood sugar) may reverse the effects of coffee on the muscles by supressing the caffeine-induced release of calcium ions from the muscles.

Magnolia salicifolia and the flowers of other magnolia species have been investigated for their neuromuscular blocking action. Perry reports that the bark of the magnolia has a quieting effect, but doesn't say the same for the flowers, though

they are "taken to relieve an unpleasant full feeling in the chest."
CHEMISTRY: The dried buds contain four alkaloids which inhibit ACh-induced contraction of skeletal muscle. Some of them, e.g. yuzirine, stimulate in small doses and then inhibit in larger doses.

Origanum compactum is a species of oregano with antispasmodic properties. A related species, **O. vulgare,** relieves arthritic joints, nervous headaches, and oral inflammations.
CHEMISTRY: O. compactum contains two phenols, thymol and carvacrol, which are also found in thyme. These act in a non-competitive way to block nerve fibre conduction, with both musculotropic and neurotropic spasmolytic action.

Lippia multiflora is found in West Africa. Its muscle relaxant properties were studied by Noamesi and colleagues. Their paper gives insight into the difficulty of distinguishing between muscle relaxant and tranquilizing effects, and into the methods of overcoming these difficulties. In animal experiments, L. multiflora reduces normal blood pressure by dilating the blood vessels. It is a local muscle relaxant and may also affect the central nervous system. It inhibits the effect of amphetamine on motor activity but does not enhance the effects of barbiturates on sleeping time: this suggests to the authors that the decrease in motor activity is not caused by sedative action. The plant does seem to be calming, but perhaps only because it relaxes the muscles.

A HERB FOR STRETCHING THE LIGAMENTS

Turmeric (Curcuma longa) is used in India for stretching the ligaments.
CHEMISTRY: Turmeric contains viscid and volatile oils, a pungent resin, and the yellow coloring agent curcumin, as well as gums and starches.

A HERB FOR SORE MUSCLES

Cayenne (Capsicum annuum, C. minimum) regulates the circulation, closing capillaries to increase blood pressure or stop a hemorrhage, or opening them to reduce blood pressure or warm up the extremities. Taken about half an hour before a performance, either orally in a glass of juice or externally, sprinkled into warm-up gloves, cayenne can eliminate tension-induced coldness in the hands (see Chapter 17), but too much of the herb could make them sweat. Because of its effects on the circulation, some herbalists recommend it for sore muscles. It is also applied externally for this purpose (see Chapter 18, counterirritants) and for rheumatism, neuralgia, arthritis, chilblains, and lumbago.

CHEMISTRY: Cayenne contains capsaicin, a pungent phenol compound, as well as dihydrocapsaicin, nordihydrocapsaicin, and homocapsaicin.

TOXICITY: Cayenne can irritate the eyes, skin, or mucous membranes, creating a burning sensation without blistering. Though some herbalists use it to heal gastric ulcers, most would not recommend it in cases of ulcers or bowel irritation.

HERBS TO STRENGTHEN MUSCLES

Ginseng (Panax ginseng) increases muscle tone, stimulates the heart and midbrain, increases resistance to stress, supports metabolic functions, detoxifies the body, stimulates the central nervous system and adrenal cortex, and increases the capacity for both mental and physical work. It is extremely popular and has been widely researched (see also Chapter 15, saponin-containing herbs).

CHEMISTRY: Ginseng contains a number of saponins, called ginsenosides by the Japanese and panaxosides by the Russians.

TOXICITY: Females who take Panax ginseng over an extended time can develop secondary male sexual characteristics. Since it detoxifies the body, too much ginseng can produce flu-like symptoms (see Chapter 11, healing crisis).

Lady's mantle (Alchemilla vulgaris) relieves many conditions arising from weak muscles. It is often combined with **Shepherd's purse (Capsella bursa pastoris).**

HERBS FOR THE NERVES

Passion flower (Passiflora incarnata, P. caerulea) has a long folk history as a tea for calming the nerves, as well as relieving headaches and insomnia. The Merck Index lists it as a sedative and analgesic, and Martindale says it is "reputed to have antispasmodic and sedative properties."

CHEMISTRY: Passion flower contains the alkaloids harmine, harman, harmol, and harmaline, as well as cyanogenic glycosides. It seems to depress spinal cord activity while increasing the respiratory rate.

TOXICITY: There have been no reports of toxicity, though Spoerke says as little as 200 mg of harmaline could cause serious symptoms. Gosselin reports no human or animal poisonings and considers the fruit edible, though unknown principles in the herb depress motor activity, increase respiration rate, and temporarily lower blood pressure. Gosselin does say harman is toxic when injected into rabbits but adds that it has been safely given to humans in doses of up to 600 mg.

Calamus or sweet flag (Acorus calamus) (see Chapter 14) appears in about half a dozen European pharmacopeias as a remedy for "hysteria" and insanity.

CHEMISTRY: The alpha-asasrone in calamus is tranquilizing, sedative, and spasmolytic. Studies have shown the essential oil of calamus to be effective against histamine-induced muscle spasms, though its effectiveness increases as its beta-asarone content decreases. The herb also contains sterol bodies.

TOXICITY: Calamus may cause drowsiness.

Catnip (Nepeta cataria) is a mild central nervous system stimulant and antispasmodic which relieves insomnia.

CHEMISTRY: Catnip contains nepeta lactone, nepetalic acid, and tannin.

TOXICITY: There is no reported or suspected toxicity from catnip.

Celery (Apium graveolens) seeds are antispasmodic and sedative and may relieve rheumatism. Since they are antispasmodic, there is a British Standard Specification for Celery Oil, published by the British Standards Institution.

CHEMISTRY: The volatile oil contains limonene, alpha- and beta-pinene, myrcene, cis-beta-ocimene, gamma-terpinene, cis-allo-ocimene, trans-farnessene, humulene, apiol, beta-selinene, senkyunolide, and neocnidilide.

TOXICITY: I once saw celery itself on a list of foods that may induce sleep; however, there is no reported toxicity for the seeds.

Chamomile (Anthemis nobilis) (see Chapter 14, digestion, and Chapter 15, other anti-inflammatory herbs) is also a nervine and relieves muscle cramps.

CHEMISTRY: Apigenin and chamazulene are probably the constituents responsible for the spasmolytic properties of chamomile. Its other constituents include anthemic acid, anthesterol, and anthemene, while **Matricaria** (German chamomile) contains matricarin.

Cow parsnip or **Hogweed (Heracleum sphondylium, H. lanatum)** has been used as a sedative.

TOXICITY: There is no reported toxicity.

Wild lettuce (Lactuca spp.) is a sedative with a long history as a soporific.

CHEMISTRY: Wild lettuce may contain hyoscyamine, which has a soporific effect. Other constituents include lactucin, lactucerol, latucic acid, and mannite.

TOXICITY: In therapeutic amounts it appears to be non-toxic, though cattle poisoning has been reported after ingestion of large amounts of the immature plants of L. Scarioa. Gosselin reports that farm animals who eat a lot of it have dyspnea and weakness, but says the "dried extracts are believed to be non-toxic."

Peruvian bark (Cinchona spp.) (see Chapters 14 and 15) is a nervous system tonic primarily used for malaria.

HERBS TO INDUCE SLEEP

Valerian or garden heliotrope (Valeriana officinalis) is said by some herbalists to be sedative when a person is agitated, and a stimulant when the person is fatigued, though it does seem to induce sleep. The Merck Index lists it as a sedative. It has been used for insomnia, nervous unrest, and hysteria for at least 1000 years and is popular in Europe as both a calming and a sleep-inducing herb. It may lower blood pressure. It is in at least twenty pharmacopeias world-wide. Most people find its odor extremely unpleasant, though oddly enough valerian is quite important in the perfume industry. If you are taking valerian to calm the nerves before a stressful performance, see the accompanying box.

CHEMISTRY: Valerian's active contituents are a number of epoxy-iridoid esters called valepotriates, including valtrate, didrovaltrate, acevaltrate, and isovaleroxyhydroxydidrovaltrate, which have a mild tranquilizing effect. It also has a volatile oil which contributes to the sedative action, containing esters including bornyl isovalerianate, bornyl acetate, bornyl formate, eugenyl isovalerate, isoeugenyl isovalerate.

TOXICITY: There seems to be no toxicity at therapeutic doses, though very large doses can cause headaches and vomiting. Gosselin says injections are moderately toxic but report no known human poisonings with oral doses. According to Tyler, valerian is safer than those synthetic tranquilizers which interact with alcohol and barbiturates, since it has no synergistic effect with either of these. Hendricks, however, found that mice on valerenic acid and pentobarbital developed hangovers, while those on either substance alone did not. Some people habituate to valerian and have to switch to other herbs to get the same effect.

VALERIAN: a herbal sleeping pill?

In spite of extensive research, it is not clear which of valerian's many constituents are the active ones. Each substance has unique effects when studied in isolation, but studying them in this way is reminiscent of the blind men investigating the elephant. Hendriks gives a good summary of the history of valerian research, with further references for those who want to pursue this topic. The author himself chose to investigate the valerenic acid component and found that it had central nervous system depressive and/or spasmolytic properties, while the other sesquiterpenoid constituents, e.g. valerenolic acid, acetylvalerenolic acid, valeranone, cryptofauronol, and patchouli-alcohol did not.

Leathwood studied the effect on sleep of an aqueous extract of valerian. This extract is missing at least one possibly-active class of constituents, the valepotriate esters, which are insoluble in water. He relied on subjective reports and activity meters attached to the wrist, rather than on EEG readings, because the EEG is so invasive that those who suffer from insomnia are not likely to volunteer for experiments. He found that 450 mg of valerian reduced the time it took a group of volunteers to fall asleep. Doubling the dose made no further difference, but the experimenters note that the lower dose itself induced sleep very quickly. He did not try smaller doses. Subjects who normally had no problem falling asleep showed no measurable change upon taking valerian, though the herb improved the subjective quality of their sleep. At 450 mg it produced no "hangover" the next morning and was free of any other reported side effects, but at 900 mg, subjects reported feeling sleepy the next morning. There was no "carry-over" effect after a single night's dose, i.e. the quality and latency of sleep on a subsequent night without valerian was back to the subject's usual level. Some sleeping pills have a "rebound" effect, i.e. their sleep-inducing effect is short-lasting, and the user has an extra restless sleep pattern later in the night. Valerian's effect is also short-lasting (about a quarter of the night), but there seems to be no rebound effect. The authors conclude that valerian is a promising alternative to the common sleeping pills.

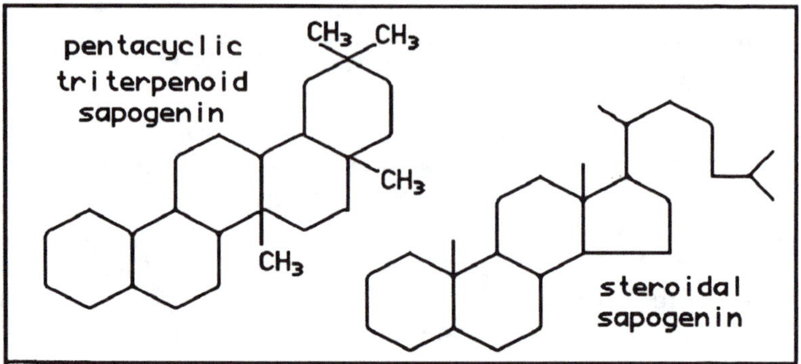

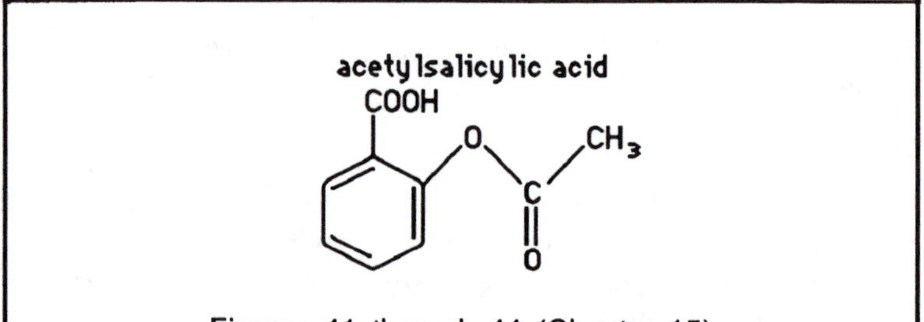

pentacyclic
triterpenoid
sapogenin

CH₃ CH₃

CH₃

CH₃

steroidal
sapogenin

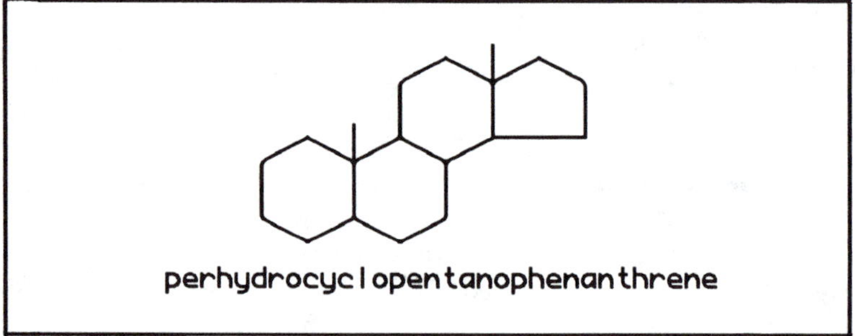

perhydrocyclopentanophenanthrene

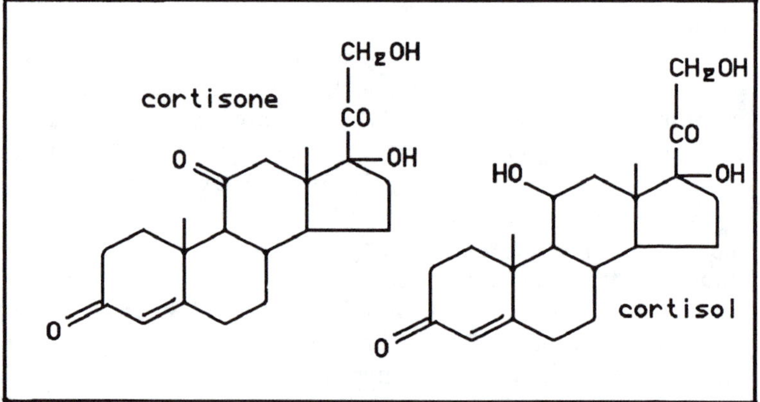

cortisone

CH₂OH

CO

O

OH

O

CH₂OH

CO

HO

OH

O

cortisol

acetylsalicylic acid

COOH

O

CH₃

C

O

Figures 41 through 44 (Chapter 15)

Chapter 17

MORE HERBS FOR THE PERFORMER:
respiration, voice, eyes, ears, memory, blood sugar, energy, and warm hands

HERBS FOR THE RESPIRATORY TRACT

Many respiratory tract problems are compounded by food allergies, Candida, or eating too many mucus-forming foods, e.g. dairy and flour products. Herbs can open the bronchials and lungs and heal damaged mucous membranes, while you reform your diet.

Ma huang (Ephedra sinica) has been used in Chinese medicine for over 5,000 years. It is related to the North American herb, **Mormon tea (Ephedra nevadensis)**, but many herbalists consider ma huang the more effective of the two. In Chinese *ma* means astringent and *huang* means yellow, a possible reference to the color of mucus for which the herb is recommended. It is commonly used to treat asthma and is also considered an anti-inflammatory agent. Mormon tea is a folk remedy for VD and can also relieve rheumatism.

CHEMISTRY: Both ma huang and Mormon tea may contain ephedrine, but ma huang has more. (Tyler says that Mormon tea has none at all, the Merck Index says it has little or none, Martindale lists it as a constituent without comment, and Morton says that none of the ten species of Ephedra found in North America have therapeutic alkaloids.) Ma huang also has pseudoephedrine, which may be lacking in Mormon tea. (Martindale says it has both). Shiu-Ying lists the constituents of ma huang as l-ephedrine, d-pseudo ephedrine, l-N-Methyl-ephedrine, p-pseudo-methyl-ephedrine, l-nor-ephedrine, and d-nor pseudo-ephedrine. It is possible that not all the constituents of ma huang have been discovered: a new alkaloid was found in the roots as recently as 1984, and two new anti-inflammatory agents were reported in 1985.

Pseudoephedrine works best on the upper respiratory tract, while ephedrine is best for the lower. Ephedrine raises blood pressure, but the roots of ma huang contain ephedradines, which tend to lower it. Pseudoephedrine raises blood pressure in large doses, but in small doses it dilates the blood vessels. In small doses, unlike ephedrine, it seems to act directly on the smooth muscles, whereas in large doses both stimulate the sympathetic nerve endings.

TOXICITY: Ma huang has been used as a cocaine substitute, resulting in at least one emergency room admission. According to Martindale, large and repeated doses of ma huang can produce giddiness, headache, thirst, nausea, palpitations, insomnia, tremor, anxiety complex, and bladder irritation. Shiu-Ying advises against taking ma huang for shortness of breath accompanied by profuse perspiration. The British Pharmaceutical Codex says that pseudoephedrine is less likely to cause the unwanted side-effects found with ephedrine.

EPHEDRINE AS A DRUG

Ephedrine is an alkaloid which was isolated in 1885. Early animal experiments involved toxic doses, so the therapeutic properties were not discovered until 1923. Ephedrine can be produced commercially by extracting it from ma huang, but it is also made chemically, in the form of L-ephedrine, essentially free of the D-isomer. The process produces an undesirable by-product, benzyl alcohol.

Ephedrine produces effects similar to the adrenal hormone, epinephrine (adrenaline), but longer-lasting, and it has the advantage that it can be taken by mouth. It is a nervous stimulant which was banned at the 1976 Montreal Olympics. Moderate doses raise blood pressure, constrict blood vessels, increase the heart rate, strengthen the heart beat, and relieve bronchial spasm, generally within half an hour. It relieves other respiratory tract symptoms, in particular those associated with whooping cough, without influencing the course of the infection. It also increases the depth of respiration and dilates the bronchi, especially when they are in spasm.

TOXICITY: Ephedrine is not considered habit-forming, and its effects are not cumulative, but after a few days patients may stop responding. It will regain its effectiveness after a week's

---

(EPHEDRINE AS A DRUG)

break. Large doses can cause nervousness, headache, insomnia, dizziness, palpitations, skin flushing, tingling and numbing in the extremities, nausea, vomiting, and possibly brief angina. It may also produce a dermatological reaction.

Ma huang contains compounds, e.g. pseudoephedrine and ephedradines, which balance the effects of ephedrine. It seems likely that the drug is more effective in emergencies and that the herb is preferable in chronic conditions. On the other hand, the herb has been successful with acute asthma, and the British Pharmaceutical Codex recommends that for cardiac stimulation ephedrine be mixed with pseudoephedrine, to balance vasoconstriction and increased coronary circulation.

Goldenseal (Hydrastis canadensis) (see Chapter 14, stomach) is known as the "King of the Mucous Membranes." It appears in many formulas for the respiratory system, and is an antibiotic which facilitates white blood cell production. Take it as a snuff for nasal congestion.

CHEMISTRY: Goldenseal contains the alkaloids hydrastine, berberine, and canadine.

TOXICITY: The metabolism of goldenseal requires B vitamins which must be replaced in the diet.

With prolonged use, the white blood cell count could become too high, and this effect could be particularly problematic in arthritis. Spoerke says large amounts can be fatal. Gosselin rates hydrastine as extremely toxic, with lethal doses of the isolated compound 30 times as great as therapeutic doses. Interestingly, an early sign of toxicity can be irritation of the throat.

Mullein (Verbascum thapsus) is a *demulcent* which is primarily effective for lung problems rather than upper respiratory conditions. It is found in about half a dozen European pharmacopeias.

TOXICITY: There are no reports of toxicity.

Plantain or **ribwort (Plantago lanceolata)** is included in many herbal formulas for respiratory problems. English plantain, or common plantain (**P. major**), relieves coughs and lung problems.

HERBS FOR THE VOICE

Take respiratory herbs for raw or sore throat or excess mucus. Try the following herbs to relieve laryngitis or improve the voice.

Bayberry (Myrica spp.) or **wax myrtle** improves the voice and clears the mind. It is an *astringent* herb which forms the basis of an old Western cold remedy and "cure-all," Composition Powder. It cleanses the digestive tract, liver, and mucous membranes.
CHEMISTRY: The root bark is considered the most therapeutic part of the bayberry plant. It contains volatile oils, tannins, astringent resins, and a saponin-like acid.

Cardamom (Elettaria cardamomum) relieves hoarseness and reduces the mucus-forming tendency of milk. Like the other aromatic spices, it reduces flatulence.
CHEMISTRY: Cardamom seeds have a volatile oil containing terpenes, terpineol, and cineol. They also contain potassium chloride and an acrid resin. Potassium chloride (KaliMur) tissue salts (see Chapter 19) reduce inflammation of the mucous membranes, after the acute stage, when the mucus is greyish-white.

Marshmallow root (Althea officinalis), recommended for for laryngitis, is a soothing *demulcent* and *expectorant* which moderates the harshness of other therapeutic herbs.
CHEMISTRY: Marshmallow roots contain calcium phosphate, pectin, asparagin, and starch and sugar. Calcium phosphate (CalcPhos) tissue salts (see Chapter 19) can reverse a tendency toward catarrh and frequent colds.

HERBS FOR THE EYES

Does reading music under poor lighting conditions and the stress of rehearsal strain your eyes? Try these herbs as eye drops. They also alleviate a number of other eye problems.

Eyebright (Euphrasia officinalis) improves eyesight, heals black eyes, conjunctivitis, and styes, and can retard or even reverse cataracts.
CHEMISTRY: Eyebright is somewhat astringent, due to what Spoerke calls an "unusual" tannin. It also contains a volatile oil which is said to strengthen and soothe many parts of the eyes.
TOXICITY: There are no reports of toxicity.

Goldenseal (see Chapter 14, stomach, and respiration, above) is an effective eyewash for eye inflammation. It is sometimes combined with eyebright to relieve eyestrain.
CHEMISTRY: Berberine may be the component that eases eyestrain.

Maria Treben recommends **Swedish Bitters** for eyestrain and other eye problems.

The **garden carrot** has been recommended for weak eyes, not only for its beta carotene content, but as a blood cleanser.

HERBS FOR THE EARS

Ear problems can range from temporary hearing loss (due to a cold) to permanent hearing loss (due to a noisy work environment). Herbs are no substitute for ear plugs, or for a good night's sleep, for that matter.

Coltsfoot or **coughwort (Tussilago farfara)** is a cough remedy ("antitussive"), especially for smokers' cough. Put drops into the ears for earache.
TOXICITY: When administered internally, the flowers have been linked with cancer in rats.

Lobelia (Lobelia inflata) (see Chapter 16) is used in eardrops to stop earaches.

The *Chinese Medical Journal* reports that thin slices of **garlic** can repair **perforated ear drums**.

Swedish Bitters has been recommended for recovering hearing loss and remedying buzzing in the ears.

HERBS FOR THE MEMORY

Forgot you had a gig? Can't remember the notes? A total program of memory improvement might include aerobics, slant board exercises (Chapter 3), elimination of food allergens (Chapter 11), vitamin or mineral supplementation, quitting smoking, and the following herbs.

Kola (Cola nitida), an ingredient in a number of "refreshing" soft drinks, improves the memory. Chewing the seeds decreases fatigue.

CHEMISTRY: Kola contains caffeine and theobromine, as well as the tannoids catechol, and epicatechol. Theobromine may increase oxygen supply to the brain. The tannoids are diuretics which stimulate the nervous system.

TOXICITY: Kola is considered low in toxicity, though in large or prolonged doses it might generate nervousness, insomnia, increased heart rate, strange "highs," or aggravation of a peptic ulcer.

Gotu kola (Centella asiatica) (see Chapter 15) is a name that seems to apply to a number of herbs, including **kola**. In India the term gotu kola refers to a herb named **brahmi**, which may be C. asiatica, or a totally different genus, **Herpestis monnieri**, or perhaps yet another genus, **Hydrocotyle asiatica**. H. monnieri relieves rheumatism, while H. asiatica relieves nervous disorders and senility. Gotu kola is found in a number of commercial preparations intended to increase mental energy. Unfortunately the Latin name is not always given, so it could be one of the four herbs which have been referred to by the common name, or yet another herb not even listed.

C. asiatica is considered a specific remedy for the nervous system and the brain, stimulating the mind, improving the memory, and moderating stress responses. Some herbalists find it so versatile that it is like a whole pharmacy in itself.

Ginkgo biloba has been used in Chinese medicine for at least 5,000 years. It relieves short term memory loss, inattentiveness, and ringing in the ears, improves both peripheral and cerebral circulation, and prevents abnormal blood clotting. It is an antioxidant and is considered a quick remedy for the common cold, asthma, and sinus congestion.

CHEMISTRY: Ginkgo improves ATP synthesis and cellular glucose uptake. It contains terpenes, flavonoids, proanthocyanidins, and flavoglycosides (ginkgo heterosides). Ginkgoide B has been proposed as a treatment for Alzheimer's.

TOXICITY: Though ginkgo can cause mild gastrointestinal upset and headache, it is not considered toxic and is not addictive.

Ginseng (Panax ginseng) is used to treat forgetfulness and nervous disorders. As a brain sedative, it can quiet psychopaths. It is covered in more detail under herbs for energy (below).

Epidmedium sagittatum, and **E. grandiflorum** are Chinese cures for forgetfulness. They are also considered antirheumatic.

Calamus or **sweet flag (Acorus calamus)** (see Chapters 14, stomach, and 16, nerves) combats memory loss by promoting cerebral circulation and is combined with gotu kola (H. asiatica) to promote clarity of mind.

HERBS WHICH STABILIZE BLOOD SUGAR

Blood sugar swings are hard on the performer (see Chapter 11). A program to regulate blood sugar should include aerobics, nutritional support, and herbs to tone the pancreas, liver, and adrenals while stabilizing glucose levels.

Licorice (Glycyrrhiza glabra) (see Chapter 15) has been a Western remedy since Roman times and is an old and versatile Chinese remedy which balances the immune system, stabilizes blood sugar, and builds muscle and bones. Despite its sweet taste, it will not induce blood sugar swings. Since it can also reduce inflammation, it could play an important role in a program for someone with arthritis complicated by low blood sugar. It also supports the adrenals and the liver, two organs which are often under stress in low blood sugar syndrome. It is a *demulcent* which may relieve ulcers and sore throat (chew the root). It also has mild *spasmolytic* and estrogenic properties.

CHEMISTRY: Licorice contains glycyrrhizic acid, a glycoside of glycyrrhetic acid, which has a structure similar to the steroidal saponins, and which gives it properties similar to those of the mineralocorticoids of the adrenal cortex. The sweet taste comes from glycyrrhizin.

TOXICITY: Licorice toxicity has been widely discussed in the medical literature. The mineralocorticoid properties can cause sodium retention and potassium loss, and anyone already on a restricted fruit regimen for low blood sugar may need supplements. If the electrolyte imbalance is not corrected, licorice can aggravate high blood pressure. Martindale gives an unusually large amount of space to anecdotes about licorice overdose. The isolated cases reported there include one person who ate 1.8 kg of licorice per week for an unspecified time, and another who ate "excessive" (unspecified) amounts for several years. Another account tells of 14 volunteers who ate 100 to 200 g every day for four weeks. In all cases, the symptoms were completely reversed when licorice consumption was stopped. Sometimes the problem was traced to licorice candy, though Gosselin states that the candy rarely has rarely more than two percent licorice extract. Gosselin also reports that eating 30 to 40 g of licorice candy a day can cause electrolyte imbalance, leading to edema, paresis, tetany, and convulsions. All symptoms are reversed when licorice intake is stopped, and potassium supplementation speeds recovery.

Guar gum (Cyamopsis tetragonolobus), a commercial thickening agent and binder, tends to correct blood sugar levels. Its mucilage content makes it a bulk-forming laxative. Its colloidal properties and a high fiber content make it a good cleanser.

Cedar berry (Juniperus monospermum) is not to be confused with J. communis, or juniper, the diuretic herb mentioned under blood cleansers. Cedar berries regulate insulin production.

Since it is important to strengthen the pancreas, adrenals, and liver while regulating the interim blood sugar levels, a herbal combination is generally preferable to single herbs. One such formula contains **cedar berries, uva ursi, licorice root, mullein leaves,** and **cayenne pepper.**

HERBS FOR ENERGY

The factors which can rob you of energy range from poor nutrition to adrenal stress. A program for raising energy levels should include diet, exercise, herbs, and stress reduction.

Ginseng (Panax ginseng, P. quinquefolium) (see Chapters 15 and 16) is one of the most popular herbs for raising energy levels. Though we think of it as an oriental herb, it has been exported from the United States to Hong Kong since the early 1700s. It is considered an adaptogen, i.e. a substance which helps the whole body resist stress of all types. It enhances brain function and memory, regulates blood pressure, restores hearing, increases visual and auditory acuity, increases stamina, and improves reflex action. It can relieve rheumatism, diabetes, anemia, and chronic cough, and has been used in place of tranquilizers.

CHEMISTRY: Ginseng glycosides dilate the blood vessels in the muscles, and increase the contractility of the heart. Though ginseng alone doesn't affect adrenal ascorbic acid (vitamin C) levels, when the body is under stress, ginseng speeds both depletion and restoration of the levels. It may stimulate glycolysis in the liver and kidneys under both aerobic and anaerobic conditions without significantly increasing oxygen consumption, and facilitate muscle tone by affecting the use of ATP. The brain works most efficiently in the aerobic cycle, but with age, the cerebral metabolism is changed to an anaerobic cycle with its burden of lactate production. Ginseng seems to reverse this process.

Ginseng contains a number of triterpenoid saponins, grouped as ginsenosides, panaxosides, and chikusetsusaponins. Panax acid stimulates the heart and general metabolism, panaquilin stimulates internal secretions, panacen and sapogenin stimulate the central nervous system, ginsenin decreases blood sugar, and panaxin stimulates the midbrain, heart, and circulatory system. Ginseng also contains vitamins A, B₁, B₂, B₃, B₁₂, C, E, and calcium and phosphorus.

TOXICITY: There are no reported cases of ginseng overdose, but some Western physicians report toxicity from long term use, "ginseng-abuse syndrome." Symptoms which have been observed include chronic insomnia, nervousness, loose stools, skin eruptions, edema, low blood pressure, and either CNS excitation or tranquilizing effects. (Those who exhibited these symptoms were also regular coffee drinkers.) In one instance, abrupt withdrawal has produced low blood pressure, weakness and tremor. Siegel suggests that the symptoms mimic those of corticosteroid poisoning.

Since ginseng increases androgen production, most women should not take it over a long time. A related herb, **Siberian ginseng (Eleutherococcus senticosus)** is considered safe for both women and men. Siberian ginseng has other advantages, especially for hyperactive people or those engaged in hard physical work, who may find it better at reducing symptoms of stress, with longer-lasting effects. The constituents of Siberian ginseng, termed eleutherosides (Eleutherococcus glycosides), are similar to those of ginseng and show less seasonal variation.

HERBS WHICH WARM THE HANDS

Nervousness can make your hands cold, and if you haven't eaten all day they're likely to be even colder. Diet and exercise can improve the peripheral circulation, and pre-performance warm-ups or external heat (e.g. hot water or gloves) are also helpful. Herbs can warm the hands, whether the problem is temporary or chronic.

Cayenne (Capsicum mimimum, C. fastitiatum) (see Chapter 16), one of the most extensively researched herbs in the pharmacopeia, is found in herbal formulas for virtually any problem. It regulates the circulation, so if tension in the neck and shoulders is squeezing blood vessels shut, cayenne will open them back up. To warm the hands, put it in a pair of warm-up mitts, or drink it in water or orange juice. It is easier to swallow in capsule form, but then you have to wait for a nervous stomach to dissolve the capsule and ask that stomach to deal with a sudden burst of cayenne. (It may come as a surprise that some herbalists suggest cayenne, taken in water, as an ulcer remedy. On the other hand, cayenne in capsules is not recommended for ulcer patients.) It takes about twenty minutes to work, though the rate will vary with both the individual and the circumstances, e.g. nutritional state at that time, degree of nervousness, etc. In chronic cases, cayenne will gradually improve peripheral circulation.

CHEMISTRY: The constituents of cayenne include capsaicin, capsacutin, and capsico, a volatile alkaloid. Its effects on the circulation are well documented (e.g. Gamse and Duckles, journals).

TOXICITY: Gosselin considers cayenne moderately toxic, since it can produce irritation of mucous membranes, possibly leading to gastritis and diarrhea.

Russell and Cormarèche (journals) question whether cayenne really makes the hands warm, or whether they just feel warm — I don't know why this is so difficult to determine.

Calendula (Marigold) tea increases circulation to the hands. Drink one to two cups of the tea daily for a week to ten days.

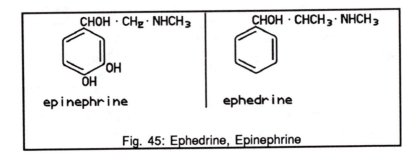

Fig. 45: Ephedrine, Epinephrine

Chapter 18

EXTERNAL APPLICATIONS
herbs that heal from the outside

While you've got that warm sock on your sore arm, why not throw in some healing herbs? They'll make it smell better, and they might calm down your -itis.

Applying herbs to the skin seems like a safe way to treat strains, bruises, muscle tears, and inflammation. However, since some herbs are toxic if taken internally, the question arises of how local these local applications are, i.e. of how much of the herb gets into the blood stream, and how toxic it is. If the toxicity produces irritation of the mucous membranes of the digestive tract, rather than any effects attributable to the herb's presence in the blood stream, then the only caveat is to protect sensitive skin. (Try coating the skin with olive oil or a similar protective base before applying the herb.) Where the toxicity is systemic, e.g. with oil of wintergreen, externally applied herbs also carry some risk.

TYPES OF EXTERNAL APPLICATION

A **fomentation** is a hot tea which is strained, absorbed into a natural fibre (e.g. cotton gauze), and placed on the skin. Cover it with plastic and a towel to retain heat and moisture, and reapply as it cools.

A **poultice** is a soft, warm, semi-liquid herbal mass prepared by making the tea and throwing out the water instead of the herb. Alternatively, the herb can be bruised, mixed with a bit of water, heated, and put on a cloth. Cover the cloth with plastic to conserve moisture.

A **tincture** is a herb dissolved in something other than water, e.g. alcohol. A tincture may retain different constituents than the fomentation would. It takes about 10 to 14 days to prepare, and the solution becomes stronger with time. An alcohol or glycerine tincture can be stored a long time. Apply it like a fomentation.

COUNTERIRRITANT HERBS

The effectiveness of many these herbs may be due to the counterirritant properties of their volatile oils. Counterirritants produce an inflammatory reaction of their own, and create a sensation of warmth, which is relayed via the afferent nerves to the cerebrospinal axis and from there to the efferent vasomotor fibers supplying the underlying internal organ, muscle, or joint. Thus they affect every place which is innervated from the same segment of the central nervous system, increasing circulation not only at the skin but also at the site of the problem. Pain is relieved further when the sensations from the skin compete with the sensations from the injured site for a common nerve pathway. Heat (e.g. from a hot water bottle) has the same effect, as does short-wave diathermy. A counterirritant should not be applied where icing is preferred to heat. Goodman and Gilman recommend counterirritants for arthritis, bursitis, and tenosynovitis, though they say that heat lamps or packs are generally preferable to medicated plasters (e.g. mustard plasters). The mildest kind of counterirritant is called a *rubefacient*, because it makes the skin red.

Some herbs, e.g. **mustard**, need to be placed between two layers of cloth to protect the skin. After a short application some herbalists recommend washing the skin with a soothing herbal tea, e.g. **chamomile** or **mugwort**. On the other hand, the Merck Index lists German chamomile as a topical counterirritant, and Martindale suggests a poultice of chamomile flowers in the early stages of inflammation.

Black or **brown mustard (Brassica nigra, B. juncea)** is the old standby mustard plaster, a classic counterirritant. The seeds should be crushed in tepid water and wrapped in two layers of cloth just before applying to the skin.

CHEMISTRY: Mustard contains a fixed oil whose principal constituent is the glycoside sinigrin. Maceration in tepid water activates the enzyme, myrosin, which hydrolyzes sinigrin to the volatile oil, allyl isothiocyanate. The seeds also contain myrosin. **White mustard (Sinapsis alba)** contains the glucoside, sinalbin, and the enzyme, murosin. On hydrolysis these yield acrinyl isothiocyanate, which is also rubefacient but is less volatile (thus less pungent) than allyl isothiocyanate.

TOXICITY: Mustard can blister the skin if left on too long. Try coating the skin with oil first.

Cayenne (Capsicum spp.) (see Chapters 16 and 17) is an ingredient in various over-the-counter remedies, including Sloan's Liniment. The cayenne plasters sold by Chinese herbalists are inexpensive, portable, ready to use, and not messy. They may relieve **rheumatism** and **lumbago**.

CHEMISTRY: Cayenne's pungent principle consists of a phenol called capsaicin and lesser amounts of dihydrocapsaicin, nordihydrocapsaicin, homocapsaicin, and homodihydrocapsaicin. The volatile oils are capsaicine, capsacutin, and capsico.

TOXICITY: Although cayenne plasters can produce intense sensations of heat, there is seldom any blistering. According to the US Dispensatory of 1943, the absence of blisters indicates that cayenne plasters don't affect circulation, while the sensations of heat are due entirely to cayenne's effects on the the nervous system.

Arnica or **leopard's bane (Arnica montana)** tincture is a popular remedy for **strains** and **bruises,** despite Martindale's contention that in this application it is of doubtful value.

CHEMISTRY: Arnica's counterirritant effects could be due to the dimethyl ether of thymohydroquinone in its volatile oil, but they have also been attributed to the two isomeric cihydric alcohols, arnidiol (arnisterol) and faradiol. Arnica also contains arnicin and anthoxanthine.

TOXICITY: Arnica can irritate sensitive skin.

Rue (Ruta graveolens) leaves, in oil, can relieve rheumatism, arthritis, painful joints, bruises, and sprains. Martindale considers it a powerful local irritant.

TOXICITY: Rue may cause redness, itching, and edema.

Oil of wintergreen is a common **counterirritant.**

TOXICITY: It contains methyl salicylate, and even external application can lead to methyl salicylate poisoning. Gosselin considers it toxic only when put on a large area or on broken skin.

OTHER SINGLE HERBS FOR EXTERNAL APPLICATION

Tea tree (Melaleuca alternifolia) oil is an Australian antiseptic and fungicide recommended for many skin conditions, from thrush to athlete's foot. As a liniment or in a bath, it relieves the pain of **sore muscles** and **arthritis**.

CHEMISTRY: Tea tree oil contains terpenes (pinene, terpinene, and cymene), cineol, terpineol, and sesquiterpenes.

TOXICITY: Though it soothes abrasions, burns, and rashes, undiluted tea tree oil may irritate sensitive skin.

Turmeric (Curcuma longa), mixed with honey, is used in India as a poultice for **strains** and **sprains**

Tansy (Tanacetum vulgare) may relieve **joint pain** and **inflammation**.

Calamus (Acorus calamus) can be made into a paste to relieve the pain of **arthritic joints** or **headaches**.

It's stretching a point to call **apple cider vinegar** a herb, but a hot fomentation of this has been recommended for all kinds of aches, including **arthritis** and **rheumatism**.

Comfrey (Symphytum officinale) (see Chapter 15, anti-inflammatory herbs) can be applied externally to heal **wounds** and all kinds of internal injuries, including **broken bones**. Treben recommends massage with tincture of comfrey for **joint problems caused by over-exertion**.

Osha (Ligusticum porteri) was introduced by Native Americans to the Hispanic settlers in the southwestern United States. It is mixed with olive oil and applied externally to **rheumatic joints**.

Shepherd's purse (Capsella bursa-pastoris) tincture is recommended by Treben for **muscular atrophy**, as well as for hernias and other conditions indicative of a weakened muscle (see Chapter 16).

Flax or linseed oil (Linum usitatissimum) softens the skin. It is listed in the Merck Index as a topical demulcent and emollient.

Aloe vera has been recommended for **blisters** and burns.

The white juice of **dandelion,** picked in the spring or fall, can remove **warts.**

For **inflamed and deformed joints** and "**wear and tear symptoms**" Treben recommends compresses or poultices of **cabbage, horsetail,** or **cow parsnip (Heracleum sphondilium).** TOXICITY: Cow parsnip may cause dermatitis.

For **rheumatism,** Treben recommends a bath of **stinging nettle** or massage with St. **John's wort (Hypericum perforatum)** and oil of **thyme (Thymus serpyllum).**

Treben also recommends oil of **thyme** for sprains.

For **muscle cramps** Treben recommends **club moss.**

HERBAL COMBINATIONS

A commercially available formula to **increase flexibility,** provide needed nutrients to the muscles, and remove **lactates** and other toxins, combines **kava, cramp bark, ginger, lobelia, lady slipper root,** and **red clover blossoms.**

Another commercially available formula to heal **sprains** and **bruises** combines **white oak bark, comfrey, marshmallow, mullein, black walnut hulls, gravel root, wormwood, lobelia,** and **skullcap.**

A liniment for **sore muscles** can be made from equal parts **cayenne** and **arnica** tinctures. Optional additions include small amounts of **birch** and **spearmint** oils.

Zheng Gu Shui, a Chinese patent remedy based on an old private formula, is a liniment which relieves the **pain** of **arthritis, sprains,** and **sore muscles.**

Tiger Balm is a popular herbal ointment developed by two Chinese brothers for **tightness in the chest, rheumatism, strains, swelling, bruises,** and **headaches.**

A Chinese "orthopœdic tincture" for **fractures, dislocations, sprains,** and **strains** contains **Croton tiglium, Cinnamomum camphora, radix angelicae, Moghania macrophylla, Inula cappa, radix pseudoginseng, menthol,** and **camphora.**

Swedish Bitters has been used externally for **sore muscles** and **swelling.**

For **stiff joints** and **rheumatism,** try a liniment of **mullein, lobelia, white poplar bark,** and **ginger,** in olive oil.

Chapter 19

OTHER WAYS OF USING PLANTS TO HEAL:
Chinese herbs, Ayurveda, homeopathy

Most of the herbs and principles covered so far come from European or Native American herbal traditions. Western herbalists are beginning to learn from China and India, and to integrate that knowledge into their practise. Each of these herbal traditions is based on a unique way of looking at health, and the herbalist who would master them must study philosophy as well as plants.

Homeopathy was developed in Europe, though there are divergent traditions in different parts of the world. Many herbalists use homeopathy in their practice, though not all of them do so in a way which would gain the approval of a homeopath.

CHINESE HERBOLOGY

Herbs and acupuncture are the primary tools of Chinese medicine. Some excellent Chinese herbal patent remedies are sold without prescription in Canada even though the government restricts the sale of Western formulas containing the same herbs. Western herbal products are usually packaged without any indication on the label as to their therapeutic effects, because Canadian and American laws prohibit manufacturers to make any claims about a product's therapeutic abilities without extensive (and expensive) testing. An experienced herbalist can scan the ingredients and know what a given remedy is for, while the layman would have a hard time guessing. (One US company, for example, has a product called H, which stands for heart, not hemorrhoids.) In contrast, labels on Chinese herbal combinations clearly indicate their uses. It is tempting, then, to go to a Chinese herb store and buy these over-the-counter remedies.

Don't do it. A remedy may give some general directions but leave out the cautions, e.g. one arthritis remedy is best if the joints are cold rather than hot, while another remedy is better for hot joints but needs to be combined with a third herb for best results. Often it seems that the symptoms listed on the package have nothing to do with the problem the herbalist is trying to alleviate: it is quite possible to come to the doctor's office with a sore throat and leave with a remedy that has dysentery or maybe "dysintary" written on the label. Even the terms "hot" and "cold" are misleading to us. For example, it is the amount of thirst rather than the presence of fever which determines whether you have "hot" or "cold" flu and thus which herbs to take. A Chinese doctor (herbalist and acupuncturist) has had years of study, just as a Western doctor has, and in China Oriental and Western medicine are often practiced with equal status in the same hospital. The Chinese agree with Western herbalists and other therapists that herbs (and acupuncture) are more effective for chronic cases, while Western medicine ("drugs and surgery") is more effective for acute or emergency cases. In China, both methods are taken seriously by the medical establishment.

Despite recent research on traditional Chinese herbs, oriental medicine places little empasis on isolating the constituents and making drugs out of them. The concept of balance is fundamental to Chinese medicine, whether it is balance between yin and yang, energizing and suppressing, hot and cold, red and white, fast and slow, or strong and weak. Chinese herbalists feel that any herb is unbalancing in the long run, so they may suggest somewhat larger doses over a shorter term or even quite a large dose ("a pound of herbs") for a single day. A remedy may have a mixture of ingredients meant to achieve balance, or it may lean toward one side, for the patient who is obviously leaning toward the other side. Remedies can include both plant and animal material, and sometimes minerals.

A diagnosis made by a doctor of Oriental medicine (OMD) is not likely to involve a diseased organ. Instead it may go something like, "a blockage of chi in the triple heater meridian." The Chinese system is not based on cutting up cadavers, but on a system of energy meridians which run throughout the body, as well as a theory of five elements which correspond to these meridians. Foods and herbs are classified according to these elements also. The Chinese base their diagnosis on careful observation and questioning of the patient. The pulse is taken, not only for its rate and strength, as in Western medicine, but to compare adjacent pulses on the wrist for a number of qualities. Thus the OMD may not want to know whether an -itis is in the bursa or the tendon, or whether an injury comes from overuse or misuse.

An experienced practitioner might show you how to speed healing by applying pressure at the relevant pressure points (see Chapter 21).

AYURVEDA

The ayurvedic system of healing has been used in India for thousands of years. It is grounded in Indian philosophy and ideas of energy. People with chronic problems are treated according to their constitution (vatta, pitta, or kapha). Balance between the patient's constitution and a herb's is the primary consideration, and the herb's therapeutic properties are secondary. The person who prepares the herbs must be in an appropriate state of mind. Herbs are rarely prescribed singly, as formulas are thought to be more capable of bringing about balance. Because there are so many sub-classifications of herbs, e.g. taste, affinity to a body system or tissue, affinity to one of five types of life-force, etc., it is unlikely that two people with the same complaint will end up with the same remedy. By the same token, ayurveda is a system requiring careful study and should be applied only with the advice of a competent practitioner.

HOMEOPATHY

Homeopathy is a system which was developed around 1800 by the German physician, Samuel Hahnemann. It is based on the theory that like (homeo) cures like, that the substance which would in large amounts cause a symptom of malfunction (pathy), would in extremely small amounts make that symptom go away. Symptoms are considered the body's way of getting well, and homeopathy seeks to further that activity on a "vibrational" level.

The concentration of herbs in homeopathic preparations starts at about one part per 1,000 (called 3x) and gets smaller (e.g. 30x would mean one part in 10^{30}). A true homeopathic remedy is considered more potent with each further dilution. At a point where no chemist can detect a trace of the substance in question, the remedy could be quite strong indeed. A mixture of dilutions, referrred to as 3 - 200x, is sometimes preferred to a single potency.

There are a number of homeopathic products on the market aimed at the athlete. They are advertised as helping muscles to unknot, microtraumas to heal, and inflammations to recede. Don't take these without the advice of a qualified practitioner.

A homeopath takes a very careful history before suggesting a remedy, asking not only about the obvious things like pain or nausea, but also about the things which might aggravate the problem, like time of day or temperature. If two people have a sore throat and one of them finds cold water soothing while the other prefers heat, they will not end up with the same remedy. Homeopaths don't treat diseases; they treat the patient according to specific symptoms. Can the remedies be harmful if the wrong ones are taken? Not according to a chemist, since there's nothing in them in the first place. However, a homeopath would say that taking a wrong remedy complicates the task of finding the right one.

Those who are used to the precision of drug prescriptions may find it odd to have a homeopath suggest taking four to twelve pills at a time. It is the strength and frequency which matter most.

A true homeopathic remedy gets stronger in greater dilution, is "proven" by people who take the substance in full strength at mildly toxic doses and record their symptoms, and is prepared by trituration, a process more complicated than simple dilution. Some of the remedies below do not satisfy all of these criteria but are effective for reasons which are clear neither from a chemical nor a homeopathic point of view.

Arnica (see Chapter 18) is to be taken internally only in homeopathic quantities. It relieves **sprains**, **pain** and **swelling**, **muscle aches**, bruises, broken bones, and various kinds of mental or physical shock.

Rhus Toxicodendron is recommended for "stiff joints, aches or bruises aggravated by rest and humidity and improved by stretching and prolonged movement," according to a product advertisement.

Ruta Graveolens is for ligament trauma, stiffness and bruising in the limbs and joints.

Hypericum is for simple trauma associated with nerve pain and aggravated by contact or jolting.

Tissue Salts

The twelve tissue salts are mineral compounds which form the core of Dr. W. H. Schüssler's "biochemical medicine". He considered them vital to cellular renewal and administered them in homeopathic form in order to facilitate assimilation. The tissue salts aren't usually considered true homeopathic remedies, because they are made from substances which are needed by the body and could be classed as nutrients. The names of the tissue salts come from the scientific names of the elements which comprise them, e.g., KaliMur is potassium chloride. Some herbs are good sources of the tissue salts, as are a few foods. They are usually taken as part of a complete health program.

Tissue salts for **sprains** include **FerrPhos** 6x or 3 - 200x every ten minutes, until the pain and swelling begin to subside, then once an hour. Make a lotion as well, dissolving three doses in a half cup of warm water, and put it directly on the sprain (renew it as it dries). FerrPhos is found in **yellow dock, hydrangea,** and **watercress.**

For **strains,** alternate **Calcfluor** and **KaliMur,** both either at 6x or at 3 - 200x, starting at once an hour, and then every two hours as symptoms decrease. Calcfluor is found in **Irish moss** and **raspberry leaves.** KaliMur is found in **crampbark, blackhaw, echinacea,** and **burdock.**

For **swellings** of all types, it might be beneficial to take **KaliMur** by itself, every ten minutes, and then once an hour according to the severity of the symptoms.

Section IV

Chapter 20

BEYOND THE PHYSICAL PROBLEM:
the emotional side of performance injury

Remember your last Great Performance? The night you "played out of control" and yet everything worked? Why do we so rarely play like that? And why do we get injured when we try so hard?

Too often we lay our egos on the line in performance. We need to do well for the sake of our self-esteem. We sabotage ourselves long before going on stage or even into the practice room. When preparing for an "important" performance, we often bypass the warmups to wrestle with the most difficult passages. Discouragement, ambivalence, or emotional fatigue make us accident prone. In our frantic desire to step up the training schedule, we may ignore the pain. Mental tension translates into physical tension, which increases the risk of injury.

What happens inside an anxious body? Emotional stress dilates muscle capillaries and increases the total blood flow without transfering more nutrients. Touch sensitivity increases, but so do glandular secretions (e.g. sweat). Muscle tension slows down the recirculation of venous blood, causing inefficient disposal of metabolites and decreased stamina.

THE STRESS RESPONSE

The stress response, first described by Hans Selye in the 1930s, is an adaptation of the atavistic "fight or flight" response to danger. The three stages of response are called alarm reaction, resistance or adaptive stage, and exhaustion stage. In the first stage the body recognizes a source of stress (the stressor), and releases the hormones necessary for fight or flight. In the second stage the acute symptoms recede, and the body makes repairs. If stress continues into the exhaustion stage, the body develops stress-related problems, e.g. emotional disturbances, heart disease, or asthma.

In the alarm reaction (first) stage, the adrenal cortex secretes the hormones adrenaline (epinephrine) and norepinephrine, depleting vitamin C reserves in the process. The liver releases glucose for quick energy. The capillaries constrict, raising the blood pressure, and the heart rate increases to get more glucose and oxygen to the tissues. The bronchial mucosa shrinks, increasing lung capacity and facilitating oxygen delivery. The pupils dilate to improve vision. The skeletal muscles tense up, becoming firmer and stronger, ready to fight or flee. Fine motor coordination deteriorates, the more recently acquired skills being lost first.

We need a certain amount of stress in our lives. Selye found that if rats were placed under stress and then allowed to recover, they became stronger. Only when the stress was repeated before they had time to recover did they become weaker. The control group of rats who were not subjected to stress did not become as strong as the first group.

RELAXATION

Many of us live under excessive stress, and the marketplace is brimming with purveyors of relaxation methods, from high-tech electronic machines to tapes evoking an ocean or pastoral scene. The proliferation is bound to be confusing to the neophyte, so some of the better established techniques are discussed in the chapters which follow.

In the laboratory, Herbert Benson had subjects repeat the word "one" over and over. They showed such signs of relaxation as decreased galvanic skin response and increased incidence of alpha waves. Followers of both Eastern and Western religions apply similar techniques, substituting their holy words for "one."

At first, relaxation may may lead to *de-stressing*, i.e. the emergence of emotional ghosts which have broken through chinks in the armor. It is tempting to send them back inside and lock the container, but these ghosts may be what prompted the development of injury-promoting armor in the first place. Performing is a high-pressure, demanding, relentless calling. Injury offers a respite, a chance to breathe and review priorities. Even the dedicated 'cellist Pablo Casals is said to have admitted to a momentary feeling of relief after a hand injury, when it crossed his mind that he might be facing the end of his career. Without blaming the victim, it can be said that virtually every injury has its payoff. Long term recovery may require dealing with that payoff.

NLP

Not everybody feels ready to face the payoffs for injury head on. It might even be dangerous to let the "ghosts" out of the box. There are those who cry "no gain without pain" (they probably play scales for eight hours a day, too), but the rest of us can be glad that Richard Bandler and John Grinder developed neurolinguistic programming (NLP), to provide a relatively painless exorcism. By letting you find new responses to old stimuli, NLP is a class of methods for obtaining the payoff without the self-sabotage, so that we can deal with the pressures of performance without getting sick.

NLP has many practitioners, not all equally qualified. Even certified practitioners vary greatly, because of differences in approach between the founders of the art. The many books on the subject make entertaining reading and give an idea of the scope of the field, but they are not really meant as self-help manuals. Some of the more traditional therapists consider NLP too shallow or perhaps too good to be true, but Richard Bandler's 20-minute phobia cure is very impressive.

SENTIC CYCLES

Manfred Clynes studied the correspondence between emotional (sentic) states and physical expression. He asked his subjects to close their eyes, listen to a piece of music, and record their emotional response by pressing a button attatched to a pressure-sensing device. When he drew a graph showing changes in pressure over time, he found that each composer had a unique sentic "signature," e.g. Mozart elicited a consistent response pattern, independent of either the composition or the listener, while Beethoven elicited another pattern.

In some of his experiments subjects recorded their responses to a series of named states, e.g. anger or love. After acting as subjects themselves for a time Clynes and his co-workers discovered an unexpected fringe benefit of their work: they became cheerful, energetic, relaxed, and free of minor ailments like migraines or digestive problems. After investigating this effect, Clynes decided to market a 20-minute tape which is packaged along with a grey plastic button (no pressure-sensing device). The tape contains a cycle of named emotions which go from neutral to mildly unpleasant, quite unpleasant, pleasant, to extremely pleasant. Each is named once followed by a series of randomly-timed clicks (the cue to press the button). Using this tape before a performance could calm the nerves while maintaining clarity of intent. However, the effects of these cycles vary among people, so try the tape out when you're not going to be under pressure.

Clynes wrote many books and articles before he attracted the attention of musicians with *Music, Mind, and Brain*. The book is full of learned articles by famous people, and if the type face were better, it might even make enjoyable reading. The other works by Clynes, most of them extremely technical, reflect his extensive and wide-ranging scientific background.

DANCE THERAPY AND OTHER ARTS THERAPIES

Strange as it may sound, even dancers can benefit from dance therapy. Here there is no right or wrong way to move: the art form is a vehicle for expressing and releasing emotions. Whether dancing your anger or splashing paint on canvas, you will get greater therapeutic value with the guidance of a sensitive facilitator. If you can bring yourself to share your painful emotions with other people, you can benefit from the extra energy generated by the group process. If group work sounds frightening, remember that most art forms can be practised at such a level of abstraction that only the artist knows what the work is meant to express.

HERBS FOR THE EMOTIONS

Around 1930, Dr. Edward Bach devised a system of healing with minute quantities of certain flower petals in water. He used 28 different plants, each associated with an emotional portrait, advising his patients to put just a few drops of the appropriate remedies under the tongue. After a time they reported relief from both emotional and physical symptoms. Bach flower remedies resemble homeopathics in containing virtually undetectable amounts of the therapeutic substance. Thus even the most skeptical don't consider them toxic.

A certified Bach flower practitioner may take a long time talking to a client about that painful finger, perhaps, or about whatever comes up. The words which make up the client's statements are more important than the statements themselves. Repetition of certain keywords yields clues to the underlying emotional state, and two clients with the same physical complaint will not necessarily receive the same remedy. Examples of targeted emotions include self-concern (heather), despair (gorse), or anticipation of failure (larch). Most practitioners will mix as many as six remedies together at a time.

Some practitioners use a questionnaire like the one included in Bormann's book (see bibliography for Section II) to determine the choice of remedies. Clients can then answer the same questions at a later date to confirm their progress. It is tempting to read a sample questionnaire and self-prescribe, but an experienced practitioner might lead the client to uncover previously unsuspected truths and is more likely to hit upon a therapeutic combination on the first try.

California essences are similar to the Bach flower remedies and come in far greater profusion. Their proponents say that these essences are more suited to the modern range of problems.

NUTRITION AND THE EMOTIONS

Before you decide it's all in your mind, check out your diet. Niacin has cured schizophrenia, where the condition was merely an extreme form of pellagra (the niacin-deficiency disease). As a less extreme example of the relationship between nutrition and the emotions, consider the effect of hunger on your patience and ability to concentrate. Food sensitivities, which are much more common than most people realize, can affect both the mind and the emotions. Schauss and Hoffer (see bibliography for Section II) are among those who specialize in the mental and emotional effects of food.

PSYCHOTHERAPY

The techniques covered so far may be newer than old-fashioned therapy, but they aren't necessarily better, and you might simply be more comfortable trying the latter route. Sports psychology has become a big field, and some practitioners have branched out to treat performers. Going to a therapist is not an admission of failure or even of illness. The aim of a sports psychologist is to integrate the physical and the mental, rather than to treat them separately. A good therapist might be able to formulate a training plan which leads to continued good health. National athletic teams often have a resident psychologist to give them a competitive edge; maybe someday the major orchestras will do the same.

Chapter 21

HOW TO GET THE BODY TO HELP THE MIND ...
to help the body ...

Still searching for the next Great Performance? Not interested in emotional ghosts? Well then, how about a nice massage? The premise that relaxing the body will in turn release tension on the mental/emotional level has given rise to a class of disciplines called "bodywork," along with an army of people ready to help you, or at least to show you how to help yourself. Whether done by you or to you, these techniques are worth investigating.

ANTIGYMNASTICS

Antigymnastics, based on the work of Thérèse Bertherat, is a set of slow, gentle movements made with directed awareness. Since everything is connected through the spine, she suggests rolling a ball around under one foot to relax the neck. And since one side of the body learns from the other, she suggests training an injured arm by exercising the opposite one. The exercises in the back of her book, called preliminaries, are excellent for focusing awareness.

To learn new skills, Bertherat advises, "before you practise a sport ... acquire muscular, sensory, and respiratory intelligence. ... Instead of limiting yourself to learned gestures, submitting yourself to the authority of specific training ... give your body and your brain the possibility of inventing the most appropriate movements." Her approach might make learning repertoire easier and performance more efficient.

ALEXANDER

In the late 19th century, F. M. Alexander, an Australian orator, kept losing his voice while on stage. The Alexander Technique is the result of his search for a cure. Today, you can consult a trained practitioner who offers a series of "lessons," consisting of very gentle touching, which let the body find balance and alignment. The verbal premise is that the neck needs to lengthen while the chin is allowed to come in. The physical lesson teaches the body what those words mean. If you have back problems, this is a great way to learn how to sit through long rehearsals without (physical) discomfort.

One lesson may well convince you that this approach is exactly what is needed, but unfortunately the effects wear off and must be reinforced periodically. After a series of lessons, the new knowledge will last much longer, so that ultimately you should not be dependent on a teacher. The effectiveness of the method depends greatly on the skill of the practitioner, so shop around.

FELDENKRAIS

Israeli scientist, Moshe Feldenkrais, developed a technique of manipulation, which he called "Functional Integration." Later he began training practitioners in his method, an extension of the work of F. M. Alexander. Some people feel that the Alexander work was complete, and that any extensions just complicate things unnecessarily. Others consider the new technique a great step forward. The manipulations are extremely gentle and merely give the body some hints about how to expand and let go.

"Awareness Through Movement," the other part of Feldenkrais's method, is a series of smooth, circular movements to be practised slowly, gently, and mindfully. The exercises are available on tapes, which encourage a leisurely pace. The combination of exercises and manipulations has brought relief from a number of ailments, including crippling arthritic conditions and **bursitis**.

YOGA

Though it can be part of a religious system, hatha yoga can be simply a safe alternative to calisthenics. Some teachers advocate gentle, flowing movements determined by the body's needs. Others are very strict in all details and insist that their

Feldenkrais neck rolls are much gentler than the more traditional version, and instead of stretching everything to the limit, this method just gently oils the system. (As with many of these methods, a good instructor can establish a mood, regulate timing, and correct errors.) Pretend that your tongue is one hand of a clock, and that the opening of your mouth is the face of the clock. Run your tongue clockwise around the circle to get the feeling. Now work on the segment from 12 o'clock to 1 o'clock. Run the tongue slowly back and forth, looking (listening? feeling?) for kinks in the movement. When you find a kink (usually you either want to go too fast or stop at this point), gently go back and forth over that spot until it feels smooth. After this five-minute segment is oiled, go from 12 o'clock to 3 o'clock, in the same way. Gradually you will have done the whole clock, both clockwise and counterclockwise. Now switch clocks. Let your nose be the pointer, making small circles in space (in about the same plane as your face). Make slow, smooth circles, proceeding as you did with your tongue. That's all there is to it — without exercising the neck at all, you can release a lot of tension.

There are similar exercises for all the joints. They take time, but they are safe and surprisingly effective.

school represents the only way to do yoga. A good instructor is essential to deriving the full benefits and practising safely. B. K. S. Iyengar and other authors recommend postures for specific ailments, but it is important to work on the whole body before concentrating on one area. Kriyananda combines yoga postures with affirmations for self-healing. Most yoga schools teach breathing and relaxation as well as hatha yoga.

MASSAGE

Most athletic teams recognize the importance of massage to the performer. When someone is massaging you, you can assist the process by concentrating, relaxing, breathing gently, and cooperating mentally as well as physically. Alternatively, you can be your own masseur with the aid of the rollers, balls, or other devices which allow the weight of your body to put gentle pressure on a passive muscle.

Schools of massage range from the traditional Swedish massage to Japanese shiatsu, and each practitioner will have an individual touch. Some schools, like Lomi massage, encourage the client to work through some of the emotional factors behind the tension.

Shiatsu massage is based on the oriental system of energy meridians and acupuncture points. A whole body massage re-establishes a freely-flowing energy field, but shiatsu can also be applied to a smaller area to relieve a specific blockage. It is a popular headache remedy and may even be able to remove the calcium deposits associated with bursitis. The "trigger points" which set off muscle spasms often correspond to shiatsu reflex points.

Acupressure is similar to shiatsu but usually means applying pressure on specific points for relief of specific problems.

One word of warning: massage can remove some of the background muscle tone which supports the joints. The hands seem to be particularly vulnerable, especially if the practitioner doesn't understand why those hand muscles are so well developed. It might be best to experiment with massage after, rather than before, a performance.

ACUPUNCTURE

Acupuncture is the stimulation of reflex points with needles or lasers. A qualified acupuncturist may be a doctor of oriental medicine (OMD) who has spent years studying both acupuncture and herbs. Acupuncture is a part of the system of oriental medicine, and it is most effective when integrated into this system.

Acupuncture can control pain, relieve inflammation, and restore mobility. Traditionally points are stimulated with needles, though some people prefer lasers. Because the needle (or laser beam) is so much finer than a finger tip, the acupuncturist must be much more accurate than the practitioner of shiatsu. This is a matter of training and experience, since each body is different. You may have a reaction to the treatment, somewhat like the healing crisis brought on by cleansing diets or herbs.

ACUPUNCTURE POINTS FOR SPECIFIC PROBLEMS

This list of points for specific problems is intended just for reference: as always, an expert practitioner will be safer and more effective than an amateur. The names in parentheses are taken from the Beijing College text (see bibliography). The book contains detailed descriptions, but for the amateur it may be best simply to look for a sore spot in the area and to massage it gently. The points are illustrated in fig. 46.

The points are associated with major organs, e.g. gall bladder (G.B.), small intestine (S.I.), large intestine (L.I.), urinary bladder (U.B.), or lung (Lu). (Sanjiao (S.J.), often translated as Triple Heater, governs the other organs.) The connection between your stiff neck and your gall bladder may be unclear, but if the search for pain relief prompts you to look at the organ and perhaps at its associated emotions (Who, me, bitter??), you may experience a real improvement in general health.

neck

For a stiff neck, stimulate G.B. 21 (Jianjing).

For a sprain in the neck, stimulate U.B. 10 (Tianzhu), or S.I. 3 (Houxi) in the hand.

shoulder joint

For a sprained shoulder joint or for pain and difficulty moving the arm, stimulate L.I. 15 (Jianyu).

For a sprained shoulder, stimulate G.B. 21 (Jianjing).

For aching and weakness, stimulate S.I. 10 (Naoshu).

For pain in the shoulder blade, stimulate S.I. 11 (Tianzong), S.I. 12 (Bingfeng), S.I. 14, (Jianwaishu), or U.B. 43 (Gaohuangshu).

For pain in the shoulder joint, stimulate S.I . 9 (Jianzhen) or S.J. 14 (Jianliao).

elbow

For a sprained elbow, stimulate L.I. 11 (Quchi), or L.I. 4 (Hegu) in the hand.

For pain and loss of movement, stimulate Lu. 5 (Chize).

There are numerous other points on or near the elbow, so if something feels sore, it probably needs gentle work. For maximum benefit, find out which meridian it lies in and which organs may be involved.

wrist

For pain in the wrist, stimulate L.I. 5 (Yangxi) or S.I. 5 (Yanggu).

For a sprained wrist, stimulate S.J. 4 (Yangchi) or S.J. 5 (Waiguan).

fingers

For numbness and pain in the fingers, stimulate S.I. 3 (Houxi) or L.I. 3 (Sanjian).

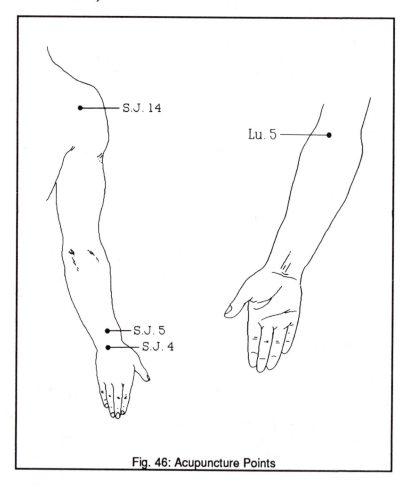

Fig. 46: Acupuncture Points

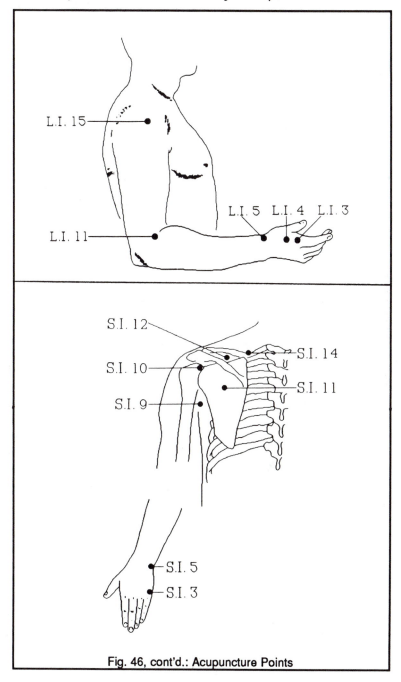

Fig. 46, cont'd.: Acupuncture Points

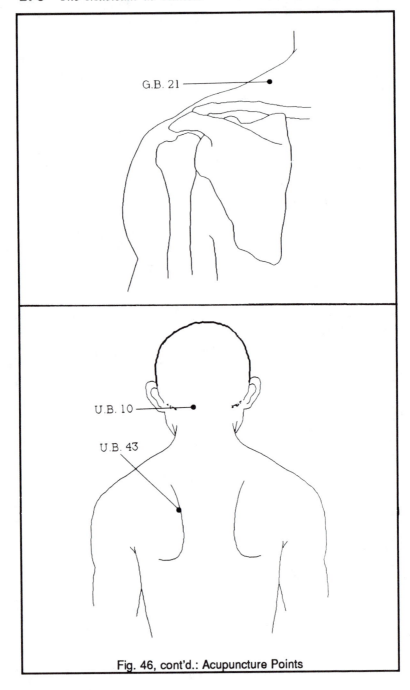

Fig. 46, cont'd.: Acupuncture Points

POLARITY THERAPY

The originator of polarity therapy, Randolph Stone, went all over the world to learn about various healing methods and synthesized a system which borrows from many cultures. Its premise is that changes in the magnetic field surrounding the body indicate an illness, and that the therapist's touch can cure that illness by realigning the magnetic field. A treatment can be very gentle or quite painful, depending on the practitioner's perception of your needs. Some massage therapists combine polarity therapy with their work.

MAGNETS

Magnets are not used for bodywork, but they are a more obvious tool than polarity therapy for realigning the magnetic field. They are particularly successful at speeding the healing of broken bones, so an experienced practitioner could help you get back to work after a fracture. Magnets are not for amateurs. Unfortunately many people selling magnets are basing their advice on poorly-controlled experiments.

Does the copper bracelet ease arthritis pains because of its interraction with the body's magnetic field, or does it work because the copper gets into the blood stream? Most people consider copper bracelets to be safer than magnets, whatever the reason for their effectiveness.

ROLFING

The deep tissue massage called Structural Integration, developed by Ida Rolf, is based on the idea that our unresolved emotional traumas result in "armoring" which in turn can be softened to release blocked energy. Known as Rolfing, a session is traditionally quite painful, though some practitioners stress that the patient can cooperate with the process rather than have it inflicted. A series of treatments can improve body alignment and increase energy and coordination.

CHIROPRACTIC

Anyone with back or limb problems might consider chiropractic. Chiropractors vary. Some are more gentle than others. Not all take x-rays. Some work on shoulders and hands, as well as the spine. Some propose a long series of treatments, while others expect to fix a problem within days. Many dispense nutritional advice and vitamins along with their treatments. (Check out their qualifications to do this before following the advice.) Many chiropractors seem to feel that health of the spinal cord is so essential that virtually any problem can be solved by a series of adjustments to the spine.

Your adjustment may hold better if you walk around afterwards, before driving home, since this practice may reduce inflammation and let the joints settle gently into their new position. If your condition seems to resist treatment, look for aggravating factors (posture? technique? diet? emotional resistance?). Some chiropractors will suggest exercises, but you may have to ask for them.

REFLEXOLOGY

Reflexology is a form of massage based on the premise that all parts of the body correspond to points on the soles of the feet, the palms of the hands, and the ears. Thus a foot massage can restore the flow of energy through the acupuncture meridians to the corresponding organs. There are many theories about *why* this works, but the most effective way of finding out *whether* it works is to try it. You may be surprised how well the tender spots on your feet correspond to your known problem areas. Reflexology is effective by itself, and it works well with nutritional and herbal therapies which encourage the body to heal itself.

You can massage your own feet, but many people feel that the exchange of energy between client and practitioner makes the healing process more effective.

IRIDOLOGY

Iridology is not a form of bodywork, but it has correspondences with reflexology: instead of mapping the body onto the feet, hands, or ears, iridology maps it onto the iris of the eye. The iris can reflect weakness or inflammation of various parts of the body, as well as acidity, toxicity, and the state of the circulatory, nervous, lymphatic, and digestive systems. Weakness in specific organs can be verified with reflexology, testing the feet, hands, or ears for tenderness in corresponding areas. A good practitioner can give you surprisingly accurate information about your medical history merely by looking in your eye.

Iridology is one of the most maligned practices in the natural healing field. Much of the criticism is based on a single test recorded in the *Journal of the American Medical Association* (see Simon et al.). Dr. Bernard Jensen, the most prominent of the three iridologists "debunked" by this test, wrote a rebuttal, but *JAMA* declined to print it (see ACA Journal of Chiropractic). The iridologists were given slides of the eyes of 143 patients and asked to screen for kidney disease on the basis of the slides alone. Jensen's answers were considered only about 50 percent accurate, or no better than chance. The other iridologists did even worse. In his rebuttal, Jensen made the following points. (1) Most iridologists stress the need to question patients while examining their eyes. Not to allow this would be like asking doctors to make a diagnosis based only on blood tests, without letting them see the patient or obtain a history. (2) The iridologists rejected 50 percent of the slides presented to them as illegible, yet they were asked to guess at kidney function, and these guesses were included in the final results of the test. (3) Medical research indicates that the criterion used by the testers to assess kidney function is not considered accurate for low grade problems or those not involving the glomerulus. Consequently many of the so-called false positives from the iridologists could just as well indicate a superior method of early detection or a warning of sub-clinical kidney weakness. (4) The criterion used by the testers generates false-positives. If these eyes were among those read as normal by the iridologists, the latter would be correct, thus further skewing the results. (5) European studies indicate a far greater accuracy for iridology (over 90 percent).

While the experts are arguing, many people are benefiting from the insights of a good iridologist.

RAYID

Rayid, developed by Denny Johnson in the 1980s, uses the iris to reveal emotional and personal history. It makes no claims of correspondence with iridology. On the other hand, some iridologists, especially in Australia, have written about the emotional implications of various physical problems. These fit very closely with the emotions revealed by rayid, as well as with other theories of body language. Many North American practitioners combine rayid with iridology.

Chapter 22

HOW TO GET THE MIND TO HELP THE BODY ...
to help the mind ...

Is the mind, then, just a slave of the body? Do we need a massage to clear our heads? On the contrary: bodywork can indeed benefit the mind, but we could also enlist the mind directly, and gain physical efficiency as a bonus.

In this chapter the focus is on awareness and energy flow, and how these things help the body relax and do what it's supposed to be doing.

T'AI CHI

As a martial art, t'ai chi might seem to have more to do with the body than the mind, but it requires mental discipline to achieve the required balance, coordinated breathing, slow and flowing motions, and attention to detail. Though any martial art will focus the mind to let you control the body (and thus feel more energetic and at ease on stage), t'ai chi is one of the gentlest. It won't lead to calloused hands, and it can be learned safely at any age. Since it stimulates the circulation and "gets the kinks out," it is an excellent warm-up for stretching exercises. On some level it lets the energy (chi) flow, so that a 20-minute session refreshes both mind and body. Neither books nor videos can replace a qualified instructor, but the books in the bibliography can give you an idea what t'ai chi is about.

AUTOGENIC TRAINING

Autogenic training is based on the discovery that mimicking the effects of mental and physical relaxation can lead to the real thing. Through gentle autosuggestion, the extremities turn limp, warm, and heavy, the abdomen becomes soft and warm, and so on. The process is learned gradually, over months.

This extremely effective technique was developed by Johannes Schultz and Wolfgang Luthe in Germany and has few qualified practitioners in North America. It has been successful in a number of therapeutic contexts, including work with arthritics. Many people have adapted the original ideas and added a few new ones. *Superlearning*, by Ostrander and Schroeder, contains one of many unauthorized introductions for self-study. Among other innovations, it starts with patterned breathing, which Luthe and Schultz explicitly reject. The originators are adamant about the need for a qualified teacher/physician, primarily to deal with any strong abreactions from relaxation. Their books make scary reading, and I don't recommend them as an introduction to the technique, because they include so many things which the authors would never advise telling a patient, and the power of suggestion could bring you unnecessary psychological and physical trauma.

Those who have mastered the physical exercises without harm might want to read the original works to learn the challenging and useful mental exercises. The books also have special instructions for specific conditions. Luthe and Schultz point out that autogenic training is especially apt for arthritics, who generally like to take responsibility for their own therapy. Any distress resulting from practice of the techniques is likely to get worse if it is not treated by a competent practitioner, so persistence is not a good idea at all. Autogenic training is a powerful therapy, to be used wisely.

AFFIRMATIONS

Affirmation is another way to bend the mind in the directions which best serve our needs. Thinking, "I am going to fail," may not cause failure, but in any case it is not a pleasant thought to entertain. Why not glow with the feeling, "I will succeed," instead? Many people believe that thoughts influence the body, and even doubters will surely find it easier to practice once they have cultivated the belief that "practice makes perfect." Affirmation techniques vary, and some people find that a gentle nudge works better than fervent repetition. Whatever the method, positive wording of the affirmation is extremely important. "I am not going to fail" contains the thought "I am going to fail," and the subconscious has a tendency to overlook the word "not."

Affirmation is more effective if you have a clear idea of the desired result. Try to involve all of the senses, visual, aural, olfactory, tactile, and gustatory. Rather than visualizing the healing process, it is generally safer to visualize a result and let the details take care of themselves. Affirmations to speed physical healing could include "My arm is strong and flexible." You may encounter resistance, especially when using the present tense to describe a hope for the future. Your responses to the affirmative thought might give a clue to possible payoffs for remaining injured. Injury is an opportunity to learn, and those who return to performing after an interrupted career often do so with a wisdom they hadn't been seeking until forced to do so.

If you are encountering strong resistance to an affirmation, perhaps on some level you think you deserve to fail. Facing this possibility can be painful. Some authors recommend writing an affirmation, such as "I deserve success," then writing your reactions to that statement, and repeating the process until the reaction is fully positive.

If you experience painful emotions and resistance, stand up and yell, hit something (with a towel, not that sore hand), go out for a run, or try a more active technique, like dance therapy. Chances are that those feelings are neither unique, pathological, nor incurable.

BIOFEEDBACK

Biofeedback is especially effective in speeding recovery from performance injuries which are aggravated by unnecessary tension. The technique was first described by Barbara Brown and subsequently adopted by many others. Some have tried to improve on the original methods, with mixed results. The concept is very simple: if you know what your body is doing, you can learn to control it. Our bodies apply biofeedback to voluntary motion. Nerves acting as position sensors, for example, monitor the motion of a limb with respect to its intended path, and trigger correcting contractions of the so-called voluntary muscles. Brown's biofeedback is novel in that electronic devices give us access to information about normally involuntary process such as blood pressure or brain waves. Thus we try to influence something external, e.g. a flashing light or a sound, in order to gain control over internal functions. There are many biofeedback devices on the market, some of them inexpensive enough for home use, but expert assistance is strongly recommended.

COLOR THERAPY

Many books have been written about the therapeutic effects of color, whether applied as colored lights, color-treated water, or "color breathing." Color breathing is simpler than buying and setting up therapeutic lights: imagine a dot of color which grows larger until it fills the visual field, then inhale it, trust it to go wherever you need it, let the body take what it needs and let the rest go. On exhalation, affirm that the color returns to the universe as pure energy, as does any undesired stress or illness this process may have liberated. To balance the colors, breathe them all in succession: red, orange, yellow, green, blue, indigo, violet. Many systems link each color to specific ailments, organs, emotions, or energy centers.

AROMA THERAPY

Scents are relayed to the least evolved part of the brain, so they affect us at a very basic level. Most people don't breathe imaginary scents, though it should be possible. Instead, they inhale the scents in oils, vaporizers, herbal baths, and perfumes. Scents affect the emotions as well as the body and are reputed to do everything from curing disease to attracting a lover. Some practitioners offer aroma therapy as an adjunct to massage or other forms of healing.

GEMSTONE THERAPY

Gemstones influence our energy and can heal or energize us. A good quartz crystal warms up the hand, but some people find its energy disturbing. Not all sellers of gem stones are knowledgeable, and not all gems seem to be equally powerful. It is up to the buyer to develop an awareness of their effects. Gems are not meant to be waved around randomly, and the stone that strengthens one person can weaken someone else. Some people find them a good adjunct to the pre-performance warmup.

Chapter 23

WARMING THE HANDS BY HELPING OTHERS:
using the hands to heal

Any dis-ease can become a learning experience. I have been lucky both in having good health and in having some learning experiences "forced" on me. I remember well the first time that I became aware of the power of my mind to heal my body (as opposed to the power of *the* mind to heal *the* body, a subject of little interest to me up to that time). It was a beautiful hot summer day, and my husband and I had walked downtown from our house. The combination of the heat and city noise had brought on a pounding headache which was in full swing by the time we turned homeward. As we still had several hilly miles to go, I felt seized by the knowledge that this condition simply would not do. For the first time in my life it occurred to me to deal with pain by welcoming it rather than by fighting it. It was easy to get into the pulsating rhythm, and the pain stopped almost immediately, to my great joy. It returned just as quickly, and I accepted the idea that I'd have to stay with that rhythm and genuinely welcome the pain for a longer time. The rhythm went well with walking, and as long as I kept up the attitude of welcome, the sensation of pain wasn't there — or was transformed into something pleasant. Whatever the case, I arrived home feeling fine. At some point on that walk, even the rhythm had faded from consciousness. My life hasn't been the same since.

How does the "headache cure" work? Physically, I relaxed my neck and shoulder muscles, which freed the blood flow to and from the head. Similarly, subjects in laboratory experiments relieved their headaches by concentrating on raising the temperature of their hands. Another great way to get your hands warm (with or without a headache) is to use them to heal. This chapter touches on one of the most powerful ideas available to the performer, whether applied in a religious or a scientific framework.

LAYING ON OF HANDS

Healing with the hands is a part of many religious traditions, so you might want to investigate the teachings of your own religion for information in this area. The practice has been found in many cultures since ancient times. The models vary, i.e. people have different explanations of what they are doing and of how it works. Does the healing energy come from the healer, from the interaction of healer and client, or from an outside source? Regardless of the answer, it is safest for the healer to feel like a channel rather than the ultimate source of healing energy. In this way, it is possible to be recharged by healing, rather than feel drained. The recharging can be explained as nothing more than the power of suggestion, but it also fits the religious model. Many churches now use some form of healing in their work, and some encourage the laying on of hands.

REIKI AND THERAPEUTIC TOUCH

Reiki practitioners transmit healing energy with their hands. Though their training includes a set of "initiations," it is based on teachings of some of the major world religious traditions. It has a Japanese name because its originator, Dr. Mikao Usui, was Japanese, but it is not really connected with any oriental tradition and is quite recent in origin (late 1800s). At higher levels of initiation, healing and thoughts can be sent at a distance. The healer can silently explore the needs of the patient, perhaps gaining insight into hidden payoffs and easier ways to realize them. Reiki can be used for self-healing, as can the methods taught by LeShan and Schwartz (below).

Therapeutic Touch is based on the principles of the laying on of hands. The originator of this system, Dolores Krieger, has introduced many people to a healing power which she feels is latent within all of us. Dr. Krieger started out teaching only nurses, but her courses are now available to people from all walks of life. She has investigated the scientific basis of her system and objectified the phenomenon as much as is possible. People who have studied both Reiki and Therapeutic Touch report that the systems seem to be equally effective and are at least subjectively quite similar.

THE SCIENTIST STUDIES HEALING

Many people have documented the search for a scientific basis for this type of healing. All of the authors have a bias, because there has to be a starting point for any sort of rational endeavor. Some of them are so intent on vindicating the healers that they verge on the incoherent. Others are so intent on debunking that they don't make much sense either. The following are among the more helpful writers in this field.

Lawrence LeShan started as a psychologist and skeptic studying the subject of healing, but he ended up developing a technique which he now teaches to others.

Jack Schwartz says he was born with the ability to heal, but he teaches others his methods through the Aletheia Foundation. The Meninger Foundation has spent quite a bit of time studying healers like him. They attest to his ability to control his body in ways considered impossible for most of us.

Douglas Dean applied scientific methods to measure the effect of sending healing energy through the hands. He asked healers to hold containers of water in their hands and send energy into the water. The energized water was measurably different from plain water. This doesn't prove that a healer can cure illness, but it does show that something is happening, other than the transmission of heat and strong thoughts.

Carl Simonton studied the influence of thoughts on the immune system. Though he used his knowledge to help cancer patients, it is applicable to all types of healing. But since arthritis, unlike cancer, is an auto-immune disease and thus the arthritic might not benefit from strengthening the immune system, the guidance of an expert is critical.

CEREMONY

In many traditions, healing is connected with ceremony. Even the white coat and trappings of a doctor's office are ceremonial in origin. A ceremony is a way of impressing the subconscious. It is a way of gathering power. It is a way of concentrating attention. It is a way of establishing a ritual, a routine which has worked many times before and will work again. It is a way of reassuring yourself that the work you are doing is safe, because it is firmly rooted in a religion or belief system. Whether establishing a pre-performance warmup or blessing food before meals, many of us make use of ceremony already. In subtle forms of healing, ceremony is particularly important.

SELF-HEALING

Taking on the role of healer can renew your own energy. Your hands may become warm, flexible, and charged up for performance. Thus, doing something for someone else helps you get well yourself. It may also help you to focus on others and thus to communicate better with your audience.

Appendices

TABLE OF CONTENTS FOR APPENDIX 1

Appendix 1

VITAMINS AND MINERALS

This appendix is intended for reference only. Supplementation with large doses of vitamins and minerals requires the supervision of a qualified practitioner.

The entry for each vitamin and mineral in this appendix is subdivided as follows: functions which might affect performance or recovery from injury, daily requirements, deficiency symptoms, toxicity, synergists, and food sources.

Functions which might affect performance or recovery from injury

This section will discuss the roles which a specific nutrient plays in the body. Those areas which might prove to be of particular interest to the performer are in **bold face**. Vitamin B$_1$, for example, is necessary for carbohydrate metabolism. Theoretically, therefore, its deficiency could push the body from an aerobic state to an anaerobic state, thus producing lactic acid, which would in turn contribute to **muscle fatigue**.

These statements do not imply that an intake of a given nutrient beyond a certain point would in any way improve performance. Even if the extra intake causes no direct toxicity, the body uses up energy to dispose of or store surplus nutrients. At best, then, taking more supplements than the body can use will make more work for the eliminative organs.

Requirements

Various government agencies have published their recommendations for daily intake of vitamins. The U.S. Recommended Daily Allowances (RDAs) are listed when available, though many of these amounts are increased with stress, pregnancy, etc. Scientists in the U.S., Japan, and Canada, with access to the same data, have come up with fairly widely varying RDAs for the same nutrients. When nutritionists' figures differ substantially from the RDAs, these too will be mentioned. The food quantities listed as examples are based on figures from the *Nutrition Almanac*. For the sake of simplicity these figures assume that daily needs are met from a single source, but this practice is not recommended.

In some cases it might be argued that performance uses up a particular vitamin, thus increasing the amount required to prevent deficiency. Stress, for example, depletes some vitamins, and though it may be better to decrease stress than to take more vitamins, a certain amount of stress may be necessary for an exciting performance. Other nutrients are needed for tissue repair, so they must be in adequate supply, lest the daily micro-traumas turn into "injuries."

Some nutrients have been proposed as "ergogenic aids," i.e. substances which increase the capacity for physical work. Rather than suggest that performance depletes "vitamin X," so that the musician/athlete needs more to prevent deficiency, this proposal implies that even in the absence of any deficiency symptoms, vitamin supplements might improve performance. This is a grey area, because it isn't clear how to draw a line between optimal functioning and superior performance. It is possible, though unlikely, that a nutritional state which allows a musician to play fast trills easily for an hour doesn't have other side benefits for less demanding life-styles. If we can achieve such a state by taking "vitamin X" should we not call anything less a deficiency state? This is a controversial question, and it is difficult to design experiments to give conclusive answers.

If a drug increases nutritional requirements, this is noted.

Deficiency symptoms

This section will mention the major deficiency diseases, but the primary focus is on the more controversial low-level symptoms which might indicate that better nutrition would improve both health and performance. Where there are many low level deficiency symptoms, those which would particularly affect performance or the rate of recovery from injury are in **bold face**.

Low level symptoms of vitamin or mineral deficiency are often "harmless" in the sense that many people have them and have learned to live "normal" lives with them. I put these words in quotes because it is unnecessary to accept sub-optimal functioning as normal, and the ambitious performer cannot afford to do so. Not everyone agrees on some of the low level symptoms, though the available evidence does indicate that they are reversible with vitamin supplementation.

The low level symptoms listed under various vitamins or minerals could be caused by a number of factors and may not in themselves indicate a deficiency. Single nutrient deficiencies hardly ever occur unless some rare metabolic problem creates a vastly increased requirement for a single nutrient. Thus the lists are not meant as a means of diagnosing specific deficiencies but rather as a reminder that poor nutrition detracts from optimal and safe performance.

Toxicity

Everything is toxic if eaten in excess. Vitamins and most minerals are generally far safer than drugs, in that the ratio of the toxic dose to the effective dose is quite large. Usually these toxicities are also reversible, i.e. the side effects disappear when the nutrient is withdrawn. Optimal health requires optimal amounts of each nutrient, and megadoses of any substance should be taken only under supervision.

Synergists and antagonists

Synergists are substances which increase the effectiveness of a given nutrient. Often these substances are themselves vitamins or minerals. Antagonists are substances which diminish the body's ability to utilise a nutrient. The synergists and antagonists are listed, sometimes with a brief explanation of their effect.

It is important to realize that we don't know all the nutrients or their synergists, so supplements can't replace a diet of whole foods.

Food sources

Since many lists of food sources are readily available, this section gives only a brief summary. In general, whole foods have more nutrients than processed foods, and even shipping and storage time destroys nutrients. Produce in the stores was probably picked before it was ripe, so it is not likely to be as nutritious as freshly picked produce. One Australian "study," using a sample of two oranges, one fresh from the tree and the other from a supermarket, found that the average ascorbic acid content was 90 mg, exactly as the charts suggested: the fresh one had 180 and the other had none.

Sometimes these lists of food sources will give the impression that animal products are needed for good nutrition. This issue was discussed in Chapter 9.

Get as many of your vitamins and minerals from foods as possible. Some nutritionists argue that you can get them all this way, while others disagree. In either case, vitamin pills are no substitute for food. They must be eaten with food in order to be digested, and since their role is so often that of processing, it is certain that they can't fulfill this role without something (i.e. food) to process.

THE B COMPLEX

The B vitamins need to be taken in the right proportions, lest the oversupply of one cause symptoms of deficiency in the others. Many

B complex supplements are based more on cost-effectiveness than on nutritional principles. For this reason, it might be best to use supplements like rice polish, liver, or brewer's yeast to get up to a baseline, and then use pills to adjust the values according to need.

VITAMIN B₁ (THIAMINE)

Functions which might affect performance or recovery from injury

Vitamin B₁ is used in **energy production,** being part of the coenzyme thiamine pyrophosphate, which is needed in the breakdown of carbohydrates and particularly in the conversion of pyruvate to acetyl CoA for entrance into the Krebs cycle (see Chapter 2) and conversion to ATP; it is also needed for synthesis of **ACh.** Vitamin B₁ is needed to produce adequate amounts of succinate, an ingredient of the **oxygen-**carrying hemoglobin. It also speeds stomach emptying time, another reason to consider eating whole grains in the pre-performance meal. B₁ is used therapeutically to speed the healing of damaged **nerve** tissue and reduce the pain. It is also used to treat **emotional** disorders.

Requirements

Like all water soluble vitamins, B₁ should be consumed daily. Since about 1 mg per day is destroyed in the tissues, the U. S. RDAs range from 1.0 to 1.4 mg daily, more for adolescent males and pregnant or lactating women. Theoretically this amount can be supplied by ten cups of cooked brown rice, a pound and a half of chicken liver, four cups of almonds, or half a cup of sunflower seeds.

   Stress increases the need for B₁, as does high caloric intake, especially of carbohydrates. Some nutritionists recommend as much as 10 to 20 mg daily for athletes, but others say that the increased caloric needs of these athletes will result in sufficient increase of dietary B₁. If supplements are taken, several smaller doses per day are more likely to be retained than one large one.

Deficiency symptoms

Vitamin B_1 is known as the **"morale vitamin,"** because early deficiency signs include **loss of stamina, depression, irritability, fatigue, increased reaction time, mental confusion,** and **poor concentration.** It has been suggested that some of these symptoms arise from impaired glucose metabolism and its effects on the central nervous system. Lack of sufficient ACh causes inflammation of the nerves (polyneuritis). Impaired nerve function can also cause **numbness, tingling,** or **increased sensitivity.** Prolonged deficiency can result in permanent nervous system damage.

Among the other symptoms of B_1 deficiency are **muscle cramps, tenderness** and **atrophy.** Since the reduced conversion of pyruvates (see functions) would result in more **lactic acid** production, there could be a reduction in **endurance** and more **muscle aches.**

Toxicity

All B vitamins need to be balanced with each other, since an excess in the intake of one of them can cause symptoms of deficiency of the rest of the B complex.

If vitamin B_1 levels are high, the body needs more vitamin D.

Passing vitamin B_1 can turn the urine yellow, but this is not considered a sign of toxicity.

Extremely high doses (125 - 350 mg per kg of body weight, or about 10 to 30 *grams* a day for a 150 pound person) can cause problems, including **nervousness** and **sweating,** also edema and rapid heartbeat. Intravenous injection of 200 mg (200 times the RDA) can cause hypersensitivity and eventual reaction resembling anaphylactic shock.

Rats have received doses of up to 100 times their requirements for as long as three generations with no apparent toxicity.

Synergists and antagonists

Synergists for B_1 include B_{12}, B_2, B_3, B_6, folic acid, pantothenic acid, and vitamin C. Caffeine increases the need for B_1. Alcohol often decreases B_1 absorption.

Food sources

Vitamin B_1 is found in whole grains, nuts, legumes, organ meats, nutritional yeast, wheat germ, wheat bran, black strap molasses, rice bran, and soy flour. Most of the B_1 in grains is in the bran and the germ, so refined grains are not a good source. Moderate amounts of B_1 are found in muscle meats and fresh green vegetables.

VITAMIN B$_2$ (RIBOFLAVIN)

Functions which might affect performance or recovery from injury

Vitamin B$_2$ plays a role in the transport of hydrogen from one compound to another (oxidation-reduction reactions leading to ATP formation), allowing a slow and controlled release of energy, so some scientists consider it important in **endurance sports**. It may play a role in glycolysis, and thus affect **anaerobic performance** as well. It helps maintain the myelin sheath around nerves and has been used therapeutically for **neuritis**. It is found in the retina of the **eye** and helps maintain **skin** and mucous membranes. It is required for **cellular growth**.

Requirements

The U.S. RDAs range from 1.4 to 1.8 mg daily, increasing with age and possibly with caloric requirements, and increasing to 1.8 and 2.0 for pregnancy and lactation respectively. Theoretically this amount can be supplied by one quart of whole milk, eight ounces of beef liver, two ounces of chicken liver, or just over a cup of almonds. More B$_2$ may be needed in periods of intense tissue growth, e.g. after an **injury** or surgery.

Deficiency symptoms

After several months' deficiency, there can be inflamed reddish skin, small **lip sores**, breaks in the skin at the corners of the mouth, a smooth purple/red tongue, inflamed mucous membranes, ulcers, oily skin, burning feet, pins-and-needles in the lower extremities, and anemia. Any **skin lesions** require the presence of vitamin B$_2$ for their repair; in its absence, minor injuries don't heal but become worse. Other symptoms include corneal vascularization, resulting in **vision** problems, especially an increase in the threshold of flicker fusion — i.e., it might get harder to see the path of that baton under fluorescent lights. The eyes may also burn, itch, or tire easily.

Toxicity
None has been reported, possibly due to the low solubility of B_2. Excess amounts and their metabolites are excreted in the urine. In rats the LD_{50} (the amount of B_2 needed to kill half of the rats in a study) has been reported at 560 gm/kg. This would work out to almost 40,000 grams for a 150 pound person, or millions of times as much as the RDA.

Synergists
Vitamin B_2 has to be combined with phosphorus to be absorbed. Its synergists include vitamin A and the whole B complex.

Food sources
Vitamin B_2 is found in milk (but is destroyed by light), nutritional yeasts, liver, kidney, shell fish, wheat germ, cheese and eggs. Moderate amounts are found in green leafy vegetables, avocados, legumes, nuts, and sprouted seeds. It is more tightly bound to the plant sources, and thus less available to the body.

VITAMIN B_3
(NIACIN AND ITS ACTIVE FORM, NIACINAMIDE)

Niacin

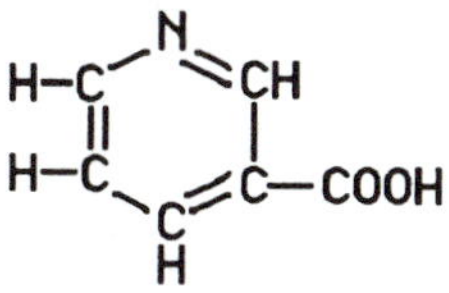

Niacinamide

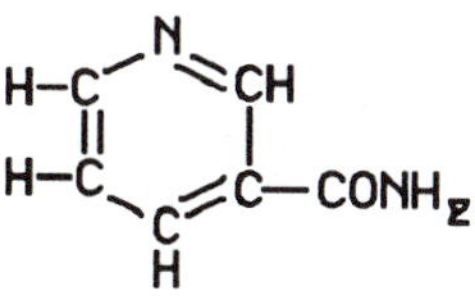

Functions which might affect performance or recovery from injury
Vitamin B_3 is necessary for the energy supply of each cell in the body. Among the over 50 metabolic reactions which depend on niacin are those involving conversion of **lactic acid** to pyruvic acid, pyruvic acid to acetyl CoA, parts of the Krebs cycle, **glycolysis**, fatty acid synthesis, formation of **steroids**, and formation of **red blood cells**. It also helps get rid of many toxins, including certain drug by-products.

Vitamin B3 is needed for proper **nervous function** and healthy skin. It may help in insomnia (possibly because it spares tryptophan, which helps induce sleep). It has been used in the treatment of high blood pressure and in alcohol withdrawal.

Niacin increases the circulation to the **extremities**. To warm up cold hands, start with a small amount of niacin (not niacinamide), maybe 50 mg daily, and increase the dose until there is a flush, maybe as much as 500 mg. Always follow with a B complex tablet about 20 minutes later. Niacin, but not niacinamide, has been used in large doses to reduce blood cholesterol, lipoproteins, and triglycerides.

Research done in the 1940s indicated that niacin was very effective in cases of **arthritis**. The excitement over the work done on steroids during the same time period overshadowed this finding, but occasionally the effectiveness of niacin in this area is rediscovered (usually as a side effect on the controls in an experiment with schizophrenics). Is it possible that niacin's role in the formation of steroids has something to do with its having effects similar to steroid drugs?

Requirements

The U.S. RDAs range from 13 to 20 mg daily, peaking in adolescence and then declining with age; add 15 and 20 for pregnancy and lactation. Theoretically 20 mg can be supplied by a cup of roasted peanuts, six ounces of turkey breast, or eight ounces of halibut.

All of these figures are complicated by the fact that the amino acid tryptophan can be converted to B3. The rate of conversion varies with each person's biochemistry, but it averages about 60 mg tryptophan to 1 mg B3. Vegetable proteins (other than corn) contain about one percent tryptophan. Animal proteins contain somewhat more, but it is less efficiently converted.

Many nutritionists feel that these RDAs are far too low. Passwater, for example, starts his program with a minimum of 50 mg, increasing to find the optimum, while Cheraskin considers about 115 mg a day to be an ideal intake.

Large doses have been used in **arthritis**, migraines, alcohol withdrawal, and mental disorders (up to 18 *grams* daily for schizophrenia).

Deficiency symptoms

Pellagra has been produced in diets with less than 4.4 mg of niacin-equivalents per 1,000 calories (about two thirds of the RDA). Symptoms include fissures in the corners of the mouth and in the tongue. Sometimes there are mental symptoms only, e.g. depression, irritability, and **anxiety**. Extreme deficiency can result in schizophrenia. Early symptoms of pellagra include **weakness**, lassitude, and indigestion. Deficiency can be detected by testing the urine for a low N1-methylnicotinamide content.

Toxicity

Niacin can cause a flushing of the face and extremities, accompanied by a burning, tingling sensation and throbbing in the head. This is not considered a toxic side effect, and occurs because the niacin opens peripheral blood vessels. (If taken in the form of niacinamide, there is no flushing reaction.) The flush is less pronounced if the rest of the B complex is taken at the same time. Some nutritionists say that the flush is an indication that the person needs more niacin, while others say it should be avoided.

Niacin occasionally causes heart palpitations. Though most authorities consider them harmless, anyone with heart problems should get professional advice.

According to the National Dairy Council, other symptoms of niacin overdose include headache, cramps, diarrhea, and liver damage. (Milk contains almost no niacin.) There are independent reports of gastrointestinal irritation, liver damage and subsequent reduced glucose tolerance, though these symptoms are rarely found, even with daily doses as high as 2,000 mg, i.e. at least 100 times the RDA.

Niacin could initially suppress free fatty acid release through decreased lipolysis, decreasing the availability of body fat as fuel and increasing carbohydrate consumption. Some experimenters have found that although work capacity did not change, their subjects experienced more **fatigue and heaviness in the limbs**, possibly reflecting the greater dependence on muscle glycogen as fuel. Other experimenters reported reduced **endurance** if niacin was taken when glycogen stores were already low. These do not appear to be long-term effects, as levels of free fatty acids in the blood of resting subjects returned to normal within an hour of taking niacin. However the findings would suggest caution about using this vitamin just before a performance: there are safer ways of warming the hands.

B3 increases the effects of barbiturates, anticonvulsants, and **tranquilizers**. Passwater suggests caution in cases of glaucoma, severe diabetes, impaired liver function, peptic ulcers. He advises starting with very small amounts and increasing them gradually.

According to Roman Kutsky, toxicity starts at 1 to 4 grams per kg daily, or about 120 to 480 *grams* daily for a 120 pound person (much higher than any amounts previously mentioned in this section).

Synergists and antagonists

Vitamins B6 and D are needed in order for the liver to convert tryptophan to B3. Other synergists include B1, B2, B12, pantothenic acid, and folic acid.

Long-term use of antibiotics depletes B_3. Excessive carbohydrate intake decreases B_3 levels.

Food sources
Tryptophan is found in milk and eggs and most protein foods besides corn (unless treated with lime water, as in Latin America, which makes the small amount present more available). Cow's milk has relatively little B_3 but is high in tryptophan and should furnish the equivalent of about 2 mg of B_3 per cup. Ground beef has 20 mg of B_3 per pound, and an additional 1,000 mg of tryptophan, for 39 niacin equivalents.

Most foods which are high in B_1 and B_2 are also high in B_3. These include rice bran, nutritional yeast, liver, tuna, halibut, peanuts, soy beans, and sunflower and sesame seeds (if well ground). Moderate amounts are found in dried figs, dates, and prunes, as well as in legumes, potatoes, broccoli, parsley, nuts, brown rice, meat, and fish. Other fruits are poor sources. Niacin is found in plants, while niacinamide is found in animals.

VITAMIN B_6 (PYRIDOXINE; ALSO PYRIDOXAL AND PYRIDOXAMINE)

Pyridoxine

CH_2OH

HO — CH_2OH

H_3C N H

Pyridoxal

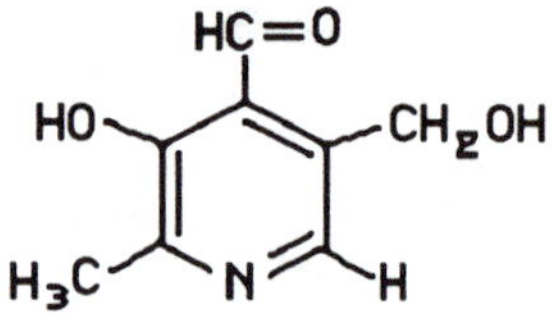

$HC=O$

HO — CH_2OH

H_3C N H

Pyridoxamine

CH_2NH_2

HO — CH_2OH

H_3C N H

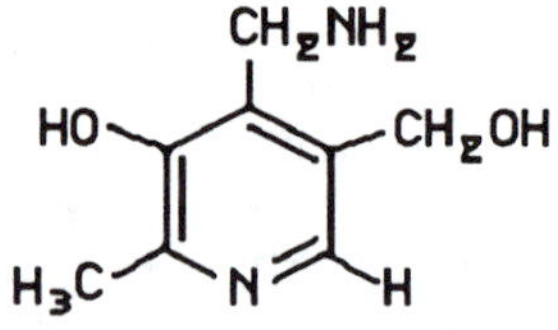

Functions which might affect performance or recovery from injury
B_6 is needed for growth and maintenance of the adrenal cortex, and for the formation of serotonin, norepinephrine, and ACh. It works with

vitamin E in slowing down free radical formation. It influences fluid balance by helping control the sodium/potassium balance. It is involved in the production of red blood cells, maintenance of healthy arteries, and resistance to **stress**. B6 is stored primarily in the muscle, and is needed for the release of **glycogen** from the muscles and liver. It is a part of over 60 enzyme systems, and plays a role in the metabolism and utilization of fats, carbohydrates, and protein. It is needed by each cell in the body to separate out the amino acids which meet that cell's needs. For **aerobic performance**, it is needed both in the breakdown of glycogen and in gluconeogenesis, as well as in the formation of oxygen-carrying or -utilizing substances such as hemoglobin, myoglobin, and the cytochromes.

Vitamin B6 has been used in the treatment of **rheumatism** and **painful finger joints**. In one experiment, a combination of B6 and alpha-ketoglutarate was found to increase **lung capacity** and reduce peak **lactate** levels in treadmill tests.

Requirements

The U.S. RDAs vary from 1.8 to 2.0 mg daily, up to 2.5 in pregnancy and lactation. This amount would theoretically be found in two large bananas, two large avocadoes, or half a pound of beef liver.

Dr. John Ellis recommends a minimum of 15 mg daily, Dr. Newbold takes 100 mg three times a day, and Carl Pfeiffer takes 25 mg daily.

Too much B1 increases the need for B6. So does a high protein intake, though some nutritionists argue that the protein foods would contain enough B6 to meet the increased need. The need for B6 also increases with use of diuretics, certain steroids, penicillamine, amphetamine, chlorpromazine, and birth control pills, with exposure to radiation, and possibly with hyperthyroidism.

Deficiency symptoms

Symptoms of B6 deficiency are similar to those of B2 or B3. The first symptoms may be **tiredness** and **weakness**. Others include **nerve and muscle pain, numbness and cramps in the extremities**, dermatitis, oily skin, cracks in the corners of the mouth, sore mouth, a smooth red tongue, and a rash near the mouth, eyes, and eyebrows. Mental symptoms include **apathy**, a loss of sense of responsibility (don't feel like practising?), **insomnia, nervousness**, irritation, and depression. There can also be **arthritis**, dizziness, anemia, hypoglycemia, weight loss, heart irregularity, increased urination, poor coordination in walking, **temporary paralysis of a limb, tremors**, and kidney stones of the oxalate type. All symptoms except for kidney stones are quickly relieved by B6 supplementation, some of them within 24 hours.

Urine tests for B$_6$ deficiency may read positive within as little as three weeks of its onset. The presence in the urine of xanthuremic acid, an abnormal breakdown product of tryptophan, signals that there is not enough B$_6$ to convert tryptophan to niacin.

Toxicity
According to some investigators, toxic amounts are about 3 g/kg of body weight, i.e. 210 *grams* for a 70 kg person, daily. (This is more than 100,000 times the RDA.) Others have found loss of peripheral sensory input and impaired gait with doses of 2 to 6 grams (still over 1,000 times the RDA).

Although high protein intake increases the need for B$_6$, it has been found that after following a low-carbohydrate (high-protein?) diet, B$_6$ supplementation led to faster depletion of muscle glycogen; however, no changes in performance capacity were noted.

Synergists
Synergists include B$_1$, B$_2$, B$_3$, biotin, folic acid, vitamin C, vitamin E, magnesium, potassium, sodium, and possibly zinc. Linoleic acid relieves the skin irritation caused by B$_6$ deficiency.

Food sources
B$_6$ is found in bananas, soy beans, wheat germ, bran, brown rice, nutritional yeast (especially engevita), black strap molasses, and dessicated liver. Some of these may look suspiciously like supplements, but they are listed here because like other food sources they contain enzymes and unknown factors missing in synthetic vitamins. Moderate amounts of B$_6$ are found in avocados, grapes, pears, beans, peas, leafy green vegetables, eggs, butter, and most cereals. Other fruits and vegetables are poor sources, as are cheese, milk, and all processed foods.

VITAMIN B$_{12}$ (ANY OF A GROUP OF COBALAMINS ACTIVE IN MAN)

Functions which might affect performance or recovery from injury
Vitamin B$_{12}$ is needed for a healthy **nervous system**, production of red and white blood cells, healthy skin and mucous membranes, function of digestive tract, and metabolism of carbohydrate and fat. Smokers and their colleagues take note: vitamin B$_{12}$ protects the myelin sheath of the optic nerve from damage caused by tobacco

smoke. It may be useful in treating **bursitis**, osteoarthritis, mental confusion, irritability, **poor memory**, inability to concentrate, depression, insomnia, and **lack of balance**.

Requirements
The U.S. RDAs are 5 to 6 *mcg* (1,000 mcg = 1 mg) for adults, less for children and more in pregnancy or lactation. Theoretically this amount can be supplied by a pound of T-bone steak, five ounces of salmon, or six large eggs.

The British Journal of Nutrition reported using 10 *mg* (more than 1,000 times the RDA) in the treatment of fatigue and tiredness in people who did not seem to be deficient in B_{12}.

Many people suffering from B_{12} deficiency do so because they lack a mucoprotein called intrinsic factor, which is produced by the stomach and needed for B_{12} absorption. They will not benefit from oral supplementation, but require intramuscular injections.

Low levels of HCl in the stomach also decrease absorption of B_{12}.

Deficiency symptoms
Pernicious anemia can take several years to manifest, because the body stores a reserve of B_{12}. It is an extremely serious condition, needing a doctor's care. Damage to the nervous system, which occurs in 40 to 95 percent of pernicious anemia cases, can be irreversible. Symptoms include **numbness and tingling in the arms** and legs, poor muscular coordination, **sore back**, **weakness**, fatigue, dizziness, pallor, dimmed **vision**, diminished **reflexes**, mood changes, poor **memory**, slowed thinking, and **nervousness**. (Any or all of these symptoms can also be caused by a large number of other, less serious conditions.) Early stages of deficiency are easily cured by B_{12} intake.

Toxicity
No toxicity has been reported, in doses of up to 10,000 times the RDA.

Synergists
Folic acid will avert symptoms of B_{12} deficiency in red blood cells while nervous system damage continues, thus masking an early warning symptom of deficiency. One study found that poor people with B_{12} deficiency tend to have anemia without nervous system damage, while wealthier people tend to have more nervous system damage along with the anemia; this may be due to the fact that the wealthy consume more folic acid-containing foods, such as fresh fruits and vegetables.

B_6 is needed for absorption and storage of B_{12}. Other synergists include pantothenic acid, thiamin, vitamin E, and vitamin C.

Food sources

B_{12} is found almost exclusively in animal foods, especially organ meats and clams. Yoghurt is another good source, as are all animal products, including fish, especially salmon and sardines.

Moderate amounts of B_{12} are found in comfrey and dulse, and alfalfa sprouts may contain some. Supplements are generally made by bacteria or molds, so they should be acceptable to vegans.

Although some B_{12} is made in the intestines, little of that is absorbed.

FOLIC ACID (FOLACIN, FOLATE)

Functions which might affect performance or recovery from injury

Folic acid is needed for protein metabolism, cell division, and the formation of hemoglobin and red and white blood cells. It has been used to treat hardening of the arteries and ulcers. It can either stimulate or sedate, depending on the individual.

Requirements

The U.S. RDA is 400 *mcg*. Supplements containing greater amounts are available only as pregnancy vitamins (800 mcg) or upon prescription. Theoretically 400 mcg can be supplied by six cups of cooked broccoli, four ounces of chicken liver, or five oranges.

Passwater puts the need for folic acid between 100 mcg and 2 mg. Therapeutic doses of 5 to 10 *mg* were used regularly before the restrictions in supplement potency went into effect. Much larger doses have been used in megavitamin therapy.

Stress increases the need for folic acid. So do infection, hyperthyroidism, alcohol, **aspirin**, anticonvulsants, streptomycin, sulfa drugs, and birth control pills.

Deficiency symptoms

Folic acid deficiency produces symptoms similar to those of B_{12} deficiency, since both are needed for healthy red blood cells. They take only about five months to appear and include hostility, **apathy**, and paranoid behavior. In case of **surgery**, a folic acid deficiency can increase the danger of hemorrhage by a factor of five.

Toxicity

Daily doses up to 5 mg have been taken without problems. (This is almost 40 times the RDA.) In rats given massive doses, the precipitaion of crystalline folic acid in the kidneys produces renal toxicity. The effectiveness of some anti-epileptic drugs has been decreased by folic acid, and very high concentrations are believed to cause convulsions.

The amounts of folic acid available without prescription are restricted since it can mask the symptoms of B_{12} deficiency. Folic acid can make body stores of B_{12} available for the production of healthy red blood cells, at the expense of the nervous system. Pernicious anemia is thus averted while nervous system damage still takes place, so that by the time symptoms do appear, the damage to the nervous system is much more serious than it would be if no folic acid supplements had been taken.

Synergists

Synergists for folic acid include B_1, B_2, B_3, B_6, B_{12}, biotin, pantothenic acid, and vitamins C and E, though vitamin C does increase excretion of folacin in the urine.

Food sources

Folic acid is found in green leafy vegetables, liver, soy beans, fresh oranges, and whole wheat.

VITAMIN B$_5$ (PANTOTHENIC ACID)

$$\text{HO} - \text{CH}_2 - \underset{\underset{\text{CH}_3}{|}}{\overset{\overset{\text{CH}_3}{|}}{\text{C}}} - \underset{\underset{\text{OH}}{|}}{\text{CH}} - \overset{\overset{\text{O}}{\|}}{\text{C}} - \text{HN} - \text{CH}_2 - \text{CH}_2 - \overset{\overset{\text{O}}{\|}}{\text{CH}}$$

Functions which might affect performance or recovery from injury

Pantothenic acid forms part of CoA, which is needed for carbohydrate, fat, and protein metabolism. It is essential for the formation of the neurotransmitter ACh. It helps protect the body against the toxic effects of antibiotics and radiation. Pantothenic acid has increased resistance to **stress** even in apparently well-nourished subjects.

Pantothenic acid has been used in England to treat **arthritis**. It has also been used in the treatment of fatigue. Haas suggests that pantothenate supplementation improves **endurance**, but cites no studies to support this.

Requirements

There is no official RDA, but the need is estimated at about 10 to 15 mg per day. Theoretically this amount can be supplied by six ounces of beef liver, two pounds of fresh salmon, eight cups of yoghurt (skim), or three pounds of fresh raw peas.

Deficiency symptoms

Pure pantothenic acid deficiency (without general malnutrition or B complex deficiency) is very rare. Even when intake is limited, the body compensates by decreasing the rate of excretion. In the only observed cases, deficiency was induced by a special diet lacking the vitamin or containing an antagonist. Symptoms included headaches, nausea, abdominal cramps, **impaired motor coordination, tingling hands**, and hypoglycemia. These were all reversed with the administration of the vitamin.

Deficiency of pantothenic acid could occur in a diet lacking in B vitamins in general, particularly in alcoholics.

Toxicity

Doses of 10 to 20 grams (1,000 times the suggested intake) have produced occasional diarrhea.

Synergists and antagonists
Synergists for pantothenic acid include vitamins B_1, B_2, B_3, B_6, C, folic acid, and biotin, as well as phosphorus, sulfur, magnesium, and manganese.
The antagonist used to elicit pantothenic acid deficiency (above) was omega methyl pantothenic acid.

Food sources
The name pantothenic acid comes from the Greek *pantos*, meaning "everywhere," because it exists in all living cells. It is found in all unprocessed foods, especially eggs, liver, herring, peanuts, and peas. Though it is found in muscle meats, their ratio of pantothenic acid to thiamin is about half of the ratio (11:1) found in human muscle tissue. Pantothenic acid is partially destroyed by virtually all forms of processing, including heating.

BIOTIN

**Functions which might affect performance
or recovery from injury**
Biotin is involved in **glycogen** synthesis and seems to be needed for **gluconeogenesis**. It is also needed for production of fatty acids, nucleic acids, and some amino acids. This makes it necessary for growth, healthy skin, **nerves**, bone marrow, and sweat glands. Biotin has been used to treat depression.

Requirements
The unofficial RDAs for biotin are 100 to 200 *mcg* for adults. The average intake appears to range from 100 to 300 mcg. Most people get enough biotin in their diets; in the few recorded cases of deficiency, the victims had subsisted mainly on raw eggs (the avidin in egg white binds to biotin) for several months. Antibiotics and sulfa drugs may destroy the intestinal bacteria needed to produce biotin, so biotin-rich foods should be eaten, along with lactobacillus culture to re-establish

the bacteria. B complex supplements are not likely to be high in biotin, as it is expensive to produce commercially.

Deficiency symptoms
Early symptoms of biotin deficiency include **muscle pain**, anemia, nausea, tiredness, sleeplessness, poor appetite, skin problems, nervous disturbances, and reduced glucose tolerance.

Extreme deficiency can result in high cholesterol, heart problems, and paralysis.

Toxicity
Excess biotin is easily excreted. There are no reported toxic side effects, even in infants under six months who were treated for seborrheic dermatitis with daily injections of up to 10 *mg* (3,000 times the RDA for that age group).

Synergists
Synergists for biotin include vitamins B_2, B_6, B_{12}, folic acid and pantothenic acid. These also appear to influence the amount of biotin synthesized in the intestines.

Food sources
Good food sources include cauliflower, peanuts, lima beans, beef liver, sardines, and whole grains. Biotin is also synthesized in the intestines.

LECITHIN (CHOLINE AND INOSITOL)

Choline   Inositol

$$(CH_3)_3 \, \overset{\overset{\displaystyle OH}{\displaystyle |}}{N}CH_2CH_2OH$$

Functions which might affect performance
or recovery from injury
Lecithin is essential to the function of the **nervous system**. It keeps cholesterol in solution in the blood, thus preventing it from forming gall stones. It is the precursor of ACh. Experiments with soya lecithin indicate that it may give increased **power and endurance**.

Choline has been used to reduce blood pressure and relieve headaches.

About seven percent of the **inositol** intake is converted to glucose. Inositol is needed for healthy brain cells and bone marrow.

Requirements

There is no official RDA for lecithin, but the intake of inositol should be about the same as that of choline. Average intake is 300 to 1,000 mg daily.

In animals, the **choline** requirements are affected by fat, protein, or carbohydrate intake, caloric intake, and room temperature (more is needed in warm rooms).

There is some evidence from animal experiments that males synthesize more **inositol**, and thus need less in their diets than females do.

Deficiency symptoms

Since a clear-cut **choline** deficiency has never been seen in humans, it is not officially classed as a vitamin. Animal experiments suggest that there could be fatty acid deposits in the liver and heart, high blood pressure, hardening of the arteries, liver and kidney damage.

No signs of **inositol** deficiency have been found in human beings. Experimental animals on inositol-deficient diets have exhibited a slowed growth rate and intestinal fat deposits.

Toxicity

Prolonged consumption of **choline** supplements (rather than eggs or lecithin) can lead to a deficiency of vitamin B_6. In the treatment of Huntington's disease and tardive dyskinesia, doses up to 20 grams per day have been used for several weeks; some patients reported dizziness, nausea, and diarrhea, as well as slight EKG irregularities. This level of intake often gives the patient a fishy odor.

People have taken daily doses of up to 3 grams of **inositol** for short periods of time with no toxic effects.

Synergists

Possible synergists include betaine or betaine hydrochloride, and vitamin B_{12}.

Food sources

Most lecithin supplements tend to be impure, so food sources might be preferrable.

Choline is found in egg yolks, legumes, whole wheat, and meat.

Inositol is found in whole grains, citrus fruits, and liver.

PABA (PARA AMINO BENZOIC ACID; A COMPONENT OF FOLIC ACID)

**Functions which might affect performance
or recovery from injury**
PABA is perhaps best known as a sun screen. It is also needed for formation of red blood cells and maintenance of healthy skin.

Requirements
None have been established. Cheraskin suggests 25 to 50 mg as a supplemental level.
   Sulfa drugs in large amounts block PABA absorption, while PABA in large amounts blocks the absorption of the drug.

Deficiency symptoms
See folic acid.

Toxicity
Most sources say that PABA is nontoxic, though there is some evidence that continued doses of 30 to 100 mg can be toxic to the liver, heart, and kidneys.

Food sources
Good food sources include liver, eggs, and molasses.

CARNITINE (VITAMIN B$_T$)

**Functions which might affect performance
or recovery from injury**
Carnitine is an amino acid which may increase the rate of fatty acid oxidation and augment **anaerobic metabolism**.

Requirements
There has been no dietary need established, and many nutritionists do not consider carnitine a vitamin at all. Most people can synthesize enough carnitine to meet their needs. In cases where the body is unable to synthesize it but is able to utilise it, dietary carnitine supplementation has helped relieve deficiency symptoms.

Deficiency symptoms
Low levels of carnitine have been associated with **muscle weakness** and lipid accumulation between muscle fibers. They are also linked to diabetes and hyperthyroidism.

Toxicity
None established.

Food sources
Carnitine is found in milk, liver, muscle meats, and yeast.

PANGAMIC ACID (B$_{15}$), OROTIC ACID (B$_{13}$), AND LAETRILE (B$_{17}$)

Functions which might affect performance or recovery from injury
Some people consider these three substances to be drugs rather than vitamins, even though they are found in food.

Pangamic acid and **N,N-Dimethylglycine**, which is thought to be its active component, are heavily used by competitive athletes. Pangamic acid is used to synthesize steroids and some amino acids, stimulate glucose metabolism, increase **muscle glycogen** levels, promote **building of muscle**, shorten **reflex time**, increase **stamina**, enhance oxygen uptake and transport, increase efficient use of oxygen, and regulate the function of the **adrenal** glands and **central nervous system**. It normalizes blood cholesterol and is needed for metabolism of proteins, fats, and carbohydrates. Methyl groups donated by pangamic acid bind to toxins, pollutants, and carcinogens, preventing them from doing damage to the body. Pangamic acid has been used to get rid of **crystal deposits resulting from strenuous exercise**. The Russians have used it to treat asthma, alcoholism, and drug addiction, as well as to help the mentally retarded. It improves brain function and circulation in those with blood sugar problems, promotes **healing of injuries**, and may **improve athletic performance**, especially in **short, intensive exercise** (it helps mobilize fat and decreases **lactic acid** buildup). With B_{12} it is used for severe compound fractures.

Orotic acid is involved in the synthesis of nucleic acids. It improves the disease-fighting ability of white blood cells, and is important in the metabolism of B_{12}.

Laetrile is the controversial cancer fighter, proposed by some as a preventive measure as well (5 to 20 apricot kernels per day).

Requirements
There are no RDAs for these substances. **Pangamic acid** is given in therapeutic doses of about 20 to 50 mg.

Toxicity
Pangamic acid toxicity has been reported only at 100,000 times its therapeutic dose. The compound is considered ill-defined, and some B_{15} preparations may contain mutagenic substances.

Orotic acid is considered non-toxic.

Proponents of preventive use of **laetrile** warn against taking more than one gram at a time.

Synergists
Synergists for **pangamic acid** include vitamins C, A, E, and the B complex.

Food sources
Sources of **pangamic acid** include whole grains and seeds, as well as apricot kernels.

The best food sources for **orotic acid** are whey and some of the root vegetables.

Laetrile is found in almonds and sprouted seeds. It is also found in apricot kernels and other things that most of us don't normally eat.

VITAMIN C (ASCORBIC ACID)

$$HOCH_2 - CH \begin{matrix} OH \\ | \end{matrix}$$

Functions which might affect performance
or recovery from injury
Vitamin C is needed for formation of **collagen**, the connective tissue found in teeth, bones, cartilage, skin, blood vessels, and the cement that holds together all the organs and tissues of the body. Collagen is the structural basis of the body, and is required to repair wounds and injured tissues; vitamin C levels have been observed to drop as much as 75 percent within 24 hours after surgery. Sufficient vitamin C prevents running injuries to ligaments, **tendons**, and bones. It is also essential for the maintenance of healthy **gums**.

Vitamin C is essential for maintenance of the **adrenal** glands and synthesis of adrenaline, formation of steroids, production of serotonin, and absorption of iron. It is considered an important factor in maintaining low blood cholesterol. It acts as an antiseptic and antibiotic, fighting infections by enabling the white blood cells to perform phagocytosis, and by increasing interferon production. Vitamin C helps detoxify or inactivate cadmium, lead, mercury, carbon monoxide, bromides, benzene, nitrosamines, strychnine, barbiturates, **Aspirin**, poison ivy, and insect bites. It is a powerful antioxidant, so it fights free radicals, and may also assist intracellular oxidation-reduction reactions.

Dr. Irwin Stone says vitamin C is useful for **arthritis** and **rheumatism** (scorbutic arthritis is considered a manifestation of scurvy). It has also been used for **back pain**, particularly disc problems.

Experiments indicate that vitamin C supplementation is of benefit in **muscular exercise**, increasing resistance to **fatigue** (measured on a **finger** ergograph!), increasing **working capacity** (bicycle ergometer), decreasing pulse rate, recovery time, and **lactic acid** buildup, increasing **mechanical efficiency**, and reducing oxygen requirements by improving **oxygen uptake** and possibly increasing the amount of oxygen available to the cell. It also increases **alertness**. Studies from Russia, Germany, and Central Europe indicate that vitamin C has ergonomic effects, but studies from western Anglo-Saxon countries do not support this conclusion.

Requirements

It may take as little as 10 to 20 mg per day to prevent scurvy in a healthy person living in a clean, unstressful environment. The U.S. RDA keeps going down: once it was aimed at tissue saturation, but now it is closer to minimal scurvy-prevention levels. In 1974 it was 45 mg, while the Canadian RDA was 30 mg. The human body, when fully saturated with vitamin C, is thought by some researchers to contain about 5000 mg, though others place this figure at 1500 mg. Some nutritionists also question the validity of attempting to maintain tissue saturation, since this level is not advocated for other vitamins or minerals.

Stress depletes vitamin C levels, as do barbiturates, sulfa drugs, and large quantities of water. Absorption is reduced by toxins, baking soda, pain-killers (e.g. **Aspirin**), pollution, smoking, disease, high fever, prolonged use of antibiotics or cortisone, and inhalation of organo-chloride pesticides or gasoline.

Not only do the RDAs fail to take these stressors into account, but they also don't seem to cover the biochemical differences among people: in guinea pigs, the amount of vitamin C required to prevent scurvy can vary as much as 20-fold.

If the animals whose bodies are capable of producing vitamin C were as big as humans, they would synthesize as much as 4.9 *grams* per day (rats), 13.3 grams per day (goats), or 10 to 12 grams per day (dogs and cats). Gorillas, who share our inability to synthesize vitamin C, eat about 4 grams per day.

One argument against such high requirements in humans is the difficulty of devising diets which would supply anything close to these amounts without supplementation. Humans maintain the same plasma concentration as farm animals on 40 to 50 mg per day. (The question is, are these farm animals getting optimal amounts?)

What do the vitamin C enthusiasts suggest? Linus Pauling says people's needs range from 250 mg to 10 grams daily, Dr. Harold Rosenberg suggests 1 to 5 grams daily, Dr. Szent-Gyorgyi takes 2 grams daily, and Dr. Fred Klenner takes 20 grams daily.

There are some indications that supplements should be taken with a snack, possibly fruit, to prevent destruction of the vitamin by intestinal bacteria. Most people recommend small doses throughout the day, to maximize absorption.

Deficiency symptoms

Scurvy is a serious but rare disease which takes 3 to 12 months of severe dietary deficiency to develop. Early signs are **weakness**, lack of appetite, and increased susceptibility to disease.

Some people consider easy bruising and bleeding **gums** to be signs of low-level vitamin C deficiency. Another clue may be decreased carbohydrate tolerance.

Toxicity

Excess vitamin C is excreted, so there is little possibility of toxicity. It can cause gastric upset, but this problem can be avoided by taking it with food or by using the sodium ascorbate form. It can cause diarrhea; this symptom is sometimes used to determine therapeutic doses, since "bowel tolerance" seems to increase with need for the vitamin.

Fears of kidney stones largely stem from a 1970 report which theorized that large doses of vitamin C would cause precipitation of the urate and cystine crystals in the urinary tract. There seems to be no evidence that this actually happens; indeed, some nutritionists have even used it to prevent kidney stones.

There is also speculation that since vitamin C enhances iron absorption, those with sufficient iron might develop a surplus, which is toxic.

One clinical study used "large" (unspecified) amounts of the vitamin to cause miscarriage.

Ascorbic acid in large doses can interfere with anticoagulant therapy, since it blocks the effect of anti-clotting agents.

Regular consumption of large doses of vitamin C may create a dependency, and may not even increase blood levels of the vitamin.

Massive concentrated doses can create electrolyte disturbances. In these doses, vitamin C is a diuretic, and could cause mineral depletion.

The presence of vitamin C in the urine can produce a positive sugar test, and thus a false diagnosis of diabetes.

Injections of massive doses of ascorbic acid can destroy red blood cells.

Synergists and antagonists

Synergists of vitamin C include vitamins A, B_6, B_{12}, E, K, pantothenic acid, folic acid, and the bioflavonoids. Some copper is needed in vitamin C metabolism. It helps prevent scurvy, and recycles vitamin C by reoxidizing it.

Antagonists include alkali such as baking soda, and possibly copper (in spite of the preceding).

Food sources
Foods supplying 100 mg or more per gram include black currants, guavas, broccoli, kale, parsley, brussels sprouts, and green and red pepper. Good sources (50 to 99 mg per gram) include oranges, strawberries, cabbage, cauliflower, and spinach. Fair sources (30 to 49 mg per gram) include grapefruit, limes, melons, asparagus, potatoes, and Swiss chard.

The vitamin C content of foods can vary widely due to factors ranging from growing conditions to processing. Vitamin C content is preserved by refrigeration.

BIOFLAVONOIDS (VITAMIN P)

The bioflavonoids are a group of nutrients, including rutin, citrin, hesperidin, nobiletin, floavones, and flavonals, which work and exist with vitamin C. They are not officially recognized as vitamins.

**Functions which might affect performance
or recovery from injury**
The bioflavonoids maintain healthy **collagen**, combine with toxic metals, act as antioxidants, and reduce the requirements for vitamin C by making it more effective. They are particularly important in the maintenance of capillary strength and permeability. They also seem to stop clumping of red blood cells, and have been used to prevent hemorrhage associated with anticoagulants. They have been used in cases of **arthritis**.

Requirements
There is no RDA for bioflavonoids. Most foods containing vitamin C also contain some of them. Average dietary intake has been estimated at 1 gram daily. As supplements, Drs. Biskind and Martin suggest 200 mg three times daily, while Cheraskin recommends 50 to 300 mg daily. Since bioflavonoids reduce vitamin C requirements, many vitamin C supplements contain them.

Deficiency symptoms
Deficiencies affect capillary health, resulting in easy bruising and bleeding. There could also be a tendency towards **rheumatism**.

Toxicity
None has been reported.

Food sources
Particularly good sources of bioflavonoids are the white pulp of citrus fruit and the pulp of green peppers. Again, most sources of vitamin C are also sources of bioflavonoids.

VITAMIN A

one form of retinol (s-all-trans-retinol)

**Functions which might affect performance
or recovery from injury**
Vitamin A is needed for healthy **skin,** mucous membranes, and **eyes,** as well as for protein synthesis in **tissue repair.** (It also affects the synthesis of **muscle proteins.**) It reduces cholesterol levels. It is essential to the health of the **adrenal glands** and maintenance of the myelin sheath of the **nerve cells.** (Saturating the tissues with vitamin A may quell **nervousness.**) One doctor who treated 2,500 **arthritis** patients with large doses of vitamins A, D, E and minerals has reported moderate to excellent success in 60 percent of the cases. There is evidence that vitamin A deficiency may slow down glycogen synthesis from lactate, and thus affect **endurance.**

Are performers, with their various calluses in strange parts of the body, more susceptible to skin cancer? I haven't heard of any evidence to this effect, but in case the possibility causes concern, there is evidence that sufficient vitamin A protects against squamous carcinoma.

Requirements
Vitamin A is found as *retinol* in animal products. It is also found as carotenoids, mainly *beta-carotene*, in vegetable sources. Carotenoids, or provitamin A, are converted to vitamin A in the body as needed, so they may be safer in large doses. On the other hand, vegetable

beta-carotene

note the symmetry –
conversion to two molecules of retinol requires only the addition of two molecules of water.

sources are less efficient: one mg retinol (one retinol equivalent) equals six mg carotene. Five retinol equivalents equal one IU (international unit), the common measure for this vitamin. Since vitamin A is stored in the liver, we don't need to meet our needs on a daily basis.

The U.S. RDA for vitamin A is 5,000 IU per day. Theoretically this amount can be supplied by ten eggs, ten cups of fortified skim milk, five carrots, or a cup and a half of broccoli flowers. There are U.S. government reports that a third of all Americans consume less than the RDA, and that forty percent of the population show clinical symptoms of deficiency. Infections increase the need for vitamin A, while decreasing its absorption rate. Exposure to bright lights, especially artificial light, reduces vitamin A stores. Some recommend as much as 20,000 IU daily for the general population.

Do performers need more vitamin A than the general population? Even **minor exertion** uses up vitamin A and decreases its absorption rate for up to four hours. There is also some Russian research which indicates that under **stress** we need more vitamin A than usual.

Deficiency symptoms
Night blindness is the best known symptom of vitamin A deficiency and is often cited as its earliest symptom, but some nutritionists argue that other low-level symptoms appear at an earlier stage of vitamin A depletion. The body protects the eyes, giving them access to the vitamin while allowing the less vital systems to become depleted. Early symptoms include skin problems (dry skin, acne) and irritable mucous membranes (itchy eyes, sore throat, increased number of upper respiratory infections), but these symptoms can be caused by a number of factors and do not in themselves indicate a vitamin A deficiency.

Toxicity
Vitamin A toxicity is widely used as an example of the dangers of supplementation. Hypervitaminosis A is characterized by nausea, loss of appetite, loss of hair, and liver and spleen enlargement. Some people report limitations to motion, weakness, joint pain, rough skin, cracking lips, and peripheral edema with aching in the extremities, as well as irritation or emotional lability. There are, however, several reasons for claiming that toxicity is not a problem for the performer:

(1) All recorded cases apparently involve doses in excess of 100,000 IU daily, over a period of 6 to 15 months. This is 20 times the RDA, and 5 times the highest amount recommended here. In addition, the vitamin A was in the form of a synthetic petroleum product. Single dose toxicity seems to be restricted to infants and those who eat polar bear liver.

(2) Symptoms of toxicity are reversible, disappearing in about three to seven *days*. Yes, there is an exception: polar bear liver may have enough vitamin A to cause death, though not all authorities agree that this has actually ever happened.

(3) There are no recorded cases of toxicity from beta carotene. The sole symptom of so-called hypercarotenosis is yellow skin, and most herbalists would argue that this coloring indicates that cleansing is taking place (with the skin acting as an organ of elimination). In any case, the symptom disappears when supplementation stops. For many people, excluding diabetics (see food sources), this makes beta carotene the preferred form of vitamin A supplementation.

These arguments notwithstanding, vitamin A should not be taken before bedtime, as it may be too stimulating.

Synergists and antagonists
Vitamins which increase the effectiveness of vitamin A include vitamins B_2, B_{12}, C, E, and pantothenic acid. Vitamins A and E work together in regulating membrane stability. Absorption of carotenoids from the intestine is highest when there are low-molecular-weight fatty acids in the diet, and absorption is reduced when the diet is very low in fat. Low protein diets will slow down vitamin A depletion, if intake of the vitamin is too low to meet current needs.

Zinc increases the need for vitamin A.

Food sources
Vitamin A in the form of retinol is found in fish liver oils, e.g. cod and halibut, also in mammalian liver, kidney, whole milk, and eggs.

Plant sources contain beta carotene, which the body converts to retinol as needed. While this attribute seems to prevent toxicity, conversion is not very efficient, and diabetics can't convert carotene to retinol. Good sources of beta carotene are parsley, carrots, and spinach. Other sources include apricots and broccoli.

The fluorescent lights in supermarkets destroy vitamin A. (Don't buy milk in clear plastic bags.) Produce which is picked before it is ripe has less vitamin A, as do leafy greens grown with nitrate fertilizers. Excessive cooking of vegetables causes losses, but some cooking of high-fiber foods, e.g. carrots, will increases carotene absorption. Frying animal livers causes losses of 10 - 20 percent.

VITAMIN D

D3 (cholecalciferol) D2 (ergocalciferol)

Functions which might affect performance or recovery from injury

Vitamin D is needed in **calcium** and phosphorus transport and metabolism, and greatly increases their absorption, as well as that of iron, magnesium, and other minerals. It helps release calcium from bones when needed, yet it enhances bone mineralization.

It is involved in **glycogen** metabolism and has also been used to treat **myopia** and conjunctivitis. It may have an impact on **aerobic metabolism** through its role in the Krebs cycle.

Vitamin D may improve muscle **strength**, though not much is known about the mechanisms involved. One experimenter reported improvement in physical performance from increased exposure to sunlight, but none from oral intake of the vitamin.

Requirements

The U.S. RDA is 400 IU for growing people, but there is none for adults, though some nutritionists point out that since our calcium and phosphorus needs don't disappear, we still need vitamin D. High acidity of the body tissues interferes with the metabolism of vitamin D. Requirements increase with lack of sunlight, and dark-skinned people need more sun than light-skinned people. Older people don't absorb vitamin D as well, and some nutritionists recommend 800 to 1200 IU daily for people over 60.

Deficiency symptoms

Rickets is the severe deficiency disease, stemming from an imbalance in calcium and phosphorus: it can be induced by a deficiency in these minerals, even in the presence of vitamin D, or conversely by the absence of the vitamin D needed for the absorption of the minerals.

Many people, including adults, may suffer from mild cases of rickets after a long and severe winter. They develop **general aches and pains**, including **back pain** from bending over, as well as **weak muscles** and weight loss. In more severe cases there are **muscle spasms** or tetany.

Toxicity

The synthetic form of vitamin D, ergocalciferol (D$_2$), is more toxic than the natural form, cholecalciferol (D$_3$), despite the structural similarities.

Doses of up 2000 IU in children do not seem to be toxic.

Overdoses in infants can cause excessive deposition of calcium in the bones and arteries, and has been linked in some cases with mental retardation. According to the Merck Manual, 40,000 IU per day for several months will produce toxicity, though Goodhart and Shils report mild hypercalcemia in infants fed one tenth that dose.

Toxic levels for adults are proportionately high, at 100,000 to 200,000 IU per day. (Once again, stay away from polar bear liver.) Symptoms include loss of **muscle tone**, nausea, vomiting, and diarrhea, as well as peeling skin and kidney damage from calcium deposits. Vitamin D overdose may play a role in sunstroke.

Since hypercalcemia can cause irreversible kidney and heart damage, anyone on massive doses of vitamin D should have periodic serum calcium tests.

Synergists and antagonists

Dietary fat is needed to stimulate the bile production necessary for vitamin D absorption. Other synergists include B$_3$. Vitamin A may reduce some of the adverse side effects of massive doses of vitamin D.

Anticonvulsant drugs deplete vitamin D stores.

Food sources

Fish liver oils (cod and halibut) are good sources. Smaller amounts are found in egg yolks, butter, salmon, herring, sardines, and tuna.

Sunlight is a good source of vitamin D, and for those who work indoors, full spectrum lighting seems to help.

VITAMIN E (D ALPHA TOCOPHEROL)

Vitamin E (∝-tocopherol)

Functions which might affect performance or recovery from injury

Many nutritionists consider vitamin E an antioxidant which combats the harmful effects of free radicals and many toxic substances. It regulates blood formation, helps form healthy red blood cells, strengthens blood vessel walls, removes calcium deposits from arteries, enlarges arteries and capillaries, regulates capillary permeability, and may prevent clotting. It also prevents formation of *ceroid bodies* in the **muscles** and vital organs, and increases absorption and utilization of iron. It increases the **efficiency** and **endurance** of the muscles, especially at high altitudes, reducing oxygen requirements and **lactic acid** accumulation. It is also thought to increase **alertness, learning ability,** and **muscle power,** decrease **reaction time,** and control **muscle cramps.** It helps prevent **scar formation and contraction** in wounds, and speeds **wound healing.** In middle-aged people it is also involved in **eye focusing.**

Requirements

Though the U.S. RDA was as high as 30 IU in 1968, the average daily intake is only about 10 to 15 IU. Consequently, in 1973 the RDA was cut in half, but it is still more than many people get. People with diets high in unsaturated fats may get as much as 60 IU of vitamin E daily, but they also need more than those on high-meat diets, since unsaturated fats produce free radicals in the body. According to some nutritionists, the ratio of dietary vitamin E to polyunsaturated fatty acids is more important than the absolute amounts. Given an ideal ratio of 6:10, they claim that most healthy people will automatically meet their needs with food intake, unless they eat large amounts of fish oils, which don't satisfy this ratio. Other nutritionists think the optimal daily intake is from 200 to 800 IU, or about 10 times the RDAs.

The absorption of vitamin E requires bile, so any supplements should be taken with fat-containing foods. Mineral oil laxatives, rancid oils or fats, and estrogen from birth control pills destroy vitamin E. Requirements are increased by heavy physical work, peptic ulcers, absorptive disorders, and low bile production.

Synthetic vitamin E is generally not of the "d" form, but of the "dl" form, and is about one third less potent than the natural, "d" form. There are other, less potent, natural forms (beta, gamma, delta, zeta, epsilon) which seem to work synergistically with the alpha forms, so the best synthetic E is dl alpha tocopherol in a base of mixed tocopherols

Deficiency symptoms

The first sign of vitamin E deficiency is hemolytic anemia, characterized by fragile, bursting red blood cells. The problem is compounded by the decreased iron absorption which results from low vitamin E levels. Further symptoms include **shrinkage of collagen tissues, wasting of muscles,** and impaired pituitary and **adrenal** function. Hemolytic anemia and the formation of ceroid pigments, known as age spots, can be relieved by using other antioxidants (ascorbic acid, selenium, SOD, sulfur-containing amino acids), but other symptoms, e.g. muscular wasting, seem to require vitamin E specifically.

One sign of temporary vitamin E need is sore bumps on the tongue. These can come from eating rancid oils, or from indigestion, particularly when too large a variety of foods is eaten at once.

Toxicity

Excess vitamin E is more readily excreted than other fat-soluble vitamins. No side effects were noted at levels of 800 IU which had been sustained for several years. In cases of high blood pressure or rheumatic heart disease, vitamin E supplements are helpful but should be increased very gradually, as they may create a temporary rise in blood pressure when a supplementation program is first begun. In cases of diabetes and hyperthyroidism it also may be best to increase the dosage gradually.

Synergists and antagonists

Synergists for vitamin E include vitamins A, B_6, B_{12}, C, K pantothenic acid, and folic acid, as well as the minerals selenium and iron (iron increases vitamin E absorption if not taken at the same time.)

Vitamin E should not be taken within three hours of iron supplementation, because the two nutrients interact to form a non-absorbable compound (most nutritionists agree on the principle, but there is considerable variation in the recommended time lapse). Chlorine from tap water destroys vitamin E.

Food sources

The best source of vitamin E is cold-pressed natural vegetable oils. These should be refrigerated to prevent their becoming rancid.

(Rancid oils contain free radicals, which require more vitamin E to neutralize them.) Other sources include alfalfa, lettuce, wheat, oats. Butterfat and meat contain small amounts. Many commercial vegetable oils have their vitamin E removed, because the vitamin can be sold more profitably in capsule form.

VITAMIN K

vitamin K1 (phylloquinone)

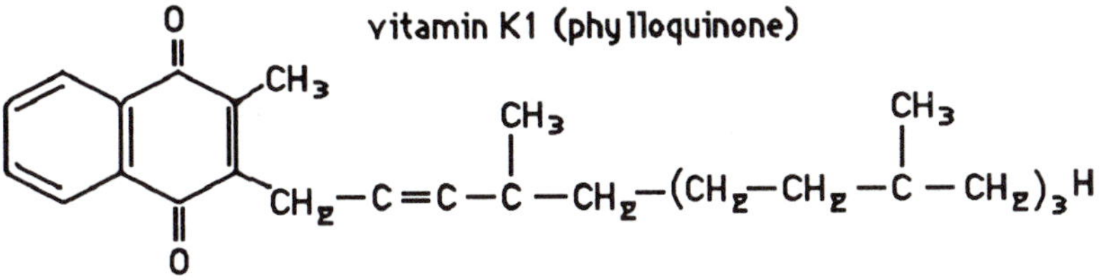

vitamin K2 (menaquinone-n)

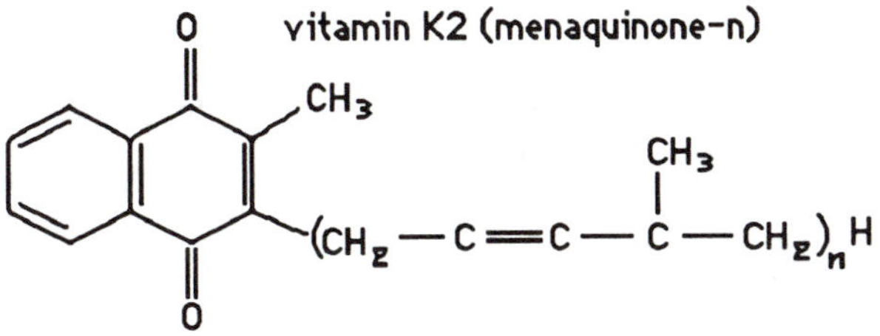

Functions which might affect performance or recovery from injury
Vitamin K is necessary for blood clotting. It is also involved in growth, electron transport, and phosphorylation of glucose. It can lower blood pressure and act as a highly effective painkiller. It may also aid in bone mineralization.

Requirements
There is no RDA for vitamin K. Suggested doses are less than 140 *mcg* per day, though the average diet supplies around 300 to 500 mcg. Since the intestines manufacture enough to meet most of our requirements, people have subsisted on an intake of less than 20 mcg per day with minimal signs of deficiency. Antibiotics kill the bacteria which make vitamin K; they can be replenished by eating cultured milk products such as yoghurt. **Aspirin** and other anticoagulants are antagonists. Fevers increase the need for vitamin K, and mineral oils, e.g. those found in some laxatives, reduce absorption.

Deficiency symptoms
Deficiency is unlikely to be due to low intake, but rather to malabsorption or liver problems. Deficiency can lead to hemorrhage.

Toxicity
The synthetic form is somewhat toxic; the natural forms (made commercially from fish meal or alfalfa) are not. Overdose causes hemolytic anemia, due to an accelerated breakdown of red blood cells.

menadione (synthetic)

Synergists and antagonists
Vitamins A and C help prevent red blood cell fragility.
  Vitamin E balances the coagulating action of vitamin K.

Food sources
Good food sources include cabbage, soy beans, spinach, pork, beef liver, and kidney.

CALCIUM

**Functions which might affect performance
or recovery from injury**
Through its role in muscle contraction and its effect on levels of the
neurotransmitters serotonin, ACh, and noradrenaline, calcium is a
natural **tranquilizer.** A high level of calcium in the blood increases
the action of the heart but decreases the action of nerve cells and
voluntary muscles, while a low level of calcium in the blood leads to
muscle cramps. Calcium relieves PMS and menstrual cramps.

Calcium is a component of all cell membranes, and is found both
inside the cells and in the intercellular fluid. It influences blood
coagulation, blood pressure, cellular adhesiveness, and a number of
enzyme reactions and hormone secretions.

Calcium supplements have been helpful in cases of **arthritis** and
rheumatism.

Requirements
The U.S. RDA is 800 mg per day, while the mean intake ranges from
400 to 1,300 mg. Theoretically this amount can be supplied by four
cups of cooked kale, two and a half cups of almonds, or three cups of
milk. Many nutritionists feel that calcium requirements increase with
age. The intakes of the three bone minerals, calcium, phosphorus, and
magnesium, need to be balanced, though not all nutritionists agree on
the optimal dietary ratios.

Drugs such as steroids and some antibiotics increase calcium
needs, though Goodhart and Shils say they enhance calcium
absorption. Factors which increase the rate of calcium excretion
include bed rest, heavy sweating, and diuretics. Calcium absorption
can be reduced by physical and emotional stress. Foods high in oxalic
acid (chocolate, spinach, rhubarb) or phytic acid (grains) bind with
calcium and thus increase the need for it. Calcium balance depends
on so many interactions among bones, kidneys, digestive system,
blood chemistry, and so on, that it is difficult to determine an
individual's calcium status or dietary needs.

Deficiency symptoms
Early symptoms of calcium deficiency include tender breasts,
edginess, depression, **tremors,** and tingling or numbness in the
extremities. Later signs include brittle bones and **teeth,** improper
blood clotting, and **muscle spasms.** There can be insomnia,
headaches, **nervousness,** and **backaches;** children may have
"growing pains."

Toxicity
Excess calcium is excreted, but when the excretion mechanism is out of balance, or when intake or absorption levels are too high, calcium may be deposited in the organs and soft tissues. Some people who use milk and calcium carbonate antacids for stomach ulcers experience constipation, nausea, vomiting, abdominal pain, and sometimes even delerium, stupor, **weak muscles,** and irreversible kidney damage. Long term hypercalcemia can be treated with phosphorus supplements. The tendency toward hypercalcemia seems to be independent of absolute calcium intake, and has been found even at the RDA levels in vitamin D sensitive people.

Synergists and antagonists
Phosphorus and vitamins A, C, and D are required for calcium absorption. Moderate fat intake and a high protein intake also help raise absorption levels, but eating a lot of meat means too much fat and phosphorus for optimum calcium balance, and overconsumption of protein results in overexcretion of calcium and may increase bone resorption. Exercise which puts some stress on the bones helps keep calcium in the bones rather than allowing it to be excreted.

Food sources
Leafy green vegetables are a good source of calcium. Milk and dairy products contain substantial amounts, though it is only absorbed well from yoghurt and other cultured forms. Almonds and sesame seeds also are high in calcium.

PHOSPHORUS

Functions which might affect performance
or recovery from injury
As part of the ATP molecule, phosphorus is vitally important to all of the cellular energy functions. Thus phosphorus plays a role in almost all body functions, including **muscle contraction** and **conduction of nerve impulses.**

Phosphorus is also an essential part of DNA, RNA, and the phospholipids, e.g. lecithin (cell membranes are composed primarily of phospholipids). It plays a role in a number of enzyme systems, activation of many of the B vitamins, and maintenance of blood pH levels.

Extra phosphorus has been used to speed healing of broken bones and reduce calcium loss. It has also been helpful in reducing mental stress resulting from the aching joints of **arthritis.**

Sodium phosphate and potassium phosphate were used by the German army in World War I to combat fatigue in its soldiers, and the use of phoshates by German athletes was popular as late as the 1950s. Research done in 1984 suggests that phosphate loading may improve **endurance.**

Requirements

The U.S. RDA is 800 mg daily, the same as the RDA for calcium. Theoretically this amount can be supplied by three cups of milk, a pound of chuck roast, a cup of raw almonds, or fifty dried figs. Many nutritionists believe that the calcium to phosphorus ratio should be 2 to 1. Phosphorus is absorbed more easily than calcium but is also excreted more easily.

Deficiency symptoms

The typical North American diet would rarely lead to a phosphorus deficiency, especially given the amount of phosphoric acid in soft drinks. Phosphorus depletion can occasionally result from excessive consumption of antacids or from a vitamin D deficiency. Symptoms include appetite loss, **nervous disorders, mental sluggishness, weakness,** aching bones, and general fatigue. There can also be hemolytic anemia and kidney stones.

Toxicity

High levels of phosphorus decrease calcium absorption. A calcium/phosphorus imbalance can result in **arthritis,** rickets, pyorrhea, and **tooth decay.** Toxic levels of phosphorus per se are rare, except in chronic kidney disorders.

Synergists and antagonists

Calcium and vitamin D may be needed for phosphorus absorption.

Excessive intakes of iron, aluminum, or magnesium interfere with phosphorus absorption.

Food sources

Phosphorus is found in meat, fish, eggs, dairy products, whole grains, seeds, nuts, and figs.

MAGNESIUM

**Functions which might affect performance
or recovery from injury**
Since magnesium reduces the irritability of the nerve cells, it is known as "the **tranquilizing** mineral." At some points in neuromuscular transmission, it acts synergistically with calcium, while at other points the two balance each other.

Magnesium is also involved in regulation of heart beat, activation of over 30 enzymes (including those involved with ATP), protein synthesis (including DNA), and function of the pituitary gland, which in turn regulates the endocrine system. It helps prevent **tissue breakdown** and is needed in the **pyruvic acid** cycle.

Magnesium can speed the healing of bones, control high blood pressure, reduce blood cholesterol, and relieve depression, senility, **nervousness**, and lack of **endurance** in thin air. It may be essential to **recovery from exercise**, and **prevention of muscular cramps**. As little as four to ten days on magnesium supplements can sometimes alleviate fatigue.

Requirements
The U.S. RDA is 300 to 350 mg. Theoretically this amount can be supplied by ninety brussels sprouts, a pound of raw Swiss chard, or a cup of roasted cashews. Some nutritionists recommend 600 to 1,000 mg daily, and Dr. Rosenberg uses 400 to 1,000 mg daily. When intake is low, more magnesium is absorbed.

Magnesium needs increase when blood cholesterol is high. Tetracycline interferes with magnesium metabolism. Alcoholism increases the need for magnesium. Dietary fat, phosphate, lactose, phytate, and oxalate inhibit absorption. Diuretics can cause magnesium loss. High calcium, vitamin D, or protein diets increase magnesium requirements, and heavy exercise lowers the blood and muscle concentration of magnesium.

Deficiency symptoms
Symptoms include **twitches, tremors, loss of coordination**, irregular heart beat, irregular respiration, nausea, anorexia, confusion, apathy, and nervous fatigue. A deficiency in magnesium can result in **overproduction of adrenaline**, blood clots in the heart and brain, and calcium deposits in the blood vessels, kidneys, and heart. It often leads to drops in levels of calcium, phosphorus, and potassium. Low magnesium levels have been related to DT in alcoholics. A mild deficiency may be quite common, since the typical diet contains few fresh green vegetables, and magnesium is lost in food processing.

Toxicity

Supplementing a normal magnesium intake increases excretion and does not alter the blood levels, but an excessive magnesium intake lowers calcium absorption. If the kidneys don't work well, then magnesium could be retained. Abuse of laxatives or antacids (milk of magnesia) can result in drowsiness, **weakness**, and lethargy, leading eventually to central depression, anesthesia, **paralysis of skeletal muscles**, and **respiratory depression**. These symptoms can be counteracted by administration of calcium.

Synergists

Absorption is aided by vitamins B₆, C, and D, and by calcium and phosphorus. Since calcium and magnesium compete for absorption sites, some nutritionists recommend taking these supplements at different times of the day.

Food sources

Food sources of magnesium include green vegetables, many fruits, wheat, corn, nuts, and pumpkin seeds.

POTASSIUM

Functions which might affect performance
or recovery from injury

Potassium works with sodium to regulate cellular membrane potential, blood pH, carbon dioxide elimination, and the amount of sodium in the body. It is involved with glycogen formation, glucose catabolism, **nerve transmission, muscle contraction**, and protein and carbohydrate metabolism. It helps transport glucose across cell membranes, is important in, and is needed for the heart to relax between beats. It has a diuretic effect, allowing the kidneys to eliminate toxins, including a number of substances which harm the heart.

A high potassium diet increases resistance to heat. Potassium has been used sucessfully for the treatment of fatigue and exhaustion.

Requirements

Safe and adequate intakes for adults are considered to be 1.8 to 5.6 grams daily. Theoretically this amount can be supplied by three bananas, three cups of grapefruit juice, three cups of millet, or a pound of turkey.

Excess sodium consumption increases potassium excretion, as do steroids and diuretics. Short bowel transit time can impair potassium absorption. **Stress** increases potassium requirements. So does very heavy **sweating**. Overheated **muscles** release potassium into the blood stream; once excreted, it must be replaced.

Deficiency symptoms

Potassium deficiency can result in **muscular weakness**, and there is some speculation that the weakness once considered a sign of aging may often be due to potassium deficiency. Fatigue is also a symptom, as are **poor neuromuscular function, slow reflexes**, listlessness, **mental confusion**, bone fragility, irregular heart beat, adolescent acne, and insomnia.

Potassium deficiency is not uncommon in athletes and is easily remedied by eating more fruit. There is a blood test for potassium deficiency.

Toxicity

Synthetic supplements may irritate the digestive tract (they are also expensive). Hyperkalemia (too much potassium in the body) is not common, but if dietary intake is suddenly increased beyond 18 grams or excretion is impaired, there can be serious disturbances in cardiac function and renal insufficiency.

Food sources

Sources of potassium include fresh fruits and vegetables, especially bananas.

SODIUM

Functions which might affect performance
or recovery from injury

Sodium and potassium work together to regulate cellular membrane potential and health, and blood pH. Sodium is necessary for **muscle contraction, nerve function**, and formation of HCl. It keeps some of the blood minerals in solution, helps eliminate carbon dioxide, and facilitates alcohol withdrawal.

Requirements

The U.S. RDA for sodium is 2,000 to 4,000 mg daily. Theoretically this amount can be supplied by a teaspoon of table salt, fifteen cups of celery, five cups of canned peas, or a cup and a half of canned chili con carne. Many nutritionists feel the RDA is too high; some put the ideal daily intake at only a few hundred mg. This supports their contention that the RDAs tend to reflect the eating habits of the average U.S. resident rather than any sort of optimal level.

Deficiency symptoms

A sodium deficiency can cause **muscle cramps, weakness** and **twitching,** low blood pressure, collapsed veins, **tissue atrophy,** apathy, anorexia, and poor **memory** and **concentration.** Deficiency is extremely rare, being restricted almost exclusively to those on special diets, e. g. fruitarians or possibly vegans. Chronic alcoholism can deplete salt in the body.

Toxicity

Excessive consumption of sodium causes edema, first appearing as puffiness or darkness under the eyes, then as **swollen fingers,** wrists and ankles, gradually progressing inward from the extremities. Excessive sodium consumption causes excretion of potassium by the kidneys, thus further aggravating the sodium/potassium balance. It interferes with assimilation of foods, especially protein, and slows down elimination of uric acid.

Food sources

Most of our sodium comes from table salt and the salt in processed foods. Alternative sources include sea salt and kelp, which have larger amounts of other minerals to balance the sodium. Celery and okra are high in a form of sodium which passes more easily into the cells, so foods may reduce a craving for inorganic salt.

CHLORINE

Functions which might affect performance
or recovery from injury

Chlorine helps maintain the blood pH and fluid balance. As a part of HCl, it is needed for digestion. It helps the liver filter out wastes, aids in hormone distribution, and is needed to maintain the health of the **joints** and **tendons.** It has been used to treat diarrhea and vomiting.

Requirements

Most people eat too much chlorine: it is even found in the potassium chloride used as a salt substitute. The estimated safe and adequate intakes for adults range from 1.7 to 5.1 grams daily, though many nutritionists feel that we need far less than this amount. The average intake is 3 to 9 grams.

Deficiency symptoms
Chloride deficiency is rare. Symptoms include hair and **tooth loss**, poor **muscle coordination, memory** loss, and impaired digestion and absorption of protein and minerals.

Toxicity
Although atomic chlorine in the form of chlorine gas is extremely toxic, the chlorine ions found in food are safe and beneficial to the body. The chlorine added to water supplies is thought by some to inactivate DNA, destroy beneficial intestinal bacteria, and form carcinogenic organo-chlorides.

Food sources
Most chlorine is consumed in table salt. It is also found in dulse, kelp, rye flour, meats, and seafood.

IRON

Functions which might affect performance
or recovery from injury
Iron is needed for the formation of hemoglobin, which carries oxygen to the cells and removes carbon dioxide, and myoglobin, which forms a reservoir of oxygen in the cells and thus helps get oxygen to the muscles when needed, and cytochrome in the mitochondria, which is involved in energy-transfer reactions in the cell. Iron is also involved in oxidation/reduction reactions, protein metabolism, and **collagen** synthesis. It is found in the brain as a cofactor for neurotransmitter synthesis. Women with **arthritis** have poor iron absorption; I don't know which is considered the cause and which the effect.

Requirements
The U.S. RDA for iron is 18 mg daily for women and 10 mg daily for men. Theoretically 10 mg can be supplied by two pounds of beef liver, half a pound of fresh oysters, or a pound of beet greens. Iron from non-animal sources is absorbed less efficiently, so vegetarians need more iron. Assimilation of iron becomes more efficient as need increases.

Dr. Price recommends 30 mg daily, and Emmanuel Cheraskin recommends supplements of 10 to 25 mg daily above dietary intake.

More iron is required for wound healing, replacement of lost blood, and rapid growth. Low levels of HCl production impair iron absorption, as do antacids, coffee, tea, cellulose, phosphates, carbonates, phytates, and oxalates. Exercise can accelerate loss of iron.

Deficiency symptoms

Many women don't consume enough calories to meet their dietary iron needs without supplements. In spite of their increased caloric needs, endurance runners and other athletes are even more likely to suffer from iron deficiency. Continued iron deficiency eventually leads to anemia, due to reduced hemoglobin levels. The symptoms include fatigue, paleness, **cold hands and feet**, headaches, constipation, brittle and spoon-shaped nails, skin problems, **difficult breathing**, lowered resistance to disease, and a smooth and sore tongue. The time needed to restore cardio-respiratory functions after exercise is often prolonged, along with a rise in **blood lactate** levels. In children there can be hyperactivity, reduced IQ, and decreased attention span. It is possible to have some or all of these symptoms without the anemia; such cases may respond to supplementation without ever showing blood changes, because other stores, e.g. those in the bone marrow and the brain, become depleted first. *Pica*, a craving for non-food substances, is often caused by iron deficiency.

Toxicity

Large doses of iron can cause constipation and upset stomach; sometimes these problems are due mostly to suggestion. Schroeder limits the safe daily dose to 2,000 mg. Intravenous or intramuscular injections of iron can produce headaches, fever, arthralgia, **back pain**, and occasionally **peripheral muscular collapse**.

Hemochromatosis is a rare and often fatal hereditary disease which results in the gradual accumulation of iron in the body. The early symptoms are similar to those of iron deficiency, and taking supplements only aggravates the problem. Later symptoms include cyrrhosis of the liver, diabetes, pigmented skin and cardiac failure.

Synergists and antagonists

Chronic alcoholism can lead to excessive absorption of iron.

Calcium is needed for effective iron absorption. Vitamin C enhances conversion of the ferric form of iron to the absorbable ferrous form. Vitamin B_{12} and folic acid assist the function of iron in the red blood cells. Vitamin E increases iron absorption, as long as the two substances are not taken at the same time. Fructose, lactose, and amino acids facilitate iron absorption.

Excessive manganese intake interferes with iron absorption, and may result in anemia which is reversible by increasing iron intake.

Food sources
Iron is found in liver (especially pork liver), oysters, lean muscle meat, heart, tongue, sardines, lima beans, prune juice, and leafy green vegetables.

ZINC

**Functions which might affect performance
or recovery from injury**
Zinc is a cofactor in about 25 enzyme reactions, including those involved in the Krebs cycle, electron transport, and **energy production**. It is needed for the absorption of B vitamins, maintenance of normal vitamin A levels, and the breakdown of alcohol. It helps regulate body pH, produce HCl, and synthesize DNA and RNA. It important to the immune system and is a component of insulin. In **building up muscles** or **healing injured tissue**, zinc is needed for protein synthesis. Zinc is found in large concentrations in the **voluntary muscles**, bones, and parts of the **eye**. It has been used to help eliminate cholesterol deposits, speed wound healing, and treat diabetes, prostate inflammation, alcoholism, and cirrhosis of the liver.

Requirements
The U.S. RDA is about 15 mg for adults. Theoretically this amount can be supplied by four cups of raw hazelnuts, seven cups of corn meal, or less than an ounce of fresh oysters. Much zinc is lost in refining foods, and many foods today are lower in zinc because they are grown in zinc-depleted soils. Therefore, the average North American diet contains only about half of the RDA of zinc. Alcohol causes zinc to be lost from the body, as does excessive perspiration. Contraceptive pills, penicillamine, and histidine lower zinc levels while increasing need. Pernicious anemia, recovery from surgery, **inflammatory stress**, **rheumatoid arthritis** and infections such as pneumonia can temporarily depress serum zinc levels.

Deficiency symptoms
Symptoms of zinc deficiency include impaired growth, **delayed wound healing**, skin inflammation, diminished sense of taste and smell, loss of appetite, scaling skin, skin ulcers, bone and **joint disease**, atherosclerosis, decreased alcohol tolerance, and decreased

fertility; there may also be high blood pressure. Low zinc levels have been linked to high suicide rates. White spots on the finger nails can be an early sign of zinc deficiency.

Toxicity
Too much zinc can interfere with absorption of copper and iron. It can also irritate the stomach. Zinc is considered relatively nontoxic, since doses of more than two grams, i.e. more than 1,000 times the RDA, are required to produce symptoms. Food stored in galvanized containers, can produce fever and digestive problems including nausea, vomiting, abdominal cramps, and diarrhea. Experimental animals which were fed massive doses developed anemia, grew little, and eventually died.

Synergists and antagonists
Phosphorus is needed for zinc absorption. Vitamin C increases absorption.

Calcium, phytic acid, cadmium, silver, and copper interfere with zinc absorption.

Food sources
Sources of zinc include whole grains, sunflower and pumpkin seeds, meat, milk, egg yolk, herring, and oysters.

CHROMIUM

Functions which might affect performance or recovery from injury
Chromium is part of the glucose tolerance factor, which is vital to the function of insulin and glucose metabolism, and supplementation has helped adult-onset diabetics. So far there is only speculation that decreased chromium levels would impair performance because of disruption of glucose metabolism.

Chromium helps produce RNA and prevent hardening of the arteries.

Requirements
The U.S. RDA for chromium is 0.05 to 0.20 mg. North Americans have considerably less chromium in their bodies than people in many other parts of the world. People who die of heart disease have lower chromium levels than those who die in accidents. Many adults' chromium levels decrease with age.

Deficiency symptoms

Chromium deficiency symptoms may include decreased glucose tolerance, slower growth, and lesions in the aorta. These effects have been observed primarily in animals since there has not been much study of human chromium needs.

Toxicity

Although chromium facilitates the action of insulin, excess amounts of chromium depress insulin activity. The effective range of chromium concentration is quite narrow.

Food sources

The chromium content of foods varies with the quality of the soil in which they were grown and with the amount of processing. Good sources include grains (except rye), vegetable oils, oysters, and pork kidney. Refining grains removes most of their chromium.

COPPER

Functions which might affect performance or recovery from injury

Copper allows iron to be absorbed, oxidized, and released from the liver. Copper is needed for vitamin C metabolism, and the two nutrients work together to form **elastin**, an important part of connective tissue. It also heps maintain strength and elasticity of the arteries, and synthesize proteins and of phospholipids, which form cell membranes and the myelin sheath covering the **nerves**. It is involved in **glucose** metabolism, bone formation, RNA synthesis, **wound healing**, and the oxidation of uric acid. It is a constituent of cytochrome oxidase, which takes part in oxidative ATP synthesis.

Requirements

The RDA is about 2.5 mg. Theoretically this amount can be supplied by one large avocado, two cups of raw almonds, or three ounces of beef liver.

Deficiency symptoms

If copper is deficient, then iron will not be efficiently used in hemoglobin synthesis, and there will be abnormal, short-lived red blood cells and possibly symptoms of anemia. Other deficiency symptoms include a low white-blood-cell count, reduced resistance to infection, bone demineralization, damaged blood vessels, **central**

nervous system impairment, patches of unpigmented skin, and kinky hair.

Toxicity

Inorganic copper is toxic, while organic copper is toxic only in large amounts. Inorganic copper can be absorbed from copper water pipes or utensils, and from beer brewed in copper kettles, milk pasteurized over copper rollers, or food containing copper sulphate (added to improve color). Symptoms include nausea, vomiting, diarrhea, headache, dizziness, **weakness,** and a metallic taste. More severe cases result in high blood pressure, tachycardia, coma, and eventual death.

Too much organic copper (found in copper-rich foods) can cause a zinc deficiency (and too much zinc can cause a copper deficiency).

Synergists and antagonists

Vitamin C is important for copper absorption.

Zinc and copper must be kept in balance. Molybdenum can interfere with copper absorption.

Food sources

Sources include avocados, almonds, beans, peanuts, seeds, organ meats, green leafy vegetables, chocolate, and shellfish.

IODINE

Functions which might affect performance or recovery from injury

Half of the body's iodine is stored in the **muscles** and 20 percent in the thyroid gland, but due to the relative sizes, the concentration in the thyroid gland is 1,000 times that in the muscle. The primary role of iodine is regulating thyroid function, and ultimately **cellular oxidation.**

Requirements

The U.S. RDA for iodine is 100 to 150 *mcg* daily for adults. Theoretically this amount can be supplied by about seven ounces of seafood or two pounds of grain. The body has no feedback mechanism for conserving iodine when intake is deficient.

Eating large amounts of the so-called goitrogens (turnips, cabbage, rutabagas, and peanuts) over a long time can inhibit the formation of thyroid hormones, thus increasing the need for iodine. So can the drug lithium.

Deficiency symptoms

Goiter, the classic iodine deficiency symptom, is indicative of an underactive thyroid. Since the thyroid regulates basal metabolism, there will be a tendency toward obesity, **lower body temperature, flabby muscles,** as well as decreasess in growth, **mental powers,** speech, skin health, protein synthesis, carbohydrate absorption, and conversion of carotene to vitamin A.

Toxicity

Although doses of up to 10 times the RDA result in little or no toxicity, the difference between required and toxic levels is relatively small. Amounts of 25 to 50 times the RDAs will eventually slow thyroid activity, though most people adapt so that function is restored fairly quickly. Those with some kind of previous thyroid disorder are less likely to adapt and may develop goiters, which disappear when iodine intake is reduced. Some people with underactive thyroids have developed overactive thyroids after treatment with 1,000 times the RDA of iodine.

Food sources

Food sources of iodine include ocean fish, shellfish, and seaweeds such as dulse and kelp. Some bread has iodine added as a stabilizer, and a single slice of such bread could provide the RDA.

MANGANESE

Functions which might affect performance
or recovery from injury

The role of manganese is less well understood than that of other minerals. It plays a role in a number of enzyme systems, including SOD (superoxide dismutase), the controversial antioxidant which may protect against cell damage from free radicals. Some of these enzyme systems can also be activated by other minerals, so it is not clear how crucial the presence of manganese is. It is needed in glucose tolerance, synthesis of mucus, metabolism and excretion of protein, and utilization of glucose, vitamin C and some B vitamins. It may be involved in blood formation, RNA activity, oxidative phosphorylation and synthesis of dopamine. It is necessary for bone formation, collagen formation, **muscle contraction**, and normal function of the **central nervous system.**

Requirements
The recommended amounts range from 2.5 to 5 mg daily. Theoretically this amount can be supplied by a cup of hazelnuts (5.7mg), half a pound of raw turnip greens (3 mg), or two cups of cooked brown rice (3.2 mg).

Deficiency symptoms
Deficiency is quite rare, though processing and refining of foods does remove much of their manganese. A high fat, high protein, low calorie diet could contain inadequate manganese.

Manganese deficiency may contribute to symptoms of diabetes. There may also be poor **muscle coordination** and dizziness.

Toxicity
Diet-induced manganese toxicity is virtually unknown, but toxicity has occurred in manganese miners or those who have ingested potassium permanganate. Although large amounts of dietary manganese will increase the liver concentrations, no subsequent symptoms of toxicity have been discovered. Excessive manganese intake interferes with iron absorption and may result in anemia which is reversible by increasing iron intake.

Synergists and antagonists
Lecithin may help prevent manganese deficiency.

Large amounts of dietary calcium and phosphorus decrease manganese absorption. Thiamine overdose results in symptoms of manganese deficiency, which disappear with supplementation.

Food sources
Most foods contain adequate amounts of manganese. Good sources include nuts, legumes, leafy green vegetables, organ meats, and whole grains.

SELENIUM

Functions which might affect performance or recovery from injury
Selenium works with vitamin E as an antioxidant, forming part of the enzyme glutathione peroxidase, which helps maintain tissue

elasticity. Selenium may be related to the health of the heart and may promote antibody production and disease resistance. It may also help protect against heavy metal toxicity (cadmium, mercury). It is found in hemoglobin, myosin, and other energy-transfer proteins, so a deficiency would theoretically impair **aerobic capacity**.

Requirements
The average intake is about 50 to 100 *mcg* daily, though a typical serving of seafood contains vastly more (a large fresh clam could contain up to 16 mg). Garrison and Somer recommend 50 to 200 mcg daily.

Deficiency symptoms
Selenium deficiency can result in decreased growth, faster aging, loss of **elasticity** of tissues, and cardiomyopathy.

Toxicity
Concentrations of selenium over five ppm are toxic, and larger amounts are as toxic as mercury or lead. Selenium can replace sulfur in the body and upset protein metabolism. The difference between required and toxic levels is not very large. Even plants grown in extremely selenium-rich soil can contain toxic concentrations (as high as 10,000 ppm), causing a condition known as "blind staggers" in grazing animals; sometimes this condition can be prevented by a high protein diet. Children raised in selenium-rich areas have developed more tooth decay than normal.

Synergists
Vitamin E and selenium are synergistic, and one will compensate for deficiency of the other, though they can't entirely replace one another.

Food sources
Because of variations in the soil, the selenium content of a specific vegetable can vary as much as 100-fold from one region to another. Good sources include seafood, organ meats, grains, cabbage, tomatoes, and broccoli. If extra selenium seems to be needed in the diet, the safest supplement is probably brewer's yeast.

MOLYBDENUM

**Functions which might affect performance
or recovery from injury**
Molybdenum helps release iron from the liver; it can be used to treat some kinds of anemia as well as iron toxicity. It is also involved in carbohydrate, fat, and protein metabolism and can assist in detoxification of alcoholics. It is needed for the function of two enzymes, aldehyde oxidase and xanthine oxidase. (Both enzymes are important in electron transport, and the latter is also needed for uric acid formation.) Molybdenum is also said to play a role in **mental attitude**.

Requirements
No RDA has been established. The average daily intake is about 300 mcg.

Deficiency symptoms
Deficiency is considered rare but has been artificially induced by increasing tungsten consumption. The results include depletion of tissue levels of the enzyme xanthine oxidase with decreased excretion of **uric acid**, and anorexia.

Toxicity
Large amounts, usually resulting from exposure to industrial pollution rather than from dietary excess, can cause diarrhea, anemia, fatigue, **weakness**, and decreased growth. Molybdenum can interfere with copper absorption.

Antagonists
Tungsten and copper can replace molybdenum in the body. Increased sulfur intake can decrease molybdenum levels.

Food sources
Good food sources include organ meats, cereal grains, legumes, and dark leafy green vegetables that have been grown in molybdenum-rich soils.

Appendix 2

KAVA
an example of a herbalist's research summary

This appendix is not meant to be absorbed in detail. Rather, it is meant to illustrate the extent to which many medicinal herbs have been studied by both scientists and anthropologists.

I chose kava because of its importance in my clinical experience, though it would be difficult to deduce from the findings below how greatly kava can benefit the performer. In relatively small doses it seems to relax strained muscles without affecting the mind or impairing physical abilities.

GENERAL INFORMATION

scientific names: *Piper methysticum* Forster, Fam. Piperaceae. (Sometimes called *Macropiper methysticum* Miq.)
common names: kava, kava-kava.
Synonyms: kav-kava, kavae, kawa, kawaka, awa, ava, ava ava, ava kava, ava root, ava-pepper shrub, intoxicating long pepper, yakona, yaqona, yangona, karae, keu, hoi, wati.
Related species: *Piper plantageneum* of the West Indies is also considered narcotic, but it hasn't been studied.
Habitat: Oceania, Sandwich Islands, Polynesia, South Pacific Islands.
Parts used: dried rhyzomes and roots.

KNOWN CONSTITUENTS

The first chemical investigation of kava was made by Gobley and O'Rorke in 1850. The active constituents are generally considered to be methysticin [M] (isolated by Cuzent, 1861), dihydromethysticin [DHM] (Winzheimer in 1908), kawain [K], dihydrokawain [DHK] (Borsche, 1914-1933), yangonin [Y] (Riedel, 1904), desmethoxyyangonin [DMY], 5,6-Dehydromethysticin, 11-Methoxyyangonin, 11-Methoxy-nor-yangonin (Hänsel et al, 1966), and small quantities of water-soluble constituents named "LE-1," "F1," and "F2."

Variant listings of constituents include the following: flavokawin and flavokawin A; alpha-type alkaloids including M, DHM, K, DHK, Y, and DMY; 5 - 10% of a resin from which six closely related styrylpyrones have been isolated in pure form: Y, DMY, K, DHK, M, and DHM; large amounts of starch; M, Y, DHM, DHK, "mostly lactones and resins variously estimated at between 3 and 4% of the root;" 50% starch, M (the methyl ester of methysticic acid), kavahin (methylene protocatechuic aldehyde, identical with heliotropin or piperonal), and the chief active principle, an acrid resin (2%) separable into the local anesthetic alpha-resin and the less active beta-resin; active resin(s) and yellow volatile oil; resins (alpha-, beta-) 2%, Y, kavaine, M (kavahin-resembles piperine), volatile oil starch 50%, ash 8%; Y is a derivative of the 6-styryl- 4-methoxy-alpha-pyrones; K and M are 5, 6-dihydro-alpha-pyrones.

Chemical formulas: K = $C_{14}H_{14}O_3$, DHK = $C_{14}H_{16}O_3$, M = $C_{15}H_{14}O_5$, DHM = $C_{15}H_{16}O_5$, Y = $C_{15}H_{14}O_4$, DMY = $C_{14}H_{12}O_3$.

PHARMACEUTICAL DETAILS

EFFECTS ON THE NEUROMUSCULAR SYSTEM

Kava pyrones are potent, centrally acting skeletal muscle relaxants, the first of natural origin to be isolated. In their sedative action, they are similar to mephenesin (see fig. 48). Large doses produce both general and local anesthesia. In animal experiments, kava has caused ascending paralysis with ataxia and loss of postural and righting reflexes, abolition of the tonic extensor component of experimentally induced convulsions, blockade of spinal and supraspinal polysynaptic reflexes, and cerebral hyperemia. The tonic stretch reflex in the unanesthetized animal is very sensitive to the depressant action of kava-pyrones. According to Ellingwood, kava "diminishes, and finally destroys, the function of the afferent nerves, by affecting their peripheral ends . . . diminishes, and eventually abolishes, reflex action, by influencing the spinal cord, and probably also the sensory nerves. The paralysis produced by Kava-kava is of spinal origin, and is due to direct action upon the cord."

In doses causing muscular relaxation and paralysis, kava doesn't have a curare-like action on the myoneural junction, nor does it affect the monosynaptic arcs or cause loss of consciousness. There is no effect on EEG arousal from stimulation of the reticular activating system, and little effect on spontaneous cerebral cortex electrical activity.

The central nervous system is stimulated by kava to a species of drowsy and reserved intoxication, similar to the effect of alcohol (but not the same), with confused dreams. Kava has mild halucinogenic properties, and is used as a beverage to allay anxiety and reduce fatigue. K and similar compounds are responsible for its sedative and intoxicating action. The solid extract has been used as a hypnotic.

Drinking kava produces a marked and prolonged (though temporary) insensibility and irritation of the mucous membrane of the mouth, also of the conjunctiva and cornea.

As a local anesthetic, its effects last several days, but it is considered too irritating for general use. Its counterirritant action is similar to pepper.

Kava has been used by athletes to promote **muscle flexibility**. It is also used for neuralgia, either idiopathic or reflex, and can sometimes relieve ocular and aural neuralgia, as well as toothache which isn't due to dental caries.

DIGESTIVE SYSTEM

Kava is a sialagogue which stimulates the salivary but not the cutaneous glands. In its tonic effect on the stomach it resembles the stimulant bitters, acting on all the GI mucous membranes, increasing the appetite, increasing the activity of the digestive glands (increasing salivary secretion "notably"), promoting assimilation, increasing peristalsis (inducing normal and satisfactory bowel movement), and reducing hemorrhoids. It is said to cure chronic intestinal catarrh, anorexia, gastric atonicity, acute and chronic diarrhea, torpidity and functional inactivity of the glands of the GI tract, and atony of the intestinal tract, "especially if nervous phenomena seem to depend upon that condition" (Ellingwood).

GENITO-URINARY SYSTEM

Kava liquid extract was formerly drunk as antiseptic and diuretic in genito-urinary tract inflammation, acute and chronic gonnorhea, vaginitis, leucorrhea, nocturnal incontinence, and other genito-urinary tract problems, including chronic catarrhal conditions. Gonosan, a kava preparation, was also considered an aphrodisiac when taken internally. Felter considers it a blennostatic in sub-acute, slow, intractable, persistent, chronic gonorrhea (with citrate of potash or oil of sandalwood). It also relieves the acute form when it is sluggish, slow to respond to treatment, and tending toward gleet. Ellingwood says kava "will cure gleet where all other remedies have failed." In more acute cases of gonorrhea, it furthers the action of gelsemium, belladonna, macrotys, though when there is marked debility, Felter recommends supplementing it with nux vomica or strychnine.

According to Culbreth, kava "increases the tone and power of the sexual and urinary apparatus and improves the general health and vigor." It relieves acute vaginitis, leucorrhea, neuralgic and spasmodic dismenorrhea, soreness or tenderness of perineum, and itching of the vulva. (He recommends that equal parts kava and glycerine be applied freely.) It also strengthens pendulous testicles and scrotum (especially if bladder irritation is relieved by wearing a suspensory), and relieves epididymitis, prostatitis with hypertrophy, and other prostate problems, especially in old men who experience a burning sensation during urination.

Kava is specifically indicated for the symptoms of Bright's disease in the absence of albumen in the urine. Conditions relieved by kava include irritation, inflammation, or debility of the urinary passages, chronic inflammation in the neck of the bladder, urethritis, nocturnal enuresis (when due to muscular atony), old feeble cases of bladder catarrh, chronic catarrhal inflammations, vesical irritation and inflammation, vesical atony, painful or burning micturition, uneasy sensations in the region of the bladder, strangury, dysuria with much residual urine, pronounced uric acid diathesis, pale and edematous tissues with scanty or irregular flow of urine and indisposition to exertion, and edema (especialy in the feet and legs).

Kava seems to pass through the kidneys almost unchanged, so that it has a profound influence on the genito-urinary mucous membranes. It decreases the blood supply to the urinary tract by contracting the capillaries, thus reducing inflammation in the genito-urinary membranes and allaying irritation, painful or difficult urination, or inflammation with mucus/pus discharge. It is a mild but efficient diuretic, promoting a watery diuresis, with proportionately less solid material being voided in the urine. It relieves acute or chronic cystitis, dropsy from renal inefficiency, and nocturnal enuresis of the aged and feeble, or of children, when the enuresis is due to temporary muscle weakness. (Ellingwood combines kava with belladonna and strychnine.)

CARDIOVASCULAR SYSTEM

Kava is a circulatory stimulant. If the heart is feeble and irregular, kava increases its power and strength, increasing the force of the heartbeat while decreasing its speed by stimulating the cardio-inhibitory centers and ganglia. It lowers arterial pressure by acting on the vagi, and later elevates it "especially after previous division of the pneumogastrics, by a direct action on the heart" (Ellingwood). It relieves hematogenous jaundice.

OTHER EFFECTS

Kava has a mild antipyretic action. Small doses increase body temperature slightly, while large doses diminish it. When grated it is a tonic for the sick and convalescent. It is also a galactagogue and diaphoretic, has antifungal properties, may relieve arterial sclerosis, and is said to have helped in at least one case of diabetes.

Kava is said to relieve both dizziness and despondency and has been used as a sedative for anxiety and fatigue.

Kava alleviates chronic bronchitis. It first stimulates, afterwards depresses, and finally paralyzes respiration. "The primary stimulation is due to excitation of the pulmonary peripheries of the vagi; the latter effect, to an influence exercised on the respiratory centers of the medulla oblongata" (Ellingwood).

Kava was used before World War I for **gout**. Ellingwood suggests the following formula for relieving acute **rheumatism**: kava 5 drams, macrotys 3 drams, citrate of potassium 4 drams, elixir of pepsin sufficient quantity to make 4 ounces. He gives 1 dram well diluted every 3 hours. For profuse sweating, he uses 2 drams hyoscyamus instead of citrate of potassium. He also suggests wrapping the joints in cotton, as well as bed-rest and a non-nitrogenous diet. (Use no salicylates: this course, he says, will prevent all cardiac complications.)

EXPERIMENTAL RESULTS (NEUROMUSCULAR ACTION)

Borsche (1933) found that none of the compounds (K, DHK, M, DHM, Y) have the full effect of kava root, though van Veen (1939) claimed that a lecithin-water emulsion of DHK worked just like kava.

In 1959, Klohs fed mice a chloroform extract of the root. He found it equal in action to the whole root. It was an effective anti-convulsant against strychnine, potentiated sodium pentobarbital-induced sleeping time, and made mice fall out of their revolving cages. He also tested M and DHM, and found them to be the most effective against strychnine, while DHM was best at increasing the effects of pentobarbital, but only the ground root or crude extract caused fall-out in roller cage experiments. He tested the hypothesis of synergistic action (rather than searching for an unknown component) by combining the known constituents in the proportions found in the kava plant. This worked better than the best single constituent.

In 1964, Meyer found that a single dose of 25 mg/kg of DHM or 60 mg/kg of DHK (intraperitoneal) raises the threshold of electroshock (prevents convulsions) in mice significantly; oral doses were about 2.5 times less effective. (Rats needed 30 mg/kg of DHM.) Though other substances are more effective (e.g. phenobarbital), their toxicity is also higher, so the "protective indices" are about the same. The effects of DHM lasted six to eight hours in non-neurotoxic doses. He also tested DHM and DHK in mice for anticonvulsive action against strychnine, pentylenetetrazol, bemergride, and picrotoxin, each of which have different types of action on the central nervous system. They worked well for strychnine. With the other convulsants, there was inhibition of maximal tonic-extensor seizure but no elevation of threshold of clonic convulsions, and the resulting purely clonic seizures were generally severe and markedly prolonged. They also work better for electro-

than chemoshock. Meyer thinks that the anticonvulsant activity comes from "inhibition of seizure spread."

In 1964, Meyer and May performed experiments on rabbit corneas. They found that K, M, DHM (but not Y) act as local anesthetics, despite a lack of structural similarities with other local anesthetics. DHK and DHM stop working sooner than the other two constituents.

In 1965, Meyer demonstrated that DHM has spasmolytic and relaxant effects on the smooth muscles of various animals, both in isolated organs and in the whole animal. It inhibits contractions induced by 5-HT and nicotine, but it is less effective against those induced by ACh, bradykinin or histamine, and even less so against barium. It is effective against epinephrine, but requires larger doses ($2x10^{-5}$ to 10^{-4} g/ml). Uterine spasms from oxytocine were inhibited by 10 – 20 mg/kg intravenous. Intraperitoneal doses of 100 – 200 mg/kg counteracted the effects of a histamine aerosol. DHM causes coronary dilation of short duration in the isolated heart. Intravenous application caused a drop in arterial blood pressure for five to eight minutes. Meyer postulates that DHM exerts a direct musculotropic action, plus a cocaine-like action on the nervous structures. It has no anti-histamine, anticholinergic or sympatholytic properties. Compared to other known drugs, however, DHM has a higher LD (lethal dose), so it does have good therapeutic ratios.

In 1965, Kretzschmar and Meyer induced convulsions in mice by electroshock or strychnine. As an antidote, they used intraperitoneal injections of water or oil solutions of lactones (M, K, Y, and DMY). With electroshock, all except DMY worked at 100 mg/kg. M was the most effective. Y worked only in doses large enough to produce a marked sedative effect. For strychnine, all four constituents worked, and M and K were the most effective.

In 1969, Krtezschmar and Meyer tested all six constituents of kava against convulsions, both from electroshock and from pentylene-tetrazol. All constituents turned out to be "pharmacologically effective." They resemble other local anesthetics in their duration of action and influence on the seizure pattern, but they differ in these respects from the anticonvulsants phenobarbital and diphenyl-hydantoin. In lower doses, they again resemble procaine, in having a weak facilitating effect on tonic extensor phase of pentylenetetrazol convulsions. They work less effectively if the subject is pretreated with reserpine. The effects of all six are similar for iv administration, while for oral or ip administration, the order of effectiveness is M, DHM, K, DHK, followed by DMY and Y. (The authors consider the differences to be due to absorption rates and the amounts eliminated.)

Using the isolated ileum of the guinea pig, Kretzschmar, Meyer, and colleagues demonstrated in 1969 that all six constituents had spasmolytic effects on the smooth muscles "mainly due to direct musculotropic action." At 10^{-6} to 10^{-5} g/ml, they antagonized responses due to histamine, acetylcholine, 5-hydroxy- tryptamine, and nicotine. (The first two toxins cause contractions by acting directly on smooth muscle fibres, while the last two act by stimulating the nervous structures of the intestinal wall.) The kava pyrones worked best on the last two. The experimenters noted the following relationships between structure and antispasmodic activity: K and M have an unsaturated hydrocarbon bridge between the pyrone ring and the benzene ring, and they are more effective than DHK and DHM, which are saturated in this position. DMY, with a completely unsaturated alpha-pyrone ring, is even more effective than K. Since M and DHM have a substitution at the benzene ring with methylenedioxy group, they are more effective, while Y, with a methoxy group at the benzene ring, is less effective. The researchers think the known alpha-pyrones explain completely the spasmolytic activity of kava

At a 1979 conference (Efron, ed.), Klohs reported that when M was turned into methysticic acid by opening the lactone ring, it was not effective. He concluded that the 5,6-dihydro-alpha-pyrone ring plays an important role in its action. He also synthesized a number of other variants, and found that several compounds could be substituted for the ethylene bridge at C6 without impairing its activity. He concluded that there is no "rigid overall specificity for drug receptor interaction."

Meyer reported to the conference that K and DHK are absorbed from the GI tract rapidly, producing their peak effect in 10 minutes. M and DHM took 30 – 45 min, but their effect also lasted longer. The pyrones inhibit smooth muscle contractions produced by histamine, barium, ACh, bradykinin, 5-HT, or nicotine. Y and DMY have only weak CNS activity when administered orally or intraperitoneally, but act the same as other pyrones when administered intravenously. Meyer blames this effect on either poor absorption from the gut or rapid elimination. The oral effectiveness of Y or DMY increases when given with the other pyrones. (This is important because they may make up as much as 1/4 to 1/3 of the total content of the root).

At the same conference, Buckley and colleagues reported that F1, F2, and LE-1 depressed spontaneous motor activity in mice but produced no loss of the righting reflex and had no effect on forced motor activity. LE-1 reduced irritability of septal rats without producing ataxia, and it also inhibited the conditioned avoidance response but not the shock response. In large doses (100 – 150 mg/kg) LE-1 blocked the EEG arousal response to visual stimulation. F2 antagonized serotonin-induced contractions of the rat uterus, but F1 didn't. DHM works on serotonin, but not bradykinin or ACh. LE-1 seems to have a skeletal muscle relaxant effect: an iv dose of 20 mg/kg completely blocked the flexor reflex for three hours in cats. It might block spinal interneurons, with weaker depressant effects on the reticular formation, subcortex, and cortex.

Marrazzi reported at the conference that an aqueous extract of kava 0.3 cc intracarotid gave similar cortical potentials to LSD25. It also acted like LSD on synaptic transmission. He hypothesized that perhaps any tranquilizer could also be a weak psychotogen.

In a group discussion at the end of the conference, Meyer said that sleep induction by kava is related to relaxed skeletal muscles rather than to any effect on the arousal response of the cerebral cortex.

OTHER EXPERIMENTAL RESULTS
(HEART, BLOOD PRESSURE, ANTIINFLAMMATORY)

In 1968 Kretzschmar and Meyer tested DHK, K, DHM, and M on isolated frog hearts and guinea pig auricles. The pyrones inhibited the amplitude of contraction in a manner similar to cocaine, and exerted "negative chronotropic action in concentrations 3 – 5 times higher than those necessary to elicit negative inotropic effects." In electrically driven guinea pig auricles, the pyrones possessed antiarrhythmic properties. In anesthetized guinea pigs, DHM protected the heart against ventricular fibrillation from electrical stimuli, and in unanesthetized rabbits, it inhibited ventricular premature contractions and arrhythmias from strophanthine or norepinephrine.

In a 1979 conference (Efron, ed.), Meyer reported that in concentrations of 1:1,000,000 or 1:100,000 the kava pyrones reduced edema produced by formalin, serotonin, dextran or carrageenin. Rapid intravenous injection of 10 – 30 mg/kg led to a transient drop in blood pressure, probably from peripheral vasodilation. In anesthetized animals, this was sometimes followed by a bradycardia lasting several hours, with a maximum reduction in heart rate of 40%.

At the same conference, Pfeiffer et al. reported on some of the few human experiments which seem to have been carried out with kava. He gave a single oral dose of 800 mg of dl-methysticin to prison inmates, and measured no significant changes in blood pressure, pulse rate, grip strength, hand steadiness, or pupil size. Subjective responses were "equally divided between stimulant, placebo, and sedative." (These people are considered "drug sophisticated," so the author concludes that there must not have been much effect.) In another test, he gave epileptics up to 6 gm/day of the crude root or 1 gm/day of the alcoholic extract, and reported some improvement in seizure control. Next he tried doses of up to 1200 mg/day of dl-dihydromethysticin (Riker Laboratories #532) and got fewer grand mal seizures, but no change in petit mal activity. Pfeiffer reports that

Saunders and Kline treated schizophrenics with 800 mg/day, with no antipsychotic effect.

Noting that aspirin affects EEG similarly to kava, Pfeiffer calls aspirin "a mild type of Kava which has been developed in modern society and used without ceremony by the tons." He reasons that since the pyrones have poor water solubility and good lipid solubility, they will always have their most marked pharmacological effects on the brain and skin, i.e. ectodermal tissues. Kava congeners, he says, are relatively inactive compared to modern synthetic central relaxants, and the most active, DHM, gives side effects (noted below), so "further study of Kava as a modern medicinal agent would not appear to be needed."

SOLVENTS

Though some sources indicate that kava is insoluble in all applicable solvents (yet remarkably quickly absorbed from the GI tract), others propose a variety of agents. It is generally agreed that the pyrones are not soluble in water, but there may be other fractions which are water-soluble. The alcohol extract, Extractum Kava-Kava fluidum, is not miscible with water. Proposed solvents for kava include peanut oil and polyethylene glycol.

Proposed solvents for the constituents include the following: DHM has low water solubility, but dissolves in polyethylene glycol; DHK, K, DHM, and M dissolve in methyl alcohol; DHK is soluble in alcohol and chloroform, moderately soluble in ether, but practically insoluble in petroleum ether or water; K is practically insoluble in water, but is soluble in acetone, ether, or methanol, and is slightly soluble in hexane; M is practically insoluble in water, but is soluble in alcohol or ether; the pyrones are soluble in "the usual fat solvents."

HISTORY AND FOLKLORE

The natives of Oceania make an intoxicating drink from the root, "that relaxed body and mind, induced refreshing sleep, and eased pain" (Lewis). They generally use one of four modes of preparation: (a) chop up and chew the root (mix with saliva), then mix with cold water or coconut milk and let stand for a few hours and strain. (b) grate and macerate the root, skip the saliva. (The first method seems to be more effective.) (c) let men and boys with good teeth chew but not swallow the root, or the saliva stimulated by it, but spit both into a bowl, add hot water and let it infuse, stir and drink. (d) select beautiful young maidens with rosy lips and white teeth, have them chew the root (while wearing hibiscus flowers but very little else), deposit the soft mass and saliva in bowls and stir by hand until the liqiud resembles milky soap suds, then strain.

The saliva is thought to make kava more effective. Proffered explanations include the alkalinity of saliva, its enzymatic action, and the presence of transitory virginal hormones (method d).

Lewis reports that kava which has been prepared with saliva has a narcotic effect, producing paralysis of the lower limbs and increasing the force of the heart beat while decreasing its rapidity. Respiration is first stimulated then depressed, and body temperature remains stable. Though mental alertness is considered unimpaired, kava produces a euphoria characterized by tranquility and friendliness, followed by a deep dreamless sleep without hangover. It is a diaphoretic which is said to counteract obesity. When prepared without saliva, the drink is only tonic and stimulant. According to Lewis, "the principle (or principles) responsible for narcotic action is still unknown."

Other observers have reported a variety of effects, including paresthesia of the lower extremities, a short-lived numbness of the tongue, drowsiness, intoxication, confused dreams, mutterings, reduced fatigue and anxiety, euphoria, feelings of comfort and peace, and increased perceptivity. Most users feel that intelligence is unimpaired, and that the flow of conversation is enhanced. Though kava produces no hangover or other side- or after-effects, some observers claim to have seen native addiction.

Because it was connected with religious cults and ceremonies, kava was suppressed by missionaries, often to be replaced by alcoholic beverages. The missionaries themselves suffered partial paralysis of the lower extremities after drinking kava, but Holmes (see Efron et al.) has suggested that this effect came from sitting cross-legged for hours during the ceremony. (The natives, who are used to this posture, have no trouble walking afterwards.)

Is the intellect impaired by kava? This question was discussed at great length during a 1979 conference (see Efron et al.). Some participants defended kava with a subjective evaluation and review of work done both by them and by natives while under the influence of the drink. Another objected that he has a colleague who writes good books, but who can only do so on a case of bourbon a week.

THERAPEUTIC DOSAGES (by form of herb)

Gonosan, an old kava preparation for gonorrhea can be taken in doses of up to 6 grams a day.

At the turn of the century, Ellingwood recommended kava for

gonorrhea, giving doses of 15 - 30 minims every two to three hours in cold water. In acute or sub-acute cases, he suggested a mild injection or irrigation (with gelsemium or macrotys) to act on "fever and nerve elements."

fluid extract: anywhere from 5 to 60 drops up to four times a day (or 1/2 to 1 dram, or 5 to 60 minims).

Tincture: 5 to 20 minims.

Powdered root: 1 tsp. of root (grated), to 1 cup boiling water, drink cold, 1 cup per day, a large mouthful at a time. (or 1 dram, or 1.0 drachm).

Solid extract: anywhere from 1 to 60 grains.

Individual constituents: effective dose (% concentration required to anesthetize against 50% of test stimuli) as *local anesthetic* (injected): Kawain = 0.36%, methysticin = 0.37%, dihydrokawain = 0.50%, dihydromethysticin = 0.60%. In higher, but non-toxic doses, May and Meyer tested the half-time of effectiveness. A 4% solution of DHK worked the longest, 38 minutes. After oral administration in rats, Rasmussen et al. found about half of the DHK dose in the urine in 48 hours, most in the form of hydrosylated metabolites (chiefly p-hydroxy-dihydrokawain), and some in the form of hippuric acid. They found less K excreted, and even less M, possibly because the low water solubility of K and M led to low absorption rates.

TOXICITY

Toxic dosages, side effects: Kava can cause drowsiness and mild sedation (in sensitive people) and has been termed a powerful hypnotic.

"The taste being agreeable, it is said one easily becomes a proselyte to its seductive qualities" (Felter, p. 546). It may be addicting, with rare cases of addiction reported in Tonga.

It can increase females' sexual appetite, but has no such effect on males.

Long term use of large amounts can cause skin coloration, dry, cracked, scaly and ulcerated skin, and lesions "closely allied to leprosy" (Felter, p. 546). If prepared *with saliva* it can cause exfoliative dermatitis.

Chewing the root over a long period of time ruins the teeth.

If prepared *with saliva*, larger doses give disturbed vision (enlarged pupils, slow light response) and **impaired muscle coordination** (staggering).

It may occasionally cause upset stomach.

The beverage may cause excessive weight loss.

Martindale reports on a patient who drank kava tea five to six times a day for six months, developing a chronic intoxicated feeling, ataxia, loss of appetite, diarrhea, skin reactions, and yellow skin (from kava pyrones in keratin?). He stopped drinking the tea, and "most symptoms had disappeared" one year later.

Pfeiffer et al. (see Efron, ed.) administered up to six grams per day of the crude root or one gram per day of alcoholic extract to epileptics. Although they had fewer seizures, the experiment was discontinued because after several weeks they developed lemon tinted skin and sclera. (The pure, more active and uncolored principles may not give this reaction.)

Toxicity of individual constituents:

DHK and DHM are lethal to mice at about 300 – 400 mg/kg intraperitoneal (equivalent to about 15 – 20 grams in a 110 lb person), and produce sedation, hypothermia, and reduction in total oxygen consumption, with metabolism reduced to basal level.

In concentrations of 0.15 – 0.2 mg/ml, DHK, K, DHM, and M cause an abrupt diastolic standstill of frogs' ventricles and guinea pigs' auricles (in vitro) by increasing the threshold for electrical excitation.

Chronic toxicity studies of K, M, and DHM in animals showed some anti-epileptic activity but no tranquilizing effects. There were some signs of skin reactions.

DHM causes exfoliative dermatitis.

Using K, M, or DHM as local anesthetics gives no local tissue damage, even with repeated applications.

The toxicity of sodium hexobarbital and pyrones are reduced when they are used together (relative antagonism).

Large oral or ip doses of K, M, or DHM can result in death from respiratory failure. The oral median paralyzing dose is about 100 – 300 mg/kg. It can depress polysynaptic responses such as flexor, crossed extensor, skin twitch, pinna — prior to corneal — and linguomandibular reflexes in doses of 20 - 40 mg/kg iv (probably about 10 times as high if given orally). Doses in anesthetized animals are about 5 - 10 times smaller. The responses of alpha motoneurons to muscle stretch were either abolished or restricted to an initial phasic response, by 15 mg/kg of K or DHM iv, with little effect on the EEG.

After 1 month of continuous therapy with up to 1200 mg/day of dl-DHM (Riker Laboratories #532), some patients developed conjunctival and circumorbital erythena, vomiting, and diarrhea. With a dosage of 800 mg/day, after 3 months there were skin rashes of the groin and axillae, but symptoms disappeared 10 to 20 days after the drug was stopped.

Antidotes: none given, most effects seem to disappear after discontinuation of the herb.

ASSAY STANDARDS

Detailed botanical description: Kava is a large, robust, soft-wooded, perennial shrub which can grow up to 10 or 12 feet high. It has conspicuous nodes and leaf scars. The leaves are simple, cordate, entire, green or purple tinged, 6 to 8 inches long and wide. There are rhizomes, stubby lateral roots, and rootlets. The white flowers grow in dense spikes, and each flower contains either male or female parts, but not both.

Varieties: Up to 14 varieties have been recorded. The stems vary from pale green to black, with a diameter from 3/4 to 2 inches There may be few or many lenticels, and these may be circular, transverse, or linear and vertical. The leaf scars range from 1/2 to 1 inch across, with internodes 2 to 12 inches long. The "white" varieties are said to make a better beverage, but they take longer to mature.

Macromorphology: The root has a faint, characteristic lilac odor and an aromatic, pungent, or bitter taste. The rhizomes have an irregular knotty crown, 12 cm thick, from which radiate many tough roots with ends separating fibro-vascular bundles, sometimes cut into angular pieces. The crown is soft, light spongy, granular, starchy, dark brown (lighter where scraped), and internally white. The powdered root yields whitish starch grains, yellow resin, oil cells, sclerenchymatous fibers, tracheae with markings, and parenchyma cells (stem).

Micromorphology:
Y = yellow crystals, melts at 155 – 157°C.
K melts at 106.5 – 108° [or 145 – 146°C: Rasmussen].
DHM melts at 117 – 118°C.
M forms needle-shaped crystals, melts at 139 – 140.5°C [or 136 – 137°C: Rasmussen].
DHK melts at 71 – 73°C.
"F1" is an amorphous solid, amber, aromatic, no nitrogen. It burns with a sooty flame, leaving little residue
"F2" is an amorphous solid, yellowish white, aromatic no nitrogen. It burns with a sooty flame, leaving no residue.
"LE-1" contains a brown gum, easily suspended in gum tragacanth.

Specific chemical tests and known adulterant tests: the natives consider it significant in what type of soil and climate the kava is grown.
The pyrones have been synthesized: see mass spectrum of kawain (fig. 49), or ultraviolet and infrared spectra of K, DHK, M, DHM, and Y in Klohs et al.

OFFICIAL PREPARATIONS

Extractum Kavae Kavae Liquidum BPC 1934.
Neuronika: proprietary drug (Germany) containing K.

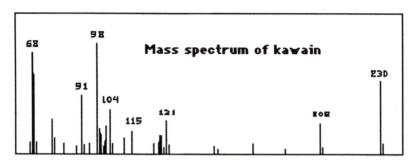

REFERENCES

Achenbach, H., J. Wörth, and B. Raffelsberger, "Untersuchung zum massen-spektrometrischen Zerfall des Kawains" (Examination of the mass spectrometric breakdown of kawain). *Organic Mass Spectography*, 1975, vol. 10, pp. 850 - 853.

Culbreth, David M. R., *A Manual of Materia Medica and Pharmacology*. Portland, Oregon: Eclectic Medical Publications, 1898 (reprint 1983).

Culpepper, N. W., *Culpepper's Complete Herbal*. Ware, Hertfordshire: Omega Books, 1985 (first published in 1653).

Efron, Daniel H. et al., eds., *Ethnopharmacologic Search for Psychoactive Drugs*. New York: Raven Press, 1979.

Ellingwood., F., *American Materia Medica, Therapeutic and Pharmacognosy*. Portland, Oregon: Eclectic Medical Publications, 1898 (reprint 1983).

Felter, H.W., *Eclectic Materia Medica, Pharmacology and Therapeutics*. Portland, Oregon: Eclectic Medical Publications, 1898 (reprint 1983).

Goodman, L.S. and A. Gilman, *The Pharmacological Basis of Therapeutics*, 4th ed. Toronto: MacMillan 1970.

Grieve, M., *A Modern Herbal*. New York: Dover Publications, Inc., 1971.

Israili, Z. H. and E. E. Smissman, "Synthesis of Kawain, Dihydrokawain and Analogues." *Journal of Organic Chemistry*, 1976, vol. 41 no. 26, pp. 4070 - 4073.

Klohs, M. W., F. Keller, R. E. Williams, M. I. Toekkes, and G. E.

Cronheim, "A Chemical and Pharmacological Investigation of *Piper methysticum* Forst." *Journal of Medicinal and Pharmaceutical Chemistry,* 1959, vol. 1 n.o 1, pp. 95 - 103.

Kreig, Margaret B., *Green Medicine.* New York: Rand McNally, 1964.

Kretzschmar, R. and H. J. Meyer, "Der Einfluss natürlicher 5,6-hydrierter Kawa-Pyrone auf isolierte Herzpräparate und ihre antifibrillatorische Wirkung" (Cardiac action of genuine pyrones of the kawaroot (Piper methysticum Forst) and their antifibrillatory activity). *Archives Internationales de Pharmacodynamie et de Thérapie,* 1968, vol. 175, pp. 1 - 15.

Kretzschmar, R., H. J. Meyer, H. J. Teschendorf, and B. Zöllner, "Spasmolytische Wirksamkeit von Aryl-substituirten *Alpha*-pyronen und wässrigen Extrakten aus Piper methysticum Forst" (Spasmolytic activity of aryl-substituted alpha-pyrones and aqueous extracts of Piper methysticum Forst (kava-root)). *Archives Internationales de Pharmacodynamie et de Thérapie,* 1969, vol. 180 no. 2, pp. 475 - 489.

Kretzschmar, R. and H. J. Meyer,"Vergleichende Untersuchungen über die antikonvulsive Wirksamkeit der Pyronverbindungen aus Piper methysticum Forst" (Comparative studies on the anticonvulsant activity of the pyrone compounds of Piper methysticum Forst). *Archives Internationales de Pharmacodynamie et de Thérapie,* 1969, vol. 177 no. 2, pp. 261 - 275.

Kretzschmar, R. and H. J. Meyer, "Zur Pharmakologie natürlicher sechsgliedriger Lactone" (Towards a pharmacology of natural lactones). *Naunyn-Schmiedebergs Archiv für Experimentelle Pathologie und Pharmakologie,* 1965, vol .251 no. 2, pp. 134 - 135.

Lehane, Brendan, *The Power of Plants.* New York: McGraw Hill, 1977.

Lewis, Walter H., *Medical Botany.* New York: John Wiley and Sons Inc., 1980.

Martindale, *The Extra Pharmacopeia,* 28th edition. London: The Pharmaceutical Press, 1982.

May, H. U. and H. J. Meyer, "Studien über die lokalancesthetische Wirksamkeit einer stickstofffreien Substanzgruppe aus Piper methysticum Forst" (Studies of the local anesthetic properties of a group of starch-free substances in Piper methysticum Forst). *Naunyn-Schmiedebergs Archiv für Experimentelle Pathologie und Pharmakologie,* 1965, vol. 250, pp. 273 - 274.

Merck Index, 10th edition, Merck & Co Inc, Rahway, New Jersey, 1983.

Meyer, Dr. Hans H. and Dr. R. Gottlieb, *Experimental Pharmacology as a Basis for Therapeutics.* Philadelphia, Pennsylvania: Lippincott, 1926.

Meyer, H. J. and J. Meyer-Burg "Hemmung des Elektrokrampfes durch die Kawa-Pyrone Dihydromethysticin und Dihydrokawain" (Inhibition of electrically induced convulsions by the kawa-pyrones dihydromethysticin and dihydrokawain). *Archives Internationales de Pharmacodynamie et de Thérapie*, 1964, vol. 148, pp. 97 - 108.

Meyer, H. J. and R. Kretzschmar, "Kawa-Pyrone -- eine neuartige Substanzgruppe zentraler Muskelrelaxantien vom Typ des Mephenesins" (Kava-pyrone -- a new group of central muscle relaxants of the mephenesin type). *Klinische Wochenschrift*, 1966, vol. 44, pp. 902 - 903.

Meyer, H. J. and H. U. May, "Lokalanoesthetische Eigenschaften natürlicher Kawa-Pyrone" (Local anesthetic properties of natural kawa-pyrones). *Klinische Wochenschrift*, 1964, vol. 42 p. 407.

Meyer, H. J., "Pharmakologie der wirksamen Prinzipien des Kawa-Rhizoms (Piper methysticum Forst)" (Pharmacology of the active principles of the kawa rhizome). *Archives Internationales de Pharmacodynamie et de Thérapie*, 1962, vol. 138, pp. 505 - 534.

Meyer, H. J., "Spasmolytische Effekte von Dihydromethysticin (DHM), einem Wirkstoff aus Piper methysticum Forst" (Spasmolytic activity of dihyrdomethysticin (DHM), a constituent of Piper methysticum Forst). *Archives Internationales de Pharmacodynamie et de Thérapie*, 1965, vol. 154, pp. 449 - 466.

Meyer, H. J., "Untersuchungen über den antikonvulsiven Wirkungstyp der Kawa-Pyrone (Dihydromethysticin und Dihydrokawain) mit Hilfe chemisch induzierter Krämpfe" (A study of the anticonvulsant properties of the kava pyrones DHM and DHK in chemically induced convulsions). *Archives Internationales de Pharmacodynamie et de Thérapie*, 1964, vol. 150, pp. 118 - 129.

Meyer, Joseph, *The Herbalist*. Glenwood, Illinois: Meyerbooks, revised 1960.

Parham, J. W., *Plants of the Fiji Islands*. Suva, Fiji: Government Printer, 1972.

Rasmussen, Anna K., Ronald R. Scheline, and Einar Solheim, "Metabolism of Some Kava Pyrones in the Rat." *Xenobiotica*, 1979, vol. 9 no. 1, pp. 1 - 16.

Robertson, T., *The Organic Constituents of Higher Plants*. North Amherst, Massachusetts: Cordus Press, 1963.

Spoerke, David G., *Herbal Medications*. Santa Barbara, California: Woodbridge Press, 1980.

Squire's Companion to the British Pharmacopeia, 16th edition. London: Churchill, 1894.

Trease, George E. and William C. Evans, *Pharmacognosy*, 12th ed. London: Bailliere Tindall, 1983.

Tyler, Varro E, *Pharmacognosy*, 8th ed. Lea & Febiger, Phila, 1981.

Willard, T. L., *Advanced Herbology 2 (Pharmacognosy)*. Calgary, Alberta: Wild Rose College of Natural Healing, 1983.

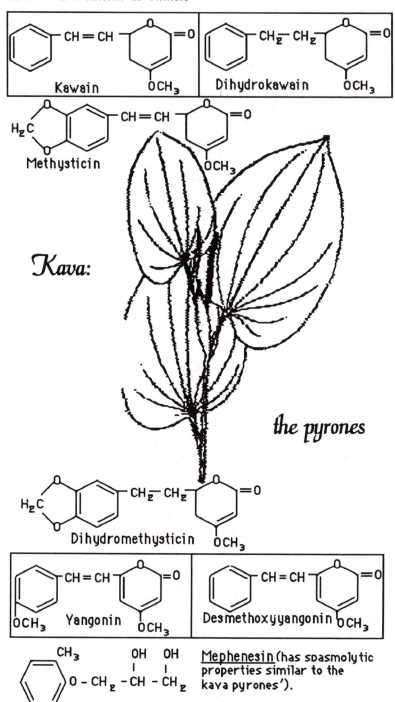

Kawain

Dihydrokawain

Methysticin

Kava:

the pyrones

Dihydromethysticin

Yangonin

Desmethoxyyangonin

Mephenesin (has spasmolytic properties similar to the kava pyrones').

Glossary

abduction - lateral movement of a limb or digit away from the side of the body.

acetyl CoA - a chemical precursor for fatty acid synthesis and for the Krebs cycle, q.v.

actin - a protein in the thin filaments of muscle tissue, needed for contraction.

action potential - an electrical charge across the membrane of an excitable cell (usually nerve or muscle cell).

adduction - lateral movement of a limb or digit toward the side of the body.

adhesion - fibrous tissue connecting two parts of the body which are normally separated.

ADP (adenosine diphosphate) - breakdown product of ATP (q.v.). Fuel is needed to reconstruct the ATP molecule from ADP.

aerobic - requiring the presence of oxygen.

afferent - conveying signals toward the center, as when a sensory nerve carries messages to the brain or spinal cord.

alveoli - the small air sacs in the lungs.

amino acids - the building blocks of proteins.

anaerobic - without oxygen.

analgesic - pain relieving agent.

antibacterial - destroying bacteria, or stopping their growth.

anti-inflammatory - reducing inflammation.

antimitotic - growth retardant (interfering with cell division by mitosis).

antipyretic - reducing fever.

antiseptic - inhibiting or preventing the growth of harmful microorganisms.

antispasmodic - relieving or preventing muscle spasm and nervous irritability.

artery - thick-walled blood vessel which carries blood away from the heart.

articular cartilage - the cartilage covering the ends of bones in a joint.

astringent - constricting agent, used to strengthen weak tissues.

ATP (adenosine triphosphate) - an enzyme which is the main carrier of energy in all cells. When work is done, ATP breaks down into ADP (q.v.) and free phosphate.

autoimmune disease - a condition in which the immune system produces antibodies against normal parts of the body, as in arthritis.

axon- a nerve fiber. It propagates action potentials (q.v.) away from the cell body.

ballistic motion - fast and uncontrolled motion.

basal tone - the tension in a resting muscle.

biceps - a muscle with two heads. The biceps brachii at the front of the upper arm flexes the forearm and supinates the hand.

blood minerals - potassium, sodium, and chlorine, the most common minerals in the blood.

bone minerals - calcium, phosphorus, and magnesium, the primary components of bone.

bowel transit time - the time required for food/wastes to pass through the intestines.

bursa - a fluid-filled sac found near the joints. The bursae reduce friction between tendons and bones or ligaments.

capillary - a network of minute blood vessels connecting the arteries to the veins. Water, nutrients, and other molecules can pass through capillary walls.

capitulum - small, rounded end of a bone, at a joint.

carminative - preventing or relieving intestinal gas.

carpals - the bones of the wrist.

cartilage - firm and compact type of connective tissue with no nerve or blood supply. Found in parts of the human skeleton, including the joints (articular cartilage).

cathartic - (from Greek, *catharticos*, purification) causing the bowels to empty.

cecum - first part of colon, before ascending colon.

clavicle - the collarbone.

coenzyme - enzyme activator, often derived from a vitamin.

collagen - fibrous protein found in connective tissue.

connective tissue - tissue which connects or supports other parts of the body. Found in skin, bone, fat, and blood cells.

Cori cycle - process in which lactic acid from glycolysis leaves the muscles, is converted to glucose by the liver, and returns to the muscles to be converted back to glycogen.

CP (creatine phosphate) - molecule that interacts with ADP to make ATP.

cytoplasm - the protoplasm of the cell outside of the nucleus.

demulcent - soothing or softening agent.

dendrite - the branched part of a nerve cell that receives input from other nerves.

diaphoretic - causing perspiration.

diaphysis - (from the Greek, to grow between) the shaft of a long bone.

distal - farthest from the center. The distal phalanges of the hand are the finger tips.

diuretic - increasing amount of urine produced and excreted.

duodenum - first section of small intestine, between stomach and jejunum.

edema - excess of fluid in the interstitial space. Can be localized or generalized (dropsy).

efferent - conveying signals away from the center, as when a motor neuron carries messages from the brain or spinal cord to the muscles.

electrolyte - mineral ions found in body fluids. (Ions carry an electrical charge.)

enzyme - a protein which speeds up chemical reactions without undergoing net change.

epicondylitis - inflammation of the epicondyle of the humerus; tennis elbow.

epimysium - sheath of connective tissue surrounding skeletal muscles.

epiphysis - (from the Greek, to grow upon) the knobby ends of the long bones.

essential amino acid - amino acid which the body needs but can't produce from other amino acids, and which must therefore be eaten.

essential fatty acid (EFA) - fatty acid which the body needs but can't produce from other fatty acids, and which must therefore be eaten.

expectorant - causing coughing.

extend - to straighten out a joint.

fascia - sheet of connective tissue which covers, supports, and separates muscles or other parts of the body.

fast twitch fibers - white muscle fibers for rapid contraction. They have low endurance.

fatty acid - one of the building blocks of fats, the one which makes each fat unique. (The other component is glycerol).

fibroblast - a cell from which connective tissue develops.

fibrosis - abnormal increase of interstitial fibrous tissue.

flex - to bend a joint.

free radical - a molecule or element with a charge. Free radicals easily form new chemical bonds, and their localized presence is normal.

free radical chain reaction - out-of-control chemical reactions which may occur if oils are exposed to light or oxygen.

gluconeogenesis - synthesis of glucose from non-carbohydrates in the liver.

glucose - simple carbohydrate which provides energy for the cells of the body.

glycogen - the form in which glucose is stored in the body.

glycolysis - breakdown of glucose to form ATP. Occurs in anaerobic conditions.

Golgi tendon organs - nerve receptors in tendons, react to distortion when tendon is under tension.

hemoglobin - the iron-containing pigment in red blood cells which transports oxygen.

herniation - a protrusion through a body opening formed by a rupture of tissue.

homeostasis - a dynamic equilibrium of the body's internal environment, maintained by feedback and compensatory regulating mechanisms.

humerus - the long bone of the upper arm.

hyaluronic acid - found in synovial fluid of the joints, as well as in connective tissue.

hydrochloric acid - HCl, secreted by the stomach to allow protein digestion to take place.

hypertrophy - increase in size, without an increase in the number of cells.

ileum - last section of small intestine, between jejunum and colon.

interneuron (internuncial neuron) - a neuron forming a link in a chain of neurons.

interstitial fluid - fluid surrounding the cells of the body. (Plasma is not considered an interstitial fluid.)

jejunum - middle section of small intestine, between duodenum and ileum.

Krebs cycle - a sequence of reactions which ultimately provide energy to the body's cells. Also called the citric acid cycle or the tricarboxylic acid cycle.

lactic acid - endproduct of glycolysis. It limits muscular activity if allowed to accumulate.

laxative - (from Latin *laxare*, to loosen) promoting bowel action.

ligament - strong fibrous tissue connecting bones at the joints, to limit or facilitate motion.

linoleic acid - omega-6 essential fatty acid.

linolenic acid - omega-3 essential fatty acid.

metabolite - any end product of metabolism, including wastes.

metacarpals - the five bones of the palm of the hand.

microtrauma - a very small lesion, generally not noticeable by itself, but frequent repetition can lead to more serious injury.

mitochondria - the part of the cell which produces most of its ATP. Also the site of the Krebs cycle (q.v.).

myelin sheath - insulative wrapping around the axons of nerve cells. Speeds up propagation of signals.

myofibril - thin bundles of filaments lying along the axis of the muscle, thought to contain the contractile elements.

myoglobin - oxygen-binding protein found in muscles, similar to hemoglobin.

myosin - a contractile protein in the thick muscle filaments. It forms cross-bridges which bind to actin (q.v.) when muscles contract.

nervine - relieving nervous excitement by acting directly on the nervous system.

neuron - a nerve cell. Structural and functional unit of nervous tissue.

node of Ranvier - constriction in the myelin sheath (q.v.).

oxidative phosphorylation - formation of ATP from ADP and inorganic phosphate, using the energy released when hydrogen combines with molecular oxygen.

perimysium - sheath of connective tissue surrounding internal bundles of muscle fibers.

periosteum - fibrous sheath surrounding bone shaft, has attachment points for tendons.

phagocyte - a cell which can surround and destroy harmful particles.

phalanges - the bones of the fingers and toes.

precapillary sphincter - smooth muscles controlling diameters of capillaries.

pronation - lying face downward or turning palm of hand downward or backward.

proprioceptor - nerve ending which receives information from within the body, about such things as pressure, position, or stretch.

prostaglandins - fatty acid derivatives which behave like hormones.

proximal - closest to the center. The proximal knuckles of the hand lie closest to the wrist.

purgative - strong cathartic, may cause watery bowel movements.

pyloric sphincter - muscle at end of stomach, opens only when food is ready to pass into the small intestine.

radius - bone on thumb-side of forearm. Attached to humerus, ulna, and wrist.

relaxant- reducing tension.

sarcoplasm - the cytoplasm (q.v.) of muscle cells.

scapula - shoulder blade.

Schwann cell - cell surrounding nerve fibers. Its plasma membrane forms the myelin sheath.

sedative - soothing, calming agent.

shoulder girdle - the scapulae and clavicles (q.v.).

sigmoid colon - S-shaped section of the colon, between descending colon and rectum.

slow twitch fibers - red muscle fibers with high endurance.

spasmolytic - arresting spasms; see antispasmodic.

sterno-clavicular articulation - joint between sternum (q.v.) and clavicle (q.v.). The only place where the arm bones are attached to the skeleton of the torso.

sternum - breast bone.

stomachic - stimulating digestive action of the stomach, strengthening the stomach.

stretch reflex - see monosynaptic stretch reflex.

supination - lying face upward or turning palm of hand upward or forward.

synapse - junction between two neurons (q.v.). Signals propagate across synapse in one direction only. Affected by drugs, oxygen deficiency, or fatigue.

synovial fluid - lubricating fluid secreted by synovial membrane.

synovial membrane - membrane lining the capsule of a joint.

synovitis - inflammation of a synovial membrane.

tendon - fibrous connective tissue connecting muscles to bones and transfers force of contraction to the bone.

tenosynovitis - inflammation of tendon sheath.

thymus - gland in upper chest, secretes thymosin and is site of lymphocyte (T cell) formation. Important in development of the immune system.

thyroid - gland at base of neck. Secretes hormones (thyroxine, triiodoghyronine), regulates metabolic rate.

tonic - strengthening or restoring tension in weak tissues, invigorating agent.

trabecula (pl. trabeculae) - fibrous cord of connective tissue extending into organ from its perimeter to form supporting structure.

trace minerals - minerals needed by the body in small (trace) amounts.

trachea - windpipe, the main trunk of the system of tubes carrying air to the lungs. Cartilaginous cylinder connecting larynx to bronchii.

trauma - injury or shock, can be physical or emotional, generally caused by an external agent.

ulna - larger bone of forearm, opposite thumb. Attaches to radius and humerus.

ultrasound - sound at a frequency above the audible range (20,000 to 10,000,000,000 Hz).

vein - wide, thin-walled blood vessel which carries blood toward the heart.

vermifuge - expelling intestinal worms.

Z line - internal fiber running perpendicular to a skeletal muscle and anchoring one end of the thin filaments.

Bibliography

SECTION I (Chapters 1 – 6)

BOOKS ON ANATOMY AND PHYSIOLOGY

Alexander, R. McNeil, *Biomechanics*. NY: John Wiley and Sons,1975.

Berkow, R., ed., *The Merck Manual of Diagnosis and Therapy*. NJ: Merck and Co., Inc., 1975.

Brauer, Marion R., *An Introduction to Kinesiology*. NJ: Prentice Hall, 1968

Carlson, F.D. and D.R. Wilkie, *Muscle Physiology*. NJ: Prentice Hall, 1974.

Gray, H., *Anatomy, Descriptive and Surgical*, Philadelphia: Running Press, 1974.

Higgins, J.R., *Human Movement, an Integrated Approach*. St. Louis: CV Mosby Co., 1977.

Hudlicka, Olga, *Muscle Blood Flow*. Amsterdam: Sweets & Zeitlinger, 1973.

Junge, Douglas, *Nerve and Muscle Excitation*. MA: Sinauer Assoc, 1976.

Knott, M. and D. Voss, *Proprioceptive Neuromuscular Facilitation*. NY: Harper and Row, 1956.

Margaria, Rodolfo, *Biomechanics and Energetics of Muscular Exercise*. Oxford, 1976, Clarendon Press.

Quiring, D.P., and J.H. Warfel, *The Extremities*. Philadelphia: Lea and Febiger, 1960.

Ott, John, *Health and Light*. NY: Simon and Shuster, 1976.

Thomas, C.L., ed., *Taber's Cyclopedic Medical Dictionary*. Philadelphia: F.A. Davis, 1985.

Thompson, Clem W., *Manual of Structural Kinesiology*. St. Louis: Mosby, 1981.

Vander, A.J., J.H. Sherman, and D.S. Luciano *Human Physiology*. NY: McGraw-Hill, 1980.

. . . AS APPLIED TO SPORTS

Bompa, Tudor O., *The Theory and Methodology of Training*. Dubuque, Iowa: Kendall Hunt Publishing Co.

Ebner, M., *Connective Tissue Massage*. Huntingdon, NY: Robert E. Krieger, 1975.

Golanty, Eric, *How to Prevent and Heal Running and Other Sports Injuries*. NY: Barnes, 1979.

Jensen, C.R. and A.G. Fisher *Scientific Basis of Athletic Conditioning*, 2nd edition. Philadelphia: Lea & Febiger, 1979.

Jokl, E., R.L. Anand, and H. Stoboy, *Advances in Exercise Physiology*. Basel: S. Karger, 1973.

Klafs, C.E. and D.D. Arnheim, *Modern Principles of Athletic Training*. St. Louis: CV Mosby and Co., 1973.

Mirkin, Gabe, and Marshall Hoffman, *The Sportsmedicine Book*, Boston: Little, Brown, and Co., 1978.

Morehouse, Laurence and Leonard Gross, *Maximum Performance*. NY: Pocket Book, 1977.

Morgan, William P., *Ergogenic Aids and Muscular Performance*, NY: Academic Press, 1972.

Muckle, David S., *Sports Injuries*, Second Edition. Stockfield, England: Oriel Press, 1977.

Reilly, Thomas, ed., *Sports Fitness and Sports Injuries*. London: Faber & Faber, 1981.

Williams, Melvin H., editor, *Ergogenic Aids in Sport*. Champaign, Illinois: Human Kinetics Publishers, Inc.,1983.

. . . AS APPLIED TO MUSIC-MAKING

Lehrer, Paul M. et al., *The Use of Beta Blockers to Treat Stage Fright in Musicians: an Evaluation*. available from the author at Dept. of Psychiatry, Rutgers Medical School, Piscataway, NJ.

Samama, Ans, *Muscle Control for Musicians: a series of exercises for daily practice*. Utrecht, Bohn: Scheltema & Holkema 1981.

Steinhausen, Dr. F.A., *Die Physiologie der Bogenführung* (the physiology of bowing). Leipzig: Breitkopf und Härtel,1920.

Szende, O., and M. Nemessuri, *The Physiology of Violin Playing*, London: Collet's Ltd., 1971.

Wilson, Frank R., *Tone Deaf and All Thumbs?* NY: Viking, 1986.

JOURNAL ARTICLES ON MUSIC AND MEDICINE

Armin, A., "Is there a doctor in the hall?," in *Performing Arts in Canada*, June, 1987, pp. 17 - 20.

Crabbe, D.J., "Hand injuries in professional musicians," in *Hand*, 1980, vol. 12, pp. 200 - 208.

Elbaum, Leonard, "Musculoskeletal Problems of Instrumental Musicians," in *The Journal of Orthopædic and Sports Physical Therapy*, Dec., 1986, pp. 285 - 287.

Frey, Hunter J.H., "Overuse syndrome of the upper limb in musicians," in *The Medical Journal of Australia*, Feb. 17, 1986, v. 144, pp. 182 - 185.

Harman, S.E., "Occupational diseases of instrumental musicians," in *Maryland State Medical Journal*, 1982, vol. 31, no. 6, pp. 39 - 42.

Hermann, L., "Dental considerations in the playing of wind instruments," in *The Journal of the American Dental Association*, 1974, vol. 89, pp. 611 - 619.

Hochberg, F.H., et al., "Hand difficulties among musicians," in *Journal of the American Medical Association*, April 8, 1983, vol. 249, no. 14, pp. 1869 - 1872.

Knishkowy, B. and Lederman, R.J., "Instrumental musicians with upper extremity disorders: a follow-up study," in *Medical Problems of Performing Artists*, Sept., 1986, vol. 1, no. 3, pp. 85 - 89.

Kollmann, H.G., "Das Karpaltunnelsyndrom. Ursachen, Symptomatik, Therapie" ("Carpal tunnel syndrome. Causes, symptoms, treatment)", *Wiener Medizinische Wochenschrift*, Nov, 1985, vol. 135, no. 21, pp. 517 - 51.

Lawton, M.B. and V. Asato, "Modification of a hand splint to permit playing of the guitar," in *Archives of Physical and Medical Rehabilitation*, May, 1986, vol. 67, no. 5, pp. 342 - 343.

Lippman, Dr. Heinz J., "The Strains of Music (Don't Be Too Sure it's Tendinitis)," in *Ensemble* magazine, Winter, 1983, pp. 17 and 25.

Morgan, R.F., and M.T. Edgerton, "Tissue expansion in reconstructive hand surgery: case report," in *American Journal of Hand Surgery*, Sept., 1985, vol. 10, no. 5, pp. 754 - 757.

Peppard, "Myotonic Muscle Distress: A Rationale for Therapy," *Athletic Training*, 1973, vol. 8, no. 4.

Polmauer, F.F. and M. Marks, "Occupational hazards of playing string instruments," in *The Strad*, 1967, vol. 78, pp. 23 - 25.

Rieder, C.E., "Possible premature degenerative TMJ disease in violinists," in *The Journal of Prosthetic Dentistry*, 1976, vol. 35, pp. 662 - 664.

Salzman, J., "Malocclusion, tongue thrusting and wind instrument playing," in *The American Journal of Orthodontics*, 1974, v. 66, pp. 456 - 457.

Wilson, Frank R., "Music and Medicine - 1985," *Piano Quarterly*, no. 132.

The *Cleveland Clinic Quarterly* did a special issue on "Medical Problems of Musicians" in Spring, 1986, vol. 53 no. 1. It includes four articles of interest to wind players, one for singers, and one on "Neuromuscular and related aspects of musical performance" (Simon Horenstein, pp. 53 - 60.)

There is an excellent new journal (first published in 1986) entirely devoted to this subject, entitled *Medical Problems of Performing Artists*, published in Philadelphia by Hanley and Belfus, Inc. It appears quarterly and includes dancers in its scope. Articles range from the medical to the historical and include interviews with prominent artists who have overcome injuries.

SECTION II (Chapters 7 – 12)
articles and books about nutrition

Airola, Paavo O., *There Is A Cure For Arthritis*. West Nyack, NY: Parker Publishing Co., Inc., 1968.

Ashmead, Dewayne, *Chelated Mineral Nutrition*. Huntington Beach, CA: Institute Publishers, 1981.

Bland, Jeffrey, *Nutraerobics*. San Francisco, CA: Harper and Row, 1981.

Borrmann, Wm. R., *Comprehensive Answers to Nutrition*. New Horizons Publishing Corp., 1979.

364 *The Musician as Athlete*

Cheraskin, E., Wm. Ringsdorf, and Arline Brecher, *Psychodietetics*. NY: Bantam, 1974.

Coca, Arthur F., *The Pulse Test*. Secaucus, NJ: Lyle Stuart, 1982.

Colgan, Michael, *Your Personal Vitamin Profile*. NY: Quill, 1982.

Colimore, Benjamin, *Nutrition and Your Body*. Los Angeles, CA: Light Wave Press, 1974.

Crooke, W. G., *The Yeast Connection*. Jackson, TN: Future Health, 1983.

Diamond, John, *Your Body Doesn't Lie*. NY: Harper and Row, 1979.

Ellis, Dr. John, and James Presley, *Vitamin B6, The Doctor's Report*. NY: Harper and Row, 1973.

Garrison, Robert, and Elizabeth Somer, *The Nutrition Desk Reference*. New Canaan, CT: Keats Publishing, Inc., 1985.

Garvey, John W., *The Five Phases of Food: how to begin*. Newtonville, MA: Wellbeing Books, 1985.

Gildroy, Ann, *Vitamins and Your Health*. London: Allen and Unwin, 1982.

Goodhart and Shils, *Modern Nutrition in Health and Disease*. Philadelphia, PA: Lea and Febiger, 1973.

Goulet, F.S., *Eating to Win: Food Psyching for the Athlete*. Briarcliff Manor, NY: Stein and Day, 1978.

Haas, Robert, *Eat to Win: the Sports Nutrition Bible*. Scarborough, Ont: New American Library/ Signet, 1983.

Hoffer, Abram, and Morton Walker, *Orthomolecular Nutrition for Physicians*. New Canaan, CT: Keats Publishing, Inc.,1989.

Jarvis, D.C., *Arthritis and Folk Medicine*. NY: Fawcett, 1960.

Jensen, B., *Food Healing for Man*. Escondido, CA: B. Jensen, Pub., 1983.

Kutsky, Roman, *Handbook of Vitamins, Minerals, and Hormones*. NY: Van Nostrand Reinhold, 1981.

Mandell, Marshall, *Dr. Mandell's 5-Day Allergy Relief System*. NY: Simon and Schuster, 1979.

The Merck Manual of Diagnosis and Therapy, 13th edition (R. Berkow, M.D., editor). Rahway, NJ: Merck Sharp and Dohme, 1977.

Mervyn, L., *Minerals and Your Health*. London: Allen and Unwin, 1980.

Mirkin, Gabe, and Marshall Hoffman, *The Sports Medicine Book*. Boston, MA: Little, Brown, 1978.

Morgan, W. (ed.), *Ergogenic Aids and Muscular Performance*. NY: Academic Press. 1972.

Null, Gary, *Food Combining Handbook*. NY: Harcourt Brace Jovanovich, 1973.

Nutrition Almanac. NY: Nutrition Search, McGraw-Hill, 1973.

Nutrition Scoreboard: Your Guide to Better Eating. Center for Science in the Public Interest, 1779 Church St. N.W.., D.C., 20036.

Oski, Frank, *Don't Drink Your Milk*. NY: Wyden Books, 1977.

Passwater, Richard, *Supernutrition and Healthy Hearts*. NY: Jove, 1978.

Passwater, Richard, and Elmer Cranton, *Trace Elements, Hair Analysis and Nutrition*. New Canaan, CT: Keats Publishing, Inc., 1983.

Percival, L., "Experience with honey in athletic nutrition," in *American Bee Journal*, vol. 95, pp 390 - 393, 1955.

Pfeiffer, Carl, *Zinc and Other Micro-Nutrients*. New Canaan, CT: Keats Publishing, Inc., 1978.

Philpott, Wm, and D. Kalita, *Brain Allergies: the Psychonutritent Connection*. New Canaan, CT: Keats Publishing, Inc., 1980

Schauss, Alexander, *Nutrition and Behavior*. New Canaan, CT: Keats Publishing, Inc., 1985.

Schroeder, Henry, *The Trace Elements and Man*. Old Greenwich, CT: Devin Adair, 1973.

Shelton, Herbert M., *Food Combining Made Easy*. San Antonio, TX: Dr. Shelton's Health School, 1971.

Slater, T..F, *Free Radical Mechanisms in Tissue Injury*. London: Pion Ltd., 1972.

Somogyi, J. C., and J. F. De Wijn, *Nutritional Aspects of Physical Performance*. Basel: S. Karger, 1979.

Steenblock, Dr. David, *Chlorella: Natural Medicinal Algae*. El Toro, CA: Aging Research Institute.

Tessler, Gordon, *Lazy Person's Guide to Better Nutrition*. Denver, CO: Better Health Publishers, 1984.

Truss, C. Orian, *The Missing Diagnosis*. Birmingham, Alabama: The Missing Diagnosis, 1983.

Williams, Melvin, *Nutritional Aspects of Human Physical and Athletic Performance*. Springfield, Illinois: Charles Thomas, 1976.

Williams, Roger, *Nutrition Against Disease*. NY: Pitman, 1971.

Williams, Roger, *Physicians Handbook of Nutritional Science*. Springfield, Illinois: C.C. Thomas, 1975.

SECTION III (Chapters 13 – 19)
articles and books about herbs

Sources of information about herbs range from the frankly folkloric to the strictly biochemical, from the innocently accepting to the stridently skeptical, from those based on practice or research to those based on hearsay, and from the well-documented to the totally undocumented. Some books are meant for the cook and gardener, while others are meant for the therapeutic practitioner, and still others are written for the vast self-help market. Some of the same phrases occur in herbal after herbal, without a hint as to who might have said them first. This is, I suppose, one way in which folklore comes about.

ARTICLES IN THE SCIENTIFIC JOURNALS
This is a small sampling of the research being done on the herbs and their constituents. Not all the articles cited are of direct interest to the performer. Rather they are given as an indication that there is

interest in the herb on the part of the scientific community. The articles are arranged alphabetically by herb name (in English when available).

ACHYROCLINE SATUREIOIDES
Kaloga, M. et al., "Isolierung eines Kawapyrons aus Achyrocline satureioides" ("Isolation of a kava pyrone from Achyrocline satureioides"), *Planta Medica*, 1983, vol. 48, pp. 103 - 104.

AGAVE:
Blunden, G. and Y. Yi, "A reinvestigation of the steroidal sapogenins of Agave sisalana," *Lloydia*, 1974, vol. 37, no. 1, pp. 10 - 16.
"Structure of hecogenin," *Act Cryst C*, 1984, vol. 40 (December), pp. 2116 - 2118.

ALFALFA:
Alcocervarela, J., "Effects of L-canavanine on T-cells may explain the induction of systemic lupus-erythematosus by alfalfa," *Arthritis and Rheumatism*, 1985, vol. 28, no. 1, pp. 52-57.
Alcocervarela, J., "The mechanism of action of L-cavanine in inducing autoimmune phenomena - reply" (letter), *Arthritis and Rheumatism*, 1985, vol. 28, no. 10, p.1200.
Dixit, V.P. and B.C. Joshi, "Antiatherosclerotic effects of alfalfa meal ingestion in chicks: a biochemical evaluation," *Indian Journal of Physiology and Pharmacology*, Jan., 1985, vol. 29, no. 1, pp. 47 - 50.
Prete, P.E., "The mechanism of action of L-canavanine in inducing autoimmune phenomena" (letter), *Arthritis and Rheumatism*, 1985, vol 28, no.10, pp1198-1200.

ARISTOLOCHIA MOLLISSIMA: (related to Virginia snake root)
Li, G.X., "Studies on the anti-inflammatory action of the essential oil of A. mollissima," *Chung Yao Tung Pau*, June, 1985, v. 10, no. 6, pp. 39 - 41.

ARNICA:
Forst, A.W., "Zur Wirkung von Arnica montana auf den Kreislauf" (Effects of Arnica montana on the circulation), *Naunyn-Schmiedebergs Archiv für Experimentelle Pathologie und Pharmakologie*, 1943, vol. 201, pp. 242-260.
Hamdy, M.K., "Healing efficacy of homeopathic arnica on experimentally induced bruised tissue" (meeting abstract), *Proceedings of the Society for Experimental Medicine*, 1986, vol. 181, no. 3, p. 472.
Labadie, R., "Arnica montana L (Literaturzusammen- fassung)" (a bibliography of works on arnica), *Pharm. Weekblad*, 1968, vol. 103, pp. 769 - 774.

BALSAM POPLAR:
Polyakov, V.V., "Carboxylic acids of Populus balsamifera," *Khim Prirs*, 1985, vol. 6, p. 834.

BARBERRY:
Manolov, P. et al., "Eksperimentalni prouchvaniia na Berberis vulgaris" ("Experimental research on B. vulgaris"), *Eksp Med Morfol*, 1985, vol. 24, no. 2, pp. 41 - 45.

BITTERSWEET:

Willuhn, G. et al., "Triterpene und Steroide im Samen von Solanum dulcamara (Triterpenes and steroids in seeds of Solanum dulcamara"), *Planta Medica*, 1982, vol. 46, pp. 99 - 104.

BLACK COHOSH:
Jarry, H. et al., "Untersuchungen zur endokrinen Wirksamkeit von Inhaltsstoffen aus Cimicifuga racemosa. 2. In vitro-Bindung von Inhaltsstoffen an Östrogenrezeptoren" ("Studies on the endocrine effects of the contents of C. racemosa. 2. In vitro binding of compounds to estrogen receptors"), *Planta Medica*, 1985, pp. 316 - 319.

BUCHU:
Casley-Smith, J.R. and Judith R. Casley-Smith, "The effects of diosmin (a benzo-pyrone) upon some high-protein oedemas: lung contusion, and burn and lymphoedema of rat legs," *Agents and Actions*, 1985, vol. 17, no. 1, pp. 14 - 20.

BUPLEURUM FALCATUM:
Ohuchi, K. et al., "Pharmacological influence of saikosaponins on prostaglandin E2 production by peritoneal macrophages," *Planta Medica*, 1985, p. 208.

CALAMUS:
Belova, L.F. et al., "Azaron i ego biologicheskie svoistva" ("Asarone and its biological properties"), *Farmaol Toksikol*, Nov. - Dec., 1985, vol 48, no. 6, pp 17 - 20.

Keller, K. et al., "Spasmolytische Wirkung des isoasaronfreien Kalmus" ("Spasmolytic action of isoasarone-free calamus"), *Planta Medica*, 1985, pp. 6-9.

CALOPHYLLUM INOPHYLLUM:
Saxena, R.C. et al., "Effect of calophyllolide, a nonsteroidal anti-inflammatory agent, on capillary permeability," *Planta Medica*, 1982, vol. 44, pp. 246 - 248.

CATNIP:
McElvain, S.M. and E.J. Eisenbraun, "The constituents of the volatile oil of catnip. III. The structure of nepetalic acid and related compounds," *Journal of the American Chemical Society*, March 20, 1985, pp. 1599 - 1605.

CAYENNE:
Biggs, D.F. and V. Goel, "Does capsaicin cause reflex bronchospasm in guinea-pigs?," *European Journal of Pharmacology*, Sep. 10, 1985, vol. 115, no 1, pp 71-80.

Cormarèche-Leydier, M., "The effect of an intraperitoneal injection of capsaicin on the thermopreferendum in the frog (Rana esculenta)," *Physiology and Behavior*, 1986, vol. 36, pp. 29 - 32.

Duckles, S.P., "Effects of capsaicin on vascular smooth muscle," *Naunyn-Schmiedeberg's Archives of Pharmacology*, 1986, v. 333, pp. 59 -64.

Duckles, S.P., "Evidence that capsaicin releases a vasodilator from guinea pig blood vessels which is not identical to substance P," *Blood Vessels*, 1986, vol. 23, no. 2, p. 65.

Dunér-Engström, M. et al., "Autonomic mechanisms underlying capsaicin induced oral sensations and salivation in man," *Journal of Physiology,* 1986, vol. 373, p. 87 - 96.

Gamse, R. et al., "Bronchial, cardiovascular and secretory responses after central administration of capsaicin in the guinea-pig," *Naunyn-Schmiedeberg's Archives of Pharmacology,* 1986, vol. 333, pp. 65 - 69.

Henry, C.J. and B. Emery, "Effect of spiced food on metabolic rate," *Human Nutrition, Clinical Nutrition,* March, 1986, vol. 40 no. 2, pp. 165 - 8.

Iwai, K. et al., "Enhancing effect of capsaicin on lipid metabolism in rats fed a high fat diet," *American Journal of Clinical Nutrition,* 1986, vol. 43, no. 6, abstract 47.

Lembeck, F. and R. Amann, "The influence of capsaicin sensitive neurons on stress-induced release of ACTH," *Brain Research Bulletin,* 1986, vol 16, pp. 541 - 543.

McCulloch, J. and J. Reid, "The effect of capsaicin on blood-brain barrier permeability in the rat," *Proceedings of the Physiological Society* (London) May, 1986, vol. 374, p. 20.

Russell, L.C. and K.J. Burchiel, "Effect of intrathecal and subepineural capsaicin on thermal sensitivity and autonomy in rats," *Pain,* 1986, pp. 109 - 123.

CELERY:

Saleh, M.M., "The essential oil of Apium graveolens var. secalinum and its cercaricidal activity," *Pharm Weekbl,* Dec., 1985, vol. 13, no. 7, pp. 277 - 279.

CHAMOMILE:

Appelt, G.D., "Pharmacological aspects of selected herbs employed in Hispanic folk medicine in the San Luis Valley of Colorado, USA: 1. Ligusticum Porteri (Osha) and Matricaria chamomilla (Manzanilla)," *Journal of Ethnopharmacology,* 1985, vol. 13, pp. 51 - 55.

Casterline, C.L., "Allergy to chamomile tea" (letter), *Journal of the American Medical Association,* 1980, vol. 244, no. 4, pp. 330 - 331.

Della-Loggia, R., "The role of flavonoids in the antiinflammatory activity of Chamomilla recutita," *Progress in Clinical Biology Research,* 1986, vol. 213, pp. 481-484.

CHAPARRAL:

Leonforte, J.F., "Contact dermatitis from Larrea (creosote bush)," *Journal of the American Academy of Dermatology,* Feb., 1986, vol 14, no. 2, pp 202 - 207.

CHINESE CARDAMOM:

Gupta, M.M. et al., "Investigation of costus. IV: Chemical studies of saponins of Costus speciosus roots," *Planta Medica,* 1983, p. 64.

COMFREY:

Gracza, L. et al., "Uber biochemisch-pharmakologische Untersuchungen pflanzlicher Arzneistoffe, 1. Mitt. Isolierung fon Rosmarinsaure aus Symphytum officinale und ihre intiinflammatorische Wirksamkeit in einem In-vitro-Model." ("Biochemical-pharmacologic studies of medicinal plants. 1.

Isolation of rosmarinic acid from *S. officinale* and its antiinflammatory activity in an in vitro model", *Archiven der Pharmakologie*, Dec., 1985, vol. 318, no. 12, pp. 1090 - 1095.

COW PARSNIP:

Rogov, V.D., "Ostryi belleznyi dermatit, razvivshiisia posle knotakta s borshchevikom" ("Acute bulbous dermatitis developing after contact with cow parsnip"), *Vestn Dermatol Venerol*, Nov., 1985, vol 1, pp 58 - 59.

DEVIL'S CLAW:

Eichler, O. and C. Koch, "Über die antiphlogistische, analgetische und spasmolytische Wirksamkeit von Harpagosid, einem Glykosid aus der Wurzel von Harpagophytum procumbens DC" ("On the antiphlogistic, analgesic, and spasmolytic effects of Harpagoside, a glycoside from the root of H. procumbens DC"), *Arzneimittel-Forschung*, 1970, vol. 20, no. 1, pp. 107 - 109.

Franz, G. et al., "Untersuchungen der Gattung Harpagophytum" ("Investigations of the genus Harpagophytum"), *Planta Medica*, 1982, vol. 44, pp. 218 - 220.

McLeod, D.W. et al., "Investigations of Harpagophytum procumbens (devil's claw) in the treatment of experimental inflammation and arthritis in the rat," *British Journal of Pharmacology*, 1979, vol. 66, pp. 140 - 141

Seeger, P.G., "Harpagophytum, ein wirksames Phytotherapeutikum" ("Harpagophyte, an effective therapeutic agent"), *Erfahrungs-Heilkunde*, 1973, vol. 8, p. 255.

Zorn, B., "Über die antiarthritische Wirkung der Harpagophytum-Wurzel" ("On the antiarthritic action of the root of Harpagophytum"), *Zeitschrift für Rheumaforschung*, 1958, vol. 17, pp. 133 - 138.

ECHINACEA:

Wagner, H. et al., "Immunstimulierend wirkende Polysaccharide (Heteroblykane) aus Höheren Pflanzen" ("Immunostimulating polysaccharides (heteroglycans) of higher plants"), *Arzneimittel Forschung*, 1985, vol. 35, no. 2, pp. 1069 - 1075.

EPHEDRA:

Hikino, H. et al., "Pharmacological actions of analogues of feruloylhistamine, an imidazole alkaloid of Ephedra roots," *Planta Medica*, 1984, vol. 50, no. 6, pp. 478-480.

Hikino, H. et al., "Pharmacology of ephedroxanes," *Journal of Ethnopharmacology*, 1985, vol. 13 no. 2, pp. 175 - 181.

Shiu-Ying, H., "Ephedra (Ma-Huang) in the new Chinese materia medica," *Economic Botany*, Oct./Dec. 1961, vol. 15, no. 4.

Siegel, R.K., "Cocaine substitutes" (letter), *New England Journal of Medicine*, Apr/Jun, 1980, vol 302, p. 817.

EUPATORIUM HYSSOPIFOLIUM, S. FLEXICAULIS, B. CYLINDRICA:

Benoit, P.S. et al., "Biological and phytochemical evaluation of plants. XIV. Antiinflammatory evaluation of 163 species of plants," *Lloydia*, 1976, pp. 160 - 171.

FAGARA:

Okpako, D.T. et al., "3,4-dihydro-2, 2-dimethyl-H-1 benzopyran-6-butyric acid; its preparation form Zanthoxylol and its antiinflammatory and related pharmacological properties," *Planta Medica*, 1983, vol. 47, pp. 112 - 116.

Oriowo, M.A. "Anti-inflammatory activity of piperonyl-4-acrylic isobutyl amide, an extractive from Zanthoxylum zanthoxyloides," *Planta Medica*, 1982, vol. 44, pp. 54 - 56.

FENUGREEK:

Bhat, B.G. et al., "The effect of feeding fenugreek and ginger on bile composition in the albino rat," *Nutrition Reports International*, Nov., 1985, vol. 32, no. 5, pp.1145 - 1151.

Cornish, M.A. et al., "Hybridisation for genetic improvement in the yield of diosgenin from fenugreek seed," *Planta Medica*, 1983, vol. 48, pp. 149 - 152.

FEVERVEW:

Heptinstall, S. et al., "Extracts of feverfew inhibit granule secretion in blood platelets and polymorphonuclear leucocytes," *Lancet*, May 11, 1985, pp. 1071 - 1073.

GARLIC:

Apitz-Castro, R. et al., "Ajoene, the antiplatelet principle of garlic, synergistically potentiates the antiaggregatory action of prostacyclin, forskolin, indomethacin and dypiridamole on human platelets," *Thrombosis Research*, 1986, vol. 42, pp. 303 - 311.

Bordia, A. and H.C. Bansal, "Essential oil of garlic in prevention of atherosclerosis," *The Lancet*, Dec. 29, 1973, p. 1491.

De Boer, L.M.V. and J.D. Folts, "Garlic extract limits acute platelet thrombus formation in canine coronary arteries," *Clinical Research*, April, 1986, vol. 34, no. 2, p. 292A.

Jain, R.C. et al., "Hypoglycaemic action of onion and garlic" (letter), *The Lancet*, Dec. 29, 1973, p. 1491.

Petkov, V., "Bulgarian traditional medicine: a source of ideas for phytopharmacological investigations," *Journal of Ethnopharmacology*, Feb., 1986, vol. 15, no. 2, pp.121-132.

GINGER:

Gugnani, H.C. and E.C. Ezenwanze, "Antibacterial activity of extracts of ginger and african oil bean seed," *Journal of Communicable Diseases*, Sept., 1985, vol. 17, no. 3, pp. 233 - 236.

GINSENG:

Baranov, A., "Recent advances in our knowledge of the morphology, cultivation, and uses of ginseng" (literature review), *Economic Botany* ,1966, vol. 20, pp. 403 - 406.

Brekhman, I.I. and I.V. Dardymov, "Pharmacological investigation of glycosides from ginseng and eleutherococcus," *Lloydia*, March, 1969, vol. 32, no. 1, pp. 46 - 51.

Etou, H. et al., "Ginsenoside Rb-1 as a suppressor of food intake in rats," *Japanese Journal of Pharmacology*, vol. 405, p. 194P.

Kim, C. et al., "Influence of ginseng on the stress mechanism," *Lloydia*, March, 1970, vol.. 3, no. 1, pp.43 - 48.

Koo, A. et al.,"Microcirculatory and cardiac effects of ginsenosides in rats," *Federation Proceedings*, 1985, vol. 44, p. 640.

Oshima, Y. et al.,"Isolation and hypoglycemic activity of panaxans I, J, K and L, glycans of Panax ginseng roots," *Journal of Ethnopharmacology*, Nov. - Dec., 1985 vol. 14, nos. 2 - 3, pp. 255 - 259.

Samira, M.M.H. et al., "Effect of the standardized ginseng extract G115 on the metabolism and electrical activity of the rabbit's brain," *Journal of International Medical Research*, 1985, vol. 13, pp. 342 - 348.

Siegel, R. K., "Ginseng abuse syndrome: problems with the panacea," *Journal of the American Medical Association*, April 13, 1979, vol. 241, no. 15, pp. 1614 - 1615.

Siegel, R. K., "Ginseng and high blood pressure" (letter), *Journal of the American Medical Association*, Jan. 4, 1980, vol. 243, no. 1.

Tsang, D. et al., "Ginseng saponins: influence on neurotransmitter uptake in rat brain synaptosomes," *Planta Medica*, 1983, vol. 48, pp. 149 - 152.

Yonezawa, M. et al, "Restoration of radiation injury by ginseng," *Journal of Radiation Research*, 1985, vol. 26, pp. 436 - 442.

GOTU KOLA:

Benedicenti, A. et al.,. "La terapia clinica delle parodontopatie, l'utilizzatione di potassa caustica, Centella idroalcoolica, in associazione alla laser terapia nel trattamento della parodontopatia espulsiva" ("The clinical therapy of periodontal disease, the use of potassium hydroxide and the water-alcohol extract of Centella in combination with laser therapy in the treatment of severe periodontal disease"), *Parodontol Stomatol*, Jan. - Apr, 1985, vol. 24, no. 1, pp. 11 - 26.

Kieswetter, H., "Experiences with treatment of wounds with asiaticoside (Madecassol)," *Wiener Medizinische Wochenschrift*, Feb 15, 1964, vol 114, pp 124 - 126.

Maquart, F.X. et al., "Stimulation of collagen and intracellular proline syntheses in vein wall and dermis fibroblasts cultures by a titrated extract from Centella asiatica (Madecassol)," *In Vitro: Cellular and Developmental Biology*, March, 1985, vol. 21, no. 3, p.34A.

Pointel, J.P. et al., "Titrated extract of C. asiatica (TECA) in the treatment of venous insufficiency of the lower limbs," *Angiology - the Journal of Vascular Diseases*, May, 1986, vol. 37, no. 5, pp. 420 - 421.

GUAIAC:

Deichmann, W.B. et al., "What is there that is not poison? A study of the Third Defense by Paracelsus," *Archives of Toxicology*, April, 1986, vol. 58, no. 4, pp. 207 - 213.

HENBANE:

Tugrul, L., "Abuse of henbane by children in Turkey," *Bulletin of Narcotics*, April - Sept., 1985, vol. 37, nos. 2 - 3, pp. 75 - 78.

LICORICE:

Delcroix, C. et al., "Tubulopathie proximale au cours d'une intoxication per le reglisse" ("Proximal tubulopathy in licorice poisoning") (letter), *Presse Medicinale*, Dec., 1985, vol. 14, no. 46, pp. 2346 - 2347.

Hikino, H. et al., "Antihepatotoxic actions of ginsenosides from Panax ginseng roots," *Planta Medica*, 1985, pp. 62 - 64. (Contains reference to licorice.)

Kimura, M., "Decreasing effects by glycyrrhizin and paeoniflorin on intracellular Ca_2++ -aequorin luminescence transients with or without caffeine in directly stimulated diaphragm muscle of mouse," *Japanese Journal of Pharmacology*, Nov., 1985, vol. 39, no. 3, pp. 387 - 390.

Shinada, M. et al., "Enhancement of interferon-gamma production in glycyrrhizin-treated human peripheral lymphocytes in response to concanavalin A and to suface antigen of hepatitis B virus," *Proceedings of the Society for Experimental Biology and Medicine*, Feb., 1986, vol. 181, no. 2, pp. 205 - 210.

Terasawa, K. et al., "Disposition of glycyrrhetic acid and its glycosides in healthy subjects and patients with pseudoaldosteronism," *Journal of Pharmacobio-dynamics*, Jan., 1986, vol. 9, no. 1, pp. 95 - 100.

LIPPIA MULTIFLORA:

Noamesi, B.K. et al., "Muscle relaxant properties of aqueous extract of Lippia multiflora," *Planta Medica*, 1985, pp. 253 - 255.

MAGNOLIA BLOSSSOMS:

Kimura, I. et al., "Neuromuscular blocking action of alkaloids from a Japanese crude drug "Shin-I" (Flos Magnoliae) in frog skeletal muscle" *Planta Medica*, 1983, vol. 48, pp. 43 - 47.

MANDRAKE:

Norberg, B. et al., "Effects on bone marrow cells of oral treatment with podophyllotoxin derivatives in rheumatoid arthritis," *Scandinavian Journal of Rheumatology*, 1985, vol. 14, pp. 271 - 275.

Truedsson, L. et al., "Complement activating rheumatoid factors in rheumatoid arthritis studied by haemolysis in gel: relation to antibody class and response to treatment with podophyllotoxin derivatives," *Clinical and Experimental Rheumatology*, 1985, vol. 3, pp. 29 - 37.

MULBERRY:

Chatterjee, G.K. et al., "Antiinflammatory and antipyretic activities of Morus indica," *Planta Medica*, 1983, vol. 48, pp. 116 - 119.

MYRRH:

Tariq, A. M. et al., "Anti-inflammatory activity of Commiphora molmol," *Agents and Actions*, 1985, vol. 17, nos. 3/4, pp. 381 - 382.

ONYCHIUM SILICULOSUM:

Ho, S.T. et al., "Studies on the Taiwan folk medicine: III. A smooth muscle relaxant from Onychuim silicosum," *Planta Medica*, 1985, p. 148.

OREGANO:

van den Broucke, C.O. and J.A. Lemli, "Antispasmodic activity of Origanum compactum," *Planta Medica*, 1982, vol. 45, pp. 188 - 190.

OSHA:

Appelt, G. D., "Pharmacological aspects of selected herbs employed in Hispanic folk medicine in the San Luis Valley of Colorado, USA: 1. Ligusticum Porteri (Osha) and Matricaria chamomilla

(Manzanilla)," *Journal of Ethnopharmacology*, 1985, vol. 13, pp. 51 - 55.

PARSLEY:

Zaynoin, S. et al., "The bergapten content of garden parsley and its significance in causing cutaneous photo-sensitization," *Clinical and Experimental Dermatology*, July, 1985, vol. 10, no. 4, pp. 328 - 331.

PERUVIAN BARK:

Puech, P. "Alcaloides du quinquina et dysrythmies cardiaques" ("Cinchona alkaloids and cardiac arrhythmias"), *Archives du Mal du Coeur*, March, 1986, vol. 79 no. 3, pp. 394 - 6.

PLAGIORHEGMA DUBIUM:

Arens, H. et al., "Antiinflammatory compounds from Plagiorhegma dubium cell culture," *Planta Medica*, 1984, p. 52.

POKEROOT:

Barker, B.E. et al., "Pokeberry poisoning" (letter), *New England Journal of Medicine*, 1966, vol. 275, no. 17, p.965.

Heilmann, C., "Secretions of immunoglobulins and IgM Rheumatoid-factor by pokeweed mitogen-induced blood lymphocytes," *ActPatMC*, 1982, vol. 92, no. 6, pp.371-376.

Hobbs, M.V., "Inhibition of pokeweed mitogen-induced immunoglobulin secretion in cultures of human peripheral blood lymphocytes by monoclonal human IGM rheumatoid factors," *Federation Proceedings*, 1985, vol. 44, no. 5, p. 1715.

Lewis, W.H. and P.R. Smith, "Poke root herbal tea poisoning" (letter), *Journal of the American Medical Association*, 1979, vol. 242, no. 25, pp. 2759 - 2760.

PRICKLY ASH:

Chen, S.W. and M.X. Lai, "Pharmacognostic study on the root of fourteen medicinal species in the genus Zanthoxylum," *Yao Hsueh Hsueh Pao*, Aug., 1985, vol. 20, no. 8, pp. 598 - 605.

RUE:

Pether, J.V.S., "Ruing rue" (letter), *The Lancet*, Oct. 26, 1985, no. 8461, p. 957.

SOLIDAGO SPP.

Bohlmann, F., "Alicyclic diterpenes from Solidago species," *Planta Medica*, 1985, vol. 6, pp. 487-489.

Kraus, J., "Antitumor-activity of polysaccharides from solidago species," *Experientia*, 1986, vol. 42, no. 6, p.670.

VALERIAN:

Balderer, G. and A.A. Borbély, "Effect of valerian on human sleep," *Psychopharmacology*,1985,v.87, pp.406-409.

Hazelhoff, B. et al., "Pharmacological effects of valerian compounds, with special reference to valepotriates. Central depressant or smooth muscle relaxant action?" *Experientia*, 1985, vol. 41, pp. 1214 - 1215.

Hendriks, H. et al., "Central nervous depressant activity of valerenic acid in the mouse," *Planta Mecida*, 1982, vol. 44, pp. 544 - 56.

Leathwood, P.D. and F. Chauffard, "Aqueous extract of valerian reduces latency to fall asleep in man," *Planta Medica*, 1985, pp. 144 -147.

YAM:
Yang, M. and Y. Chen, "Steroidal sapogenins in Dioscorea collettii," *PLanta Medica*, 1983, vol. 49, pp. 38 - 42.

YUCCA:
Ali, M.S. et al., "Isolation of antitumor polysaccharide fractions from Yucca glauca," *Growth*, 1978, vol. 42, pp. 213 - 223.

Backer, R.C. et al., "Phytochemical investigation of Yucca schottii," *Journal of Pharmaceutical Science*, Oct., 1972, vol. 61, pp. 1565 - 1566. (Inflammation.)

Stohs, S.J. et al., "Sapogenins of Yucca glauca tissue cultures," *Lloydia*, 1974, vol. 37, pp. 504 - 505.

MISC:
Bunim, J.J., ed., "A Decade of Anti-inflammatory Steroids, from Cortisone to Dexamethasone," *Annals of the New York Academy of Sciences*, Oct. 14, 1959, vol. 82, art. 4, pp. 797-1014.

Heftmann, E., "Biochemistry of steroidal saponins and glycoalkaloids," *Lloydia*, Sept.,1967, vol. 30, no. 3, pp.209 - 230.

Segelman, A.B. et al., "Biological and phytochemical evaluation of plants; False-negative saponin test results induced by the presence of tannins," *Lloydia*, March, 1969, vol. 32, no. 1, pp. 52 - 58.

BOOKS ABOUT HERBS

Angier, B. *Field Guide to Medicinal Wild Plants*. Harrisburg, Pa.: Stackpole Books, 1978.

Bellew,B.A. and J. Galaz Bellew, *The Desert Yucca for Health and Arthritis*. Printed in the U.S.A., no publisher listed. (pamphlet)

The British Pharmaceutical Codex. London: Pharmaceutical Press, 1934.

Chen, K.K. and C.F. Schmidt, *Ephedrine and Related Substances*. Baltimore: Williams and Wilkins Co., 1930.

Christopher, J.R., *School of Natural Healing*. Provo, Utah: BiWorld Publishers, Inc., 1979. (classic textbook)

Coursey, D.G., *Yams*. London: Longmans, Green, and Co. Ltd., 1967.

The Dispensatory of the United States of America, 23rd edition. Montreal: J.B.Lippincott, 1943.

Goodman, L.S. and A. Gilman, *The Pharmacological Basis of Therapeutics*, 4th ed. Toronto: Collier-Macmillan Canada, Ltd., 1970.

Gosselin et al., *Clinical Toxicology of Commercial Products*, 5th ed. London: Williams & Williams, 1976.

Grieve, M., *A Modern Herbal*, Harmondsworth, Middlesex, England: Penguin Books, 1982. (large number of listings, good reference)

Henry , T.A., *The Plant Alkaloids*, 3rd ed. Philadelphia, Pa: Blakiston's Son & Co. Inc., 1939.

Herbal Pharmacology in the People's Republic of China; Trip Report of the American Herbal Pharmacology Delegation. Washington, D.C.: National Academy of Sciences, 1975.

Hutchens, A.R., *Indian Herbalogy of North America.* Windsor, Ont.: Merco, 1982. (good reference book, covers several traditions)

Kloss, J., *Back to Eden.* Santa Barbara, California: Woodbridge Press, 1939, reprinted 1981. (from the era of the classical herbalist)

Lad, V. and D. Frawley, *The Yoga of Herbs.* Santa Fe, N.M.: Lotus Press, 1986. (ayurveda)

Lewis,W.H., *Medical Botany: Plants Affecting Man's Health.* N.Y.: Wiley & Sons, 1977.

Li, C.P., *Chinese Herbal Medicine.* U.S. Department of Health, Education, and Welfare, Publication No. (NIH) 75 -732, 1974.

Lucas, R., *Secrets of the Chinese Herbalists.* West Nyack, N.Y.: Parker Publishing, Inc., 1988.

Lust, J., *The Herb Book.* NY: Bantam, 1980. (brief introduction to herbs)

Martindale, *The Extra Pharmacopeia.* London, England: The Pharmaceutical Press, 1982. (medical reference)

Moore, M. *Medicinal Plants of the Mountain West.* Santa Fe: Museum of New Mexico Press, 1979. (beautifully written, by a doctor and herbalist)

Morton, J.F., *Major Medicinal Plants: Botany, Culture, and Uses.* Springfield, Illinois: Charles C. Thomas.

Perry, L.M., *Medicinal Plants of East and Southeast Asia.* Cambridge, Mass.: MIT Press, 1980.

Robinson, T., *The Organic Constituents of Higher Plants.* Minneapolis, Minn: Burgess Publishing Co.,1963.

Shadman, A.J., *Who is Your Doctor and Why?* New Canaan, Conn.: Keats Publishing, Inc., 1980. (homeopathy)

Sim S.K., *Medicinal Plant Glycosides: an Introduction for Pharmacy Students.* University of Toronto Press,1967.

Spoerke, D.G., Jr., *Herbal Medications.* Santa Barbara, Calif.: Woodbridge Press, 1980. (critical, out of print)

Trease, G.E and W. C. Evans, *Pharmacognosy*, 12th ed. Eastbourne, England: Baillière Tindall, 1983. (text)

Treben, M., *Health Through God's Pharmacy*, 5th edition. Steyr, Austria: Wilhelm Ennsthaler, 1985. (European tradition)

Tyler, V. et al., *Pharmacognosy*, 8th edition. Philadelphia, Pa.: Lea & Febiger, 1981. (text)

Veninga, Louise and B. R. Zaricor, *Goldenseal, etc; A Pharmacognosy of Wild Herbs.* Santa Cruz, CA: Ruka Publications, 1976.

Vithoulkas, G., *The Science of Homeopathy.* NY: Grove Press, 1980.

Wallis, T.E., *Textbook of Pharmacognosy.* London: J. & H. Churchill, 1967.

Windholz, M., *The Merck Index,.* Rahway, N.J.: Merck & Co. Inc., 1983.

SECTION IV (Chapters 20 – 23)

This section of the bibliography is divided into four parts, one each for Chapters 20 through 23. The divisions are arbitrary, and many books have relevance in more than one area. Some of the entries are annotated, because works in these fields range from the purely speculative and highly biased to the thoughtful and well researched. Some are classics in their fields, some are reviews of what is available, and others are popularizations of more basic work.

Some authors suggest exercises for the reader. Some also give workshops. These have the advantage that the leader indicates the pace and focus, and the group often generates an energy which gives everyone a more intense experience. Books and workshops can become habit-forming, providing an escape from the responsibility for solving the problem. If approached with clarity of purpose, however, they can renew enthusiasm and lead to ever freer and safer performance.

BOOKS AND ARTICLES ON STRESS, RELAXATION, EMOTIONS (CHAPTER 20)

Bach, Edward, and F. J. Wheeler, *The Bach Flower Remedies*. New Canaan, CT: Keats Publishing, 1977. This is a re-issue of the original classics by Dr. Bach, along with a repertory by a student and colleague. Rather than rely on quick-and-easy questionnaires for assigning a person an appropriate set of remedies, with this book we can see the greater picture and to sense how these remedies were used by their discoverer.

Bandler, Richard and John Grinder, *Neuro Linguistic Programming*. Moab, Utah: Real People Press, 1979. This is but one of many books by the authors and is a good introduction to NLP. It is a composite transcript of a number of workshops, and the authors' presence and effectiveness are strongly felt. Readers will probably find that some of the techniques and observations resonate with their own experience enough to be useful at once, though none of the books is likely to be a substitute for study with a good teacher. The authors have a refreshing way of looking at change: you don't have to have a problem in order to improve.

Benson, Herbert, *The Relaxation Response*. NY: William Morrow, 1973. This is the book on how to do transcendental meditation, without religious overtones.

Clynes, Manfred, "Cybernetic Implications of Rein Control in Perceptual and Conceptual Organization" in *Annals of the New York Academy of Sciences*, vol 156, art. 2, pp 627-968, April 21, 1969. A precursor to his sentics book, this paper is very technical. Only for those who are interested in a deeper understanding of the subject.

Clynes, Manfred, "Sentics: Biocybernetics of Emotion Communication," in *Annals of the New York Academy of Sciences*, vol 220, art. 3, pp 55 - 131, July 9, 1973. This is briefer than his sentics book and harder to understand, but it contains some information which is not in the book.

Clynes, Manfred, *Sentics, the Touch of Emotions*. NY: Doubleday, 1977. This is a fascinating book, in which the author moves from psychology to mathematics to music without catching his breath.

Who but Clynes could talk about "the mathematical relationship of what has also been called *satori* "? I'm not always comfortable with his conclusions about the nature of our minds and emotions. On the other hand, sentic cycles work — you don't have to read the book to benefit from them.

Cousins, Norman, *Anatomy of an Illness.* NY: Bantam, 1979. This is a classic, chronicling Cousins's journey back from illness to health. Though the author is best known for healing himself with laughter, he also describes a world view, and a large number of techniques arising from that world view, which made him well again.

Ellis, Albert, Ph.D. and Robert A. Harper, Ph.D., *A New Guide to Rational Living.* No. Hollywood, CA: Wilshire Book Co, 1975. This book seems simplistic and full of unlikely-sounding argument/dialogues, but Ellis has helped people, notably Warren Johnson (below).

Grindea, Carola, ed., *Tensions in the Performance of Music.* NY: Alexander Broude, Inc. 1982. These are the proceedings of the first of a number of symposia on the subject, held in both Europe and the United States. The well-known and respected contributors to this book include performers of all categories of instruments and voice, as well as a psychologist and an Alexander teacher. Most of these people have written more on their topics, so this is a good introduction to their work. The papers appear to be written rather than transcribed from talks, and this makes them better reading.

Jacobsen, E., *Progressive Relaxation.* Chicago: U of C Press, 1958. This is the classic in its field, and many people have since misused the term to connote simplified (and probably less effective) versions of the same thing. Other books by the author include *Tension in Medicine*, Springfield, Illinois: Charles C Thomas, 1967, and *You Must Relax,* New York: McGraw Hill, 1978.

Johnson, Warren R., *So Desperate the Fight: An Innovative Approach to Chronic Illness.* NY: Institute for Rational Living, 1981. This man has a severely disabling and usually-fatal disease which he learned to control through exercise, massage, and diet. To work effectively on the physical level, he first had to deal with his emotional response.

Pelletier, Kenneth R., *Mind as Healer, Mind as Slayer.* NY: Delacorte Press, 1977. In spite of its pop-sounding title, this is a thoughtful book by a well qualified practitioner of psychosomatic medicine. Selye's book on stress is a classic, but Pelletier's presentation is probably easier for the layman to understand, though it doesn't appear to oversimplify. The same goes for the chapters on stress management.

Ristad, Eloise, *A Soprano on Her Head.* Moab, Utah: Real People Press, 1982. Ristad died while working on a second book, but she has left us with this gem. I don't know whether reading the book will make you play better, or even teach better, but it has to be one of the most enjoyable and inspiring books around. Ristad's bag of tricks is infinitely deep, and she encourages us to know that we, too, have her resources.

Selye, Hans, *The Stress of Life*. NY: Longmans, Green, and Co, 1956. This classic book arose out of the author's observations that the same set of symptoms preceed many diseases, and that these symptoms can be seen as the effects of stress. It is the first book that the author wrote for the general public, after many years of writing for the medical community.

Selye, Hans, *Stress Without Distress*. Philadelphia: JB Lippincott, 1974. This book is more concerned with the necessity of stress to a productive and healthy life.

Stroebel, Charles, *The Quieting Reflex*. NY: Berkley, 1982. This is one of many popular books on dealing with stress. It describes a six-second technique for preventing excess stress.

BOOKS AND ARTICLES ON "BODYWORK" (CHAPTER 21)

Alexander, F.M., *The Resurrection of the Body*. NY: Dell Publishing Co, 1969. This collection of the author's writings contains the theoretical basis of his teachings. I don't really think his method can be learned from a book, and might even get in the way of letting the body understand. There are many other books on the subject, but if you are going to read just one, you might as well go to the source.

Beijing College of Traditional Chinese Medicine, *Essentials of Chinese Acupuncture*. Beijing and Foreign Languages Press, 1980. This is a text which explains the theories behind acupuncture. It includes lists of ailments and corresponding points, but as the book makes clear, you need more than a roadmap to be an acupuncturist.

Bertherat, Thérèse and Carol Bernstein, *The Body Has Its Reasons: anti-exercises and self-awareness*. NY: Pantheon Books, 1977. The book is about the Mézières method, which can ameliorate a surprising variety of conditions by releasing posterior body tension. It contains many anecdotes supporting a rather depressing view of how we use our bodies. The exercises, called preliminaries, at the back of the book are excellent for focusing awareness, but they would probably work better if led by an experienced teacher. Courses based on Bertherat's work are sometimes called anti-gymnastics.

Davis, A. R. and W. C. Rawls, *The Magnetic Effect*. Smithtown, NY: Exposition Press, 1975. This is one of many books by these and other authors on how magnetism affects the body. It contains specific techniques for a large list of complaints. This shouldn't be used as a how-to book without further guidance, but it is a clear introduction to an important subject.

Feldenkrais, Moshe, *Awareness Through Movement*. NY: Harper and Row, 1972. This is one of several books by the originator of the "Feldenkrais method." It gives good detailed descriptions of exercises which can be done alone. It may be faster to read the book than to listen to a tape, and the exercises could then be done at your own pace. The slow pace of a tape, however, forces you to take the time to notice your body's response. (An instructor would be even better.) Feldenkrais studied with, and then moved on from, Alexander.

Heckler, Richard Strozzi, *The Anatomy of Change: East/West approaches to body/mind therapy*. Boston: Shambhala Publications, Inc., 1984. Heckler helped develop the Lomi method of deep tissue massage, which works on emotional as well as physical blocks. He is influenced, as are so many of the workers in the release-of-tension field, by the martial art, aikido. Drawing on his background as a psychotherapist, the author facilitates change by breaking up old patterns. With its anecdotes and exercises, the book is fun to read, though it does not appear to be really life-changing.

Holmquist, Karl V., *Home Chiropractic Handbook*. Forks, Washington: One 8 Incorporated, 1985. This book comes with the warning that, of course, you should go to a chiropractor for adjustments rather than trying the techniques out at home. A bit like brain surgery, self-taught, but the book might help a patient understand and cooperate with the adjustments done by a chiropractor.

Iyengar, B. K. S., *Light on Yoga*. NY: Schocken Books, 1966. Considered a classic, this book is only for the serious yoga student, and is not meant to be used without a teacher. The Iyengar approach is one of the more rigorous, but it is only for the advanced student. There are many other books which can be read by the beginner, though none is a substitute for a good teacher.

Jensen, Bernard, D.C., "Reply to Western Medicine's Study of Iridology," in *The ACA Journal of Chiropractic*, March, 1980. This is the reply to the Simon article, q. v.

Johnson, Denny, *What the Eye Reveals*. Goleta, CA: Rayid Publications, 1984. This is the introduction to the Rayid method, by its originator. It is only one step in his process of development, but it stands well by itself. The color photographs and diagrams clarify the text.

Kriyananda, *Yoga Postures for Self Awareness*. Nevada City, CA: Ananda Publications, 1967. This is a good companion to any study of hatha yoga. It gives instructions for doing the postures, with comments on how each one can enhance awareness. For each posture there is a brief mental affirmation.

Lawrence, Ronald M. and Stanley Rosenberg, *Pain Relief with Osteomassage*. Santa Barbara, CA: Woodbridge Press Publishing Co, 1982. Osteomassage means massaging the periosteum, i.e. the thin covering of the bone. The authors apply this technique to relieve both acute and chronic pain from a number of causes, not necessarily related to the bone itself. By a means called "hyperstimulation analgesia," it is supposed to erase from the nervous system old patterns created by physical traumas or anything that activated the fight-or-flight response. The technique uses the finger tips, and bears the same relationship to osteopuncture (developed by Lawrence) that acupressure bears to acupuncture. There are other similarities, and some of the points have similar locations. Rosenberg describes a pulse which increases in speed as trauma is removed. Not for the amateur.

Maxwell, Jessica, *The Eye/Body Connection*. NY: Warner Books, 1980. This is one of the best short introductions to the subject of iridology. It has fairly good color photographs to illustrate key ideas, with case histories attached, and it has charts of both the North American and the European systems.

Rywerant, Yochanan, *The Feldenkrais Method: Teaching by Handling*. NY: Harper and Row, 1983. This book, authorized by Feldenkrais, explains "functional integration," which the practitioner does for the client. Though the theory is somewhat mysterious, the descriptions of the manipulations are clear, and the anecdotes are convincing. Like any form of bodywork, the Feldenkrais method requires instruction and experience, The book might help clients understand what is happening during a session.

Simon, Allie, et al., "An Evaluation of Iridology," in *Journal of the American Medical Association*, vol. 242, September 28, 1979, pp 1385 - 1389. This is the article which debunks iridology. See Jensen for a reply.

Stone, Randolph, *Health Building: the Conscious Art of Living Well*. Reno, Nevada: CRCS Publications, 1985. This book, published posthumously, summarizes the work of the originator of polarity therapy. Based on learning gleaned from years of travel throughout the world, the book presents an eclectic view of wellness. It contains advice on diet and a series of exercises for balancing the energy. Polarity therapy is best learned from a good teacher, but the exercises will help you experience and understand this form of energy.

BOOKS ON "AWARENESS" (CHAPTER 22)

Birren, Faber, *Color Psychology and Color Therapy*. Secaucus, N.J.: The Citadel Press, 1961. This is the classic book on the effects of color on the body and the mind. It is both scholarly and witty, thorough and entertaining. Though the medical establishment does not agree with everything Birren says, they have been fairly receptive. In addition, he has developed a large following in industry, architecture, and government.

Brown, Barbara B., *Stress and the Art of Biofeedback*. NY: Harper & Row, 1977. Brown is the original authority on biofeedback, the one quoted by most others. She gives details of the theory and suggestions for instrumentation. Her writing style is not easy to read, and there may be more up-to-date books on the subject.

Campbell, Don G., *Introduction to the Musical Brain*. St. Louis: Magnamusic-Baton, Inc, 1983. I don't like the theory in this book, but some of the many exercises are fun. The book is addressed mainly to elementary school teachers.

Gallwey, Timothy, *The Inner Game of Tennis*. NY: Bantam, 1984. This is the first "inner game" book. It shows how to replace destructive inner dialogue with awareness.

Gallwey, Timothy and Bob Kriegel, *Inner Skiing*. NY: Bantam, 1979. This is one of a number of collaborations extending the inner game principle to other sports. If you really get the idea, you won't need the new books, but if you want a booster, it's fun to learn by analogy from another field.

Gallwey, Timothy, *Inner Tennis*. NY: Random House, 1976. This is Gallwey's extension to the original book, providing more exercises for applying the principles. Even more effective than any of his books is the video made for one of the major US television networks, showing Gallwey teaching a reluctant beginner to play tennis: in twenty minutes this non-athlete was playing a surprisingly good game, and subsequently went on to develop her own course, "inner game of weight loss."

Green, Barry, and Timothy Gallwey, *The Inner Game of Music*. NY: Doubleday, 1986. The officially sanctioned extension into music. Bass player Green spent many years preparing this book, and its exercises are tailored to the musician. It suffers, as do the sports books, from being in the shadow of the original.

Irvine, J. and R. L. Levine, "The use of biofeedback to reduce left hand tensions for string players," in *American String Teacher*, 1981, vol 31, pp 10 - 12. The article applies Brown's work to string playing only, but it could be relevant to muscular tension generated anywhere in the body.

Leonard, George, *The Silent Pulse*. New York: Bantam, 1978. This is one of my favorites, about pulse and rhythm, the power of the mind, and letting go, written by a student of the martial art, aikido.

Levee, J. R. et al., "Electromyographic biofeedback for relief of tension in the facial and throat muscles of a woodwind musician," in *Biofeedback Self Regul*, 1976, vol 1, pp 113 - 120. Extension of Brown's work for wind players, and anyone else who wants to get rid of excess tension in the face and throat (in other words, someone who wishes to communicate more freely?)

Liang, T.T., *T'ai Chi Ch'uan for Health and Self-defense*. NY: Vintage Books, 1977. This is just one of the many books on t'ai chi. This book would make a good companion to lessons, since it includes some history and philosophy and some principles behind the techniqes. T'ai chi itself is best learned from a master.

McCluggage, Denise, *The Centered Skier*. NY: Bantam Books, 1983. This is one of the books Ristad recommends to musicians. It talks about learning Chinese as an aid to learning how to ski. (Do we get the idea that a bit of lateral thinking never hurt anyone?) It has some great material on breathing.

Millman, Dan, *The Warrior Athlete*. Walpole, NH: Stillpoint Publishing, 1979. This book is purposely general at times, to encourage readers to devise appropriate exercises for themselves. The focus is on integrating mental, physical and emotional factors to become a "natural athlete."

Morasky, R.L. et al., "Using biofeedback to reduce left arm extensor EMG of string players during musical performance," in *Biofeedback Self Regul*, 1981, vol 6, pp 565 - 572. An extension of

Brown's approach to string players and others with muscular tensions.

Nideffer, Robert M., *The Inner Athlete: mind plus muscle for winning.* NY: Crowell, 1976. The author discusses hypnosis, autogenic training, "progressive relaxation" (not his term), TM, active meditation (martial arts), mental rehearsal, biofeedback, systematic desensitization, and other aids for controlling physical and mental states. The first part of the book lets you decide which techniques are for you, providing tests to determine your patterns of narrow/wide focus, and internal/external focus. If you like the numerical approach but don't mind the skewed scales on his graphs, this book might help you to choose among the many techniques available.

Ostrander, Sheila, and Lynn Schroeder, *Superlearning.* NY: Dell Publishing Co., Inc., 1979. This popular exposition of a method developed by Dr. Georgi Lozanov in Bulgaria has spawned a host of courses and tapes, most of which claim to teach foreign languages effortlessly. The book also summarizes the methods of Schultz and Luthe, below.

Ott, John N., *Health and Light.* NY: Simon and Schuster (Pocket Books), 1976. This book is considered a classic on the subject of how our lighting conditions affect us. If you've wondered why some people are switching to full-spectrum lighting for the office, this book may persuade you to do the same.

Schultz, Johannes H. M.D. and Wolfgang Luthe M.D., *Autogenic Therapy, vol I, Autogenic Methods.* NY: Grune & Stratton, 1969. Luthe, Wolfgang M.D., and Johannes H. Schultz M.D., *Autogenic Therapy, vol II, Medical Applications.* NY: Grune & Stratton, 1969. Luthe, W. and J. H. Schultz, *Autogenic Therapy, vol III, Applications in Psychotherapy.* NY: Grune and Stratton, 1969. These books give the impression that the details of the autogenic therapy techniques can be unexpectedly important, and that competent guidance is essential. All of the other books I've read on the subject give slight variations, which definitely contradict the instructions here — whether this makes them wrong is hard to say. The reader gets the impression that this therapy is as dangerous as it is effective. If you're planning to do-it-yourself, this book just might give your suggestible subconscious too many ideas about possible problems. The bibliography (vol. IV) has 2,450 references.

Tisserand, Robert B., *The Art of Aromatherapy.* NY: Destiny Books, 1977. This book discusses the history of aromatherapy and its applications, including fairly detailed massage instructions. It covers 29 aromas, or essences, from both the scientific and esoteric points of view.

Zi, Nancy, *The Art of Breathing: Thirty simple exercises for improving your performance and well-being.* NY: 1986, Bantam. This is a singer's adaptation of the Chinese art of chi kung. The techniques, called chi yi, can improve health, relieve pain, center the mind, and increase energy.

BOOKS ON "HEALING" (CHAPTER 23)

Achterberg, Jeanne, *Imagery in Healing*. Boston: New Science Library, 1985. This book takes a good look at ways in which the mind can heal the body. The author, a professor in rehabilitation science, has worked with Simonton and others in applying her ideas to cancer patients and has written a number of books and articles on the subject. This book starts with a survey of techniques from other cultures and times, and then reviews current attempts at integrating these techniques into today's scientific paradigm.

Bennett, Hal Zina, *The Doctor Within*. NY: Potter, 1981. The reasoning in this book is extremely loose, but he has some good ideas, e.g. "Those physical and mental functions that make psychosomatic disease possible evolved within our bodies not to create disease but to maintain health at its optimal level. ... Creating health through them is not a matter of exerting control over them. On the contrary, it is a matter of learning to recognize when you're standing in their way, and then developing techniques to get out of their way." (p73).

Dossey, Larry, M.D., *Space, Time & Medicine*. Boulder, CO: Shambhala Press, 1982. For those interested in modern physics and its possible impact on healing, Dossey gives a good introduction. This book is more theoretical than *Beyond Illness* (Shambhala, 1984).

Krieger, Dolores, Ph.D., R.N., *The Therapeutic Touch*. Englewood Cliffs, NJ: Prentice Hall, 1979. This book describes the method Krieger has taught to many nurses in the last decade. It is based on her observations of the famous healer, Estebany, and on her further studies in healing. As far as this technique can be taught in a book, it is done extremely well. In any case it will help understand the transmission of healing energy.

Krippner, Stanley and Alberto Villoldo, *The Realms of Healing*. Millbrae, CA: Celestial Arts, 1976. The authors discuss psychic healers from many countries and make recommendations for conducting a proper scientific examination of psychic healing. Not at the top of my list, but it does cover a lot of ground.

LeShan, Lawrence, *The Medium, the Mystic, and the Physicist*. NY: Ballantine, 1982. A skeptical psychologist becomes convinced of the possibility of healing another person without drugs or manipulation.

Lingerman, Hal A., *The Healing Energies of Music*. Wheaton, Illinois: Theosophical Publishing House, 1983. This is one of many books on using music to heal, rather than healing ourselves so that we can make better music. By using music to heal, we may well remove the blocks which keep us from playing as we would like to in the first place. The book is easy to read and relatively non-technical in the esoteric parts. It gives many examples of music for various occasions.

MacNutt, Francis, O. P., *Healing*. Notre Dame, Indiana: Ave Maria Press, 1974. A Catholic healer talks to doctors and fellow Catholics. Compassionate and insightful, the author talks about the relationship between his work and medicine, healthy habits, etc. This is an extremely helpful book for anyone practising laying on of hands.

Oyle, Dr. Irving, *The Healing Mind*. Berkeley, CA: Celestial Arts, 1975. This book discusses alternative modes of healing, as seen by a doctor, not a scientist. Dr. Oyle has been trying out a number of approaches (mostly visual imagery and sonopuncture) which engage the mind of the patient in self-healing. He accepts as evidence a few things which some readers would question, e.g. the psychokinesis of Uri Geller and the psychic surgery in the Philippines. Other books by the same author include *Magic, Mysticism and Modern Medicine* (1976), *Time, Space, and the Mind* (1976), and *The New American Medicine Show / Discovering the Healing Connection* (1979).

Schul, Bill, *The Psychic Frontiers of Medicine*. Greenwich, CT: Fawcett Books, 1977. This is a review of some healers and their work.

Schwartz, Jack, *Voluntary Controls*. NY: E.P. Dutton, 1978. The author is one of North America's most famous healers, the man who was investigated by the Meninger Foundation. This book explains Schwartz's philosophy and gives techniques for self-healing. It suggests many alternatives, to encourage the student to develop a personal program.

Simonton, O. Carl, Stephanie Matthews-Simonton, and James Creighton, *Getting Well Again*. NY: Bantam, 1980. This is the classic on imagery and cancer, but the ideas have often been applied in other settings.

INDEX

ATP (adenosine triphosphate) 17, 26, 27, **29 – 30**, 31 - 33, 39, 41, 58, 99, 237, 239, 288, 290, 322, 324, 332

abrasions 246

acetyl CoA 31, 33, 288, 291, 300

acetylcholine (ACh) 26, 224, 288, 289, 294, 300, 302, 321, 343

Achyrocline 218

acidosis 107

actin 17, 18, 26, 27, 60

acupressure, acupuncture 56, 249, 250, 251, **266 – 270**, 272

additives **131 – 132**, 145, 164, 165

adhesions 65, 68, **71 – 72**, 74, 77

adrenaline (epinephrine) 38, 133, 232, 258, 324, 343

adrenals 131, 134, 142, 143, 202, 203, 225, 237 - 239, 294, 305, 307, 311, 318

aerobic **30 –32**, 33, 34, 36, 38, 41 - 43, 58, 59, 83, 115, 133, 145 - 147, 236, 237, 239, 295, 315, 336

affirmations 265, **276 – 277**

agave **199**

agility 17, 54, 60, 84, 91

aging 168, 326, 331, 336

agrimony 214

alcohol 134, **135 – 136**, 137, 145, 156, 157, 228, 289, 299, 326, 330

alcoholism 133, 292, 300, 305, 324, 327, 329, 330, 337

alertness 38, 133, 307, 317, 347

Alexander, F. M. 35, 88, **263 – 264**

alfalfa 180, **187 – 188**, **199**, 213, 298, 319, 320

alkaline diet **150 – 153**

allergies 116, 120, 128, 139, 141, 145, **147 – 149**, 185, 186, 189, 203, 231, 236, 261

alterative **191 – 193**

aluminum 136, **138**, 323

amino acids (see also purine, tryptophan) 106, 108, 115, 117, 118, 124, 135, 292, 295, 301, 304, 305, 318, 329

anaerobic **32 – 34**, 35, 36, 38, 58, 59, 111, 115, 160, 239, 290, 304

analgesic (see also pain) 196, 205, 207, 210, 215, 226

androgen 240

anemia 115, 118, 137, 208, 211, 239, 290, 295, 297, 299, 302, 318, 320, 323, 329 - 332, 335, 337

anesthetic (see also drugs) 188, 218, 339, 343, 349

antibacterial 183, 193

antibiotic (see also drugs) 233, 294, 295, 307

antigymnastics **263**

antihistamine 209, 210, 212, 220, 343, 344

anti-inflammatory 184, 188, **191 – 216**, 220, 221, 231

antimicrobial 189

antimitotic 195

antioxidants 102, 118, 131, 192, 212, 221, 237, 307, 310, 317, 318, 334

antipeptic 184

antipyretic 205, 207, 209, 211, 341

antiseptic 184, 194, 246, 307, 340

antispasmodic 193, 208, 215, 217, **218 – 224**, 227

anxiety (see also emotions, nervousness) 78, 132, 140, 148, 212, 217, 232, 257, 292, 339, 341, 347

arnica 245, 247, **252**

aroma therapy **278**

Artemesia 214

arteries 20, 23, 35, 117, 130, 132, 134, 137, 138, 295, 298, 303, 316, 317, 330 - 332, 341, 343

arthritis 66, 67, 86, 102, 108, 115, 117 - 119, 124, 135, 139, 140, 145, 146, **149 – 154**, 155, 156, **191 – 216**, 224, 225, 233, 238, 244, 246, 248, 250, 264, 271, 276, 281, 292, 295, 297, 300, 307, 310, 311, 321, 323, 328, 330

arts therapies **260**

ascorbic acid: see vitamin C

aspen, quaking **205 – 206**

aspirin 64, 69, 183, **206 – 208**, 299, 307, 308, 319, 346

asthma (see also lungs, respiratory

NOTES

NOTES

NOTES

NOTES

NOTES

NOTES

About the Author

Dorothy Bishop graduated from Brandeis University (Waltham, Mass.) with a degree in mathematics and then joined the 'cello sections of the Calgary Philharmonic and CBC (radio) Strings. She has also served as guest-principal in the Saskatoon and Okanagan Symphonies and participated in master classes of Mstislav Rostropovich and Paul Tortelier. In 1975 she obtained government grants for two years of study with Antonio Janigro. Solo, chamber music, and orchestral positions have taken her throughout Europe, Japan, Canada and the United States. Recordings include the Eckhardt-Gramatté Concertino and the Britten Sonata in C, with pianist Delores Keahey (Discopaedia). For the past ten years she has been a member of the Allegra String quartet, recording and performing live and on radio and television.

In 1979 a minor injury prompted studies in physiology, herbology, nutrition, and other healing arts, leading to the degree of Master Herbalist. Since that time, the author has given lectures and workshops on both sides of the continent and maintains a practice at Wild Rose Clinic in Calgary, Alberta, where she resides with her husband and son.